# GOTTA GET THEROUX THIS

Also by Louis Theroux

The Call of the Weird

# Louis Theroux

# GOTTA GET THEROUX THIS

MACMILLAN

First published 2019 by Macmillan
an imprint of Pan Macmillan
20 New Wharf Road, London N1 9RR
Associated companies throughout the world
www.panmacmillan.com

ISBN 978-1-5098-8036-2 HB
ISBN 978-1-5098-8038-6 TPB

1 3 5 7 9 8 6 4 2

A CIP catalogue record for this book is available from the British Library.

Typeset by Jouve (UK), Milton Keynes
Printed and bound by CPI Group (UK) Ltd, Croydon, CRO 4YY

*For Nancy, Albert, Freddie and Walter*

# Contents

# GOTTA GET THEROUX THIS

# Sensual Eating

Though I knew him to be a business executive and samba instructor, the poised man who came to the door in his t-shirt and pyjama bottoms, with his well-tended white beard and faint air of naughtiness, looked more like the sensei at an erotic dojo.

I was a little out of breath. The house – tall, with wooden decks around it – stood on the side of a pine-covered slope on a street on the edge of Portland, Oregon, and I'd had to climb a steep drive in inappropriate leather footwear to get there, being met at the top by Cliff, my host.

He ushered me inside – my crew followed behind – and I took my shoes off in a cloakroom, then ventured into a large kitchen where little Indian statues of couples in coitus sat beside generic holiday snaps of Cliff's children.

Trays and bowls of food were arrayed on countertops – a buffet of the type you would find in the business lounge of a regional airport: grapes and apple slices and small slabs of cheese – but there was cling film over them. It wasn't yet time to eat.

The kitchen filled up: couples, a handful of singles, male and female in roughly equal measure, most in their thirties and forties.

Many of the guys were in plain collared shirts, and the women in knee-length dresses – they might have been at a church mixer.

But there was also a sprinkling of more flamboyant partygoers. A bearded man in a blue sarong, his shirt unbuttoned to show a huge blue pendant resplendent on his hairy chest. Another, older, dread-locked man, in black leggings and a little leatherette waistcoat. A heavyset lady in an orange kimono that was open to reveal a gener-ous helping of cleavage.

A woman, probably in her thirties, was smiling at me with a daffy air of free-spirited bonhomie that seemed to invite further inquiry.

'Are you excited?' I asked.

'I'm *so* excited!' she replied.

'Are you nervous too?'

'Nuh! Why would someone be nervous? It's just a night of fun and freedom! It's all about the pleasure.'

'Yeah, the pleasure – of the food,' I added hopefully.

'Yeah! Well, you know, the food *and . . .*' Eyes wide, she trailed off.

'Have you been fed food before?' asked a grey-haired older lady with dangly earrings. She placed her hand on my chest. 'I think you're going to really enjoy the experience. You're pretty safe. We're a good group of people.'

'Oh, it's good to hear that,' I said.

At Cliff's direction, we separated into three groups. Group one began loading up plates with food and pouring drinks into plastic beakers with sippy-cup lids. Then we all made our way downstairs to a basement where mats were laid out and gentle music was playing.

'As those who have been to my events before – the massage-à-trois, the tantra events – know, I'm really into putting together events where you learn something about yourself,' Cliff said. 'You learn to connect more deeply. This is an L2 event, so genitals stay covered. No genital touching. But whatever else you would like to take off, feel free to take off. If you don't have any underwear I've got plenty of my sarongs you can wear.'

Group one sat down with their plates and beakers next to them. Some took their tops off.

'If you like what's happening, say yes. If you really like it, say yes please,' Cliff said. 'If you're feeling overwhelmed and you need a pause say "ground".'

Then, at Cliff's command, group one put eye masks on, and the rest of us – groups two and three – set about massaging, stroking and feeding.

'Givers, feed slowly,' Cliff said. 'Feed off part of your body, but do everything slowly. Slow is always better.'

It was a little like a starter's pistol had gone off but, instead of running in a straight direction, the masked athletes had begun swaying and groaning with their mouths open like little baby chicks. I was immediately feeling a little out of my depth. *Oh Christ*, I thought.

I circulated slightly aimlessly, trying to stay in the orbit of receivers who already had a giver next to them, to take the pressure off me. But even with a two-to-one ratio, it still occasionally happened that I was left alone with a receiver, which induced mild feelings of panic, having the sole responsibility of imparting profound feelings of connectedness and emotional well-being. In a way the feeding was the easy part: you pop a chocolate in someone's mouth, they go 'mmm!' But you can't just keep feeding and feeding, and it wasn't totally clear what the next move was: you squeeze the shoulders, massage the arms a little bit, but then what? I was running out of ideas. A bit more chocolate? A strawberry?

As the minutes passed, there was a palpable escalation in the groaning and gyrating. Cliff was keeping up a patter of encouragement. 'Find connection on a deeper level,' he intoned as he paced up and down. Across from me, a long-haired woman, who I knew to be a doctor, was squirting whipped cream onto one of her breasts and with a big smile on her face feeding it – the cream and possibly portions of breast – to her receiver. Meanwhile the man in the leatherette waistcoat was moaning and spasming in ecstasy. I looked over at my director Arron to try to gauge his reaction: was this what he'd been expecting? His eye was fixed to his camera.

And then it was my turn: group two was called. And what, after all, was I doing here if I wasn't going to get involved? I loaded my plate with some chocolate, some strawberries, slices of apple. I'd heard someone recommend a combination of savoury and sweet, so I added a couple of slabs of cheese. I took my shirt off, and I put my eye mask on, noticing a strange sense of liberation as my vision was obscured. I felt invisible and some of my self-consciousness ebbed away.

'Human connection is one of the most precious things we can experience in our lives,' Cliff was saying. 'This is an incredibly safe space to explore touch, to explore sensuality.'

Strawberries and cream were tickling around my mouth. I was aware of a low throaty sound and a soft face pressing against my cheeks. Then a warm hairy body was at my back – I had the impression of a pendant and then more flavours: chocolate, whipped cream. I was saying my 'yeses' and 'thank yous'; there was the sensation of other bodies and bits of chocolate and more strawberries entering my mouth and cheese – possibly a little too much cheese, though I didn't like to mention it because I thought it might spoil the mood – and above all there was a growing feeling of connectedness, the faint echo of the tingling sensation of a first kiss with a new lover. I had to admit I was enjoying it.

And then it was all over. I took my mask off to see Cliff sambaing up and down in a transport of satisfaction at the tableau he had created. But for a moment the idea of a community in which the currency of sex and love was more free-flowing made a tiny bit of sense. I rubbed my eyes at a world that felt a little friendlier, a little closer to home.

A little later I said my goodbyes and drove back to my hotel with the crew. In the minivan I felt slightly sheepish at how far I'd gone with my commitment to experiencing the workshop. I had the familiar sensation of being assailed by multiple ironies, of having been in control of an experience and at the same time out of my depth.

I thought about my wife, Nancy, aware that the scene I'd told her we'd be filming – involving me being fed a couple of strawberries by scantily clad women – had turned out to be more outré than I'd expected. I wondered whether she would be upset and annoyed.

And I thought, here I am, aged forty-seven, still making a fool of myself for the purposes of a TV show, creating connections in unlikely places, in a spirit in which the boundaries between silliness and seriousness, sincerity and role-playing, self-exposure and canny journalistic revelation weren't always clear even to me. Here I am, telling stories, using myself, my feelings, for real – after so many years, still doing it.

# Chapter 1

## Boisterous

Growing up, if anyone had suggested I might one day be on television, I would have looked at them, quizzical and confused, racking my brains to imagine what set of steps could possibly lead to it happening. It wasn't that the people on TV seemed remote. If anything, the reverse: they were familiar – they turned up in your home, their faces beamed onto a piece of furniture, sometimes on a daily basis. But there was no sense that you could ever aspire to be them.

One of my earliest memories is of watching an episode of the daytime legal drama *Crown Court* with my au pair. She told me the surprising fact that, although we could see the people on the television, they couldn't see us. Years later I was able to confirm this is quite true.

I probably watched too much TV. From the earliest days grazing on *Play School* and *The Clangers, Pipkins,* and *Chorlton and the Wheelies* on through *Blue Peter* and *Swap Shop* and then *Jim'll Fix It, It's A Knockout,* and *Beadle's About,* television was a constant companion. During the holidays there was a show called *Why Don't You?* that had the paradoxical brief of encouraging viewers to stop watching TV and do something else, develop a hobby like falconry or trainspotting. I never did the things they suggested, though. I was fine just watching the programme.

It may be that I missed out. But I also tend to think that deprivation and narrowness bring their own compensations. The hours of watching Open University or Eastern European expressionist cartoons with atonal music or even test cards because nothing else was on were an education of a sort, the beginning of an understanding of storytelling and a shared language that connected you to friends at school. The strange images and random phrases from programmes you liked or remembered were like flotsam and sea wrack – rubbish that could be reconstituted and repurposed, as jokes and impressions, or just to provide the reassurance of something recognizable and familiar. Held prisoner by the television, a kind of Stockholm Syndrome set in and I fell in an ambivalent love with my captor.

As I grew older and my tastes became more decadent, one of my pleasures was TV that *went wrong*. A game-show contestant called Floyd on an American episode of *The Price is Right* who got nervous and fluffed his prepared anecdote. 'He-hey! Floyd! I didn't quite get that!' the host said. My brother and I would impersonate it and collapse in giggles. An episode of *Record Breakers* in which a truculent child contradicted the house expert – and keeper of the records – Norris McWhirter, who everyone knew had a photographic memory, presuming to tell him that he'd given the wrong weight for the Cullinan Diamond, drawing him into an undignified squabble. The following week the presenter Roy Castle came on with a pile of reference books and, in grave tones, assured viewers that the child had been mistaken – figuratively crushing him with the books – and order was restored.

Later, I loved programmes like *The Kenny Everett Video Show* and *The Young Ones* that broke the rules by drawing attention to their own artifice. Kenny Everett would wander off the set, showing the wires and cameras you weren't supposed to see. It felt daring and transgressive. *The Young Ones* made jokes about its own fictional nature, diving down rabbit warrens, using what would now be called 'meta humour'.

Sometimes I'd enter TV competitions hoping to experience the vicarious fame of having my work featured. I drew pictures and sent them in to the art programme *Take Hart*. They didn't get on. I also entered two different *Blue Peter* competitions, one to design a logo for the UN's International Year of the Child and another to do an illustration for an anniversary card for the Natural History Museum. Every time they read out the address, 'That's London W12 8QT', I couldn't find a pen in time to write it down.

If I ever did send them in, they didn't win. Nor were they shown in a wide shot of entries-that-didn't-win.

I couldn't even get my stupid pictures on television. That's how not-on-TV I was.

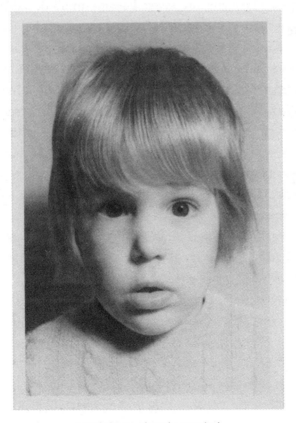

Aged three, already worried.

I was the second of two sons and I had the space and licence to be the silly one. My brother, Marcel, was the prodigy, the dauphin of the kingdom of literature: a precocious reader, a writer of poetry, a star actor at school. I was light relief. This was the natural order of things. Everyone had his place: Marcel's was reading about Greek myths and *Beowulf*. Mine was knowing all the words to the nursery rhyme 'Solomon Grundy'. My English grandma, who had a gift for simplifying people's characteristics, pegged me early on as someone who was 'good with his hands'. It took me years to realize it might not be a compliment.

A word that got used a lot about me was 'boisterous'. My mum would sometimes recall a performance at my pre-school. We were singing 'Peter Hammers with One Hammer', with accompanying gestures, and she noticed that instead of hammering my own knee, I was hammering the knee of the boy next to me.

I had a very loud voice. I was adenoidal, my Ms sounded like Bs. A family impression had me quailing after my mother, 'Bub? *Bub!*' They took me for tests to see if I might be deaf. I was probably three or four, given headphones for the first time while the doctor dropped tiddlywinks into a jar then whispered numbers into my ear that I had to repeat back. When the results came in, the verdict was: not deaf, just loud. Another impression my dad used to do involved me saying, 'But why does the man have his mouth open?' It was based on a dimly remembered incident on a bus or a train or somewhere in London when I'd embarrassed my parents by making loud enquiries about a fellow passenger who was, presumably, mentally ill or had weak jaw muscles.

My 'But why?' questions were my sallies at a world full of mystery and strangeness, and often they drew attention to taboo subjects, things you weren't supposed to say: the homeless, people with disabilities, the mentally ill muttering to themselves on streets. And yet I was also very worry-prone, finding causes for anxiety in the most unlikely scenarios. That I would never be able to read and write. That I would be unable to pay my taxes when I was grown up. That 'Winkie' – of the nursery rhyme 'Wee Willy Winkie'– was out 'running through the town' and specifically running towards my bedroom with undefined malice in mind. That our family was going bankrupt. That I wouldn't learn how to maypole dance in time for the summer fete.

Many of my anxieties focused on events at school. When I was still at primary school my mum went in to explain to the teacher that I was perhaps more fragile than they realized and needed special attention. The teacher was sympathetic but confused – she didn't recognize me in the description. On the way out, my mum passed by my classroom and through the door she could see me running along the tops of the desks.

My parents met in East Africa – in Kampala. My dad was American, a lecturer in literature at Makerere University and already a published novelist. My mum, English, was studying to be a teacher so she could take a position at a girls' school in rural Kenya. They fell in love, married, and my brother followed less than nine months afterwards. Later they moved to Singapore, where my dad had taken a job teaching at the university, and it was there that I was born, in May 1970, at Gleneagles Hospital, and issued a US passport.

We moved to England when I was one year old. My mum joined the BBC as an arts producer for the World Service. She was a feminist, a proud working woman, and we had live-in au pairs. There is an early photograph – from a newspaper feature about mums that work outside the home – that shows her resplendent in flares and a short-sleeved jumper, with puffy shirt sleeves poking out, as she strides off to her BBC office in London's West End. I am looking on from the doorway with my brother and our au pair Catherine.

My dad worked from home, tapping away on a manual typewriter, wreathed in pipe smoke. Photos of him from that time show he too was a prisoner of the era: long sideburns, big-collared shirt, a

Mum going to work. I'm in the puffy shorts on the left.

tight little tank top that his mother-in-law had knitted for him, and jeans that were as loose around the ankle as they were tight around the crotch.

Until I was four, we lived in Catford, a scruffy area of south-east London, in a small terraced house. My memories of this period are dim and of the surreal do-I-really-remember-this? variety. I thought there were tiny musicians that lived inside the radio, and my favourite toy was a tin robot that shot sparks from its chest.

The family fortunes changed in 1975 when my dad wrote a bestselling travel book, *The Great Railway Bazaar*. The success was enough to make him a literary celebrity at the young age of thirty-four.

Dad in *The Great Railway Bazaar* era.

The impact on my parents must have been huge: recognition, financial security. In my world it meant seeing him on the flyleaves of copies of the book, and international editions arriving from around the world, with foreign stamps that, for a while, I collected in an album. Gradually our lifestyle changed. The car, a Singer Gazelle, was replaced with a canary-coloured second-hand Renault and then a sleek new Rover that was the least reliable of the three and often failed to start or broke down.

We moved to Wandsworth, which was, back then, a little rough but more central and leafier than Catford, with trees and commons and Victorian housing stock built for people with servants who lived below stairs. Our house on Elsynge Road felt mysterious and grand, organized over four storeys, with weird nooks and draughty sash windows and creaky stairs and folding shutters. It had been chopped up into bedsits and still showed signs of multiple occupancy, but my parents began fixing it up. They got it carpeted, and the chimney was refurbished, they painted an upstairs bedroom avocado and wood-panelled the entire ground floor. And it was here, seated on the bottom of a flight of slatted wooden steps, aged five or six, that I had the strange realization, thinking about my parents' lives before I'd been born, that I had not always been here, alive, on earth, and by extension that I would, one day, not be here again. For a moment I was filled with a weird giddy feeling of cosmic insignificance mixed in with a tang of fear, and then I heard a voice saying 'DPYN' – an acronym that stood for 'Don't Pick Your Nose' that my parents used with me, and the moment was gone.

I attended Allfarthing Primary School, which was full of kids in Bay City Rollers t-shirts playing rounders, beanbags that smelled of chocolate, and road-safety films that they showed on a portable screen in the assembly hall. The school was famous for its choir that, by tradition, appeared on *Blue Peter* every Christmas. Though it went unrecorded in annals and history books, 1978 was a year of great moment in our house, when John Noakes rested his hymn book on my brother's head on national television. I dug up the tape from the BBC archives as a gift for his thirtieth birthday. You can freeze it and see my brother's face looking angelic. The year I was due to go on, there was an industrial dispute and all the Christmas programming was cancelled on the BBC. We still got *Blue Peter* badges, but it seemed all too typical – me missing my shot at the big time. Another piece of evidence that I was at best a warm-up act to the main performance.

As a consolation for missing out, the school arranged for the choir to make a recording at a professional studio. We were singing 'Zulu Warrior'. 'Here he comes, the Zulu warrior / Here he comes, the Zulu chief!' I didn't sing that bit. I just had to chant, 'Chief – chief – chief – chief'. What stays with me, though, is the recollection of being asked, after one of the takes, if I wanted to see the control room. I went in, marvelling at the banks of buttons and knobs. I peered through the internal window and was surprised to see the choir singing again, doing another take *without me*. Only years later did I realize – in an innocuous version of recovered memory syndrome – it must have been a ruse to get me out of the studio, though to this day the question of what was wrong with my *chiefs* – whether they were too loud or possibly offbeat – remains a mystery.

It was also around this time that I composed what may turn out to be my most enduring contribution to posterity and the arts. Ill and off school, I had an idea for a poem called 'The Beggarman'. It was about a man . . . who begs. He comes to town and plays on an old Mandalay and people put money on his tray. That was one of the rhymes. Then one day the beggarman leaves town and no one knows where he's gone. It was the saddest and most mysterious poem ever written, so far as I was aware. At the bottom I drew a picture of the beggarman holding his Mandalay and showed it to my brother. He told me a 'Mandalay' isn't an instrument, it's a city in Burma. So I changed it to mandolin and 'tray' to 'tin'.

I don't know what became of the manuscript of 'The Beggarman'. It is a text only known from references to it, like the second book of Aristotle's *Poetics*. But it represents an ideal for the kind of sad beauty and wistfulness I'd hope to achieve in all my work.

My dad came from an immigrant family of slender means, half Italian, half French Canadian. He'd grown up in Medford, a shabby suburb of Boston, with seven siblings all shouting and crying and hugging. My mum came from a south London family of worrywarts, steady and conscientious, but occasionally brittle and overly concerned about appearances.

My parents were very different, ill matched in some ways, him more emotionally expressive and freewheeling, her more steady and contained. But I suppose that was also the yin-and-yang of what kept them together, until they separated. Both were first-generation university-educated and placed a high value on literature and the written word. They encouraged us to view the artistic life – and specifically fine writing – as the highest calling, and reading as an essential part of our moral and intellectual sustenance. The house was full of books. Editions of Yukio Mishima, Graham Greene, Patrick White, Albert Camus, Anthony Burgess. Without them saying it – without them needing to say it – we were encouraged to think of ourselves as perhaps slightly better than other people, whose children didn't read Tolkien or know who Shakespeare was.

I didn't question the indoctrination. I was too young to. But it could be a little confusing, especially when it conflicted with signals from outside the home. Later, when we were sent to a fee-paying prep school, the children all advertised their Tory leanings. I knew my mum supported Labour. I kept it quiet. We were not patriotic, nor were we royalist, we did not support a football team, nor did we watch sports as a family.

On religion, my mum said she was agnostic. I wasn't sure what this meant. 'Is that the same as being atheist?' 'No, it means I don't know,' she said. But she had a soft spot for squishy spiritual thinking and there were books about Gurdjieff, the Armenian mystic, on her study shelves. Once or twice she spent the weekend at meditation retreats.

They had both been raised in churchgoing households but were lapsed. I once asked my mum why they never had me baptized. She said she thought it would be better if we chose our religion when we were old enough to make up our own minds – something I haven't yet got around to doing. When my brother was about seven, my mum gave him a book on the world's major religions. Partly this was to broaden his cultural horizons, though I also have an inkling she was hoping he might pick one out.

'Mum, I've decided. I'm becoming a Hindu.'

'Great! That's a *lovely* religion!'

She was conscious of trying to counteract the lazy assumptions that were then part of the cultural climate and which her parents had occasionally been guilty of trafficking in. 'Do you know, Africans think *we're* backward because we sit in baths and not running water,' she would say. 'Buddha was preaching the idea of pacifism long before Jesus was.'

My dad seemed to find British people in general ridiculous, though he also admired a small selection of British and Irish writers of an older generation, like V. S. Pritchett and William Trevor. He had a non-specific English accent he would put on to amuse himself, loosely based on a cleaning lady we had called Mrs Tarpy. 'Wayew, the sun's trying to come ou', innit?' 'I go' a new compu'ah!'

We were, in many respects, a seventies-style family. My parents were attempting, in a way that was in equal parts ridiculous and admirable, to find a new way of doing things that was less constrained than their own upbringing. I think they were both conscious of not wanting to live the narrow, untravelled lives of their parents.

There was a copy of *The Joy of Sex* that used to lie around the house, showing line drawings of an old hairy man and a young woman making love, and *Our Bodies, Ourselves*, which encouraged readers to look at their vaginas with a mirror and a speculum . . . 'Touch yourself, smell yourself . . . taste your own secretions.' I was less puzzled by the vagina concept than by the speculum.

My father published short stories in *Playboy* so there was also, conveniently, a stash of pornography in the house. I borrowed these and I find it hard to believe he never noticed them becoming more battered throughout the eighties. It's possible he thought I was reading his fiction.

I think my parents felt that whatever we were old enough and interested enough to read, we were old enough to deal with. When my brother turned eleven or twelve, my parents gave him a copy of Colin Wilson's *Order of Assassins*, an omnium gatherum of grisly murders, for his birthday. Evidently they had their limits because either he or my mum tore out one chapter. But thereafter, Marcel rejoiced in telling me about Jack the Stripper, a serial killer whose

MO was to choke prostitutes to death using his penis – not something you necessarily need to know as an eight-year-old.

Later, drugs became part of the conversation, and I overheard my mum saying to my brother, 'When the time comes and you're a little older and you want to get high, you can do it with us.' So when, aged fifteen or so, I told my dad that I'd been smoking spliff with friends the night before, I slightly expected him to say, 'Hey, cool, man! Did you dig it?' Instead he flared his nostrils and said, 'You know, Lou, that's not very smart. The school will throw you out if they find out.'

Along with the vaguely hippy-ish ethos went a certain relaxing of the rules on monogamy. My mother had a policy of being OK about sex on location when my dad was away and, to be fair, in the early days his trips could last as long as several months. Eventually his relationships with other women became more consuming, and the strain too much for the marriage to bear. But, like most parents of that era, they were figuring it out as they went along.

Looking back, I'm conscious of being able to pick out a number of different narratives that cover some of the facts, all equally true and at the same time contradictory. There is one that celebrates the free-spiritedness and open-mindedness my parents brought to their duties, a benign neglect that allowed us to find our own fun and meant they weren't overly worried about us having long hair or staying out late or reading weird books or watching films with sex in them. Then there is another version of the story that sees them as part-timers, preoccupied with their work, delegating their responsibilities to au pairs, intermittently present, under-interested, and unmindful of the impact their semi-detached relationship with each other was having on us.

I go back and forth but in general I'm grateful for the space my mum and dad allowed us. They were ahead of their time in some ways, mindful of the need to promote tolerance and understanding about other cultures, trying not to carry on the unexamined racial attitudes of their parents.

In the years that followed – thinking about their infidelities, the discord, and the way it ended, and the sense I sometimes had of being an afterthought and someone marginal – I would occasionally feel confused and resentful. But those feelings have ebbed away as I and they have grown older, and now I am mainly thankful – for the curiosity they shared about the world, for their love of knowledge, their good humour and indulgence, and more than anything that there was never any doubt how much they loved us.

## Chapter 2

# The Fulani People of Nigeria

I f ever in my life there was a lapsarian moment of loss of innocence it was in 1978, when I was eight, and my parents moved us to a fee-paying prep school called Tower House.

I'd been excited about the change. As befitted its name, its premises were a house with a small turret in a quiet suburban street in south-west London. The children all wore uniforms and did homework. They studied French and Latin. After the relaxed all-must-have-prizes attitude of my primary, it seemed exotic.

The excitement wore off pretty fast.

It was as though I'd time-travelled back into some earlier, more narrow-minded era. All boys. Surnames only – the children even used them for each other. The teachers were almost all men. You had to stand up when they came into the room, and several were subject to strange rages, lashing out, demented with anger. 'If you can't remember it now, *how are you going to remember it in three years when you take your Common Entrance?*' Corporal punishment was common: a whack on the hand with a ruler or plimsoll or a visit to the headmaster's office for a taste of 'The Sword'. The ex-headmaster, and school founder, a half-fossilized Edwardian leftover called Mr Martin-Hurst, garaged his Jaguar at the back of the playground. When he wanted to take it out, all the children had to stand aside as he drove past, like spectators at a Lord Mayor's procession. It was said that only one boy had ever been expelled from Tower House, and that was for selling copies of the Socialist Workers Party newspaper in his school uniform.

My brother had swanned through the school, beloved by all. I thought I would do the same, but it didn't work out that way. Notwithstanding my dedication to my studies and the fact that I generally did well in tests and homework, I had absorbed from my dad a certain iconoclasm and swaggering attitude. I thought being cheeky made me lovable. The teachers of Tower House disagreed. Our English teacher, Mr Townsend, was an effeminate Irishman who lived with his mum and modelled his personality on Noel Coward. He carried a cigarette holder and wore a cravat, telling stories, almost certainly fictional, about a fiancée who died in a tragic accident. Pausing on one long anecdotal ramble, he said, 'To cut a long story short.' 'It's a bit late for that,' I interjected, thinking he might appreciate a well-crafted zinger, but almost immediately realized I'd made a mistake as I saw him pause and look momentarily as though he'd been slapped.

At the same time as I was making enemies of the teachers, I was also, slightly paradoxically, becoming increasingly fixated on work. Without really being conscious of it, I tried to control my anxiety through study: an obsessive dedication to making my homework neat, headings all underlined twice. A single crossing-out meant I had to start again.

In a way, this was akin to doubling down. If work *wasn't* going well, I felt even more distraught. In family lore, one legendary night, aged ten or eleven and preparing for a geography exam, I became fixated on not knowing enough about the Fulani people of Nigeria. My mum did her best to assuage my concerns but I was way beyond reach, in the emotional equivalent of deep space, weeping, raging, hyperventilating. She called my dad, who was away, travelling, maybe even in Nigeria, and through the phone he tried his best to talk me down but, not knowing much about that herding people who count their wealth in heads of cattle and seasonally traverse the Sahel, he was ill equipped to help. For years afterwards the phrase, said hoarse-voiced, 'Fulani people of Nigeria!' became a byword for a kind of extreme stress and emotional exhaustion.

As the culture of Tower House rubbed off on us, my dad noticed we were turning into little twerps. 'I was worried you were becoming too English,' is how he put it later on. He wrote a short story, 'Children,' based on overhearing our conversations with friends, full of mild bigotry and boasts about skiing holidays – it's in his collection *The London Embassy.* 'We went to Trinidad on a yacht my father chartered!' says one. 'American schools are rubbish!' He must have had ambivalent feelings about our education. There was a side of him that liked the idea of us learning Latin and showing off to his American family – a side that, in a way similar to the Fulani people, measured his wealth in heads of privately educated children. But he was still enough the Medford-raised boy to also think we were pampered ninnies, nincompoops who would be better off pinging tin cans with an airgun and learning how to tie sailors' knots, as he had done as a boy.

In Tower House school uniform (the hat was my dad's).

Our summers on Cape Cod became a chance to toughen us up and connect us to the homeland. He'd bought a house on the north shore, East Sandwich, and for six weeks a year we'd go there while our mum stayed and worked in London. But we had few friends and, though we sometimes saw our extended family for 'cook-outs' and trips to the beach, it was more often the case that my brother and I were left alone while our dad wrote in his study in an annex. We'd grow demented with boredom, torment one another – one morning Marcel drove me into a frenzy by repeating the meaningless phrase 'Bonjouro, Monsieuro Duro' purely for the pleasure of seeing my rage; we would hack paths through brambles and sumac trees with machetes, or go camping and build fires in the woods, or if it was raining we'd peer into the electronic blizzard of a small portable TV, trying to make out images of distant stations.

Marcel and I were objects of some curiosity to our American relatives. With our English accents, we were aware we came across as exotic and quaint. We played up to it, conjugating verbs in Latin to impress them – *video, vides, videt* – speaking with exaggerated courtesy, like royals visiting a savage colony. 'I like to read. Tolkien is my favourite. I only wear corduroy trousers.'

At the end of the summer we'd fly back to London and our other lives, saddled with a sense of doom.

Aged twelve, learning how to brood.

In 1983, after four years of Tower House, I took my Common Entrance, and got a place at Westminster School. My brother had started two years earlier – I assume my parents had picked out Westminster because it had a reputation for academic excellence and also for catering to the children of the London media and arts crowd, unlike its rival St Pauls, which, supposedly, was all bankers' and stockbrokers' children.

After Tower House, Westminster was a definite improvement – we'd joined the second half of the twentieth century – and the only odd thing looking back is that our parents should have sent us off to board, instead of enrolling us as day boys, when we lived only a half-hour cycle ride away. I suppose the arrangement allowed them to focus more on their work – and anyway we came home at weekends – but it's also true that my brother and I had had a brief and embarrassing love affair, one summer on the Cape, with a series of Enid Blyton books called *St Clare's* about a fictional girls boarding school, full of midnight feasts and pranks played on wacky French teachers. I can't say for certain but I tend to think it was these books, at least partly, that made my brother want to board.

Situated in the heart of London, Westminster was founded by Elizabeth I, in fifteen something – or maybe refounded – you can google it if you're interested. The playwright Ben Jonson went there, the poet John Dryden, and also Shane MacGowan of The Pogues. Its buildings, several of them designed by Sir Christopher Wren, clustered around a cobblestone yard and connected to Westminster Abbey via a network of cloisters. The school charged huge fees, though its proximity to the West End meant its atmosphere was arguably a little less fusty than some other public schools. Those students so minded could study their Cicero, then race up to the Slots o' Fun on Leicester Square to play video games called Rolling Thunder and Out Run.

Still, it had its share of ridiculous traditions such as the annual tossing of the 'Greaze', a huge inedible pancake that was thrown, each Shrove Tuesday, 'Up school', amidst a melee of pupils who fought to see who could retrieve the largest portion. 'Up school' was Westminsterese for 'in the assembly hall', where the walls were emblazoned with coats of arms with horses, all of them weirdly sporting erections. Another strange bit of terminology was calling normal non-uniform clothing 'shag'. 'Good Lord, Theroux, why are you in shag?' 'My school trousers were giving me a rash, sir. I have a chit from Matron.'

Assemblies – 'Up school' – started with a recitation of the Lord's Prayer in Latin, pronounced in a special Westminster style, and it was said that the dining tables in College Hall, a separate roof-beamed building, the other side of the cloisters, where the boarders ate breakfast and supper, had been hewn from the wreckage of the Spanish Armada. At that time, Westminster also had a system known as fagging. This involved the new boys acting as servants to the older boys, waking them up, delivering newspapers, making toast on boxy industrial machines with conveyor belts. Among those I aroused was the future deputy prime minister of the United Kingdom, Nick Clegg. He was a deep sleeper and needed a lot of pushing and hump-ing. Years later, when I mentioned this fact in an interview, Nick issued a statement: 'I have no recollection of Louis Theroux waking me up in the morning.' I didn't mind, though it makes me wonder if I was humping him hard enough.

The school uniform was a black suit. The children tended to be bespectacled and hunched over and pale. They'd stalk around the yard like a phalanx of miniaturized undertakers, hands thrust into pockets, coughs wracking their etiolated limbs, or lean against the Wren-designed buildings, heads too big for their tiny necks.

It was in some ways perfect for me, inasmuch as it was founded on the two lodestars of my life: withering repartee and academic work.

My geekiness, already in evidence, was about to be turbo-charged. In those days, Westminster ran a programme of 'accelerating' the top two classes of each fresh intake, moving them up a year so they took their exams early. This had the effect of isolating them from the rest of their older peers, making them even more freakish and socially disadvantaged, which was probably the idea behind it – to make them likely to work harder. I was among those accelerated and – a late developer anyway, hairless and high-voiced until I was nearly sixteen – I became even more socially maladapted: aged fifteen, I knew twenty different sexual positions by name and the effects of most illegal drugs but I had never touched a girl's breast or smoked a joint.

For most of that O level year of 1985, I kept a diary, which I can't now put my hand to but can probably summarize without too much difficulty: *I don't have any friends. When will my life start? Why don't I have any pubic hair?* These sentiments interleaved with Big Thoughts About Life, the death of God, *Crime and Punishment*, which I had recently read, a paisley shirt I'd bought at the Great Gear Market on the King's Road and was excited about, meditations on whether I might be a Nietzschean *Übermensch*, and a sense of doom at my prospects of ever getting a girlfriend or in fact even speaking to a girl or standing near one at a bus stop.

In the sixth form, when we were joined by an intake of female students, I must have made a strange apparition, piccolo-voiced androgyne that I was, rubbing shoulders with classmates some of whom were already shaving and starting to go bald. My efforts at seduction put me in mind of those pictures they used to run in the *National Enquirer* of tiny yappy dogs that have managed to mate with Great Danes.

By now I'd at least found some friends, a small gang of arty types who, like me, were a little bit pretentious, over-interested in music and comedy, and scared of girls. Two of them, Adam Buxton and Joe Cornish, went on to success in TV, radio and film, and it's striking how fully formed they were as young teenagers. Joe, aged fifteen, was tall and angular, with a dry sense of humour and an occasionally haughty attitude that didn't win him friends among the clique of sporty brooding boys who were nicknamed The Lads. He'd already set his sights on being a director and written four or five screenplays, making posters for them, which he put up in his bedroom. Adam, cuddly and ingratiating, was an obsessive diarist, a Bowie fan, and maker of 'compies' – compilation tapes of music – for friends. He was also an early adopter of video technology. On shoebox-sized cameras he and Joe would film improvised skits in which I occasionally appeared. Parodies of adverts. A spoof French art film called *L'Homme Avec La Tête*. Our version of an American TV show we'd seen called *Danger Freaks*. We filmed a friend called Daniel Jeffries as he squirted lighter fluid on his sleeves and set them on fire. 'This is called the *Danger Freaks* double hander!' he shouted as he whooped and cavorted under the low wooden ceilings of the highly flammable Westminster buildings.

Under Joe's influence, our weekends revolved around a regimen of movie-going, of whatever happened to be on at the Cannon Oxford Street – often horror, sometimes comedy, occasionally art house, many of them films that posterity has done the favour of consigning to oblivion: *The Stuff, The Incredible Shrinking Man, American Ninja 2, Remo: Unarmed and Dangerous*. Others I still remember fondly, like *Reanimator, The Burbs*, the first *Nightmare on Elm Street*. Another friend, Zac Sandler, introduced me to the world of comics – *The Fabulous Furry Freak Brothers* by Gilbert Sheldon; *Viz* – and in history class we'd compose strips, doing alternate panels, under the noses of our teachers. For the first time I began to feel that I had a little team of likeminded compadres, that I wasn't quite so alone.

In the first term of sixth form, Adam and Joe, with another friend, Ben Walden, put on a production of an American play called *Pvt Wars*, in which the three public school adolescents took roles as grizzled Vietnam vets with PTSD in a mental hospital. It was all oddly predictive of the Wes Anderson film, *Rushmore*. Joe and Adam had announced they were now co-proprietors of their own media corporation called Joe/Adz and they approached the production with a seriousness and ambition that verged on the comical, but the scariest part may have been how skilled they all were – the years of immersion in American movies and television meant their accents were pitch-perfect, better than those you might hear on the professional stages of the West End. Later, feeling jealous, I announced I was founding my own corporation with Zac, called Lou/Zac. 'It sounds like a toilet cleaner,' Joe said.

Also with Zac I took a role in a production of *Ritual for Dolls*, an allegorical play about repressed Victorian society written in 1970, featuring children's toys. Zac was in the role of 'Golliwog', which was questionable even then, while I played the Wooden Soldier. For my climactic speech, I had to confess my forbidden love for my sister, the doll, and declaim the line, 'I spill my seed on the sheets of my fever-soaked bed.' It was supposed to be dramatic but caused a school colleague, recognizable even in the dark as Reed Smith, to snort involuntarily with laughter.

Towards the end of the year, when Joe and Adam made plans for an ambitious staging of the children's musical *Bugsy Malone*, I was cast as Dandy Dan, which led to several weeks of anxiety on my part as I thought about going back on stage. After my first rehearsal, feeling self-conscious about my performance, I went off and brooded, then finally sought out Joe and told him, 'I'm so sorry, I don't think I can do it, I'm just no good.' He was understanding. 'I'm sure we could have sorted it out, Lou,' he said. But he accepted my resignation and gave me a couple of tiny walk-on roles. When the show finally went on – preceded by a massive promotional blitz masterminded by Joe/Adz and based on the publicity campaign for *Ghostbusters* – it was a triumph. My performance as Looney Bergonzi would be the last time I ever attempted to act, unless you count a role in a porn film for *Weird Weekends* many years later.

When we weren't watching movies in the West End we'd some-times spend the evening at Ben's flat in Kentish Town – he lived with his mum who was often away – and we'd smoke cigarettes and drink gin there until morning. There still exists some video of these evenings shot by Adam. If Vladimir Putin is ever minded to blackmail me, I'd suggest he take a look at them. There's no pee-ing, but there are definite homoerotic undertones. I come across as a squealing drunken ninny, giggling and prancing around like someone auditioning for a comedy update of the Merchant Ivory film *Maurice*. Sometimes we'd watch fifteen minutes of whatever film Joe had brought on video before conking out on Ben's mum's double bed.

When, around 1988, Joe made me a compilation tape that intro-duced me to Eric B and Rakim's 'Paid in Full' (the Coldcut remix), I felt I'd found some kind of missing piece: a popular art form that was infectious and vital but which – I told myself with more than a touch of self-importance – was also socially significant, an authentic expression of the streets. It was swaggering and confident, occasion-ally angry, unapologetically masculine, with hints of criminality – in short, everything that I was not and secretly aspired to be.

At the beginning of my last year at Westminster I sat what was called 'Fourth Term' – an entrance paper to study at Oxford. Weeks of memorization of history essays followed. A month or two after I sat the exams I was summoned for an interview. Thanks to being accelerated, I was only just sixteen years old. My voice had recently broken. I borrowed a suit of my brother's, but I'd grown so fast I had to wear the trousers prison-style round my bum so the cuffs could reach my ankles.

It would be hard to imagine someone in whom book learning and emotional maturity were more out of balance. I was like something created in a laboratory, a freakish man-child in culottes, offering opinions about the Valois kings of France in a voice that went up and down like a broken radio.

I took the train up the night before, then spent the best part of a day waiting for my fifteen-minute slot, strolling around the Magdalen grounds, its gracious configuration of quads and cloisters, and its deer park. Steeped in the atmosphere of its centuries of history, the chiming of the bell tower, heavy oaken doors and lawns and rose gardens, I felt overawed but also oddly as though I was enacting a drama of myself as a candidate self-consciously thinking big thoughts about 'the death of the Middle Ages' and 'baronial power'. When the time came, I climbed a narrow stone staircase that led up from a cloister, to find three professors, all male, who ushered me into a seat so yielding that it felt a little like falling through a trap door.

The dons seemed kindly. One looked old enough for me to be concerned about his ability to live out the duration of the interview. Another, a little younger, in tweeds, smiled and, after some throat-clearing remarks, said, 'You quote a comment of Vaughan's describing Philippe de Commynes as having been "a mendacious charlatan". Why do you suppose "charlatan"?'

Nerves had made my voice little more than a whisper.

'Because he wasn't who he claimed to be?'

There were nods. I imagine, looking back, they were registering my evident anxiety and wondering whether, if pushed too hard, I might burst into flames or just short-circuit, emit a 'bzzzzt' sound and a ribbon of smoke waft out of my ears.

When the acceptance message came, I read it with a weird blank feeling of inevitability. *Well, of course.* They also sent a letter to the school, which my head of house was kind enough to read out to me. It made reference to 'this remarkable young man', and I remember thinking how odd it was that they called me a 'man'.

## Chapter 3

# Bird-dogging Chicks and Banging Beaver

In some ways, Westminster spoiled Oxford for me. By the time I went up, in the autumn of 1988, I had already done medieval cloisters and archaic slang like 'subfusc', which meant formal clothing, and 'battels', which meant bills. Half the people at Oxford were *from* Westminster or Westminster-ish places – academic public schools like Eton and St Paul's and Winchester – and, like me, brimming with entitlement and floppy hair. Crossing Magdalen Bridge, I nodded at many of the same faces as in Westminster's Little Dean's Yard: the location had moved fifty-six miles down the M40 but the population was to a great extent the same.

I was by now eighteen, having taken a year off to give nature a chance to make me a fraction more man-like. The less said about that year, the better. It's a tradition of British public school children to travel to the developing world between school and university. The idea, I think, is that the imperial powers of yore did *too little* to harm their former colonies and so it falls to the younger generation to hobble them further by arriving in hordes as unqualified and incompetent volunteers.

My stay in Zimbabwe was definitely educational, though sadly not for my students as I quit halfway through the posting, unable to keep control in the classroom. I had been struggling from the get-go:

with no natural authority or instinct for the job, I had tried to bond with students by being silly and making them laugh, which turned out to be a short-term strategy. My classes became unruly; fewer and fewer homeworks were handed in. I was putting children in detention en masse, trying to claw back some control, to little avail. Then my dad wrote to say he was coming to the country and wanted to visit. I sent him a mealy-mouthed letter of non-encouragement, feeling it undermined the purpose of my being there, which was, I supposed, to remove myself from my normal milieu and develop my autonomy. The Great Traveller dropping by, checking up on things, would have felt like being upstaged.

He arrived unannounced in the middle of a maths lesson, having taken a two-hour taxi ride from Harare. 'Lou, I couldn't reach you on the phone.'

I hugged him. He began taking photographs and the students erupted. I still have the photos. I'm smiling, surrounded by overexcited children. Maybe it was what I needed: to recognize the whole misadventure of 'teaching in Africa' as play-acting, something I was too young and too immature to know how to handle.

I muddled on to the end of the term, then handed in my notice and went travelling in Zambia, Malawi, and Botswana. Given that the idea was to teach and help out, not up stumps halfway through the job, you could say that my going and then leaving was worse than not going at all – and I wouldn't argue with you. I sometimes wonder how different the fate of the African continent might have been had I stuck it out.

Arriving at Oxford, I'd planned to take it easy, kick back a little, start to enjoy life – go out bird-dogging chicks and banging beaver. Or if that couldn't be arranged, maybe take a long walk through Magdalen deer park, holding hands and talking about Ian McEwan and Paul Auster. But, despite my best resolutions, working *less* proved more difficult than you might think. Something in me kept driving me to study. My subject was 'Modern History', which in classic Oxford style meant everything after the end of Roman Britain. During a one-to-one midway through my second term, Magdalen's head history tutor, Angus Macintyre, told me he thought I was on track to get a first in the end-of-year exams. This had not previously occurred to me as a possibility but from then on I saw it as an obligation. The beaver banging and tail-chasing, already delayed, now drifted further behind schedule as I applied myself to essay writing and rote learning with my wonted obsessiveness while all the time being aware, like a rider on a startled horse, that I needed to slow down, that I was in danger of missing out, of letting student life pass me by.

At the end of my first term I struck up a romance with a fellow student. She seduced me, coming round to my bedroom half-drunk one evening and saying, 'Kiss me.' She'd also been at Westminster – she was, by coincidence, the 'doll' I'd 'spilled my sheets over my fever-soaked bed' about. In the play. And possibly in life. Her name was Sarah. (Her name wasn't Sarah.) Fiercely intelligent, thoughtful and argumentative, she came from a Jewish family in north London that was in its way as status-conscious and idiosyncratic as my own, though less liberal and less at pains to signal its bohemian credentials. There was no question of smoking ganj with the parents in Sarah's family. Raised like a caged veal, as the American writer Shalom Auslander once wrote of his upbringing, she'd been shielded from pop music – or maybe had just taken no interest in it – until her adolescence. She was intensely self-conscious of her privilege and spoke an English so correct that people sometimes thought she was foreign. Around her I could pass as something of a hipster.

Once every couple of terms I would break up with her, imagining a wealth of romantic opportunity waiting to be taken. Then reality would sink in, I'd be alone and she'd call, or on at least one occasion she climbed through the window and we'd find ourselves back together again. My relationship with Sarah continued, with breaks and intermissions, over the next twelve years.

At the weekend, when I'd finished studying, I'd hunt for house parties among the student lodgings up and down Cowley Road and Iffley Road, senses primed for any open doors and the sound of music emanating from them – it was a little like a game in which the objective was to become inebriated in a stranger's kitchen. Sometimes I'd take the coach down to London to visit Adam and Joe, and Zac, who was starting a career as a comic-book artist. These were my most dedicated years of pot-smoking and, with Joe, I'd walk down to Armoury Way, round the corner from the Arndale Centre in Wandsworth, to buy an eighth or a sixteenth of hash from a West Indian dealer called The Professor who lived in a flat in a twenties Peabody Estate-style housing block. Later The Professor gave way to an older man named Coarsey – the spelling of his name is pure conjecture on my part – whose services we used for five or more years.

The flat was barely furnished, with a TV and a bed. It was a little like visiting a B&B, the awkward feeling of doing business in someone's home. Joe and I would joke that we worried Coarsey seemed lonely or that business had dried up, since we never saw much evidence of other customers. I'd try to start small talk about rap. 'So, what do you think of the new Big Daddy Kane album?' For some reason these conversational gambits did not lead to the fantasy of respect and comity that I'd dreamed of, and occasionally I wondered whether Coarsey might *not* be pining for a transracial friendship that could be a beacon of brotherhood for the world. One time Joe returned from a solo journey to Armoury Way to announce that Coarsey had asked, 'Where's Glasses?' That was about as far as we got in the warmth stakes.

Often we'd go to Zac's place in his dad's flat off Finchley Road in North London. Zac's dad was a Napoleon obsessive, his sitting room a vast library of leather-bound books about the armies of the French Empire and Waterloo. Early in the evening he'd sometimes come and say hello and we'd make conversation. 'They got so desperate they drank horse piss, didn't they, Dad?' Zac said. 'All right, lads, have fun,' Zac's dad would say. Then, surrounded by the walls of dusty volumes, we'd get high and listen to whatever new hip-hop was out – BDP, Public Enemy, EPMD, Schoolly D – or tapes of Tim Westwood, the Capital hip-hop DJ, flattering ourselves that we were plugging in to important bulletins from dissident America. We'd put tracing paper on the record player and scratch records and improvise rhymes over break beats.

I subscribed to *Hip Hop Connection*, a British rap magazine. It mainly covered American hip-hop but the editors tried to support the nascent UK scene. British rap was then spotty at best. There was Derek B, who was a pale photocopy of an American MC. MC Duke was more interesting – he styled himself like a country squire, with tweeds and jodhpurs and a shotgun, ready to hunt some grouse. The least embarrassing UK rapper was Silver Bullet, a verbal spitfire from Aylesbury who used alliteration in his lyrics in a manner reminiscent of the *Beowulf* poet.

I bought a couple of British rap albums out of a sense of obligation, one by the Demon Boyz, another by Ruthless Rap Assassins. Neither

Left to right: Zac Sandler, me, Joe Cornish, and Adam Buxton.

was very good. Feeling burned, I wrote to *Hip Hop Connection*, complaining about their uncritical promotion of British artists. 'Let's face it, UK hip-hop sucks,' I said, signing off, 'King Lou-E, Oxford.' They ran the letter. A couple of months later there was a special letters page given over to replies, all of them negative. One began: 'King Lou-E, dope name, pity about you being such a fucker.' The editors wrote, 'This is just a small sampling of the literally sackloads of mail we received.'

In my third year, with finals on the horizon, my world became smaller still as I redoubled my academic efforts. When the time came to choose a specialization, I focused on philosophy and sociology, areas of inquiry that purported to provide world-encompassing solutions, frameworks for understanding the big questions in life. History came easily – the memorization and grinding through reading lists, the marshalling of arguments, 'on the one hand this, on the other hand that' – which prejudiced me against it. I romanticized subjects that struck me as more mysterious and difficult: the grand narratives of figures like Marx or Hegel or Auguste Comte, the pessimistic liberalism of Max Weber, the idea that lives in the West are becoming bureaucratized and regulated and imprisoning, that society *isn't* progressing but getting worse, and the post-structuralism of Michel Foucault and his view that our bodies and lives are always being shaped and disciplined by dimly understood cultural forces, that even apparently benign concepts like freedom and justice are masks for deeper and more insidious forms of power. I spent a term studying the Scientific Revolution of the seventeenth century – Galileo, Kepler, Descartes, Boyle, Newton. I read philosophers of science like T. S. Kuhn, who maintained that scientific progress is much more erratic and less purely empirical than it appears, and Paul Feyerabend, who went further, holding that the supposed methodology of science was no better and no more truthful than mythology or magic.

At the same time, I enjoyed these concepts more as a spectator than as a believer, in the spirit of George Orwell when he wrote, 'There are some ideas so wrong that only a very intelligent person could believe in them.' I found myself drawn to fundamentalist figures like Robespierre or the thinkers in George Woodcock's book, *Anarchism*: Sergey Nechayev, the Russian revolutionary who slept on bare wood and advocated terrorism and murdered a former comrade. I was fascinated by people who acted at odds with norms of behaviour – people unmindful of conventional ethics or even of commonly acknowledged reality, expressing the darkest parts of the human heart often out of a misplaced idealism.

If there were any ideas that stuck me with me from my entire three years at Oxford, they were to do with the contingency of beliefs, the ways in which we are all prisoners of our own place and time. Slaveholders and pederasts in Ancient Greece. Godbotherers in the Dark Ages. Torturers and witch-hunters in early modern England. And, as much as I enjoyed the ingenuity of the theories of philosophers and sociologists, where I found writing to admire and connect with tended to be in the surprise of tiny commonalities and little beacons of shared humanity across the centuries, in the humane and intimate essays of Michel Montaigne, in the gossipy little biographies of John Aubrey. Something in their combination of remoteness and familiarity was oddly reassuring.

As time went on I saw friends making plans for their future, setting up appointments with careers advisers, going to jobs fairs, meeting emissaries of big companies. It was faintly worrying. I had no idea what I might do in the future. By now I had contributed the occasional article and film review to Oxford publications, and drawn some comics and written a humorous rap for a student comedy magazine – the Queen delivering gangsta verses in the style of NWA, boasting about her riches and sexual prowess. But the idea of being a writer didn't seem especially realistic and as my graduation date approached I looked out at the inhospitable world feeling like a prison inmate after years of incarceration who doesn't know what the Internet is or how to work a mobile phone.

I wondered about pursuing a postgraduate degree, maybe becoming an academic, and I applied for and got a place at SOAS, the School of Oriental and African Studies. The embarrassing part of my brain began to hope I might do well enough in my finals to get the nod from All Souls, the semi-secret Oxford College for the crème de la crème of academics, a kind of brains trust where the fellows are released from having to do any research. They sit around at their formal dinners having big thoughts. It's like something from a James Bond film except, instead of a shadowy group of supervillains bent on world domination, they are tweedy academics dribbling into their soup – that seemed like a job that wouldn't be too demanding. Professional boffin insulated from the world.

When the finals results came, I got a first. With the amount of work I did, it would have been pretty weird if I hadn't. The notice came by post – there was also a message from one of the history dons. It said how many Magdalen history students had taken firsts that year, going on, 'but yours was by some way the highest and must have been close to the top of the entire year.' The phrasing, which I unintentionally memorized, warmed my spirits in low moments for several years afterwards.

The summer after I graduated I postponed my place at SOAS and flew to Boston. I did it on a whim, wary of the London jobs market, which was then in the throes of a recession, thinking I could postpone any decisions about my future and work by taking a few months off in America. The first Gulf War had been fought earlier in the year. Margaret Thatcher had recently left office, and the mood in Britain was bleak. The hectic and high-paced era of the eighties – all shoulder pads and yuppies in braces and 'when it hits eighteen *buy it all*' – had given way to a hangover of gloom and joblessness and shoulders tragically reduced to their natural proportions.

By now, Sarah had taken a job teaching English in a remote area of China for a year. We were spending some time apart, by mutual agreement sowing some wild oats, and for several weeks I mooched at my dad's house at Cape Cod, visited family, hung out with Marcel, who had taken a job writing the news for a start-up cable station in Boston, the Monitor Channel. On a whim, I took the train to Los Angeles, riding over in an Amtrak sleeper car, spending much of the time in conversation with the train attendants, who were all black and – confusingly – fans of Phil Collins.

I was staying with my uncle Peter, an author and Arabic translator, at his apartment in Long Beach, a small city south of Los Angeles. For several days I made sorties to sites around LA: a pilgrimage to Compton, spawning ground for the rap group NWA; a road trip down to to the Mexican border city of Tijuana. But the trip was mainly memorable for an outing to Hollywood where, amid the array of flea-bitten attractions, shops selling plastic Oscars, fly-by-night guys with vans advertising 'tours of stars' homes', I passed a tall old distinguished-looking building advertising the L. Ron Hubbard Life Exhibit, a museum dedicated to the life of the founder of the religion of Scientology.

I had heard a little about Scientology – my uncle Peter, who like me had a certain fascination with the macabre and the taboo, had described it to me as a mysterious and secretive spiritual organization, created by a science-fiction writer, which numbered Hollywood stars among its devotees and used hard-sell tactics on its parishioners to make money out of its religious services. Going into the museum, I'd expected a half-hour ramble around an unintentionally humorous slice of roadside Americana. Instead I was dismayed to find I was chaperoned by a very slow-moving docent. The displays about Hubbard's early life worked hard to create the required impression of a spiritual prodigy of world-changing stature. They made a great deal out of his having been an Eagle Scout at an unusually young age – my dad had also been an Eagle Scout; impressive as it was,

I reflected that it didn't necessarily qualify him to start his own religion. There were illustrations of LRH as a teenager trading gnostic insights into life's big questions with Native American shamans in Montana and wrinkly Asian holy men in Lhasa or Ladakh.

Finally, after forty-five minutes or so, I overcame my natural urge to be obliging, and said, 'I'm so sorry, but I really have somewhere I need to be.' The staff looked at me as if to say, *What could possibly be more important than finding out you are actually a trillion-year-old space alien?* Eventually I made my way out, having promised to return the following day, which needless to say I didn't do.

I'd been planning to head back to London at the end of the summer, but as September approached, figuring I had nothing pressing to do there, I decided to stay in America.

For several months I lived in Boston with my brother, sleeping on his futon. I found a job in a glass-blowing studio next door to an Asian bookstore where Marcel had briefly worked as a sales assistant. The studio, which belonged to a sleepy young glass sculptor called Tony Devlin, mainly produced cherub goblets. These were ostentatious gold-coated *objets d'art* – the kind of goblets Uday and Qusay Hussein might have enjoyed using to drink the blood of their enemies. They sold in high-class stores for large sums and, supposedly, were made in accordance with an age-old Venetian glass-twisting technique. In fact our guilty secret was that only the cherubs themselves were sculpted. The base and bowl were cannibalized from mass-produced glassware. It was my job to remove the stems from the store-bought goblets, grind the ends down and fix the cherubs in the middle using a glue that was activated by UV light – I had to wear special goggles when I did it.

My other job was to hold Tony's punty rod until the blob of glass on the end heated up – this is not a weird sexual euphemism but technical glass jargon, as any fellow glassworkers among my readership will recognize. Later on, after I left, Tony told me he'd found a brick that did the same job of holding his punty in place just as well as I had done. He said he'd nicknamed the brick 'the Louis'.

Never having aspired to make cherub goblets, I was feeling directionless and unfulfilled. My parents had split up by now, and while it had been abundantly foreshadowed, it was still weirdly upsetting and at the same time a little bit exciting. I felt licensed to feel a level of anger and alienation that was already in me. I had the feeling that at the point of leaving home, home itself had disappeared – and not just disappeared but been exposed as hollow, based on lies and improvisations. A Potemkin village erected by its own inhabitants to convince themselves that they were normal and well cared for. Looking back, with my own children as my future judges, I see these characterizations as unfair, but it was how I felt. And in a positive way, emerging from the fog of my own indoctrination, I felt what was probably a salutary urge to make something of myself, to separate myself from my family, to prove something, though exactly what was as yet unclear.

If I'd been predisposed to become a jihadi or a white nationalist terrorist, it probably would have happened around this time. Instead I started trying to teach myself Russian. That lasted about two days. I thought about joining the marines. I read books full of angst and grandiosity: *Ecce Homo* by Friedrich Nietzsche and *Hunger* by Knut Hamsun and *Notes from Underground* by Dostoevsky. I jotted down philosophical aperçus and wrote 800 words of a memoir. Based on paper-thin knowledge of the then-fashionable theories of postmodernism, I said things like, 'Art is like a chicken running around with its head cut off. It's dead, it just doesn't know it yet.' Full of ambition but with no clear sense of direction, I had the strong sense it was time to start my life, and no idea how to do it.

Chapter 4

## The Way to San Jose

When I told my dad I was going to San Jose, his reaction was to say several times, 'Do you know, I have never been to San Jose,' as though this in itself was an interesting fact about the place. Given that he had travelled throughout the world, the idea of finding somewhere he hadn't written about and left his mark on was, in fact, one of its main attractions.

It was an internship – I would be working for next to nothing for three months in California at a weekly newspaper. One dark winter afternoon I had visited the august reading room of the Boston public library and found a book called the *Directory of Internships* and applied for work placement schemes at a far-flung selection of US newspapers and magazines – one in Colorado, another in New Orleans. A few weeks later, a call came from *Metro*, a weekly in San Jose, California, saying they'd like to take me on.

I had thought San Jose might be on the sea, confusing it with San Diego. In fact, San Jose is landlocked, a farm town that, as they say of cancer cells, forgot to stop growing. It lies a hundred miles south of San Francisco and numbered, in those days, around a million souls. It has no claim to fame other than featuring in a Burt Bacharach song about someone unable to find it, and its connection to Silicon Valley, in which it notionally sits, though in fact most of the big tech companies are in smaller towns outside the San Jose city limits, like Santa Clara and Cupertino. It is a city in which the natural relation between centre and periphery is reversed. The life of its community takes place in vast malls, secondary towns, suburbs, freeways, and office parks, far away from its largely empty downtown. All these peculiarities – its soullessness, the indistinguishable strip malls, the gun stores and fast-food places, franchise outlets and the weird scattered non-belonging of people, many of them from elsewhere – had a perverse charm for me. After a lifetime of cloisters and Victorian suburbs, I saw exoticism and romance in San Jose's anomie and unplanned sprawl. It seemed utterly different to anything I'd experienced, and its strangeness and lack of judgement combined to make me feel, for the first time, invisible and liberated.

*Metro* was a free newspaper, given away in metal bins around the city. The editorial team was a ragtag band of ageing punks and ex-hippies – what might today be called hipsters. The deal on offer from management involved allowing those on staff the liberty of coming in late, wearing what they liked, and playing Tetris late into the night on office computers, on the condition that they did their work and didn't expect to be well paid. Several of the writers were graduates of the nearby University of California, Santa Cruz, a cradle of radical activity and progressive politics, and I don't think it's too grandiose to say that faintly in the background were the stirrings of new ideas and subcultures that would prove influential through the rest of the decade – whispers of the Internet, 'modern primitives', techno-shamanism, and Burning Man. Sadly, there was only a limited outlet for many of these ideas in a newspaper dedicated to the prosaic concerns of a very average American city, in which it was widely acknowledged the only feature anyone read was the horoscope.

My news editor, Jon Vankin, was a polymath of US politics, with a righteously angry punk edge, a devotee of the British music acts The Pop Group and Gang of Four, liable to quote lyrics about the death of the campaigner Blair Peach during an anti-Nazi rally in London in the seventies and rant about oligarchic corruption in the US body politic. He and another *Metro* writer later compiled several books of American conspiracy theories propagating the idea that we are all brainwashed drones existing in a sinister confected reality in which nothing is really what it seems – the Kennedy assassination, Iran–Contra, the cancellation of the TV series *The X-Files*.

Embattled amid the surrounding blandness of San Jose, *Metro* felt like the citadel of a small counterculture. We were lonely hold-outs flying the flag of strangeness in a vast indifferent sea. God knows what they made of me – the pale and awkward recent Oxford graduate, turning up six thousand miles from home in one of America's most boring cities. A city that didn't even have the inverse allure of high crime or deprivation.

A news intern, my duties involved fact-checking articles, undertaking bits of research for other writers, transcribing tapes, and pottering around looking confused. A few weeks in, they let me have a small column, the 'Polis Report', where I wrote quirky articles about the city. An interview with a Jamaican psychic who was predicting an earthquake in the Bay Area. A business story – largely fictional – about a rise in vibrator sales in sex shops. In the middle of the year, in the wake of the Rodney King verdict unrest – San Jose experienced this in the tiny rippling form of a small downtown protest – I phoned an anarchist thinker and writer, John Zerzan, and wrote up a short account of his view that the disorder was overall 'a positive act' that should be celebrated, under the headline 'Paperback Rioter'.

After three months of interning, I got hired as a staff writer on a smaller newspaper owned by the Metro media group, the *San Jose City Times*, that shared offices with *Metro* and was known among staff as Shitty Times. Supporting myself with words was still new enough to feel exciting. I wrote about City Council meetings, budgets and zoning, fires, charity fundraisers, shake-ups at City

Hall, some political gossip, and the occasional human interest story about local characters. I turned in an early story about a fire that had gutted a Chinese restaurant. It began with a description of clouds scudding across the sky as the smoke rose.

'Do you know about the inverted pyramid?' my Shitty Times editor, Lorraine, asked. 'Most important facts at the top. Was anyone hurt? How much damage? The clouds scudding can come further down.'

Once in a while I got to range more leftfield. I wrote a satirical account of my past-life regression experience at the 'Berkeley Psychic Institute' and another about making a donation to a sperm bank in Palo Alto, for which I had to masturbate into a little cup. (My donation was turned down – they said it didn't freeze, though that's hard to believe. Presumably it froze but the sperm were all dead when they thawed it out. Either that or I am missing my true calling as a manufacturer of organic automotive products.)

I look back now at those times from a distance of twenty-five years and I see myself totally dedicated to doing my work, to making a mark, and finding a small measure of success with my articles . . . but I also see emptiness. In that entire year I had no romances. My social life revolved around work and though I enjoyed being removed from

My *Metro* press card.

my usual milieu, stranded on a kind of frontier of middle America, I was in a deeper way cut off from real life, as though it was taking place behind glass or being conducted secretly in rooms away from me. In the end, the idea of getting close seemed complicated and entangling, fraught with all sorts of potential for embarrassment, more trouble than it was worth. I would play the encounter out in my head and get ahead of myself. How will this end? How will I get out of it?

Towards the end of the year, feeling I might have gone as far as I could in San Jose, I made plans for another move. I wondered about joining my brother, who was now living in New York. 'We'll have larks, Lou!' he said. 'We'll get an apartment in Hoboken! It'll be wicks!' I applied for an internship on a magazine there called *Spy*. But I was also missing Sarah, who was still in China, but coming to the end of her teaching assignment. We'd been writing to each other and discussing the possibility of me joining her and us living somewhere in South East Asia. By coincidence, my uncle Gene, an international lawyer, told me he had a connection on a paper in Mongolia called the *Mongol Messenger*. Gene mentioned he could hook me up there. The randomness of the connection, the fact that I knew almost nothing about the place, tickled me. I liked the idea of making big life decisions based on very little information. At the same time, I didn't take Gene's offer too seriously – he had form as an over-promiser – but on this occasion, to my surprise, he came through: an offer of a position on Ulan Bator's leading English-language newspaper arrived by post.

*Spy. Mongol Messenger. Mongol Messenger. Spy.*

At this distance I can't recall what decided me one way or another. I just know that in December of 1992 I drove in my Honda Civic, not west to Mongolia, which would have been tricky with the Pacific in the way, but east to New York and *Spy*.

# Chapter 5

## Have You Seen *Roger & Me*?

I was a latecomer to *Spy*, like someone who mistook the timings of a wild party, arriving fresh-faced long after the action had abated and all the bottles had been emptied and all the coke snorted, finding a depressing scene of depletion – a handful of semi-comatose guests and the afterglow of excess and missed opportunities. 'They mount, they shine, evaporate and fall', Dr Johnson's assessment of 'The Vanity of Human Wishes', applies to celebrity, the subjects of *Spy*, and *Spy* itself.

In its heyday in the late eighties, the magazine had enjoyed a status among its readership that verged on the cult-like. I'm not sure there is an exact analogy that exists now – its combination of satirical journalism, pranks, cultural commentary, and playful graphics. It was said the founders – Kurt Andersen and E. Graydon Carter – had drawn inspiration from *Private Eye*. Certainly it featured industry gossip and muck-raking reporting. But unlike *Private Eye*, *Spy* was glossy and full-colour. It ran big essays making fun of fashionable people and pastimes. A survey of multi-millionaire female powerbrokers called 'Too Rich and Too Thin'. Another on short billionaires, calculating their 'adjusted height' if each hundred million was worth an extra inch. Often there were pages of unflattering photos of people at high-society parties. Parts of the magazine read like an issue of *Tatler*, but a *Tatler* where the staff had stayed up too late and gone feral, Gremlinized, and turned on the socialites they were supposed to be celebrating.

For an overly cerebral young man fixated on popular culture, the *Spy* tone and approach was irresistible. Its satirical profiles of creepy directors or cryogenic facilities or Scientologists spoke to the side of me that was fascinated by bizarre cultural phenomena. The magazine managed to be simultaneously switched on and unstuffy and brainy, a cocktail of high- and low-brow sensibilities, as clever in its way as those books by French philosophers and critics about 'the postmodern moment', but unlike those books it was also very funny.

Alas, it turns out insulting high-profile industry leaders and celebrities on a monthly basis in a glossy magazine is not a long-term business strategy. By the time I arrived the advertiser base was drying up. The magazine had fewer pages, afflicted with the publishing world's equivalent of a wasting disease. 'You work at *Spy*? Is that still going?' was a common question at parties. At the office, I would gaze at the grandeur of the back issues, fat and full of ingenious features, eviscerations of the rich and powerful, satirical takes on lazy pop-cultural tropes. I'd wonder if this was what Ancient Britons had felt as they gasped at the plumbing and viaducts and pooped amid the ruins of the columns and mosaics left behind by the Roman Empire.

An intern again, my duties involved photocopying and stapling 'gossip packs', culled from the five or six New York newspapers, and also doing research for the editors. Occasionally I was allowed to contribute waspish items about celebrities or write the table of contents or headlines or take part in brainstorming sessions for pun-based captions for photographs. 'It's a picture of Michael Jackson with what looks like a bread roll.' 'Er, how about "boulangerous"? Or . . . just "Michael Jackson, roll model"?'

Over the months, I worked my way up the masthead, becoming an editorial assistant and then a staff writer. I did a couple of pranks.

When a little-known TV writer called Conan O'Brien landed a high-profile gig as a talk show host, it fell to me to call up the eminent historian and writer Conor Cruise O'Brien at his home in Ireland and interview him as though *he'd* got the job – the comedy arose from the historian-O'Brien's bafflement and confusion at the direction of my questions, his polite and bookish bemusement at being asked if he would be doing 'Stupid Pet Tricks' on his new TV show.

I didn't much like the bad faith that went with prank calls. All I can say in my favour is that I brought a kind of comedy-jihadi zeal to work that was at times embarrassing and morally hard to justify: I could usually summon the necessary ruthlessness to call unsuspecting people and ask them obtuse questions.

Probably the only thing I wrote from that time that sort of holds up was a series of interviews with rappers in which I asked them about the importance of gun safety and then invited them to freestyle a rap on the subject. This had been the idea of a talented comedy writer colleague from Canada called Chris Kelly.

Ed O.G., a 'positive' rapper from Boston who probably nobody but me remembers, stopped halfway through his freestyle, unable to find a rhyme. Schoolly D and Everlast and Sir Mix-a-Lot all refused to do it. The only rapper who distinguished himself was Fat Joe the Gangsta. 'I once knew a sucka who tried to play me and slay me. And make me do a muthafuckin' rap about gun safety. Yo check it! Fat Joe. On the freestyle tip. A nigga you don't wanna fuck wit.' For me, a fan of rap, being mentioned by Fat Joe was a kind of baptism.

After San Jose, New York had taken some adjustment. The slow-paced, supersized farm town was no preparation for the noise and scale of Gotham: the asperity of the people, the cold of the winters, the heat of the summers, the inescapable round-the-clock hum of the traffic, the city's apparent lack of interest in me. I've sometimes thought the quintessential New York moment was a scene I once witnessed on a subway platform at 7th Avenue and 42nd Street.

A businessman put his briefcase into the closing metal doors of a train, trying to force it open, but instead the doors gripped the bag and the train took off. For a moment, the man jogged alongside, shouting and pulling. Then the handle snapped, leaving the man holding it, as the train disappeared with the rest of his bag. That was New York. You may think you can crowbar its doors open but you are just as likely to lose your precious briefcase.

For the first week or two I'd been sleeping on my brother's floor in a studio apartment in Chelsea. Then, having encouraged me to come, he landed a job in London and I took over his place.

The manager of the apartment was a Puerto Rican crack addict called Ray. His voice was broken and husky from drug use and he spent the warmer evenings playing dominoes on a folding table in front of the building. In an apartment across the hall was a gay man with an alcohol problem who was dying of AIDS. Next door was a couple who had arguments that sounded borderline abusive, after which they'd have noisy make-up sex. Without many friends in the city, I found myself taking an interest in the lives of these people.

New York still had the reputation of being dangerous in those days. The era of the mythic super-predators, and feral youth raised on crack as one of their five-a-day, was part of the recent past. There was a simmering sense of racial tension. A year and a half earlier there had been riots after a young black boy, Gavin Cato, was run over by an Orthodox Jewish man. A Jewish student, Yankel Rosenbaum, had been killed in the unrest. In uptown salons it was whispered that there were no-go areas of the city and that to travel by subway after dark was to take your life in your hands. With the foolhardiness of the young, I ignored this advice, riding the subway into the small hours, returning drunk from parties and bars. The intimate mood of the carriages late at night, their galleries of homeless and mentally ill and inebriates and red-eyed partygoers, the smell of metal and refrigerated sweat, became one of my favourite moods of the city.

Midway through the year Sarah joined me in New York. She found work making origami boxes for a living, which she sold to chichi shops, cash under the table. She had to work illegally because of her immigration status. I don't know what it's like now but back then the origami black market was pretty niche and not terribly lucrative.

Our cohabitation in that tiny apartment added to a kind of claustral isolation. We lived in a bubble of pot smoking and backgammon-playing, working our way through rented videos, by director, almost like we were programming a season: Alfred Hitchcock, Bob Fosse, Sam Raimi, Sergio Leone. We were more like conjoined twins than boyfriend–girlfriend, existing in a feedback loop that much of the time was loving and some of the time malign, with feelings of resentment and irritation going back and forth like a game of 'it'.

Sometimes I'd be seized with worry, realizing we were in our early twenties in the greatest city on earth and all that teeming craziness and life was passing us by. We'd go to a club or a bar or a friend's party then head back to our apartment in the spirit of someone who's had their fifteen minutes of fresh air and can go home.

My cousin Justin was also living in the city. He was someone I'd grown up seeing every summer on the Cape, when he'd been an excitable little ball of nervous energy. He'd visit, with his siblings and my Uncle Gene, and afterwards my dad would point out footprints on the hallway walls where Justin had been climbing up them. Once, when he was probably only six or seven, I'd seen him eat part of a polystyrene cup, and then, a few minutes later, vomit it back up again. I was slightly in awe of his untrammelled Dionysian style. But he was also a talented mimic and natural performer. He'd grown up in Washington DC, raised by his mum, and as a teenager embraced hip-hop culture. One year he arrived at the Cape in a shell suit and spent the whole summer body popping and breakdancing: spinning on his back, undulating his arms, doing robotics. After the shell suit went, he adopted a Velvet Underground look – black jeans, dark glasses, tight t-shirts over his skinny torso, usually a roll-up in hand. He was always switched on to whatever was happening in the culture, the latest music and fashion, in a way that was completely unforced. Coolness came to him as though it was his first language.

In New York he was trying to make it as an artist, producing works influenced by graffiti and street art, or a stage actor, ideally both. One night he and I and Sarah headed up to 42nd Street to visit the sex shops. Rudy Giuliani had recently been elected mayor and it was said he was cleaning up the seedy side of the city, making it safe for tourists, and we thought we owed it to ourselves to experience something of old-time unsanitized New York before it disappeared. In booths, dirty old men were watching screens – on one of them the women seemed to me smeared in Marmite, though I think it may have been something less edible, an image that has never left me. At the back of the shop, there were live shows, and the three of us crammed into a single booth and put quarters into a slot. A screen came down to reveal an ample smiling woman. She squeezed a breast and a dot of milk appeared on her nipple. 'I got a baby at home,' she said.

'That's great! Congratulations!' I said.

She squeezed a little more.

'Save some for the baby,' I said, and she took this as her cue to squeeze again, and this time a white filament of milk reached the booth, spraying over us as we squirmed and laughed like spaniels cavorting in the water from a garden hose.

As it became clearer that *Spy* was going under, I half-heartedly thought about an exit plan. I wasn't sure what it would look like. I made desultory approaches to other New York magazines, writing letters to editors I knew at *Time* and *Entertainment Weekly*. They went nowhere. I wondered about applying to a news service as a stringer. Or maybe working for a small local free-sheet called the *Manhattan Spirit*. That at least seemed somewhat realistic.

Sarah thought we should move to another country, possibly Vietnam. The choice of Vietnam was fairly arbitrary. Far away from family. Friendly seeming. A chance to practise my French.

Occasionally I would wonder what it would be like to write for television. But that did *not* seem very realistic. Early in the year I submitted some multiple-choice questions to an MTV quiz show. None were used. Painfully, they *had* used some of the questions written by my *Spy* colleague Daniel Radosh and tasked him with telling me the bad news, which he did with a little too much ease. 'Yeah, they just felt your questions weren't sharp enough somehow. Sorry.' I'd also performed a short monologue for an MTV pilot, which wasn't used either – this was completely fine as I wasn't sure why they'd asked me to do the monologue – but they also hadn't invited me to the wrap party, which did sting a bit. Was the monologue so wooden and laugh-less that it disqualified me from socializing with other members of the team?

In other words, my track record with respect to TV was somewhere between poor and whatever is below poor.

At the same time, I was aware that a kind of television renaissance was taking place, and particularly in the area of comedy. Shows like *The Simpsons* and *Larry Sanders* and *Seinfeld* were bringing a new level of intelligence and craft to the medium. It was said that many of those who wrote sitcoms in Hollywood were high-achieving graduates of top universities. Nowadays this hardly seems worthy of comment but in the early nineties in America evidently this was still considered surprising. An article appeared in *Variety*, suggesting that the money pots of Hollywood were tempting the best and the brightest away from their destinies as composers of sonnets and novels. Literary marvels were going unborn due to the lure of television. It seemed a frankly ridiculous thesis. But I also, if I'm honest, found it appealing. A little part of me wondered if I might be able to measure up to my dad and his literary success by distinguishing myself in a field that was word-based and maybe more relevant in this day and age than books about riding the trans-Siberian express. 'If Shakespeare were alive today, he'd be writing on *Caroline in the City*,' I did not say but maybe thought.

When *Spy* finally folded, at the beginning of 1994, it was hardly a surprise. Well, we hadn't been paid for a couple of weeks, so that was a clue. One morning, it was announced that the magazine was done and we were to leave immediately. I took a single copy of every back issue and put them into a crate, and walked home.

I found part-time work as a fact-checker in the legal department of a large publisher. Most of my *Spy* friends had already found work elsewhere by this time, at other magazines and news agencies, and a couple on a new TV show named *TV Nation*. It was the brainchild of the film-maker Michael Moore, and a pilot episode had been shot the previous year. A mixture of satirical stunts and humour reportage with a left-wing point of view, it was similar in style and feel to *Roger & Me*, Michael's documentary about the death of the auto industry in his hometown of Flint, Michigan. One of these friends, Chris Kelly of the rappers on gun safety idea, suggested I might want to send over a packet – a collection of ideas for jokes and sketches. NBC had financed the pilot, he said, but the network had balked at paying the full amount for the series. The BBC had stepped in, providing one-third of the budget. According to Chris, the BBC commissioners had told Michael, given they were chipping in, they'd quite like him to hire a British correspondent.

'Hmm,' Chris said one evening after work. 'If only we knew a British person who was intelligent and had a sense of humour. I just can't think who that could be.'

'Ha ha!' I said. 'I'll let you know if I think of anyone.'

I didn't take the teasing seriously, mainly because the idea of me as a TV correspondent seemed so unlikely. Still, I remembered my ambition to write for television, on a sitcom or a talk show.

I wondered if pretending I wanted to be on TV might be the price of being offered a more menial job.

Chris encouraged me to send Michael some segment ideas. I sat in front of the computer and tried to come up with something – the only one I recall had to do with the fatwa against Salman Rushdie. I wondered if it might be funny to go to the Iranian Embassy and offer our services as hit men. I sent off the packet and then didn't think much more about it.

I didn't know it then, but I was far from being the ideal hire for Michael Moore. Hailing from Michigan, from a family of autoworkers, Michael had an unapologetic loyalty to the American working class of the Midwest. My background, private education, bookishness, soft hands, university degree, effete interests and lack of enthusiasm about sports were all likely to be marks against me. Still, Chris said he was feeling optimistic about being able to get me an interview and he began prepping me for what to say to Michael.

'You are willing to do anything on the show,' he told me. 'Make coffee, do messenger work, phone bash.'

'Fine,' I said.

'You saw the *TV Nation* pilot and you absolutely loved it.'

'Sure,' I said.

'And you've seen *Roger & Me*, right? He will definitely ask you about it. It's your favourite film.'

'OK,' I said. 'Got it.'

In fact, while I had seen and enjoyed many of Michael's TV segments, including some short comic pieces he'd done on *The Tonight Show*, and had paid money to watch his *Roger & Me* sequel, *Pets or Meat*, at the cinema, I had never actually seen *Roger & Me* itself. Naturally, I decided I should probably see it, but life being the way it is, I delayed, at some level not really believing Michael would call. I read *In Cold Blood* by Truman Capote. I wrote an article about Charles Manson's latest parole hearing for a small British magazine.

I got stoned and played Tetris on the computer. I stared at the red-eyed figure in the bathroom mirror, looking for answers to who I was and what I was supposed to be doing, finding none.

I did any number of things, except watch *Roger & Me*, with the result that when Chris phoned to say Michael was ready to meet *right now* I realized I still hadn't seen it and it was too late now.

Michael was then working out of the Brill Building in Times Square, hallowed headquarters of many composers and songwriters of the early rock-and-roll days: Goffin and King, Leiber and Stoller. It was late in the afternoon when I arrived, having pedalled up from Chelsea – a cold winter's day, just beginning to get dark. He was then finishing up post-production on his first non-documentary feature, *Canadian Bacon*. He was with my friend Chris when I arrived. Michael looked tired and harassed, slumped in the corner at his desk, his body language barely registering that I'd entered.

He asked about my previous jobs.

'How was it working at *Spy*?' he said.

'Good. I enjoyed it a lot.'

Chris, acting as my corner man, added: 'Louis did the piece about rappers. Free-styling raps about gun safety.'

'And you also worked at *Metro*?'

I was surprised he'd heard of Santa Clara Valley's free alternative weekly. 'It was great,' I said. Later, I discovered Michael had got his start in journalism by founding and editing *The Flint Voice*, which was his hometown's left-wing weekly and its equivalent of *Metro* – part of the same network of papers – and that, for him, my time in the salt mines of alternative newsprint may have been my greatest selling point.

'Did you see the *TV Nation* pilot?' he now asked.

'Yes, I did. So funny. And the segments you did on *The Tonight Show*.'

'What do you see yourself doing on the show?'

'Anything. Whatever I'm asked. Photocopying. Phone bashing . . .'

I was trying to be as ebullient and enthusiastic as possible – buoying the mood and compensating for the sense of *Weltschmerz* Michael was giving off. My overall feeling was that it was going OK, and that Michael, having had his arm twisted by the BBC to consider a British correspondent, liked the idea of having one that wasn't *too* British: someone who understood American cultural references, who wasn't too establishment. Also, strangely, he didn't seem too bothered by my lack of TV experience.

Then Michael asked, 'Have you seen *Roger & Me*?'

'Yes, I have. I loved it,' I said. 'It's one of my favourite films.'

I'd like to say it cost me some pangs of conscience to lie about having seen *Roger & Me*, but it didn't, it slipped out very easily, though I did make a mental note to watch the film as soon as I got home, thereby making my lie into a truth retroactively, if you can do that.

The interview ended soon after. I cycled back home. I have no idea what I thought about on the way back. Possibly Lucretius's *De Rerum Natura*, which I was reading, or, just as likely, the Texan supermodel Bridget Hall who was on billboards at the time . . . I do know I had no inkling of being on the verge of a momentous change.

Chapter 6

# Millennium

When I picked up the ringing phone and the voice said, 'Louis? Jerry Kupfer. *TV Nation*,' I put my spliff down and stood up, not feeling equipped to conduct a high-stakes professional conversation. I didn't normally answer the phone high and I was regretting doing so now. I tried to gather my thoughts – he was talking about 'the millennium piece', an idea I had discussed with Michael and Chris Kelly, and when could I fly. It seemed I was being offered the job of presenting the segment and I did my best to reply appropriately and sound on-point and alert.

It was to be a satirical investigation cross-referencing the predictions of various apocalyptic groups for when the end of the world was going to come and how it would take place. I would be leaving the following night. It was weird and surreal – the idea of me being a TV correspondent. I was struggling to process it and after I put the phone down, I realized I had been so clouded with anxiety and dope that I probably hadn't sounded keen on taking the job. I called Jerry back. 'I just want to say how pleased and excited I am,' I said. 'You caught me off guard. Thank you for this wonderful opportunity.'

'OK!' Jerry said. 'That's good to hear. Yeah, good to know you're excited. I didn't know if I caught you in an off moment.'

'Ha ha! No!' I said. 'I'm very much . . . on! And excited! Thank you!'

Truthfully, though, I was mainly panicked and worried.

It was now several weeks since my first interview with Michael. There had been a follow-up interview, at which, afflicted with toothache, I was aware I'd been less effervescent. Michael had mentioned a possible segment about hockey fights. 'That sounds amazing,' I'd said but maybe without enough conviction – Michael was exquisitely attuned to body language – and afterwards he'd told Chris, 'He doesn't seem very enthusiastic.' Dubious about my knowledge of US culture, he'd also pointed to his ballcap, which had a 'p' on it.

'What does this stand for?'

'Philly?' I said. I am still not sure whether this was the right answer.

After that, it had all gone a little quiet, though Chris had mentioned the millennium segment. It had been offered to Merrill Markoe, the author and comedian who'd been a writer on *Late Night with David Letterman*, but she'd been worried that talking to religious loonies might disturb her mental equilibrium. Then the performance artist Karen Finley had been in the frame, but it was said she'd wanted to bring her baby and partner, making the flights prohibitively expensive.

And to be fair, seriously, why *was* I being offered a network TV job? Weird-looking, gawky, socially awkward, unqualified, anxious, twenty-three years old . . . Yes, I was cheap and keen and, in being British, a sop to the BBC paymasters, but I was very far from conventional TV material. I thought of all the people I knew who were funnier than me . . . school friends like Adam and Joe and Zac, family members, random people down the pub. I tried to reassure myself that my sense of curiosity about the story itself would see me through. I had no idea whether I'd be any good at asking questions on TV but I did know I was excited to meet the various religious groupuscules making their lonely cataclysmic prophesies. I thought back to university and my interest in offbeat sects, millenarians and chiliasts, the fanatics that flourished during the English Civil War . . . I'd once bought a copy of *The Pursuit of the Millennium* by Norman

Cohn, a landmark overview of apocalyptic religious movements – one day I planned on reading it – and maybe that enthusiasm would carry the day . . . Or, you know, maybe it wouldn't.

The next afternoon, having given notice on my legal fact-checking job, I went into the *TV Nation* offices with my bags packed to pick up my tickets and have a quick briefing chat with Michael. We sat in a conference room with a couple of the writers. On the wall were segment ideas on index cards. 'Pets on Prozac'. 'Move the Show to New Jersey'. And also: 'Apply as Hit Men to Whack Salman Rushdie'. That was mildly encouraging.

Michael screened a rough cut of a segment he was working on in which he visited the Serbian Embassy and they explained the Balkan conflict using slices of pizza. An embassy aide, reaching over for some pepperoni, said, 'I think I would like a slice of Montenegro because my mother is from there.'

This was supposed to be my speed-education in presenting fact-based comedy on TV, and Michael began throwing out pieces of advice: how to play to the camera in reaction shots and elicit small moments of humour. 'That *Monty Python* guy, on PBS, Michael Palin. He's great but we're not doing gentle comedy, Americans don't want that. You've got to kick ass and take names. Get in there and shake it up. This camera guy – I'm not happy about how he shot this. He needs to stay on the interviewees, he's coming back to me too much. You can always repeat your own lines but the gold is in what *they* say so you make sure you get that.' There was more advice but it was flying by and for some reason the main pearl of wisdom that stayed with me was to be careful not to interrupt or talk over my interview subjects as it made the segments hard to edit.

I was going to San Francisco. US union rules meant network TV shows had to fly writers and correspondents business class. This somehow exacerbated my sense of unworthiness – there I sat with my sparkling wine and free packet of socks, thinking about all the money that was being spent on a segment I would probably end up making a complete hash of. I looked at sheets of funny questions written for me by the *TV Nation* writers. Of a Christian fundamentalist I was supposed to ask: 'Let's say I worship the devil. Should I be worried?' I couldn't imagine having the gall. Then I began to fixate on how I would remember all the questions – could I carry a little notebook? Or maybe a clipboard? I thought I'd seen people on television doing that.

I arrived at San Francisco airport to find a limo driver holding a card with my name – the first time I'd ever been privileged to such a welcome.

At breakfast the next morning I met up with the segment producer.

'Hi, Daniel!' I said.

'David,' he said.

'David, of course. Such an interesting subject,' I said. 'Really keen to get started. Have you read *The Pursuit of the Millennium*, Norman Cohn's landmark history of late medieval apocalyptic movements?'

'No,' he said.

Looking back, I am struck that David must have thought it strange to be saddled on a network show with a presenter with literally zero hours of television experience. But he showed no disquiet. Entirely professional, he said he was excited to have me on board.

'Ve fing is,' he said now, betraying a very slight speech defect, 've important fing is to have fun.'

For the first day of filming we were in the San Francisco Bay Area to speak to a radio evangelist named Harold Camping, based in Oakland, who was predicting the end of the world for later in the year. Camping's outfit, Family Radio, had listeners in the thousands. He'd written a book, *1994?*, outlining the biblical basis for his prophesy, with the question mark to indicate the small possibility that the apocalypse would not materialize.

We arrived at his radio headquarters: me, David the director,

Chris Kelly – who'd flown out on Michael's orders to hold my hand through the four-day shoot – and the sound recordist and camera operator. Inexperienced as I was, I felt self-conscious around the crew, imagining them sizing me up as a jumped-up chancer. Presumably they had worked with hundreds of presenters and could recognize a greenhorn when they saw one.

The sound recordist miked up Harold Camping. We sat in his office, me with my questions folded in the inside pocket of the thrift-store jacket I was wearing. Craggy and deep-voiced, Camping must have been in his seventies, and he droned on and on about his bible studies and how he'd arrived at the conclusion that 1994 was God's appointed year of doom. 'The evidence in the Bible points to the fact that September 6 of 1994 will be the last day of the final tribulation period,' he said. Christ was coming back – on the Tuesday or possibly the Thursday and 'every mountain and island' would be 'moved out of their places.'

Bearing in mind Michael's advice, I waited for Camping to finish what he had to say before asking follow-up questions. But there weren't many breaks in the torrent of theology. And so Camping had free rein to deliver long rambling biblical monologues, instead of the peppy tongue-in-cheek repartee I'd been hired to provide.

Camping took me on a tour of his radio studio, pointing out the collection of Christian records – some of whose tracks had been marked with little stickers to indicate they had 'too much beat'. I asked a couple of the silly questions that had been scripted for me: 'Are you any relation to the beast spoken of in the book of Revelation called "Camping"?'

'Heh heh,' Camping said.

That night, I felt relieved to just have got through the day but, without anyone saying it, I could tell I wasn't doing very well.

'Good just to be underway,' David said as we rode up in the hotel lift.

'Yes,' I said.

'I always fink everyfing relaxes when you've got somefing in ve can.'

'Yes,' I said.

'One small fing. I would just say you could maybe interrupt if someone is really going on?'

'Oh, OK, will do.'

The next day we flew down to San Diego.

On the plane, David passed along a packet of information about our next group. They were called the Unarius Academy of Science, and their predictions involved a cargo cult-style prophesy of a vast number of flying saucers landing in the near future, bringing gifts of technology way beyond our mortal imagining and ushering in an age of peace and tranquillity on Earth. They didn't seem to have many members.

'They make their own films,' David said. 'Very far-out space films wiv wacky special effects. They're rahver fun.'

The Unarius headquarters were on a low-rise commercial strip in El Cajon, a small city in the mountains some miles east of San Diego. Their spokesperson was a past-life regression teacher, Lianne Downey. Lianne was in her early thirties, fawn-like and bright-eyed. In her teacherly dress with sparkly jewellery and big earrings, she had the air of an intergalactic primary school teacher – which, with her advanced extraterrestrial-derived wisdom, is perhaps what she felt like.

'We're not predicting doom and gloom or fearful of doom and gloom,' she said. 'In the year 2001 we expect the first spacecraft to land from another planet in our galaxy.'

She laid out a vision involving the arrival of thirty-three space ships, which would stack one on top of another like a cosmic game of Jenga. In its strangeness it was oddly appealing – not that I believed it, naturally, but there was something intoxicating about her conviction. To someone like me, who struggled daily with uncertainty about far more banal matters, her complete faith in something so silly felt enviable.

Before arriving I'd learned that the Unarians enjoyed dressing up in space-themed costumes for big celebration days and also to make their visionary films. I thought it might be funny to interview them while dressed up in one of their outfits. I raised the idea with Lianne. She seemed a little surprised but took me to a storage room where they kept their costumes. I settled on a blue nylon space suit with a little gold hat – I looked like a bellhop at the Hotel Liberace.

We were joined by Lianne's superior at the Unarius Academy, director Charles Spiegel. Charles was in his seventies and had been married to one of the founders of Unarius, Ruth L. Norman. Ruth had been a glamorous, larger-than-life figure, reminiscent of Glinda the Good Witch in *The Wizard of Oz*, in puffy skirts, with diadems and wands and sparkly jewellery. Charles, in sober suit and tie, lacked her over-the-top clothes sense, but he had brought an unlikely accent of outlandishness by styling a wholly unconvincing wig.

The plan was for us all to drive to the future landing site of the intergalactic federation fleet. Charles, Lianne and I would be riding in the Unarius 'space caddie' – a bright blue Cadillac with a model of a flying saucer fixed to the top and the message 'Welcome Your Space Brothers' written on the side – and the crew would follow behind. We took off, appropriately enough, like a rocket, leaving the crew vehicle in our dust. Alas, it was several minutes before we realized we'd lost them and – this being before mobile phones – had no way of contacting them. As we travelled, Lianne and Charles were wondering aloud – given the screw-up – which of their various past lives they were now reliving. They couldn't seem to agree, and were becoming irritable. In the back seat I was having flashbacks to long car journeys growing up, feeling hot and bothered, my parents arguing, not to mention the nylon space suit which, in the heat, was becoming itchy and increasingly unfunny.

Having failed to rendezvous with the crew, we drove back to the Unarius headquarters and there I sat in my space uniform, wondering about my next move. Charles and Lianne disappeared. It was strange and depressing: comedy and high jinks had curdled into a feeling of being lost and forlorn. A woman who was plainly mentally ill wandered into the building and began asking me questions about the space brothers, which I didn't feel well qualified to answer. Finally, what felt like hours later, the crew called, from a payphone. They had found the landing site and would meet us there.

We drove out again and when we arrived, the light was going. We had about fifteen minutes and captured a short sequence of me at the landing site: an expanse of scrubby desert.

'It doesn't look as though it would be the ideal landing place for a spacecraft just because it's so uneven,' I said.

'Oh, the technology they possess – the space brothers – is entirely in advance of anything we know,' Charles said.

'Is it OK to call them aliens?'

'No! They're not aliens. They're homo sapiens, like you and I. They have the same anatomy.'

'They're homo . . . ?'

'Sapiens.'

The mix-up with the crew and the ensuing delay blew out the schedule. We were able to film the Unarian choir singing a bizarre space song about the flying saucers coming, but an interview with a small cult in Los Angeles, scheduled for the following day, had to be cancelled and I felt guilty – I couldn't help feeling it was my fault due to my failure to stay in contact with the crew vehicle.

We were now three days into the shoot and clearly it wasn't going brilliantly. I probably should have felt bereft. But the truth was I had such low expectations for myself that by my own lights I was doing sort of OK. I hadn't burst into tears on camera or shat my pants. In a way, I was ahead of the game.

On day three, we flew to Montana then drove several hours through a wild landscape of snow-patched fields and lonely farmhouses, and in the distance the Bitterroot Mountains, to the far west of the state, arriving late in the afternoon at a small trailer. This was the headquarters of the Church of Jesus Christ–Christian, a white supremacist Christian group. There were only two of them: Archbishop Carl Franklin and Pastor Wayne Jones. They came to the door in matching uniforms modelled on those worn by the Nazi Brownshirts. They were vague on when the apocalypse would happen and when Jesus was coming; they just knew it would be soon and who he was coming *for*: specifically, white people, with other races banished to other planets.

'We teach the gospel of the Kingdom, which Jesus teached,' Franklin said. 'He did not teach a gospel of so-called brotherly love with other races . . . He came only for his own race, the white race, the Aryan or Adamic race.'

Jones chipped in, 'Each race will have its own territorial imperative, its own place. There will be no integration.'

'And will it be on Earth?'

'No. See, the Earth was the inheritance of His children only.'

'So only the white people get Earth,' I clarified. 'So the planet the black people get, will it be better than the white people's planet, about the same, or not quite as good?'

'Well, it'll be whatever they make it.'

'So they could make it as nice as they want?'

'Exactly.'

'So what about if there are white people on Earth and Earth's not doing so well and they see the black people have done a good job on their planet, would they be allowed to maybe emigrate?' I asked.

'No, there is no interracial mixing. No.'

It was a paradoxical mood – as the conversation progressed, the Nazi Christians settled into an attitude of teacherly indulgence. They seemed grateful for some attentive company, and my questions, ludicrous as they were, had a soothing effect. Later, I found out that the two of them had a long history in far-right politics – they'd been involved with Aryan Nations, as chief of staff and chief of security – but in that moment they came across as a pair of lonely bachelors, enlightening their visitor in a friendly way on the secret knowledge of their theology.

We retired to their small kitchen, where they made me tea. They talked about *Star Trek* and *Star Wars* – they believed that the mythology of the two franchises contained a great deal of historical truth about the grand cosmic plan.

'*Star Trek* does actually represent some of the battles that were fought when Lucifer actually came to the Earth and declared himself a God.'

'How about *Star Wars*? Pretty accurate?'

'Pretty accurate.'

By now, I had the impression I had cast a kind of benign spell over them and that there was almost nothing I could say that would break it. I sang a space hymn that the Unarians had taught me, and wondered whether our rapport was now strong enough that it could possibly cause them to recant some of their racism.

'I have one teensy-weensy, eensy-*speensy* bit of Jewish blood,' I said. 'Do you think I might be allowed to stay on planet Earth?'

'You will have some place to call your own,' Jones said.

As I left, putting on my woolly hat and stepping out into the cold dark Montana night, I said, 'After the race war, when we're all on other planets, maybe we can keep in touch by phone.'

'Communications are unlimited when things are put back right,' Franklin said.

Over the years I've been tagged with the epithet 'faux-naive' – sometimes unfairly, I feel – but that encounter with the two millenarian neo-Nazis was one time when I definitely earned the description, lobbing fake-sincere questions that ostensibly attempted to put a humane gloss on a weird space-Nazi vision, thereby satirizing it. After the encounter, back at the hotel, the sound recordist came up to me. He looked a little pale.

'I'm Jewish,' he said. 'Kind of weird spending a couple of hours with people you know would like to see you annihilated. But I thought you handled it rather brilliantly.'

The camera operator, an older guy from the Bay Area, also sought me out. 'You've been on this journey the last few days and I've seen you grow,' he said. 'I've worked with a lot of correspondents. Your voice, your inflections are beautiful, because it's the voice of an ordinary person.' Then, perhaps feeling he'd overdone the compliment, he added: 'I find all the voices of ordinary people beautiful.'

In characteristic fashion, I toggled from the insecurity of the preceding days to an overweening feeling of self-satisfaction. I began to think what a shame it was that such rich material would have to be whittled down to an eight-minute segment. It seemed to me we had enough interviews and moments to deliver a spin-off project, possibly of feature length. That night, at our hotel in Missoula, Montana, Chris and I got drunk as a celebratory valediction to the shoot. I overslept the next day and very nearly missed the flight back to New York.

After I got back I fell ill, possibly related to the stress of the preceding week. I called in to say I was unwell.

'Don't worry,' Jerry Kupfer said. 'Take your time, no need to rush in.'

Later I realized that I'd been in a holding pattern – kept away from the office while they decided whether I'd done a good enough job to be offered more work.

On day three Jerry called and asked if I wanted to come in to the office.

I was hired.

Chapter 7

# Don't Burn Me Now

For a year and a half, up the Amazon in a rickety motorboat, in the revolutionary hills of Mexican Chiapas, among religious crazies in Jerusalem and good old boys in the backroads of the Deep South, and occasionally amid the almost-as-alien milieu of a well-funded workplace with ambitions to change American television and society, I worked at *TV Nation*. But it was all a salutary apprenticeship – I was learning, without realizing it, skills and techniques that I would rely on through the course of my TV career.

That was all in the future. When I started I was simply intent on lasting from week to week, working from segment to segment. I remember thinking if I could get enough together for a reel, maybe I could find more TV work when Sarah and I left for Vietnam. Later the Vietnam option receded as my position at *TV Nation* became more secure. I figured I should keep going as long as they would have me.

It was a summer replacement series, commissioned for six episodes on a trial basis. My beat was, more or less, offbeat cultural phenomena – or, for want of a better term, weirdness. For an idea to work, there also needed to be some political or social relevance. A branch of the Ku Klux Klan whose leader was rebranding it a civil rights group for white people. Avon sales ladies who worked in the Amazon rainforest, selling cosmetics to dusty villagers. A company in Baltimore that specialized in cleaning up the mess left by crime scenes and suicides.

At the time I didn't have enough TV experience to know how far from being a typical show *TV Nation* was. Much as he had reinvigorated the documentary form with *Roger & Me*, Michael was attempting a new way of making TV. He would often say he wanted to see meaningful political change in his lifetime, and the production had an enjoyable mission-focused atmosphere of being about something bigger than making entertainment. It was part TV project, part political advocacy group, with a sprinkling of religious cult. 'Behave as if you are never going to get another job in television,' he would say. He told us we should consider it a good sign if we were ever arrested while making a segment.

Michael had a year-zero attitude to the work. In long story meetings in his office, he would slouch back in his chair and ramble about his pet subjects, mumbling out of the side of his mouth: his theory that OJ had been framed for the killing of his wife Nicole; the liberationist properties of rock and roll for the baby-boomer generation; random people in the media he had a grudge against for their reviews of *Roger & Me*. Prior to working at *TV Nation*, I had thought of myself as being politically liberal, though not in an active way. But *TV Nation*'s undercurrent of Jacobin anger appealed to me. It spoke to my unacknowledged resentful side that saw the world as corrupt and inhospitable. To be fair, this was driven as much by my own callow angst against those older and more comfortable – and a world I viewed (ridiculously) as having taken insufficient notice of me – as it was by any righteous political attitude. At least as much as the politics, I enjoyed the weirdness and danger of the show and its writers and, in the spirit of Shakespeare's third life-stage, I was seeking 'the bubble reputation' in the camera's mouth, in charged encounters with excitable extremists on the American fringe.

One of my proudest moments came during the second season of

*TV Nation* while making a segment about Ted Nugent, the right-wing rocker, when I was manhandled and shoved by a gatekeeper at the Washington office of the NRA after being repeatedly told to leave. Later, back in the office, Michael commended me, using me as a kind of object lesson for other staff and drawing attention to the irony that a person born to privilege should end up his fiercest soldier.

Without realizing it, I began to breathe in Michael's way of making television. There was a house style that dictated everything should be shot hand-held; when a correspondent met a contributor for the first time you captured it for real; there were no sit-down interviews. Everything was geared towards creating a sense of liveliness and authenticity. One of the few times I saw Michael annoyed was when a producer showed a rough cut that had a reverse shot from inside a door as it opened, signalling to any thoughtful viewer that the sequence had been set up in advance. 'I never want to see that shot in this show,' Michael said solemnly.

Many of the show's most memorable segments involved satirical stunts and pranks. In one, Michael hired a '*TV Nation* lobbyist' to see 'how much democracy $5000 could buy' – they managed to get a '*TV Nation* Day' passed in congress. Another involved Michael flying to Britain and buying a Lordship. In another, a black *TV Nation* correspondent, Rusty Cundieff, attempted to hail a cab – and was repeatedly passed by in favour of criminals and men in clown suits. All of the segments were supposed to serve the show's political agenda of advancing socialism.

*TV Nation* was justly lauded for the inventiveness of these satirical pieces, but what made them work wasn't just the concepts but their execution and in particular Michael's eye for reality-based comedy and the moments of tension and awkwardness it created. Interviews that went sideways. The corporate handler putting his hand over the camera. Random people shouting abuse. Michael had a gift for taking situations into extreme terrain by nudging and twitting his interviewees in a friendly way, threatening to run into the back of a factory across the Mexican border to check out working conditions or gatecrashing political conventions in a quixotic attempt to hug all fifty US governors.

*TV Nation*'s strange mix of comedy show and political documentary was reflected in the way the show was staffed. There was a team of writers who came up with ideas and who tended to be younger and less ideological than the rest of the staff but who were in a way – certainly at the beginning – Michael's inner circle. Then, at one remove, there were segment producers, some of them distinguished documentary film-makers with Oscar nominations to their credit. At marathon meetings, Michael and his wife Kathleen, who was also an exec on the show, would sit in session with the writers as producers came in for progress reports on the segments they were developing. For all his political bent, Michael seemed to view his writers in an almost talismanic way, recognizing that for the show to work it needed first and foremost to be funny.

Always there was a hunger for ideas, to the point where 'What else ya got?' – Michael's question to a writer or producer who was pitching him – became an office catchphrase.

While many of the segments on the show were high-concept satirical pieces, my own bits tended to be less stunt-driven. Usually they involved me visiting a weird or eccentric character with questionable views and then shooting long days and pushing him or her until something funny happened.

In a way, the millennium piece, with its mixture of crazy religion and racism, set the template for much of my subsequent work. My second shoot was the one about the Klan rebranding. Before we flew to the location, the segment producer, Kent Alterman, convened a bull session in the conference room. Someone suggested it might be funny if I wore a Klan robe and hood during filming. Michael advised against it. 'You don't want that photo out there,' he said.

Michael felt the segment wouldn't require any big gestures on my part for it to work. In the mid-eighties, before he made *Roger & Me*, Michael had collaborated with the director Kevin Rafferty on a feature documentary about the racist right called *Blood in the Face*. He knew how the Klansmen operated, he said. 'If you just go down there and film, without them meaning it to, all the racist crap will slip out. They can't help themselves.'

We flew out to the location a couple of days later. Having already made one segment involving white supremacists, I imagined it might be the same drill with the Klan: be nice, and wide-eyed, and gently satirize their ludicrous racial vision. But it quickly became clear these were a different calibre of racist – they weren't sequestered in the mountains of western Montana, lonely and maladapted. They were in mainstream America. Their spiel, about being for white civil rights, had a surface plausibility, and they had an instinct for the need to cover up their more outlandish beliefs.

Our first contributor, Michael Lowe, lived in a quiet unassuming single-storey home outside Waco, Texas, which he shared with his mother. Probably in his forties, slightly built, mullet-haired, in jeans and a short-sleeved collared shirt, he came to the door, seeming both a little friendly and a little wary. Much of that day is lost to me but I can reconstruct it from viewing the finished segment. He led us out into his extensive yard, green and overgrown and backing onto fields, centred around a vegetable patch. Nodding to my heritage, he smiled and said, 'Those are my English peas.' With that old footage as evidence, I'd like to make fun of Michael's appearance but what is clear is that, of the two of us, it is I – in an ill-fitting thrift-store sports jacket, hair shaggy and uncombed – who am the more ludicrous to look at.

'You're the Grand Dragon of the Knights of the Ku Klu Klan,' I said.

'Yes, sir.'

'How is your Klan group different from other Klan groups?'

'Well, one, we promotionalize. We have items to sell to the public and that's an advantage. It's the nineties and you need to sell yourself to the public and let them know about the Klan.'

The conversation continued – I was asking about women he found attractive and whether it mattered what race they were. The name Roseanne came up. 'She's Jewish, ain't she?' Michael said. Other *TV Nation* writers had written up some sheets of goofy questions, which I tried to slip in alongside the more normal ones. One written by my colleague Stephen Sherrill was: 'If you were in a plane crash and you had to eat human flesh to survive, would it make more sense for you to eat the white people or the people of other races?' 'It has happened,' Grand Dragon Michael conceded, and attempted a thoughtful answer, before returning to his media script: that their branch of the Klan didn't hate anyone but just preferred their own.

In a shed at the bottom of the yard he showed me a sign they used for roadside sales. The wood of the sign was old and battered – 'rethered', to use Grand Dragon Michael's word. Still, it wasn't so rethered that you couldn't read that it said: 'For the discriminating individual', with the word 'discriminating' in red.

'And it's kind of catchy,' he said. 'For the discriminating individual.'

'Is that because you discriminate?'

'No, we do not discriminate. No, sir.'

'It's not a pun, there?'

'Course not,' Grand Dragon Michael said, not quite able to keep a straight face.

'A slight one?'

'Well, maybe just a slight one,' he allowed, in the spirit of someone conceding that he might be a 'wee bit of a Nazi'. The moment was so odd that both of us giggled awkwardly.

A little later he let us into his bedroom, where we found more racist pictures. One showed a cartoon of a petrified-looking black boy – Grand Dragon Michael said he was planning to put it on a t-shirt. There were also Klan figurines doing what looked like Nazi salutes.

'Why is he sticking his arm in the air like that?' I asked.

'It is a salute,' Grand Dragon Michael replied. 'A lot of times the media will think it's a Nazi salute.'

'It looks a little bit like a Nazi salute.'

'Yes, sir, but it is a right-hand Roman salute. Like the Roman Empire, they gave the right-hand salute, to legions.'

'But that's his left hand.'

The mood in the room had become awkward again, and though, truthfully, it really didn't matter which arm the Klan figurine was saluting with – it was as racist either way – the revelation of the mistake momentarily broke the tension. 'They made 'em wrong!' Grand Dragon Michael said, and we both laughed nervously.

I continued, in as gentle a way as I could, asking to look at other objects until Grand Dragon Michael lost patience. The mood shifted again. 'Now, now. Don't burn me. Let's face it. I been nice!' he said, and ushered us all out of the room.

Our other main contributor – Michael Lowe's Klan colleague and superior, Thom Robb – lived in a rusticated old house up a long driveway on the outskirts of Harrison, Arkansas.

Robb was smoother than Michael Lowe. He wore glasses; he didn't have a mullet – if anything, with his rumpled bearing and air of educated indigence, he came off like a professor at a community college. On the top floor of his house he had an office – family members were stuffing envelopes with his Klan newsletter, to give an impression of activity.

'What would you say is the traditional negative image of the Ku Klux Klan?' I asked.

'The *image* is that every Saturday night you put on your Klan robes and go out and lynch a black person or burn down somebody's home. This is the image – of a bunch of yahoos out night-riding in the back of a pick-up truck . . .'

'Do you hate being called a hate group?'

'The white people are my family. I love 'em, but it doesn't mean I hate anybody else. Hating people is stupid.'

We filmed him printing out a flyer – 'New leadership! New ideas! New direction! . . . We're not in the cow pasture any more' – then he took me on a visit to a local store that made up little pieces of branded Klan merchandise – keychains, ballpoint pens, fly swats. It was all fairly low-key, less obviously fractious than the encounter with Michael Lowe, and I wasn't too sure how much useful material we were getting. As ever, there was a balance of 'normal' questions and sillier satirical bits of business. I had thought it might be funny to suggest other rebranding ideas, like giving their outfit a classier pronunciation: 'Ku Klux Klaaahhn'. He batted this away, likewise the 'which human meat would you eat' hypothetical dilemma, and a sophomoric riff about whether, if you were checking out an attractive woman from behind and then discovered it was actually a man, that made you gay. In the end it wasn't Thom Robb who lost patience but my camera operator, who stopped filming in the middle of a testy exchange about the Holocaust, exhausted from holding his camera for so many hours while I frittered the time away going down conversational blind alleys, needling about nonsense.

By the end of the shoot, I had no clear sense of whether we had what we needed to make the segment work. I was aware that I hadn't been in control of the encounters in the way I had on the millennium segment. If the mission had been to build rapport with the contributors, put them at their ease and gently satirize them, I was fairly sure I'd failed. In the edit, most of my sillier questions were cut out; I worried we didn't have much of a story, that I'd been bumbling and hadn't built the necessary trust.

But in the course of cutting down the material, something surprising happened: the tension and the sense of me being out of my depth combined to give the encounter a power I hadn't expected. The encounters were stronger for my being *less* in control. There was comedy in seeing me diffidently probe Michael Lowe and in his fumbling attempts to explain away the unexplainable. There was a winning quality in the juxtaposition of mildness and malice and a kind of maturity in the way the segment did not push its judgements too hard. Michael came into a screening of a rough cut and said simply, 'You got it.'

For a final *coup de grâce* in the story, we found news footage of Michael Lowe and Thom Robb at rallies, facing off with counter-protesters, being less guarded and more openly racist than they had with me. We edited these against the blander statements they'd made when we filmed, making the point that the main difference between the old and the new Klan was how careful they were about what they said in public. From a mild soundbite of Robb telling me he didn't go around saying 'He's a Jew, he's not a Jew' we cut to footage of Robb at a Klan event saying to a protester: 'You're a Jew, I'm not going to talk to you.' From another clip – of Robb saying he didn't hate black people – we cut to a speech of Robb declaring in strident tones: 'America belongs to the children of the Republic! Not those from Mexico! Not those who came on slave ships from Africa!'

We also had a clip of Michael Lowe claiming, with a display of sensitivity, that Nazism 'turned his stomach' – then showed him on stage shouting about 'taking back' the country 'for White America' and doing what looked like a Nazi salute. He might have called it a Roman 'right-armed salute' but, once again, he was doing it with his left arm.

Time passed. I did more segments. There were some rifts on the show, and several writers departed – including Chris Kelly, who had been so instrumental in getting me hired. Much of it had to do with disgruntlement over an occasionally eccentric work environment. Coming from Flint, Michael and Kathleen sometimes gave the impression of viewing the *TV Nation* staff as spoiled and pampered and insufficiently grateful for their jobs, while the writers understandably took the view there was a contradiction in Michael, tribune of the working man, skirting union rules on his own TV show.

Working on my own segments, I was insulated from the office politics. Having been rescued from publishing drudgery and set to work in TV as a writer and correspondent, I was still enjoying the novelty of a busy, well-funded workplace. I loved spitballing with the other writers, wisecracking, trying to come up with ideas for segments, and writing 'sheets' – questions and ideas for bits of shtick for other correspondents on location.

I'd gone from being a confused and insecure magazine underling to a TV correspondent flying around the country to talk to the wild and weird denizens of the American extremes. I liked and admired Michael, while also being grateful for the break he'd given me, which felt undeserved. Given how green I was, looking back I'm surprised at how much latitude Michael afforded me to do my work. He was far from being a conventional mentor. He wasn't huge on bonding. But just his keeping me on board felt like a huge endorsement.

I knew I was doing well at *TV Nation* because I kept being brought back – for more segments, for a year-end special, for a second season, by which time the show had moved from NBC to Fox. I thought back to Michael's hiring me and as time passed I began to realize how much my own unfitness for TV was part of what worked. It was my lack of the conventional qualities of a TV presenter – smoothness, self-assurance, maturity, good looks, half-decent wardrobe – that marked me out and made a funny contrast with the American characters I was reporting on – and in fact, more than that, which licensed them to express themselves to me, confide in me, and sometimes in amusing ways dominate me.

But I also had pangs of conscience. Increasingly I worried I was taking something real and abusing it – building trust and making it a basis for ridicule. I suppose I came to see myself as a bit of a hatchet man, doing hit jobs on racists, members of the far right, religious kooks. At the same time, I didn't see myself as a satirist, and my guilty secret was that I rather liked some of the supposed crazies I was spending time with.

With many of the alpha-type ideologues, I had a reassuring feeling of invisibility when I was in their presence. In certain ways it was a little like being around my dad – himself an American gun-owner of decided opinions. It was comfortable, like listening to an oldies station on the radio. I found I could switch off a bit, surrender control, and go with the flow. It was almost a secondary side effect that whatever friendliness arose turned out also to be useful for the creation of a candid and revealing TV segment.

I made about fifteen pieces for *TV Nation* in the end. Most of them are forgettable and in all of them I'm embarrassed now to see how weird my hair looks, the strange way it is sort of stacked on my head, the size of my spectacles, and the puffiness of my shirts.

Looking back, those segments that worked best were the ones that relied on me forming good-natured relationships with contributors, in which the comedy flowed from an unlikely bonhomie between me and someone utterly unlike me, usually a gun nut or a religious crazy. It may sound obvious – the idea that some chemistry and goodwill might be a helpful ingredient in making a TV segment – but in fact the idea that we were satirizing the enemy or trying to get one over on people we viewed as malevolent or wrong-headed meant that there was sometimes a gravitational pull towards an antagonistic approach, which could end up being ugly and unkind. Minute for minute, the best piece of television I appeared in at that time was probably a very short segment about a visit to an exotic weapons shooting range in Arkansas, called The Farm, and advertised as 'the safest place on Earth'. The owner, Robert Lee Warren, a droll good old boy and Vietnam vet, had laid out a selection of high-calibre guns on a table, like a paramilitary buffet.

Robert's enthusiasm for his weaponry was infectious, and by the time we had blasted off a thundering round from a fully functioning military-grade mortar I had more or less forgotten about the angle of the segment and was enjoying the intoxication brought on by discharging heavy-duty artillery. 'That was coo-ool!' I heard myself exclaim.

Later, I heard a British colleague refer to the segment as a piece of satire, and I was a little surprised. Not that I didn't think it was weird that such powerful firearms should be freely available to the citizenry. It was just that an encounter that I'd viewed as textured, ambivalent, warm, he'd seen as a kind of exposé.

From colleagues I kept hearing that the BBC was taking an interest in me – an exec had visited from London. 'He wrote down your name,' I was told.

Towards the end of the second season of *TV Nation*, when it became clear that the US network wouldn't be renewing the show, a BBC producer named David Mortimer took me to one side to let me know there was an appetite 'at the channel' for a spin-off project from me. This all felt rather theoretical. I didn't lend it much credence. It felt premature to begin outfitting my own escape vessel when the mother ship was still afloat, albeit listing badly.

It was never officially said that *TV Nation* was over. In a way, it was classic Michael. He would never admit defeat and even after it was clear she'd gone to a watery grave, I stayed around to find out whether we might be called upon to do the show on cable or in some other incarnation. For a while Michael developed a sitcom for Fox, called *Better Days*, which Jim Belushi was supposedly attached to. It was to be a more political *Roseanne*. He sent me a copy of his script and I tried to offer constructive feedback. Then he began writing a book that would appear as *Downsize This*. Once or twice we spoke on the phone and I suggested ideas, but by now I was distracted because David Mortimer had made good on his word and offered me a BBC development deal to come up with ideas for my show.

# Chapter 8

## Popular Documentary

It should have felt like a kind of redemption – *my own show*. From a state of directionless obscurity I had been vaulted into a realm of possibility I hadn't ever dared imagine. And one part of me saw it this way. But another, greater part was dubious, suspecting that the transformation was not wholly earned and therefore not really mine. I wasn't exactly sure what the shadowy execs at the BBC who were taking a chance on me imagined they were buying and I worried I was on a conveyor belt trundling towards something I'd never aspired to be – a presenter on BBC2, making light-hearted documentaries that pandered to a superior view of America as a benighted haven of misfits and morons, with the further paradox that I was myself half-American and something of a misfit, with occasional moronic tendencies.

David Mortimer had explained that I should be thinking of ideas in the 'popular documentary' genre. 'You're probably aware of the boom in popular documentary programming,' he said, like a man at a corporate seminar. I had never heard the term before. I was wholly *unaware* of the alleged boom. When I finally got around to watching some examples of 'popular documentary', I didn't like them. The travelogues with comedians and raconteurs were self-satisfied and lifeless. They didn't follow any of Michael's rules of style – they were well lit and they looked nice and nothing weird or surprising ever happened in them.

The only example of British television I found in anyway relevant to what I hoped to do was a couple of episodes of a series called *The Ronson Mission*, hosted by a comic journalist called Jon Ronson. It followed him around the UK on absurd quests. I'd only seen two episodes on VHS, one about mega-fans and another in which his mission was to increase the ratings of his own show. There was something about the weirdness of Ronson that I enjoyed, his sly subversiveness mixed with awkwardness, and the feeling the shows had of always being in motion. I mentioned *The Ronson Mission* to David and he was dismissive. 'That didn't do very well,' he said.

Meanwhile I'd also been continuing my education in independent documentaries, immersing myself in films that pushed the boundaries of subject and approach: Todd Phillips' documentary *Hated*, a portrait of the disturbed punk rocker GG Allin. There was a scene in it in which a super-fan peed in Allin's mouth as a birthday treat, causing Allin reflexively to vomit. You didn't see *that* on a BBC2 'popular documentary'. The same director made another film about the pornographer Al Goldstein, called *Screwed*, which had a scene on an adult film set that was both funny and imbued with a surprising dignity and pathos – an actor reeled off a list of theatrical credentials in mainstream productions before the film cut to a ludicrous bit of dialogue ('Would a blow job go well with that?' 'A blow job would go great with this') as a precursor to an energetic sex scene.

In those days, in New York, those so inclined could investigate the world of niche film-making at a legendary video store in the East Village called Kim's. Kim's is gone now, rendered obsolete by the Internet and streaming, but in an era before YouTube and WorldStar and Twitter it was like the nether regions of Web 2.0 in physical form. Racks of underground films organized by director, esoteric documentaries on bizarre subjects. *Chicken Hawk*, an access-based documentary about NAMBLA, a group that advocated in favour of paedophilia; *Blast 'Em*, about obsessive fans and paparazzi who stood in gaggles outside stars' homes in New York; *Dream Deceivers*, about a pair of teenagers in rural America who attempted suicide under the influence of a Judas Priest record. One of them lived, but with the bottom of his jaw missing so he drooled and had to be subtitled during his interviews.

In general I was drawn to the sort of stories of strangeness and deviance that were the opposite of how I was living my own life, which was domesticated and quiet.

Sarah and I were still in the same studio walk-up in Chelsea and also, by this time, married. We'd tied the knot one cold December day at New York City Hall in a gambit intended to make it easier for her to work in America, though clearly we were in a real relationship. The term 'a small ceremony' doesn't really do justice to the minimalism of the occasion. We didn't tell any friends and family. We were the only ones present, and to make it legally binding we had to ask a passing stranger to witness the event.

Even afterwards, I didn't think of myself as married; I imagined that if we ever did decide to marry 'for real', which I thought we might, we'd get married again. It was a little confusing. If you *are* ever thinking of marrying someone, I don't recommend marrying them before you marry them.

Now able to work lawfully, she found a job as a writer on a trivia quiz website called Riddler – the Web was just then taking off as a force and everyone seemed suddenly to be finding work at e-zines and dotcoms – while I rented a cubicle a short walk from our apartment. I spent my days there, staring at my laptop, at least part of the time trying to think of ideas for my putative BBC TV show. Most of these revolved around my persisting fascination with macabre and taboo themes. Jumping off from the work I'd done at *TV Nation*, I wanted to go further into the realm of deviance and the really weird.

The undercurrents of American culture fascinated me. The backward-looking, the bizarre. Drawing from the then-flourishing world of zines – self-published fanzines, like Donna Kossy's *Kooks*; Jim Goad's *Answer Me!*; another called *Snake Oil*, which ran tongue-in-cheek appreciations of miracle workers and carried the slogan 'For Fans of Kooky Kristian Kulture' – I found a wellspring of stories on hidden worlds of misfits but also a Middle American milieu so aggressively retrograde and antithetical to my own bourgeois, liberal upbringing that it struck me as exciting and transgressive: snake handlers, infomercial celebrities, preachers taken over by the personalities of millennia-old cavemen, people who cut off their own body parts for sexual thrills.

In my days working on a paper in San Jose, I'd been turned on to Adam Parfrey's *Apocalypse Culture*, a book-length anthology of outrageous behaviour and assorted diablerie on the American fringe, loosely themed around the idea of pre-millennial disquiet. I had reason to pick it up again recently and found much of it, frankly, repulsive and awful, but I'm a father of three now whereas back then I was a dyspeptic young pup who viewed revoltingness as a positive quality. Articles about Nazis and sexual predators felt like forbidden literature. The interview with Karen Greenlee, 'The Unrepentant Necrophile', in which she talked candidly about having sex with corpses while working at an undertaker, made a particular impression.

I was also reading widely in more mainstream magazines, and a few articles caught my attention as possible source material for documentaries: a long piece from the *New Yorker* by an author named Susan Faludi, which looked at the stresses and emotional strain attendant on making a livelihood out of the vagaries of one's erections; and two stories about the militiamen and survivalists in Idaho and Montana – one by Philip Weiss, another by William T. Vollmann – that depicted them as rather romantic figures, confused idealists making a stand for their idea of freedom. All three of these articles were imbued with a combination of emotions, finding human qualities of pathos and warmth and, on occasion, an almost mythic level of commitment to causes that were on the face of it ludicrous and laughable.

It was quite a weird time. I was freelancing the odd article for British magazines. I was writing odd bits for low-budget cable TV pilots that never went to series. Meanwhile, in a tiny circle of programmers and producers in the UK, it seemed I was viewed as a coming man of TV presenting and being paid to write my own ticket on BBC2.

I bumped into a friend, a young editor I'd known at *Spy* called Larissa.

'What are you working on?' she asked.

'I've got a development deal with the BBC. They say they want to do a series with me, so we'll see.' It sounded like something I was making up.

Sporadically I emailed ideas to David Mortimer for series with me in them, long incoherent rambles with statements of intent and philosophical underpinnings. Not much came back and I sensed his real attention was elsewhere. And truth be told, so was mine.

With time on my hands, and enough of a safety net with the BBC offer, I had decided I wanted to take the leap of following a dream I'd been thinking about for a couple of years: to write for an American sitcom.

With the doors of the BBC documentary department swung wide open to me, I can understand the idea of turning my back on them to pursue a career in sitcoms – a world where I didn't even know where the doors were – may seem quixotic, and especially with the twenty-five years of work as a TV documentary presenter weighing against the counterfactual version. The best I can explain it is that I was conscious of wanting to move away from my ordinary life, my upbringing, London, my parents, and that even the BBC represented something too close to where I'd come from. I craved success on my terms, that wasn't academic or literary or British. Possibly, too, I still felt the need to prove myself. Somehow me being on TV as myself felt like cheating. In my mind I was as much the subject as I was the creator of the segments I'd done at *TV Nation* and whatever gifts I had were in some way accidental and unintended. But if I could write my way into a job in Hollywood it would all seem more *earned*.

I began work on a spec script for a new sitcom called *NewsRadio*. I had chosen *NewsRadio* partly because I liked it, it was quite new, and because its showrunner, Paul Simms – oddly enough, a *Spy* magazine alumnus who I'd been told looked like me – had previously worked on *Larry Sanders*, HBO's groundbreaking sitcom about a fictional chat-show host, that featured celebrities playing themselves. *NewsRadio* had potential, but it also wasn't so good that the idea of writing on it seemed unrealistic.

I brought a monastic level of commitment and purpose to my spec script. It took one whole day to figure out how to do the formatting on my computer, with all the indentation and spacing. I'd been told that a half-hour script should take a couple of weeks to write, but I honed mine over the course of two months at the end of 1995, going through ten or more drafts. When I had finished, I showed it to my comedy-writer friends. 'The good news is it looks like a sitcom script,' was one of the more positive remarks. Conventional wisdom held that you were supposed to write two scripts and use them to get an agent. But by now I was so spent I didn't have it in me to come up with a second one. You also weren't supposed to send a script for a particular show *to that show* – the writers would be so attuned to lapses in voice, they'd see everything that was wrong with it. But having decided to break the agent rule, I thought I'd break the other rule too. I labelled the final draft 'first draft' then sent it off to Paul Simms.

I also submitted some ideas to David Mortimer at the BBC, just to keep that plate spinning. There was one for a millennial-themed magazine show, provisionally titled *The End of the World News*. It would have segments about women who had sex with corpses and super-fans who peed in people's mouths. Another, *Brief Lives*, took its cue from John Aubrey, the seventeenth-century diarist. It would be ten-minute profiles of random weird people I found intriguing. There was an idea for a travelogue in which my brother would appear – he'd been working as a camera operator and reporter at a start-up local TV channel. The conceit was that he would be shooting our TV show, which would take us to trouble spots around the world, but he'd also be appearing in it. Thinking of the then-popular band Oasis and two famous TV-presenting brothers, I'd pitched it as, 'The Gallaghers meets the Dimblebys!' Hence, *The Gamblebys*. On his reworking of my pitch document, David had renamed it *The Boys from the BBC*.

The last idea was for an immersive documentary series, a longer-form version of my *TV Nation* segments. Borrowing from a programme I'd watched as a child called *In At the Deep End*, I'd added the device of following my attempts to participate in the worlds I was reporting on. In each episode I would get hands-on in a different weird subculture – take a role as a porn performer or make contact with a space alien. Riffing on the popular cookery programme *Ready Steady Cook*, I joked we might call it *Ready Steady Kooks*. David renamed this one *Louis Theroux's Weird Weekends*.

In spring 1996, David Mortimer flew out to New York and took me to lunch in a posh restaurant called Canard something where the butter pats were shaped like ducks. David always enjoyed those professional duties that involved a sense of occasion – especially when he was in the role of bestower of largesse – and he drew out the reveal like a judge on a talent show, as he spread some duck-shaped butter on his crusty bread.

'So they have decided . . . to commission . . . *Louis Theroux's Weird Weekends*.'

'Oh, OK, great,' I said. 'Yeah, I thought they might go with that one.'

'So.' Big smile. More buttering. 'Are you pleased?'

'Yes. Of course. That's great.'

Truthfully, though, I was already having the usual bouts of anxiety and seeing a vastness of downside.

'Do you think it has to have my name in it? *Louis Theroux's Weird Weekends*. No one really knows who I am.'

'Well, it builds brand recognition,' he said. 'We have another one we're working on, *Ray Mears' Extreme Survival*. It's how the commissioners like to develop talent in the popular documentary genre.'

'So there are four of them?'

'Yes.'

'Fifty minutes each?'

'Yes.'

'Do you suppose there's a case for just doing one to begin with? And then sort of seeing how it goes?'

I don't recall his response to this remark but his expression, if translated into English, would have said, 'You are a tiny child who doesn't have the first clue about how TV works.'

David flew back to London, presumably to make plans to start production imminently, while I disbelievingly commenced a one-man Bataan Death March towards making my own series – a series that, for some reason, had the name of a nonentity in its title. I felt disappointed in myself and intensely self-conscious about having been commissioned.

A few days afterwards, I returned to the studio apartment to find the message light on the machine flashing.

'Hey, Louis. This is Paul Simms at *NewsRadio*. I read your script and I, ah, liked it. So give me a call.'

It's a little strange to admit, but in my entire working career – BBC commissions, BAFTAs, academic plaudits – *that call* engendered the most profound feelings of relief and gratitude.

A month or two later, and *Louis Theroux's Weird Weekends* was postponed, possibly indefinitely, and I was making my new life as a comedy writer in LA.

Chapter 9

# Deadheads for Dole

wasn't, in fact, working at *NewsRadio* but for a topical HBO sketch show about the presidential elections called *Not Necessarily the Elections*. I'd sent the producer a packet of material months earlier, in the fallow period after *TV Nation* had ended, and been hired based on a single funny idea, about fans of the acid-folk group the Grateful Dead following Republican presidential candidate Bob Dole around on the campaign trail in the wake of Jerry Garcia's death.

The gig was for two months, but for me a big part of the appeal was that my day job could be combined with the active pursuit of my destiny as a sitcom writer. Sarah, my girlfriend-now-wife-kind-of, had stayed in New York. If anything she was a little *too* relaxed and philosophical about our separation, saying, 'It'll be good to have some space.' Later, in LA, I recounted the story of this parting to a friend's girlfriend. She explained that in women's language that meant we were splitting up. I took this on board. *Splitting up.* In a human-like way, I attempted to do soundings of my inner depths about how I might feel about 'splitting up'. Or like a ham-radio operator trying to make out a signal through a fog of static. No clear emotional response came back.

I'd also had to send David Mortimer an email telling him to postpone production on *Louis Theroux's Weird Weekends*. I was aware it was tricky emotional ground – that it could be construed as a strange move on my part and maybe a little ungrateful-seeming, as schedules and budgets were now presumably having to be reconfigured, and vast BBC cogs screeching and sparking as they went into reverse – and I got Sarah to read the message to make sure I'd struck the right tone. I'd signed off, 'I hope you will continue to view me as your boy from the BBC' or something equally cringe. Though I said I'd be back in September, I was secretly thinking I might bail on *Louis Theroux's Weird Weekends*, get hired on *NewsRadio*, and never come back.

Los Angeles was a vast sun-drenched factory town. For a couple of weeks I was back staying with my uncle Peter in Long Beach, an hour's drive from Hollywood. Later, I rented a sub-let that came with a very needy kitten that had been weaned too young and was always mewing for attention and treadling me with its paws. I entered into a dysfunctional relationship with the kitten similar to ones I'd had with other people close to me. It needed me and I seemed to need it to need me.

The city was the reverse. Aloof and indifferent, it ignored me and I fell hard for it as a result – in pick-up artist parlance they call this 'negging', seduction by insult. Pale and skinny and bespectacled, I had little or nothing to offer the city of beautiful bodies and success, which made it all the more tantalizing.

I loved the morning adventure of driving to work on a Hollywood lot – Sunset-Gower studios – down roads colonnaded with palm trees. In my borrowed car, I felt like a knight riding into battle. The lot itself had the air of a medieval town, circled by high walls with guarded gates, and in place of a portcullis an electric pole that went up.

I turned out to be oddly ill qualified for my new job. The show was a US cousin to the eighties comedy format *Not the Nine O'Clock News*. It had been commissioned for four episodes over the summer – Bob Dole was then running against the incumbent Bill

Clinton – and was hosted by the comedian Dennis Miller, though he was never around until we taped. Several of the other writers had come over from a live chat show Miller hosted, which was dark over the summer. With their day-jobs on the live show in their back pockets, the Miller writers were faintly dismissive of the hoary old eighties holdover they now found themselves working on. Even when I was staying an hour away in Long Beach I was the first one in the office and the last to leave. I shared a room with a talented stand-up comedian and writer called David Feldman. Alas, having had the one idea involving Deadheads for Dole, I struggled to come up with anything else.

By coincidence, also on the Sunset-Gower lot were the *NewsRadio* offices. By now I'd had a first, cursory meeting with Paul Simms – he'd seemed friendly, though a little distracted – and I'd sent some follow-up plot ideas along. But the line had then gone quiet and I wasn't quite sure what the next move was – I didn't want to badger him too much – and during breaks or just going about my day I wandered the central courtyard, hoping I might bump into him.

Finally, through his assistant, another meet-up was arranged. It was early afternoon when I arrived. Tinfoil had been put up on the windows to keep out the light. There were classic video machines about the place. Probably it says more about my own state of mind and the weird level of emotional investment I had in the whole notion of being a sitcom writer – I was like an airport frisking wand on its highest setting – but I had the disquieting feeling of there being no adults around; it was like being back in a sixth-form common room or a frat house the afternoon following a big party.

Paul, in a large back office, was in conversation with a PA called Spider, who was lounging on a sofa. 'Wooden Ships' by Crosby, Stills and Nash played – 'Wooden ships on the water! Very free!' – and someone remarked on the ridiculousness of the lyric about eating 'purple berries.'

I nodded and tried to think of something funny to say about Crosby, Stills and Nash or purple berries.

One of the story ideas I'd sent over involved a character on the show becoming obsessed with Dungeons & Dragons and having a psychotic break, going down into the sewers of New York, thinking he's an elf or a wizard.

'Yeah, thanks for your ideas,' Paul now said. 'We're actually working on one about Dungeons and Dragons already . . . So you're based here now? You should come to a taping.'

'I'd love to,' I said.

He mentioned that the Writers Guild required a minimum number of scripts to be farmed out to freelancers each year. Maybe I could write one.

'Wow, that would be great,' I said.

Then he went to work editing a scene and complaining about one of the extras, who was over-acting. 'This fucking guy at the back is killing me,' he said.

Afterwards I was a little deflated. I had been trying to think what the office had reminded me of and later I realized it was of a story in *Twilight Zone: The Movie* in which a child with superpowers has taken the rest of his family hostage and they exist in a fearful state of forced fun. I wondered if this was the life I had dreamed of. Was I giving up my own BBC TV series for the possibility of freelancing a single script? And handing it in to a man in a room with tinfoil on the windows? And what was wrong with the lyric about eating purple berries? I trudged back to the *Not Necessarily the Elections* offices, wondering what exactly had I imagined life writing on a sitcom would be like.

We began taping segments, including the Deadheads for Dole skit, but not much else by me, since in the six or so weeks I'd been there I'd written virtually no other usable material. My office mate, David, had been kind enough to include me as co-writer on some of his sketches – one based on the idea that the language was running out of words and we needed to invent a new letter, the 'triple-you', and another about the Vice Presidential Republican nominee Jack Kemp and a fictional prehistory he had as a singer in a doowop group called The Kemptones. I'd had an idea about a robot running for president but that hadn't made the cut and another about a makeover show for homeless people. That one was produced but bombed so badly in front of audiences in rehearsal that it was also tossed out.

One evening, eating a lonely meal at a fast-food restaurant called El Pollo Loco at Fountain and Vine in Hollywood, I stared into my 'Pollo Bowl' and realized I was being ridiculous. Of course I should do my TV series. With a new gust of anxiety generated by the idea that *Louis Theroux's Weird Weekends* might become real, I went back to my apartment and sent a long venting email to David Mortimer, starting 'Dear Dave', and confessing all my doubts and misgivings – about my competence, about his competence, about the folly of embarking on a set of four hour-long programmes when I wasn't sure he understood my basic concept, and that I wasn't interested in making piss-taking shows that pandered to British prejudices about Yanks.

David sent back a considered email taking my points one by one and ending by saying he didn't like to be called Dave.

## Chapter 10

## Head for the Hills

In the dog days of the summer of 1996 I arrived back in New York, with a plan to move back into the Chelsea studio apartment and reoccupy my old relationship with Sarah. I found to my dismay that she was ambivalent about both ideas, viewing me with an attitude of semi-detachment – she was thinking of moving on. 'You need to get serious or hit the road,' she didn't say, but that was the subtext. But we still loved each other – I more than I realized – and we were also alone, knowing barely another soul in the city in any intimate way. After a few days of importuning on my part, I prevailed on her to think about her own creative projects – a book she was working on, her lack of funds. In a purely pragmatic way it made sense for us to live together, and, you know, probably continue the relationship, too, 'or whatever'. And so, in this spirit, not quite knowing how committed we were to one another, but carrying on regardless, we found a new apartment in a semi-desolate but supposedly up-and-coming area of Brooklyn just across the East River called Williamsburg, which was then being settled by a small vanguard of artists and urban pioneers.

We borrowed a van from a friend and moved one afternoon with the help of a couple of Sarah's colleagues from Riddler, then sat amid the boxes that evening, eating pizza that had to be delivered from ten blocks away and listening to the Biggie Smalls CD that was blasting from a stoop across the street.

David, who was coming on as my series producer, had by now moved himself and his girlfriend from London for the nine-month duration of the production – the BBC was paying for some sweet digs in Greenwich Village. Alongside our production, he was also working on a BBC-funded film with Michael Moore, which would later come out as *The Big One*. Making this only slightly awkward was that my getting my own series – and the BBC's and my failure to keep Michael informed – had apparently annoyed him. I once heard the process of hiring me from *TV Nation* to do my own series referred to as an 'extraction'. In a way, the dental metaphor is apt; it was painful but I suppose necessary, though probably it could have been handled better. At one point, it was mentioned that lawyers might get involved, since some of my *Weird Weekends* ideas were similar to segments I'd pitched at *TV Nation*, but no suit ever materialized. It was about twenty years before Michael and I spoke again.

David would be a close collaborator for seven years and would guide me, with varying degrees of involvement, through three series of *Weird Weekends*, the *When Louis Met . . .* documentaries, and a period of confusion afterwards. Tall, lantern-jawed and perma-stubbled, he looked undeniably like a TV executive, and it was easy to forget that he was only in his twenties. He shared a quality of many of the best producers: an ability to absorb anxiety, to keep the faith in dark times, and recognize when decisions needed to be made. His natural authority was the inverse of my total lack of authority. Along with it came a taste for the perks of senior office, like fine dining and taxis. I only once saw him on public transport, on a subway in New York, and he made the best of it but I had the impression he felt like he'd been dropped at midnight in a *favela* in Rio.

While I was in LA, David had found two assistant producers, Jim Margolis and Simon Boyce, and in them may have been our best hope of salvation. They were both whip-smart, and funny, and excited about whatever ill-defined comedy-documentary-travelogue project it was that we imagined we were working on. Jim was small and a little neurotic, hailing from Ohio; Simon, tall and skinny and fastidious about his appearance, came from Oxford. They were like a transatlantic cop team, a Dempsey and Makepeace of the lower echelons of the TV world. Both could also shoot with the small cameras that were then still relatively new as a format. David had had the idea of using them on location, supplementing the material from the 'real' camera to get more intimate after-hours footage or shots from hard-to-reach spaces.

A director named Ed Robbins came on, a thoughtful and urbane collaborator of a slightly older generation. Ed's strength was a contemplative approach, a feel for mood and nuance. On occasion this tipped over into a certain dreamy, spaced-out quality. Sometimes the delays in his replies meant it was like conversing with someone on a long-distance crackly phone line – or possibly an astronaut in orbit. He'd look at you expectantly after you finished speaking as though one more word or phrase was still needed for everything to make sense.

Huddled in three small windowless rooms on a high storey of a tall office building in midtown Manhattan, three thousand miles from the documentary unit in Bristol, we spent those first few weeks developing our ideas. My years of accumulating cuttings and zines on the offbeat and bizarre finally paid dividends as I brought in a pile of manila folders stuffed with research and shared them with the team.

It was clear from the off that our two strongest ideas were the militia/survivalist story and porn. David made the decision to do survivalists first. This made sense for a couple of reasons. One was that porn, given the sexually charged material, was easier to get wrong. It was also a more confusing world to penetrate (pardon the pun) – there were too many directions to go in: fetish films, fans, awards shows, sex toys, magazines. It stood to reason that we would fare better if we worked out our style and approach with a story that was more manageable and less high-risk.

Militias and the associated community of ultra-constitutionalists and patriots had been thrust blinking into the spotlight of national media attention in the wake of the Oklahoma City bombing, in which 168 people had died in 1995. There had been a wave of shock and outrage, news stories and TV profiles, but by late 1996 the movement seemed somewhat in abeyance. My main aperçu regarding that world was that its true believers, while undoubtedly dogmatic and paranoid, were slightly less hateful and less racist than was commonly understood. The idea of someone putting all their noble qualities of dedication and bravery at the service of a cause that was so weird struck me as funny but also touching. I saw an opportunity to create a mood in the show that was weird, comic, and moving by turns.

David said he shared the same ambition for the programmes, though occasionally I sensed he was troubled by my enthusiasm for showing contributors with unsavoury political views in three dimensions. I told him it was important that in the mix of characters we find a 'bigot with a heart of gold'. I was aware this was a ridiculous phrase; I'm not too sure how seriously I took it. I just knew we needed to challenge viewers' prejudices and that a moment in which an interviewee went from being cartoon-like to something more rounded, and eliciting compassion, would create an interesting emotional tension.

Many long conversations were had trying to figure out the degree of my participation. I wanted to show willing in the worlds I was investigating but I also didn't want to hijack the narrative and I was aware that, while it might be funny to see me running around with a gun and pretending to declare war on the federal government, it would also be an odd break in tone. How involved could I get in something I was personally opposed to? How did the idea of me 'going native' in a slightly tongue-in-cheek way jibe with our deeper ambition for the programmes, of giving time and consideration to people putting their lives at risk for ridiculous dreams?

The focal point of the militia episode was to be Almost Heaven, a purpose-built 'covenant community' in the central Idaho panhandle, founded by a much-decorated ex-army colonel called Bo Gritz. In the media, Almost Heaven had been characterized as a semi-apocalyptic gathering of fire-breathing zealots who'd moved up there, seduced by Bo Gritz's canny exploitation of their bible-based fears, to be safe when the end times came. There was much talk of a UN-backed plot to take over the world. We hoped Bo Gritz might be a central character in our episode.

Ed and Simon went on a recce – a pre-filming trip to scout locations and characters. A week or so later, they returned sounding broadly positive about what they'd found. The only hiccup was that many of the hours of tape turned out to show thin air or ground or background. 'I wasn't looking through the viewfinder,' Ed said by way of explanation. 'I like to maintain eye contact.'

Then we learned that Bo had a narrow window of availability. He spent his winters in Nevada, whereas we needed him to be in Idaho at his home in Almost Heaven. We rushed to ready a first filming trip. I wrote a sheet of humorous questions to ask Bo. We also added a stop-off in Beverly Hills. In my reading of militia literature, I'd come across a Hollywood producer called Aaron Russo who'd produced *Trading Places* and managed Bette Midler but more recently had devoted himself to promoting quasi-apocalyptic militia-tinged views that the Feds were taking over and eroding the precious right to carry firearms and not to pay income tax. He lived in LA in Beverly Hills. I liked the odd contradiction of his Hollywood connections and his militia leanings, and I lobbied to interview him on the same leg of filming.

I have vivid memories of that shoot. Not good ones.

Three of us – me, Ed the director and Simon the AP – flew out to Lewiston, Idaho, then drove an hour and a half through a rough-hewn landscape of farmland, rolling hills and sinuous rivers to Kamiah, a scenic little logging town on the banks of the Clearwater River, population 1,100. It's the kind of town where they have jell-o at the salad bar. We'd arranged to meet Bo at his house early the next morning. The call time was five a.m. In order to give myself more of a lie-in, I'd decided to shave the night before. In hindsight, this strikes me as a bizarre thing to do.

We drove up a narrow winding country road in the early morning darkness. It was November and snow was everywhere. Almost Heaven lay on a small plateau: 200 acres, divided into thirty or so lots, a motley scattering of unprepossessing homes. We arrived at Bo's house, an incongruously bland and suburban triple-wide trailer. He answered the door – white-haired, well built, in a tight black t-shirt and big buckled belt – and growled in way that wasn't entirely friendly: 'What's goin' on?'

'Colonel Gritz. How are you doing? We're from the BBC.'

'Well, you're too early, it's tomorrow, isn't it?'

Later I was grateful that we had captured this bit of unintended comedy on film – it was a perfect illustration of Michael's documentary precept about always filming the 'hello' for real in case something unexpected happens – but at that moment I was confused. In the footage you can see me glance off camera for help.

'No, it's supposed to be today,' I said.

'Well, you can come in but I'm supposed to be doing my radio show in just a couple of minutes. And I was told it would be Tuesday!'

'OK, well, sorry about that . . .'

'Take your shoes off!'

When the radio show was over, the delays, the sense of occasion, the undeniable fact that I was now starting filming on *my own TV show* – after a break from being onscreen of a year and a half – combined to create a sense of pressure that momentarily disabled my faculties. Shaking Bo's hand emphatically, I began: 'Well, let me just say, General Gritz – Colonel Gritz, excuse me, it's a real pleasure for you, for *me* to—' I sputtered to a halt and Bo peered quizzically into the camera as if to say *Who is this moron?*

We resumed, I tried again, and the interview proceeded. He took us on a tour of the house, which I can only assume was decorated to his wife's tastes, with cute little bits of Christian kitsch, figurines of angels, framed inspirational messages, and paintings of Jesus that looked like adverts for shampoo. It was an odd contrast to the gruff macho figure Bo cut. He had supposedly been the real-life model for Rambo, though I had the impression it was mainly him who put that rumour about. He had had a distinguished career in Special Forces, as attested by his forty or so medals framed on the wall. His war exploits had naturally made him a hero and role model to many on the far right and, combined with a commitment to a fringe brand of evangelical Christianity, he had built up a devoted following of listeners to his short-wave radio broadcasts, which were big on cataclysmic events and signs of the end.

One of Bo's promotional spiels was that he had settled on Kamiah after taking a map of America and crossing off every area associated with any kind of risk. I proposed that we re-enact this exercise, for illustrative purposes, and I pulled out a map and magic markers.

'OK, so you founded a patriot covenant community here in rural Idaho, would that be correct?'

'You'd be exactly correct,' Bo said. 'I went to every state and everywhere I went I saw people afraid. They were paranoid.' He enumerated the various sources of the people's paranoia – the government, natural phenomena, nuclear power plants. 'So I went to FEMA – the Federal Emergency Management Agency. They have a great database of catastrophic events. And I started taking a magic marker . . .'

At this Bo began scrawling over great swathes of the country, ruling out areas in the 'tornado belt', the 'giant flood belt', 'the blizzard zone', nuclear waste in Nevada, earthquakes in California. 'What could be wrong with North Dakota? You've got NORAD!'

This went on for several minutes, after which the resulting map was a mess of scribbles of torpedoes, tornadoes and other hazards.

'So it doesn't leave that much, does it?' I said.

'Well, we ended up with a little tiny spot up here – we are *right here*,' he said, making a little cross in northern Idaho. 'This place is the safest place in all of America.'

In the afternoon we took a drive to the far side of Bo's 'constitutional covenant community', to Almost Heaven 'Too' – 'That's T-O-O,' Bo felt impelled to point out. The bizarre details piled up: the shock troops of the UN might be planning try to grab Americans' guns or implement a mass programme of computer-chipping the citizenry; there was also the possibility of a UN military assault, though it was all rather vague and I wasn't sure how much of it Bo really believed and how much was a marketing pitch designed to help him make money selling parcels of land to the credulous. But if the extent of Bo's good faith was hard to figure out, what was more worrying was a more basic issue: the growing sense as we filmed that Bo's steamrolling style was simply a bit boring. My sheets of amusing questions were redundant – they either led to rambling, unfunny answers or simply went unused. Bo was right in his comfort zone of delivering a kind of ad hoc radio show to an audience of one.

The shoot with Aaron Russo was even more lamentable. We met him at his Beverly Hills mansion. He had the over-tweaked attitude of someone who has seen through the matrix of programmed reality and can liberate you from your brainwashed, sheeple consciousness, if only you're brave enough to follow him down the rabbit-hole. He made it his project to school me on the dishonesty and inherent instability of the Federal Reserve. In hindsight, I don't know quite what I'd been expecting. I just know it wasn't this – a tubby Hollywood producer delivering a learning annex style lecture about the US treasury in his pool house. I have a recollection of Ed – God bless him – stepping in about fifteen minutes into a Russo monologue, confessing that it was a primetime show for a general audience and we would have to be realistic about how much detail about the US financial system we would be able to get across.

The experience of watching the rushes with David back in the office was funereal. I looked a mess: unshaven with long floppy hair. The supposed presenter, I was the least presentable person anywhere near the camera. This might have been excusable but the conversations were borderline unwatchable. Bo Gritz never shut up. The Aaron Russo material was so poor, I don't think we ever spoke about it from that day on. It was like a national tragedy or a terminal illness: just to mention it would have been bad juju, eating away at our fragile production morale.

The elephant in the room – which no one mentioned but to my mind was all but snorting and hosing us with its trunk – was my total incompetence. Any other job, I might have been fired at that point. I realized there was an advantage to having my name in the title after all. And yet, along with the feelings of doom, and the embarrassment, was a vague sense of relief. I cycled home in the late-autumn gloom, down the concrete defiles of Manhattan, thinking at least it was all out in the open now. No longer was it my solitary concern. There was a general awareness that it was *possible* we were embarked on a monumental folly. A failure. We were all thinking it. Everyone was worried, which meant maybe I could worry slightly less.

Over the following weeks, we retooled our efforts, focusing more on the need to make the programme a coherent whole. We started with a sense of location. No more jetting off to Hollywood – Aaron Russo was off the menu. The whole thing would be shot in and around Idaho. It was also clear Bo couldn't be our main contributor. Instead we committed two days to filming a less elevated character, an Almost Heaven resident and true believer called Mike Cain – Ed had met him on the recce – who had a Mexican-born wife and showed signs of having the paradoxical qualities we'd been looking for of being radical and crazed but also sympathetic.

We slotted in another couple of characters. I was keen to include a lefty-hippy survivalist. We found a man who lived in an underground home named Mike Oehler, a freak-flagged Mr Natural who was also knowledgeable about the broader milieu of the radical right and happy for me to stay the night in one of his subterranean lodgings. We found another non-racist Almost Heaven-ite, a slightly crazed born-again called Don – he'd once worked in computers and donated to Friends of the Earth – who lived in a house made from straw bales. In bull sessions that stretched into the evening, we plotted a rough outline for the story and the beats of my immersion. I would overnight with Mike Cain at Almost Heaven and bunk down with Mike Oehler in his underground home, and I would help build a little straw-bale annex next to Don's house. It wasn't quite clear what the story was leading up to.

By the time we were ready, Christmas was nearly upon us. To squeeze in the shoot and still make it back home to England on Christmas Eve, I realized I'd have to fly straight from Idaho. The night before I was due to leave, after the disaster of the first shoot, I was crazed with anxiety. I was packing and planning, cursing the world for putting me in a position that was, in fact, entirely of my making. I made my TV segments for *TV Nation*, a nasty part of my brain was saying. I have nothing to prove. If my show is a disaster, it's on David and my new collaborators.

As I packed, along with my clothes, I also had some Christmas gifts I'd bought for family members back in England. Rather than drag them around with me on the shoot, I thought it might make more sense to send them via FedEx. I took them down to a local office and then later I realized that, in my heightened state, I had accidentally included my airplane tickets in the package of gifts.

The production had to pay for new flights.

Hindsight has telescoped that second militia shoot into a golden idyll of productive days and cascading good fortune. From our first scene in a Montana survivalist store (where I indulged in some good-natured teasing of the owner while he showed me his emporium of preparedness items: imperishable meals, night-vision goggles, guns, and his ultimate safety item – a kind of habitable plastic pod that you were supposed to bury in the ground), through the subsequent days in Idaho, at Almost Heaven among the militia families, then further north in a visit to a neo-Nazi compound and a drunken night with Mike Oehler the underground hippy – those days stay with me as a redemption from all the doubt that preceded them.

Without thinking about it too much, I took on the persona of a slightly hapless but enthusiastic reporter who was intent on making friends and also getting his questions answered, but equally awkward at both. Though it would be just as true to say that was who I was. I still chuckle at the moment in a wide shot (to signal it is 'overheard') when I plead with Steve, the owner of the survivalist store, to let me know where his survival shelter is so I can join him in the event of the apocalypse. There was also a bizarre encounter on a visit to the headquarters of the Aryan Nations, a White Power group, where my elderly neo-Nazi chaperone and guide around the compound, 'Reverend' Jerry Gruidl, turned out to be a huge fan of Benny Hill and *Are You Being Served?*.

But what made the shoot – and subsequently anchored the TV episode when we came to edit it – was the time we spent with Mike Cain, the Almost Heaven survivalist. Shooting over the course of two days, giving his story a chance to breathe, we were able to allow Mike to reveal himself in surprising ways. The man who'd stopped paying his taxes and was intent on declaring war on the federal government, turned out to be warm and welcoming, a self-described 'ex-hippie' who loved his Mexican-born wife and was by turns comical and self-deprecating, friendly and unhinged.

By prior arrangement, we'd shot a greeting on a hillside, where Mike and his friend Pat were building a house – wearing carpenters' overalls, clambering amid a carcass of two-by-fours, surrounded by a dirty sea of snow and fields, and lit by the lowering sun.

'What do you want?' Mike asked.

'We're doing a little story on Almost Heaven, finding out what life's like up here,' I replied.

He drove us back to the homestead: it was dark when we arrived, but the lights on Mike's battered truck lit up a ramshackle construction of breezeblocks and logs. Inside was a basic country dwelling with a freestanding stove in the middle. Mike's wife Chacha had prepared an evening meal of Mexican food, and while we ate Mike outlined his unlikely vision.

'There has been a conspiracy for some years by a group of people that have become known loosely as the New World Order,' he said. 'The problem with the New World Order and the one-world government is that it requires a benevolent dictator. You show me in history any time when there has been a benevolent dictator ever. And if you don't have a benevolent dictator you have a tyrant.'

Over that night and the following morning – when we went out on a dawn patrol of the local area, presumably looking for the advance guard of the UN invasion – I grew to like Mike, enjoying his strange combination of qualities, his warmth, his ability to see himself as he described it as 'a radical nut'. He told me his story: a building contractor in Las Vegas, he'd struggled financially. The IRS had raided his bank accounts. He'd also been one of Bo's short-wave radio listeners, and Bo's pitch of a mutually supporting 'patriot' community geared towards communality and self-defence in the end times had appealed to him, though I had the feeling that Mike viewed Bo as a disappointment – that, having encouraged them all up there, Bo wasn't doing enough to organize the patriot believers and provoke the feds.

On our last afternoon, he took me target shooting.

'When's it all going to happen, do you think?' I asked.

'Maybe before the year two thousand,' he said.

'And what will it be?'

'All-out war. I'm sorry. One day. We've all fought wars before. But one day it'll happen.'

'You against who?'

'Us against the New World Order.'

'I've really enjoyed being around you and it just makes me worried because, the more convinced you are that this is going to happen, it seems in a way the more likely it is that it will happen.'

'Louis, I appreciate what you say, I really do. I can promise you this: if it happens, it won't be because we started it . . . We pray daily it doesn't take place. We lift a standard of peace always. But if they're going to have a war then let it begin here.'

Mike was cradling his rifle all through the conversation. His delivery was utterly poised and he gave the impression of having waited years for this moment to make a public declaration of his willingness to violently resist those who would deny him his free-born American's right not to pay taxes or have a social security number. His dignity was so seductive, it created an odd dissonance between the power and the emotion of what he was saying – the very real sense of connection I felt with him – and the fact that it was fundamentally nonsensical: a quilt of overheated far-right rhetoric and paranoid religious craziness.

Mike's hillside declaration of war gave us our ending. We filmed a goodbye at his house, where I hugged him and Chacha and thanked them for their hospitality. As we were leaving, the camera operator let me know he was running out of tape. I liked the authenticity of the video stopping mid-goodbye. We did in fact have other blank tapes. Later, back in the office, David Mortimer was perplexed that we hadn't bothered to reshoot the scene to cover ourselves in the edit.

I don't think I said anything in response, but I remember thinking, in my almost fanatical zeal for realness: *You really don't get it.*

The idea of going back inside and re-enacting a heartfelt farewell would have struck me as almost sacrilegious.

And in fact, my obsession with authenticity, while it occasionally went overboard, was probably my greatest asset. When I look back at what worked in that first episode about militias and survivalists, what strikes me – other than my questionable wardrobe, the leather donkey jacket that is several sizes too big, the wonky wire-rim specs, and a faint mid-Atlantic twang in my accent – is the sense of there being something true in the relationships.

The planned bits of comedy had mostly fallen flat. The clever questions I'd written had mostly gone unasked. What had saved us was a quality of relaxed intimacy with our contributors – how they felt licensed to express themselves, be affectionate, laugh at my lame jokes, occasionally bully me. Shooting using the small cameras – on car journeys, in hard-to-reach locations – had also allowed us to expand the frame and include moments of unselfconscious actuality.

I felt pleased with how it had all gone. I felt something real – almost magical – had taken place and for the first time I felt that it was possible my series might be a success.

Chapter 11

# Weird Christmas

That first *Weird Weekend* with the militiamen and survivalists – and the sense of belonging I'd felt on location among people utterly unlike me – taught me something about my own survival in the world of television. It seemed paradoxical: the success of the shows would hinge on my ability to open up on location, lose perspective, go native, and though elements of it were an act, there was a large part of it that was real. Later, when the time came to do publicity interviews, I would say that I felt more comfortable among the supposedly weird people I documented than I did in the corridors of the BBC, and I was only half-joking.

We made three more episodes in the first half of 1997, one on male porn performers, another on UFO contactees, a third on Christian evangelists of the healings-and-miracles variety. I tried to remember the lessons I'd learned from that first excursion in Idaho. For each episode I spent a concentrated period of time in a subculture alien to my own outlook and way of life, in which the subjects had a commitment to something I viewed as wrong-headed, weird, ludicrous or self-destructive. Each focused on a defined area of the country. This helped give the show an organic quality, a unity of place and look. And with each I tried to stick to the idea of giving the programme a sense of pathos and imbuing our contributors with dignity while also not ignoring the fact that they and their worlds were often quite funny.

The episode about male porn performers, in particular, benefited from this double-edged approach. Having sex for a living – staking one's professional fortunes on an unpredictable physical organ – is strange, kind of funny, and potentially pretty sad, all at once. The young performer we featured, J. J. Michaels, went on to become a friend. As I write this, he is living in Ukraine with his fourth wife, very happily if his Facebook posts are anything to go by. The UFOs episode was arguably the closest to the freaky Americans Yank-tacular that I'd been telling myself I'd been trying to avoid. It is faux-naive and undoubtedly mickey-taking. The emotional stakes are low. The voiceover is over-the-top and silly. But all of that is outweighed by the sheer otherworldliness of the Nevada and Southern California desert terrain and the self-seriousness of the true believers – one of whom, Reverend Robert Short, was a 'space channel', able to give voice to a being on another planet, and another of whom, Thor Templar, claimed to have personally killed ten aliens.

Not long after finishing the shows, word came that the BBC2 controller Mark Thompson had seen them and wanted to commission more. I signed up to a two-year deal for twelve more episodes. I think there may also have been a clause about doing some specials – I'm not sure what was in the contract because I don't think I read it. Contracts made me tense: they made everything too real and I just thought about the pressure of having to fulfil them. But there was no word on when the new shows would actually go out, and there followed a weird interval of a few months.

Around this time Sarah and I separated. She initiated the break-up, possibly thinking a little bit of a reality check would focus my mind and shock me into a more serious commitment to my future with her, or perhaps intent on following her own romantic interests.

One of my periodic episodes of unsought celibacy soon followed. I took an apartment in Fort Greene, a historically black neighbourhood of Brooklyn that was battling the tide of gentrification. The apartment was on the second storey of an elegant brownstone, overlooking Fort Greene Park, on a street lined with towering plane trees. I bought furnishings second-hand at thrift stores and junk shops. The city's lower income areas were full of these emporia of cast-offs, records, old clothes and board games, kitchen utensils. I enjoyed the air of abandonment that hung over them – the other lives they testified to; the sad way they were arranged; the weird mothball smell and the benign lack of interest of the salespeople. It was the antithesis of the typical commercial encounter's hard sales and constantly moving inventory, an antidote to the lie we'd been told that we needed new stuff. Thrift stores were like animal shelters, and shopping there was an act of rescue. The fact that the drawers in the dresser didn't work or the clothes didn't really fit felt a small price to pay for the chance to build a friendship with an object with its own sad back story.

I was in a strange limbo. I wrote some articles, smoked and drank my nightly allocations of red wine and spliff, watched old movies. It was a little like the interval between taking exams and getting the results. Nothing was quite solid and it was difficult to commit to doing anything in particular. It may be that this otherworldliness contributed to my decision to embark on what, in hindsight, is probably the strangest and most wrong-headed of all the TV documentaries I've ever been in involved in.

No one likes to dwell on failure. In certain self-actualization philosophies there is an expression: there is no such thing as failure, only feedback. As someone who took four goes to pass his driving test, I'm not sure that's true. ('Well, Mr Theroux, congratulations on once again getting feedback on your test.') But I do think failure is often more interesting and revealing than success. Second-rate works, pieces that don't quite come off, are more likely to reveal how they're done. It's like watching a magician perform a trick badly.

It started with David Mortimer's mentioning that the channel was looking for Christmas programming for the following year. At the same time, I'd been thinking about how much I'd enjoyed my time in the worlds of the first four shows, and specifically what great characters we'd found. The idea began gestating of making more out of those contributors. In concert with the Yuletide theme, I wondered about bringing one person from each of the first four programmes to New York to spend Christmas with me at my apartment. As funny as it was seeing me on location in Idaho talking to a neo-Nazi, wouldn't it be twice as amusing to see a neo-Nazi interacting with a UFO contactee who was channelling a space being from another planet? I mentioned the idea to David, who liked it and encouraged me to put calls out to contributors to test their enthusiasm for taking part.

One of the first calls went to Jerry Gruidl, the *Are You Being Served?*-loving neo-Nazi from Idaho. Once on the phone with him, I had a feeling I've had many times when talking to contributors after taping is concluded: an irrational surprise that it isn't an act and that they are still exactly who they were on screen: in his case, a poisonous neo-Nazi and anti-Semite.

I asked him about Christmas.

'What do you normally do?' I said.

'The normal thing is I try to thwart the Jews' plan for the takeover of the world,' he replied. 'Anything I can do to screw a Jew, I'll do.' He paused, then added, 'I don't mean sexually.'

The strange reality check engendered by the call – the ugliness of his discourse and his complete inappropriateness as a candidate for what was basically a reality-TV format – might have been the first red flag if I'd been paying attention, which I guess I wasn't. There is a world of difference between stumbling across funny contributors in weird situations on location and, on the other hand, flying them out of their normal environment to engineer comical shenanigans on demand. What was I thinking – that we would go a-wassailing around Manhattan with a neo-Nazi while he handed out racist pamphlets? I had enough sense to rule Jerry out of contention for the show, but not enough to wonder if there might be a problem with the concept itself.

We pushed on with other less toxic contributors: Mike Oehler, who lived underground and whose political views were relatively mainstream, other than thinking society was on the verge of collapse; J. J. from the porn show; a Christian preacher called Randy James from the episode we made in Dallas about evangelism.

We began thinking of how we might structure the shoot. This was before *Big Brother* and the idea of rigging a house. We figured we would put our contributors up in a hotel but our days would involve small missions – one for each contributor – that the other members of the group would help out with.

Filming went smoothly enough, taking place in the week leading up to Christmas – 'smoothly' in the sense that there were plenty of made-for-TV arguments between the contributors. Early on it became clear that Randy would be providing the necessary conflict, as so many of our activities seemed to clash with his hard-line Christian beliefs. Unsurprisingly, he was not totally cool with watching J. J. getting it on in a porn shoot and wandered off in a huff to proselytize to passers-by, which then led to a set-to between them about J. J.'s chosen path. 'You're dead, spiritually,' he said with utter gravity.

On Christmas Day, Reverend Robert Short arrived and channelled his alien friend Korton in the front room of my apartment, issuing horoscope-like space messages for each of us for the coming year. Randy's feeling was that New Age prognostication of this sort was demonic. He opted out of this session, too, and when he came back he accused Reverend Short of being a satanist, whether or not he knew it. I tried to broker a peace on camera.

Afterwards I remember feeling the shoot had been successful.

Certainly we'd had our share of explosive arguments. The interventionist, high-concept dimension felt ballsy and brave – like we were real TV makers as opposed to documentary chroniclers of a slightly dull but worthy sort. Only afterwards did I realize how dubious it all was – not so much ethically (since the contributors all knew more or less what they were signing on for) but dramatically: the entire undergirding of my shows, namely that 'Louis Theroux' is at the mercy of forces beyond his control, the correspondent who has gone too deep, was short-circuited by the inescapable sense that 'Louis Theroux' was also an insincere on-camera ringmaster. The whole exercise was haunted not so much by the ghost of Christmas past as by shades of Jerry Springer past. When it finally aired – almost exactly a year after taping – the public agreed: *Louis Theroux's Weird Christmas* was a cracker that made no noise. A few months afterwards, I was approached at a party, in a friendly way, by someone who described himself as a fan – he'd loved the first four *Weird Weekends*.

'But that Christmas episode. What was that about? I sat watching it with a friend and I'd built it up to him and it just . . . oh dear.'

'Well, you weren't really supposed to *enjoy* it,' I offered. 'It's more of an avant-garde piece.'

Much later, David tried to claim that we had invented the *Big Brother* format two years before the fact, which – given that we had no 'house', no 'rig', no public voting, no evictions, plus me in it – was a bit of a stretch, but I applaud him for trying and any residuals to which I am entitled can be forwarded to my agent.

Chapter 12

# Habits of Work

At the beginning of 1998, word came that the BBC had finally scheduled the first four episodes of *Weird Weekends*. I was still living in America, so the production flew me to London for a few days of publicity. There wasn't a massive demand on my time. There was only one TV appearance, on an ill-fated Channel 5 chat show hosted by the Scottish comedian Jack Docherty, and I did a couple of print interviews. I was also on the Radio 4 show *Loose Ends*, where the host Ned Sherrin criticized my approach in the Christianity episode, accusing me – possibly accurately – of making fun of my interviewees. He played a clip of me talking with a born-again Christian lady who anointed her car with holy water. 'You're taking the Michael, aren't you?' Ned said. I should have been prepared for this but I was so wrapped up in the ambiguous rapport I had built with contributors that the question took me by surprise and I didn't know quite what to say.

We had no photos from the locations so we arranged a shoot with a photographer and props relating to each episode. It took place in a studio in the basement of BBC Television Centre in Shepherd's Bush. For the Christianity photos I held a large wooden crucifix and shouted at the camera – which wasn't at all the feel of the episode but I have a regrettable habit of agreeing to do what I'm asked by photographers. For the porn one I stripped off and made antic faces while wearing only a pink feather boa and a pair of boxer shorts. That image still makes me sigh inwardly whenever I see it in random places on the Internet, where it lurks like a ninja awaiting the right moment to assassinate my ego. David Mortimer was at the shoot offering suggestions, one of which was that I should take my boxers off. He said they'd use an effect – possibly blurring or maybe a little box – to make sure nothing would be seen that didn't need to be. To this day I'm thankful I declined this idea.

We also did some straight portrait-style photos of me wearing a ribbed turtleneck jumper that I'd recently bought at Gap. When combined with my two-sizes-too-big leather jacket I imagined it gave me a roguish seventies appearance, a bit like Bodie from *The Professionals*. This photo would return, years later, on the Internet and spread like a cancer across various media in meme-form. Time has somehow erased its roguish qualities; I looked less like Bodie than a missing child on the side of a milk carton. It was picked up by shadowy unlicensed makers of merchandise and began appearing on t-shirts and tea towels and other bits of product for reasons that are obscure but which I'm fairly sure have nothing to do with its roguishness.

When the shows finally came to air, it was more than a year since I'd begun making them. I felt a little disconnected from them. At the same time, I was fairly confident that they were doing something different – showing in an unvarnished and honest way the intimate lives of various unlikely American dreamers – and without me wanting it to, the embarrassing parts of my brain began entertaining all sorts of visions of grandiose success, with BAFTAs dancing around in a conga line.

Critics had their own opinions – mostly positive but not wildly so. I had the sense they hadn't really understood how much in them was new. Many saw them as exactly what I hoped they weren't – mickey-taking and anti-American. Of the TV reviewers, the only

Trying to look like Bodie from *The Professionals*.

one I much cared about was Victor Lewis-Smith, who wrote for the *Evening Standard*. By the time his piece appeared I was back in America. I couldn't find it online – this was before newspapers were routinely on the Web – and I had to resort to calling up the *Evening Standard* offices. It was late in the day in London and I asked a security guard to read it to me. It took him a while to find it, and he also couldn't read very well, but it soon became clear that the write-up was not positive – my encounters with the UFO believers reminded Victor of someone 'arm-wrestling a thalidomide victim' – and so I found myself enduring the indignity of straining to understand a long, stumbling rendition of an unfavourable review down a transatlantic phone line.

'OK, that's probably enough,' I broke in. 'Thanks.'

Some of the negative feedback was a result of how the shows were scheduled. The Christianity episode went out first, followed by the UFOs one. Critics concluded we were taking a predictable anti-religious perspective on hoary examples of American flim-flam. When the porn and militia episodes came out, some reviewers expressed surprise at the more complete palette of emotions they showed. Some wrote as though I must have been shocked to meet sensitive and appealing characters in far-out worlds, as though I hadn't planned for them to be included in the shows.

A few months after those first four episodes went out, in May 1998, I moved back to the UK. I'd been living out of the country for nearly seven years. There were several reasons to return. Closeness to family and friends. Also, David Mortimer was based in London and I'd come to value him as a collaborator. I figured, if I was going to make programmes for the UK, I might as well live in the UK. And, oh yes, fame. I had never dreamed of being famous. But when I saw TV celebrity, of a modest sort, coming down the tracks towards me, I won't pretend I wasn't curious what it might bring in its train.

The answer was, first, random interview requests. I agreed to these with alacrity. I did one with a Welsh railway magazine and another with two fans from a student paper who asked questions like, 'If you were a Quality Street, which one would you be?' Occasionally people shouted at me in the street. Sometimes nice things like 'We love you, Louis' or more mystifying remarks. 'Are you the bloke that does that thing?' 'Are you who I think you are?' One I didn't know how to respond to was, 'I love the way you take the piss out of those cunts.' (Said to me by three young men from Motherwell. I replied, 'Oh, wow. Thanks!') Another frequent interaction involved being complimented on shows I hadn't made. I don't just mean the title was wrong ('Wacky Weekends' is a common misnomer and I don't bother to correct it); I mean praise directed at actual shows and documentaries made by other people. Over the years, I've been praised as Ruby Wax, Nick Broomfield, and Mark Dolan, among others. If any of the aforenamed is reading this: someone loved that thing you did about snake handlers/tiny people/the Grim Sleeper.

More than once I had the disconcerting impression that people expected me to be other than I am on screen, and that they felt a little insulted to find that that is more or less who I am. They thought I was making fun of them. Once or twice I overheard people I was working with say, 'He really is just like he is on camera!' which I found odd. The question I heard more often than any other was: 'Is it an act?' or 'Are you playing a character?' I don't know that I ever found a satisfactory answer to this, except: yes, a little bit but possibly not as much as you might think.

The other storied side benefit of fame – sexual opportunity – was little in evidence, though this was at least partly due to my now being back with Sarah, my girlfriend-wife, and living in semi-married semi-bliss.

In the two years that followed I settled into habits of work that were to serve me well – with some changes and adaptations and a few hiccups – for the next twenty years. Programmes on husband-and wife-swapping sex-party enthusiasts, and devotees of Indian gurus. South African Boer nationalists, and gangsta rappers in the Dirty South. Some episodes I'm still proud of, some I'm a little embarrassed of. All have their moments, and – if Twitter is anything to go by – there are many people who would prefer if I went back to that light-hearted and slightly antic style and who regard everything that followed as a bit of a creative diminuendo.

Having suffered through the ructions and self-doubt of the first episode, I'd like to be able to say that the process of making the shows became easier. It didn't. Story generation was always an issue. For the first four episodes, I had my subjects pretty well mapped out. It was a bit like making a debut album. Like a bag of songs, I'd been thinking about those shows for a couple of years at least – reading and cogitating and collecting cuttings. After that, it was second-album syndrome.

I still have a list from 1996 of possible ideas – a brain-dump of fifty or sixty subject areas from 'Anarchists' to 'Toad Licking'. Some are so wrong-headed I am a little baffled as to what I was thinking. I had a preoccupation with US culture's colonization of the world. Hence

'Exporting Baywatch' was one idea and 'Game Show Missionary'. Malls and theme parks and fast food all feature prominently. I wrote:

Don't want it just to be 'fringe'. Need mix: fringe, sex, celebrity, violence, villainy, fun.
   Keep it broad but still focused.
   Also: is there a place for sadness? for people searching for meaning?

A small handful made it into the pantheon of commissioned episodes of *Weird Weekends*. Some we covered but not until many years later. The list includes 'Eating Disorders', which I made a programme about twenty years later in 2017. Scientology is on there too. *My Scientology Movie* came out in 2016. For some topics, because of their weightiness and lack of obvious comedy, it was a case of needing to gain the confidence to know how to handle them – or maybe earning the right to cover them. It's also always been true that as a production we've had trouble focusing on more than one idea at a time. A little like air traffic control: you land the planes one by one. And sometimes they crash.

I used to say that each story rested on a kind of tripod of qualities: comedy, pathos, participation. But as much as I liked to think there was a formula, we didn't always get it right. In the second series, I became aware that we had over-emphasized the 'participation' leg of the tripod and ended up doing stories that lacked moral complexity or gravity. It was usually a bad sign if my moment of becoming involved was the climax of the film: selling paper shredders on the home-shopping network or auditioning for a Norwegian cruise line. My participation worked best as a device – a tongue-in-cheek motivation, an opportunity for incongruous comedy – but the real story needed to be bigger: my connection with a contributor who'd pledged his life to something immoral, dangerous, even life-threatening. I'd sometimes reference a children's TV programme that starred the *Blue Peter* dangerman Peter Duncan trying his hand at exotic pastimes like sumo wrestling: 'We're not making *Duncan Dares*!'

If I had to distil a single lesson in the selection of story ideas – which I still try to stick to – it would be to make sure there is something at stake for the contributors: life, limb, freedom, sexual or mental health. I tried to stay vigilant and look after the seriousness and the journalistic side of the story, but there was a countervailing pull towards comedy: the need for the shows to be funny and also that there should be opportunities for me to participate. It wasn't always easy to find the balance.

Many of the techniques we relied on in that first episode about militiamen in Idaho became central to how we worked. Always we looked for subjects with a geographical focus. This had the practical benefit of allowing us to revisit characters we liked and to build their stories with multiple scenes. But it was also a sign that the story really existed in the way it needed to, suggesting a depth and real-ness to the relationships within the worlds we were exploring. I was suspicious of stories that were too spread out or only held together by Internet-based friendships. Furries (fetishists who dress up in mascot-like outfits and have sex at conventions) were considered but dismissed based on their having a part-time and largely virtual connection. The world of porn performers, on the other hand, is a village in which people live and work and even die together. It is not a hobby; it is a job and an all-consuming identity, which puts its practitioners at loggerheads with the mainstream world.

Even when we had an idea, there followed weeks of research – led by the director and his or her AP – in which magazines and news-papers were gone through, phone calls made, old films watched, until there came a moment of commitment to the recce. During the recce the director and AP visited locations and met and interviewed a variety of potential contributors with a view to deciding who would be in the eventual film. Usually, they filmed a little taster tape of each contributor. This might take a week or ten days or sometimes longer. Back in the office, they'd show the highlights of their favourite candidates. Based on these conversations, we would plan the journey of the story on index cards blue-tacked to the wall. 'LOUIS MEETS MASTER P. HE ENCOURAGES HIM TO RAP.' 'LOUIS AND RANDY ORGANIZE EVANGELICAL CAR RALLY.' 'LOUIS RETURNS TO MELLO T TO CONFRONT HIM ABOUT HIS CHOICES.' These index cards were only ever a rough guide: they tended to feature more contributors than we would end up using and the shape would change as characters dropped out. Still, they were almost always helpful, allowing us to plan action and have a vague structure in mind.

In general, when I arrived to meet someone on screen, we made sure it was my first meeting. But usually the team would have met the person already on the recce. This raises what is probably the biggest misapprehension about our programmes: how much I do. The shows all carry a 'directed by' credit at the end of them. And yet I am always surprised at the credulity of viewers – even those in the TV industry – who assume I am the sole author of the films. The directors are the motors of the film to which they are attached. They guide the research, do the recce, they are in charge on location, and they sit in full-time on the edit with the editor, while I drop in and out for screenings in between drinking martinis and being massaged with hot stones.

It's for this reason that I try to remember never to call myself a film-maker but a journalist. To be honest, I sometimes think I'm closer to being the lead singer of a musical group – not a very glamorous or exciting one, maybe a glee club or a barbershop quintet – I'm the one doing the shrill coasting falsetto, I'm not sure who the deep bass *dooby-dums* are coming from, maybe the series producer? – but probably even that does me a little too much credit. Still, there seems to be no end to viewers' naivety. I'm amazed when intelligent people worry that Bear Grylls might starve to death in the woods or drown falling off his raft when he is clearly being filmed by someone who presumably has sandwiches and/or a buoyant vessel. It's flattering that people imagine I do more than I do. I used to try to explain it by comparing the 'Louis Theroux' on screen to Homer the poet, in that he is more like a committee of people operating under a single moniker. And yes, I did just compare a TV show about weird people to the *Iliad* and the *Odyssey*.

It also has to be said that getting disproportionate credit has its downside. When the shit hit the fan with the Jimmy Savile business, I was surprised to find that while I got called before various inquiries – including the BBC's Janet Smith Inquiry – the director and executive producer on my Jimmy Savile doc were overlooked.

Acting headshot for the *Weird Weekends* 'Off-Off Broadway' episode.

I'd like to think I improved at my job as time went on. My strength had always been that I was an attentive listener and a hard worker. I flattered myself I was good at building relationships on location. It may be that whatever sense of anxiety I had always laboured under stood me, in certain ways, in good stead. I found shoots a welcome break from my routine. I felt many day-to-day cares dissolved when I was embedded in the odd worlds I investigated on location. I surrendered to the priorities of whoever I was with. I tried to pitch in. I felt it was my job to be fully present and available. And if there was a little bit of 'going native' – a mild dose of Stockholm Syndrome – then that was perhaps a salutary part of getting stuck in to a story, a way of understanding more deeply. And truth be told it was also just something I enjoyed: the release from my normal existence and sometimes an occasion to imagine myself in a wholly other life.

I had made the welcome discovery that the participatory element of the *Weird Weekends* concept – while it had been intended as a storytelling device and occasion for comedy – had the surprising effect of endearing me to my hosts. It helped win trust with those I was among when I rapped/did dynamic meditation/walked on hot coals. For the porn show, as a comic bit, I had stripped naked in the offices of the main porn agent and had my Polaroid taken. It was a funny moment, but the real revelation was the effect it had on other performers when I showed them these photos. They warmed instantly, seeing me somehow as no longer aloof or antagonistic. They made me part of the club.

In a way, the key to the whole enterprise was walking a line between winning over contributors and, at the same time, trying to keep my journalistic focus. Always, whatever the story was, I had an idea of what I was trying to understand: a simple ten-words-or-fewer contradiction, paradox, or tension, which I would worry away at, asking question after question while trying not to overly fatigue the contributors.

And yet, as much as I liked to flatter myself that I had a technique and knew what I was doing, I was aware that much of it was adventitious and undeserved, hingeing on lucky breaks and collaborators who took up the slack of my incompetence. And even those positive attributes I brought to the production were accidental much of the time – a certain quality of ingenuousness or maybe gormlessness that won people over, a willingness to get involved that was also twinned with an unworldliness that was for the most part unintended and unconscious.

In our office bull sessions I'd sometimes say, 'The real participation is the emotional connection.' If there was a trick to this whole thing, it was nothing more complicated than finding quasi-friendships in unlikely places – among people widely viewed as suspect or questionable or flat-out predatory and wrong. As much as the shows were still viewed as mickey-taking by some, there was also enough humanity that they worked as the opposite: exercises in rounding out people usually seen in two dimensions. I was trying to show the *other* as not wholly other. Even among those unapologetically devoted to ways of life I viewed as harmful – a pimp in Mississippi, a Boer nationalist in South Africa, an unscrupulous spiritual figure like a space channel or a miracle-working televangelist – I attempted to see them as up-for-grabs, salvageable, not so different from me.

Chapter 13

# If You're Going to Puke, Puke Chunks

In 1999, while coming to the end of the second series of *Weird Weekends*, running dry of ideas, I began circling around the subject of muscle men in strange uniforms (capes, tights, leather jackets, with canes and little hats) slamming each other to the floor, sometimes cutting themselves with tiny concealed razors, in front of screaming crowds – in other words, professional wrestling.

It was a natural subject for us. Unlike Olympic-style grappling, pro-wrestling is a semi-fictional activity in which the bouts are choreographed and the outcomes predetermined. The code of secrecy that surrounds wrestling is sometimes called kayfabe, a term whose origin is disputed but which means presenting staged performances as though they are real. People describe pro-wrestling as 'fake' but that isn't really accurate. The athleticism is real and so are the injuries. Wrestlers have to perform night after night, taking body slams and chairs to the head, and risking brain trauma. They are actors, stuntmen, and athletes all rolled into one. This gets lost because of the benign deception at the heart of pro-wrestling that it's a competitive sport. Which it isn't.

To direct, we brought back Ed Robbins, the thoughtful and slightly eccentric veteran of the 'Head for the Hills' programme. He and an English AP, Will Yapp, began working the access. The biggest wrestling league, Vince McMahon's WWF, turned us down but its rival outfit, the WCW, said they were open to filming. How much they'd be likely to let us see backstage was unclear. To cover ourselves we also approached a much smaller local wrestling league of part-timers in South Carolina called the AIWF. This would, we hoped, fill in some of the gaps, and maybe provide intimacy and pathos as well as giving the programme a sense of range, showing the entire food chain of the wrestling world.

It went without saying that I would not be maintaining kayfabe in reporting my documentary. In fact, I saw the wrestlers' refusal to break character or acknowledge the fictional aspect of their craft as both a bit of a problem and also a potentially helpful source of conflict.

Early in the filming, I flew down to Florida with my crew to visit a WCW road show called Monday Night Nitro. It was a bright, sunny day, and fans in ballcaps and a few in wrestling masks were streaming into a vast arena. I'd been hoping for free-range access backstage at the event. That was how we'd filmed the doc about the porn industry, being allowed to wander around more or less willy-nilly, if you'll pardon the pun. In my fantasy of how the wrestling shoot might go down – which is always a dangerous place to dwell, and extremely alarming to directors because it is often so out-of-whack with a sense of reality – I'd envisioned myself in a huddle with the wrestlers, helping them on with their trunks, and planning story-lines for the bouts. Yeah, right. After protracted negotiation, the WCW PR guy – an Elton John lookalike called Alan Sharp – had permitted us to stand at the entrance to the dressing room, inter-viewing the dribble of wrestlers as they arrived. I was like a little press gauntlet of one.

A wrestler named Randy 'Macho Man' Savage walked past, incognito in dark glasses and a tight black t-shirt. For a moment he appeared on the verge of saying something, then thought better of it and walked on. An old-timer called 'Rowdy' Roddy Piper, also in dark glasses and a leather jacket, asked me my name then, mishearing it, said, 'Louis LaRue.'

'Theroux,' I corrected him. 'But you can call me LaRue if you want, being a wrestler.'

I asked how old he was.

'April 17, I turned forty-five,' he said. 'And they still can't beat me! All right? So you should have caught my act when I was twenty-nine! I would have made love to *you*!'

'Ha ha! Steady on!'

Next came a young German wrestler in dark glasses, with Mohawk hair and a trench coat. He was debuting a new character, he said in accented English. 'I used to be Alex Wright in WCW and I used to dance techno. But the American people are not very familiar to techno so I changed to be a bad mean guy and I came up with my new look.'

'So tonight you're debuting a new persona?' I asked.

'Yes,' he replied.

'And is there a new name?'

'Yes. Well, like I said, before I was Alex Wright. Now I am *Alexander* Wright.'

He was there to give his new 'Alexander Wright' character a soft launch, not by wrestling but by walking the aisles and the ringside, creating a buzz around the new identity, '*Achtung! Achtung!* Alexander Wright!' he exclaimed. (Sadly, I later heard that the news of the Columbine School shooting – and the negative association around trench coats – put paid to the 'Alexander Wright' identity.)

The show was an extravaganza of ultra-muscular men in boots, slamming and swinging one another around the ring and tumbling over ropes. A study in paradoxical violence, it was a ludicrous simulation of combat that was at the same time extremely dangerous. I don't like to think about the amount of concussion that was sustained. In the entire display, more than the stunts and the danger,

I most enjoyed the grace notes of the over-the-top storytelling, which had a tongue-in-cheek quality. At one point, a camera feed outside the hall showed an injured wrestler being helped into an ambulance before the door closed and the camera revealed the name of a *mental* hospital as the wrestler pounded on the windows to escape.

It was only after the show – possibly prompted by its outrageous storytelling – that I realized I hadn't asked any of the wrestlers about the choreographing of the bouts. Not that I expected any of them to break kayfabe, but it was less about getting an answer than being seen to have asked the question. By now, with the crowds streaming out of the venue, it wasn't clear whom I could speak to. There was no sign of the publicity guy, Alan, and I was running out of options. I spied Sarge, a bullet-headed muscle-bound man I knew to be the head wrestling trainer, breaking down the ring.

I approached him, camera in tow. After some pro forma compliments about the excitement of what I'd just seen, I said: 'One thing I don't totally understand is to what extent they know what's going to happen in the ring when they come out. Do you know what I mean?'

'No, I don't,' Sarge said.

I sensed a hint of irritation, so I retreated and made a fumbling concession to the 'enormous amount of athletic and acrobatic ability' of the wrestlers, and 'tremendous strength and that type of thing', and then wobbled to the end of a vaguer and now slightly nervous question about 'how it worked' in the ring.

'I don't have any idea,' Sarge said, ending the interview, though not explosively, and I didn't give much further thought to whether I might have annoyed him with my gentle sally at the is-it-real question.

After the big-bucks show business of the WCW, the AIWF was a different proposition. Based in Mount Airy, North Carolina – quintessential small-town America, and supposedly the real-life model for the fictional Mayberry of *The Andy Griffith Show* – it was like a hillbilly am-dram troupe getting together at weekends to put on a performance for the local crowd.

The owner-manager was Dean Puckett, a friendly mullet-haired carpet fitter whose *nom de guerre* was Rick Deezel. As an outfit, they were friendly and hospitable, flattered by the attention of a foreign film crew. Rick's boast was that they were the most extreme wrestling troupe in America: 'Fire, barbwire, thumbtacks, glass doors. That's our claim to fame. Most hardcore extreme wrestling federation *anywhere*.'

One of their wrestlers, Jody Rushbrook, worked nine to five changing the oil in cars at a Jiffy Lube. The afternoon I arrived in town we spent a couple of hours at his workplace, hitting each other with a tin tray so I could get a flavour of how it all worked. Their star wrestler fought under the name Brian Danzig. Brooding and a little withdrawn, he worked in a sock factory, but for his bouts Brian had a horror-clown persona with ghoulish black-and-white make-up. An hour before showtime, he would take five or six aspirin to thin his blood, tape little razors to his thumbnail and then, once in the ring, lacerate his forehead out of sight of the crowd to make blood pour down his face. In the wrestling world, this sort of self-inflicted bleeding was called 'getting colour'.

The venue for the AIWF event was a school gymnasium. I helped them set up the ring, and quizzed them on how it worked – unlike the wrestlers at WCW, they were fine with acknowledging that they planned fights and happy to let us in on their professional secrets. Clearly they had less money at stake than the big-name wrestlers. I also tend to think their self-mutilation was so sanguinary and extreme that they didn't feel the need to lay claim to any other kind of authenticity.

'It's a soap opera for men,' Rick said. 'A lot of people they think, "Oh well, these guys know who's going to win, who's going to do this, so it's fake." That may be one side of it, but this is not fake.' He picked up a coil of barbed wire that was stapled to a plywood board.

Then, pulling Brian's hair away from his forehead to show a patch of skin that was etched with a multitude of tiny scars, he said: 'And this right here is not fake.'

The ensuing carnage and gore of the evening's performance took place before a crowd of seventy or so, some of them small children. The wholesome atmosphere of the school gymnasium, its association with nativity plays and beanbags, made a strange contrast to the extremity of the display. Brian's bout had him pitted against some 'kung fu fighters' from a local martial arts academy, 'The School of Hard Knocks', who were bald-headed and dressed in only pyjama bottoms. One of them was blading for the first time, but as he went to gouge himself he got jogged and cut too deep. His face as he came off stage after the fight was a horror mask of pale white skin doused in red. Yet he appeared thrilled with how it had gone, beaming as a nurse patched up his wound. Brian, too, was transformed – no longer shy and introspective, he had become ebullient.

'Well, as long as you're not really hurt,' I offered, though truthfully I was a little freaked out at how much gore was on display.

'Other wrestlers'll be like, why do you get out there and half-kill yourself? But I don't! I don't half-kill myself! I'm fine! I'm going to go tear the ring down and go to the Waffle House.'

A few weeks later I flew to Atlanta to see Sarge the trainer at the Powerplant for a follow-up interview and what had been planned as a light-hearted workout session with some of the wrestlers-in-training. I didn't think too much about it in advance. The sequence we were shooting had 'unpromising' written all over it. I suspected most of those present would be second- and third-division wrestlers hoping to make it. It felt potentially like a segment for breakfast TV. 'Ever wondered how wrestlers get in shape? Our presenter Darren went to find out.'

Arriving at the airport, for some reason I treated myself to a greasy breakfast – possibly it slowed us down because when we reached the gym we were a little late: thirty or so budding made-for-TV monsters were already doing squats and chanting in a cavernous space under Sarge's tutelage. Ripped and shiny and hairless, the wrestlers combined extremes of masculine and feminine in classic bodybuilding style – like a hair-metal band that had been overfilled with air.

Sarge was wearing a loose tank top. The armholes were so wide that from time to time the taut red rivets of his nipples would poke out distractingly. I had the sense Sarge was irritated by our tardiness and I jumped into the workout, squatting, doing sit-ups and press-ups, trying to keep up, but it was clear I wasn't so much fifteen minutes late as ten years too late – ten years of crunches and pull-ups and squats that I'd been too busy reading and drinking wine and smoking spliffs to bother with. Still, I tried my best.

At first I was enjoying the liveliness of the scene, the shouting and chanting. Then I got tired and that's when things got slightly weird. It seemed it wasn't as simple as saying, 'Right, lads, thanks, we've got what we needed.' Sarge had no intention of letting me stop.

'We been doing this since ten o'clock,' he shouted as I attempted a kind of human coffee table posture, pushing my belly in the air and bending my arms back like a crab. Sarge was bending over me, sweat dripping off his nose and on to me.

'It's hurting my back!' I said.

'I was here yesterday doing this, I'm here today doing it and I'll be here tomorrow. Get up now!'

'It's killing my back.'

'I don't care!'

I was experiencing muscle failure. I protested that I couldn't do any more press-ups. The trainee wrestlers gathered around me in a throng, all shouting in a way that was somewhere between turbo-pep-talk and psychological gangbang. I waved my hands to try to let them know that – in a friendly and respectful way – I was withdrawing from the field of battle.

'Everybody back up!' Sarge shouted. 'Lie down. Move your arms. Move your legs. Say, "Sir, I'm a dying cockroach."'

This I was more than happy to do. I wondered if it might be the 'safe word' that would end the torture. Thinking it might help, I added: 'I am a dying cockroach because I haven't got the will to win!' But there was no noticeable lessening of the verbal assault.

'These guys go through this every damn day!' Sarge said, sweat spanging off his shiny head and nipples. 'And you got the nerve to ask me that bullshit down at Nitro. What the hell? You think we aren't athletes? Hell, we're the best athletes in the damn world!'

*Fine.* I did some more 'hindu squats', some running on the spot and screaming, then, feeling I really *had* had enough, I retreated to a small dressing area, only for Sarge to come literally running after me to pull me out.

'Where in the hell you think you're going? No! You're coming out and watching everybody else! I don't give a shit. Get your ass back in the ring . . . Do you see how stupid the questions were you asked at Monday Night Nitro?' he asked.

'Yes, I do, yes.'

'Do you see why I am the Sarge? Huh?'

'Yes, I do.'

'SPEAK UP! Say "Sir, yes, sir!"'

'Sir, yes, sir!'

'Look at these guys! They started at ten o'clock. Now you see why this is the toughest sport in the fuckin' world. Bar none. And they gotta put up with my short irritable ass every fuckin' day.'

I was happy to agree with him, and was nodding and shaking my head as vigorously as I could, as cued, my discomfort only somewhat relieved by the awareness that everything was being captured on tape and might be helpful for the documentary.

The workout continued. 'I give up,' I said, not for the first time. The greasy breakfast was now making its presence known; I was beginning to feel nauseous. 'I'm going to throw up,' I said and went to get a small paper cup of water from the cooler. Seeing this, Sarge slapped the cup out of my hand and sat me down – dunce-style – on an upside-down plastic bucket. The workout moved outside and, still feeling the need to prove my willing to the wrestlers, I joined them as they ran lengths in the gym parking lot.

It's possible I might have managed to keep the sick down if I'd tried – or at least in my mouth. But I was secretly hoping my vomiting might have a shaming effect on Sarge. Up it came – a couple of small acid mouthfuls that went splat onto the parking lot tarmac. Its chastening effect on Sarge, however, was nil.

'That ain't nothing! You ain't done nothing!' he shouted. 'If you're gonna puke, puke chunks!'

This may have been the weirdest part of Sarge's critique of my performance – his disappointment at the consistency of my vomit.

After that, seeming to feel he'd made his point, Sarge disappeared. We shot a couple more bits. In one, with some other wrestlers, I practised delivering hyped-up speeches to camera, talking up fictitious future bouts under the new ring name they'd given me, Waldo.

Weeks later, I viewed Ed's rough assembly of the episode and was surprised to see he hadn't included the moments of the workout spinning out of control or the regurgitation. Possibly he was a little embarrassed that he hadn't done more to stop it in its tracks, even though he had been right not to intervene – the entire episode was an exercise in humiliation but not physical danger. I encouraged him to put it all in, including wobbly shots, to give the sequence its flavour of authenticity. When the episode appeared on TV, at least one reviewer thought the whole sequence faked, which I could sort of understand. Given how intrinsic fakery is to wrestling, it would have been a sly but understandable storytelling device. In fact, it is real, though clearly there was a performative quality to the moment, with Sarge enacting a ritualistic humiliation of the visiting journalist.

It is also true, though, that what I experienced was business-as-usual at the Powerplant. Five or six years after my visit, a well-respected wrestler, Dave Bautista – who went on to find success as an actor, playing Drax in the *Guardians of the Galaxy* franchise – described a very similar experience in an interview: being shouted at and forced to work out until he vomited, and being told by Sarge that he would never make it. I also heard that puking during workouts was a regular occurrence – in which case, the only surprising part was that Sarge was holding me to his usual standards of what he expected from young wrestling try-outs.

It was only later that I came to see it as an example of a certain kind of documentary making: those moments when the contributor takes over control and 'produces' the encounter. In dramatic terms, it is the satisfaction of seeing the protagonist find himself at the sharp end of the story in a way he hadn't expected.

The paradox of wishing for moments of unplanned jeopardy is, of course, that they can't be planned. The expression that comes to mind is hoping for lightning to strike. This isn't as difficult as it first appears. If you run around a hilltop during a thunderstorm, waving a long copper stick in the air, you're likely to get struck by lightning.

You may also get burned to a crisp.

Chapter 14

# The Godfather

Several times over the years it has seemed to me that I was coasting onto the off-ramp from the TV highway, heading towards the gritty surface streets of obsolescence. Late 1999 was one of those periods. The second series of *Weird Weekends* seemed a decline from the first – ratings softer, reaction more muted – and I was still under contract to make six more episodes.

I'd been back in London a little over a year, living in a flat in Shepherd's Bush with Sarah. The BBC had leased some offices in west London within a short cycling distance. Later I would come to value the unsupervised atmosphere of working away from the BBC campus. There are benefits to not being caught up in the politics of the corporate hive, but at that time I was still new enough to TV that I was curious what it might be like actually inside HQ and, if I'm honest, slightly interested – in a theoretical way – in the romantic opportunities it might afford, being in the swim of hordes of media types of a similar age.

David had been encouraging me to think of other ideas that might work as single documentaries. It was still my habit, from time to time, to write up lists of half-baked concepts for new formats. One I came up with was for an occasional series I was calling 'Hotspots'. It would involve me doing gonzo first-person reportage at the site of major international incidents: wars, natural disasters. I've always had a secret yen to be a more respectable journalistic figure – a foreign correspondent covering big international stories. This never seemed to get anywhere with the channel. International disasters come and go but 'Hotspots' remains uncommissioned.

Another, more promising, avenue was the idea of a documentary portrait of an intriguing cultural figure. I had a file on Lemmy, the lead singer of Motörhead. I liked the pathos of an unregenerate rock beast approaching the winter of his dotage. I imagined living with him in his Hollywood house, doing tequila shots for breakfast. I'd also read he collected Nazi memorabilia, which sometimes suggests unhealthy political interests. Bernard Manning, the northern comedian given to racially charged humour, was another perennial – bunking up with him at his place in Manchester.

And then the name of Jimmy Savile came up.

It's a little hard to see him through the miasma of everything that has been uncovered since, but the first thing to recall about Jimmy Savile was that – to many of us – he was weird and creepy even then.

I'd grown up watching his wish-fulfilment show, *Jim'll Fix It*, which aired on Saturdays and which was, in fact, the creation of its long-time producer Roger Ordish. He'd presented an odd figure in his tracksuit and with his pageboy platinum hairdo, affecting the style and air of someone younger than he was. Later, he'd worn suits and dressed more conservatively, but the hair was still dyed and he still passed himself off as a curiosity, an un-fancy man of the people and self-described con artist or pirate.

On his show he was a granter of wishes – 'fix-its' – to those who wrote in with a special request: to drum with a favourite pop group or to indulge a whim like, as a boy scout troop famously did, asking to eat packed lunches on a rollercoaster. He was also on the radio when I was growing up, a weekend oldies show, and he presented ads for road safety ('Clunk click every trip') and British Rail ('This is the age of the train'). Not to mention his indefatigable charity work, running up and down the country and raising the millions required to build a new spinal injuries unit at Stoke Mandeville hospital.

His private life was famously obscure. For almost as long as I can recall – certainly since my early teens – I'd heard there was something sexually untoward about Jimmy Savile. But one didn't attach any more significance to these rumours than to the idea that a certain film star had a furry animal removed from his rectum or that a rock star collapsed on his way to a gig and had his stomach pumped of six pints of semen. Later, when it was said (as it was by many) that 'everyone knew', I took it to mean that 'everyone knew there were rumours'. But the phrase 'everyone knew' was misleading and suggested a wider circle of complicity than was warranted or fair.

One day in 1999 I'd been at a lunch for a women's magazine I was freelancing for. Most of those present were in their late twenties and early thirties and it came out that every one of us had written in to *Jim'll Fix It* as children. One had asked for 'Jim' to fix up his bedroom with new furniture and gadgets, because he'd seen the same fix-it done the previous week. Another had written in, offering to make a cup of tea for Jimmy as his fix-it. This one had actually been granted. I recounted writing in, aged eleven or twelve, asking to shoot my teachers at Tower House with *Bugsy Malone*-style splurge guns. This request, not surprisingly, had gone unfulfilled.

Back in the office I told David about the conversation. He turned out to be a trove of weird Jimmy Savile facts. 'He's got a cell at Broadmoor where he sleeps,' he said. 'He keeps his mother's clothes in a closet and gets them dry-cleaned once a year.'

I mentioned that I'd heard rumours that he was a paedophile or even into necrophilia. This was all discussed in a spirit of unreality. Naturally one assumed that if he'd really been a paedophile or a necrophile, then forty-plus years in the spotlight of British entertainment would have brought something solid to light.

An AP, called Leeanne, went up to Leeds to visit Jimmy at his penthouse for a recce, to test his appetite for filming. It was surprising in a way that he agreed to do a recce, which is basically a kind of documentary audition. He was famous enough that he might have viewed it as beneath his dignity. She spent an afternoon with him, filming on a little camera as he showed her how he would make two cups of tea with a single bag. He prided himself on his thriftiness. His two *This Is Your Life* red books were on display. He announced that he was the only person to have been featured on the programme more than once – a first taste of the unverifiable Jimmy Savile self-mythologizing. The flat was furnished with the mementoes of a life dedicated to show business and charity fund-raising: certificates and trophies were everywhere. It was also visibly a bachelor's den. Most of the furnishings were merely functional; the smaller items were informative and commemorative rather than decorative – the detritus of forty years in the business.

He took Leeanne to Harry Ramsden's, the fish-and-chips chain, where he paid for their meal with a collection of loose change, counting it out with theatrical frugality. For the meal, they were joined by two friends of Jimmy's – local Yorkshire characters of an unstarry sort.

Jimmy was clearly keen to be involved. He came across as to-the-point and businesslike but also obliging on Leeanne's recce tape – up for answering questions and showing off his Rolls-Royce, which had the licence plate NNNN. 'It stands for nice natural naughty nookie.' 'Discos open and close,' he said. 'Hospitals never close.' He was seventy-two, or in his argot, 'thirty-six twice'.

He spoke of an encounter with Cherie Blair – 'When The Cherie came to see me, I put a fixed penalty parking ticket on her car' – and his connection to Chequers, which he said was only four miles from Stoke Mandeville. 'I spent eleven Christmases and eleven New Year's Eves there,' he said. This segued into chat about his hopes for the documentary. There were jokes about turning the camera off and what would happen.

'What if Louis wanted to dye his hair like yours?' Leeanne asks.

'Yes, but that's not real,' Jimmy says, in words that – when I see them now – I allow as perceptive.

In his bedroom, Jimmy gestured at the double bed and said: 'There it is – the altar.' Leeanne's voice from behind the camera – its brightness and cheeriness – is striking throughout the tape and at this moment she asks: 'Why do you call it the altar?' 'Because that's where the sacrifices happen,' he says.

Still, he seemed a marginal figure and I continued to hesitate. What was he actually doing? What would we be filming? I was used to doing stories about weird people – but weird people with a sense of vulnerability, which in the end made them relatable and sympathetic. This didn't apply to Jimmy. I was worried he was simply irritating. What hope did we have of making him interesting? I watched a documentary made in the early seventies, entitled *The Amazing World of Jimmy Savile*. Shots of Jimmy riding his bike, going to church, talking about his OBE and his relationship with 'The Man Upstairs'. It was boring beyond belief.

We started filming another UK-based project: a profile of the owner of Harrods, the multi-millionaire Mohamed Al-Fayed. His son Dodi had been dating Princess Diana when she died, and Fayed blamed her death on a racist conspiracy orchestrated by the royal family. Having been promised access, we took occupancy of a small back room at Harrods while we waited for him to appear. We filled time with interviews with his support staff. Fayed enjoyed collecting pedigreed businesses – like Harrods and Fulham Football Club – and he was the same with people, accumulating soigné names. Princess Diana's stepmother, Raine Spencer, was on staff. An ex-BBC royal correspondent, Laurie Mayer, was doing PR. We interviewed both, to little avail. After two days, Fayed finally appeared, taking us on a tour of a central staircase that he had expensively remodelled on an Egyptian theme. He denounced Prince Philip for fifteen minutes, then disappeared. We pulled the plug.

One morning I read a story in the papers about Jimmy attempting to comfort a depressed tiger at a zoo. There was a photo of the tiger with its paws over its ears. The implication was that Jimmy's help was making the beast feel even more desperate and forlorn. The idea that Jimmy's good works were increasingly regarded as ludicrous and seized on as an opportunity to lampoon him helped focus my thinking. I saw there was pathos in the prospect of a huge celebrity coming to his life's final chapter – an illustration in grand form of the indignity and decay that awaits us all. That sadness, which contrasted with the slightly irritating qualities of show business and banter, might make for an intriguing portrait.

My hesitations and the resulting delay meant that by the time I arrived at Jimmy's penthouse in Leeds he was a coiled spring of excitement – like a rodeo bull waiting for the gate to go up.

'Is that the Spice Girls?' a voice said through the intercom. Then, through the letter slot of his penthouse door: 'I don't believe you exist!'

The door opened to reveal an old man in a Nike tracksuit, his white hair pulled back in a ponytail, and an unlit cigar in his hand. He bore a resemblance to Jimmy Savile, but a much older version whose platinum locks were now thin and indistinguishable from the ordinary white hair of an OAP. 'You're better looking than me, you can't come in,' he said. 'Anybody better looking than me, that's it.'

Preparing for filming, I'd made a decision to try to be more aggressive than usual in my questioning. In the months between having the idea of filming with Jimmy and our arrival I'd acquired a new executive producer. David Mortimer had been kicked upstairs – or possibly to one side – and replaced with Kevin Sutcliffe, who'd come out of the BBC's flagship current-affairs programme, *Panorama*. Kevin was from Blackpool, marinated and seasoned in the rough-and-tumble world of news coverage, and he had put me on my mettle to be more than usually feisty. We were all aware that Jimmy, the experienced broadcaster and leathery self-caricature, would be in full Jimmy mode and that it was up to me to try to knock him off balance, to stop him disappearing into his comfort zone of catchphrases.

Quickly it became clear it would be unlike any other filming I'd ever done.

In a marathon session of interviewing that lasted several hours without a break, I poked around his penthouse, asking questions as I went, while Jimmy kept up a perpetual stream of jabber – about his physical fitness ('fitter and stronger than a butcher's dog'), his lack of interest in a conventional family or social life, and his friends in high places (Margaret Thatcher, the royal family). His level of energy and backchat was unflagging. It was like a big game: tantalize and retreat. He wanted both to be asked about the mysteries and contradictions of his life and then pointedly not answer. He was keen to be seen as well connected (pointing out a place-setting that appeared to come from Buckingham Palace) and at the same time he enjoyed ostentatiously parrying and deflecting the questions that followed, using bits of prison or mafia slang – 'Because when you're not a grass, you're not a grass; *Omertà!*' – and references to himself as a mob boss: 'The Godfather' and '*Il capo di tutti capi*', which he pronounced in Yorkshire-Neapolitan.

When I pushed him harder on some of his evasions and ellipses, letting the silence play out, he looked into the camera, saying, 'He's on the ropes! He's on the ropes!' in a way intended to take control of the moment. Then he said, 'And there's that Louis smile again!' I wasn't sure I'd been smiling. But alongside his gift for being combative without ill will was a knack for being friendly without benevolence. In presuming to assert that we were still on good terms, he was in fact leading the mood, like a hypnotist: acting as if everything was happy and friendly in order to make it so.

The most striking phrase from the morning came on the subject of his relations with women. He viewed them as 'brain damage'. He said it with enough irony to give himself some deniability. 'Wonderful,' he went on. 'That's what makes them interesting.'

We'd budgeted the morning for the tour of the penthouse, but past lunchtime we were still going. I asked about virtually anything I could put my hand to. Jimmy seemed to enjoy the idea that every-thing was up for grabs – that his life was an open book. The stubs on his chequebook. The contents of his drawers. I noticed that there was no computer. Jimmy did not do email. He made a point of saying that he was not part of the high-tech generation, in a veiled way appearing to fend off the idea that he could ever be accused of having anything inappropriate on a hard drive. Around that time, figures like Gary Glitter and Pete Townshend were being accused of downloading images of child abuse on their computers.

When the time came to see his bedroom he duly referred to it as 'the altar'. With the recce tape in mind, I asked: 'Why do you call it "the altar"?'

'Because I go to sleep in it and I smile and it's nice to be there.'

'Yeah,' I said, stalling while I pondered this unexpected reply. 'That doesn't sound like an altar to me.'

'It just sounds like one to me.'

'Really? The altar – is that because you sacrifice people on the altar?'

'No, no, no, no, no, that's negative, I'm positive.'

As the day wore on, with our stomachs empty and no let-up in the questioning, the mood became more captious and irritable. We were in danger of getting bogged down in a rhetorical slugfest, exchang-ing blows, both of us trying to grind out a points victory. I was a little confused about whether we were generating any usable material.

When the time came to drive to a cafe in Otley, in a moment I'm fairly sure he thought was off camera, Jimmy suggested I take a 'more positive' approach to my questioning. 'Instead of negative things which keep cropping up, try and work out two or three things that I can give you a piece of wisdom . . . A lot of people on their way up, for instance, what's it like for somebody today to get into the business? Or something like that.'

Moments later we were in the car, with me driving and Will filming, heading towards the cafe. Ordinarily, a contributor might feel he was off the meter when driving to a location, so Will's grabbing a small handheld camera and continuing to shoot while the crew followed in a separate vehicle was, in a sense, a statement of intent: Jimmy wouldn't get to relax.

Jimmy was in the back seat. He was exasperated. The constant questioning was wearing on his nerves.

'It's a lot easier to make negative TV shows than it is positive ones,' he said. 'And if we are doing nice things and good things and happy things, imagine how many millions of people you will cheer up. And they'll say, "That Louis Theroux, he's a fabulous geezer. He doesn't just do interviews with unusual people that leave us with nothing except, 'Ho! How unusual they are!' Look at the wisdom he extracted."'

'It can't all be positive, though, can it? That's just not reality.'

'Right,' said Jimmy, his manner becoming brusque. 'Make it as negative as you like. That's all right. See you in court. Take a few quid off you same as I take a few quid off anybody. Money has no conscience.'

I didn't think too much about this exchange and the suggestion that he might resort to legal action if he didn't like the finished documentary; I simply enjoyed it as a bit of barbed repartee that we had managed to capture on camera.

After a cup of tea at the Otley cafe, we drove back to Jimmy's penthouse. Now, off camera, Jimmy struck me as more direct, less playful – he talked about TV longevity and, for some reason, Ruby Wax, whom he called 'The Rube'.

That night I called my exec, Kevin. I told him I wasn't sure how well it was going. Jimmy was subjecting me to a barrage of banter.

At the same time, I had the feeling there was almost nothing he wouldn't endure to carry on filming. 'I feel as though I could kick him in the balls and he'd just keep going,' I said.

Day two followed in the same vein. In his kitchen, after I asked him playfully about a stash of spirits I'd discovered in his – the famous teetotaller's – cabinet, he gave me a mini tutorial about how to conduct an interview. I was too aggressive and accusatory, he said. Picking up on a phrase from the previous day, he said: 'Next!' And then, at my exasperation, he practically sang: 'I love it! I love it! I love it!' He was packing for a two-day cruise, and he itemized the contents of his overnight bag, making sure I noticed a packet of condoms. 'Hope springs eternal in the human breast, especially when you're single,' he said. What was more striking was that he hadn't packed a change of underwear. 'Wash it in the sink,' he said, 'let it dry overnight.' I didn't believe this, incidentally. You only needed to look at his teeth to see that hygiene wasn't his strong suit.

We took the train down to Liverpool docks – at my invitation, en route, Jimmy made a verbal inventory of his accolades and honorifics: OBE, knighthood, papal knighthood. We arrived at a star-studded celebration of the relaunch of the cruise ship, the *Caronia*. John Prescott gave a speech. Random celebrities milled about: Michael Buerk, Kenny Lynch, Liz Dawn.

Towards the end of the day, as the festivities were winding down, Jimmy took me and Will up to his cabin – he stalked about, jabbing his cigar at its luxurious features: it was, he said, one of only two penthouses on board, the best lodging to be had.

A bell rang to announce that the ship would soon be departing. Jimmy saw us out of the cabin, and we passed a smiling crewmember carrying a jacket with gold epaulets and a peaked naval cap – he seemed a figure of some authority, an officer or maybe the captain. 'Mornin', guvnor,' Jimmy said, looking suddenly shifty. On instinct I mentioned Jimmy's boast of having one of only two penthouses. The naval man looked confused as Jimmy nodded at him in pantomime fashion and said, 'That's right, yes.' 'No, that's not *the* penthouses,' the man said. 'The main penthouses are on the next deck.'

Jimmy barely missed a beat – 'Servants quarters! It'll do for me!' – but I felt I had scored a small victory, redeeming the preceding hours of fruitless filming, by showing his habit of brazenly and untruthfully self-mythologizing, albeit over a trivial exaggeration.

Back in the office, a meeting was convened to figure out whether it was worth continuing with the idea – me, Kevin, Will, and my old exec, David, who came down from the lofty citadel of his new job. We looked at the rushes – the atmosphere in the room was reminiscent of a team sent to survey the wreckage from an accident. The material wasn't like anything I'd seen before and Kevin seemed unimpressed. He commented that he wasn't seeing the unselfconscious Yorkshire miser he'd enjoyed on the recce tape. Jimmy was more 'on' around me. 'I wanted to do Cliff Richard,' he said with the air of someone whose confidence in an idea is ebbing.

But David saw reasons to keep the faith – whether because he enjoyed the fractious quality of the encounter or possibly just because he knew Jimmy was still enough of a name to pull in viewers. And so, with various misgivings, and with a redoubled sense of the need to get through Jimmy's showbiz armour, it was decided we would go on.

Chapter 15

## Zero Tolerance

It is striking, looking back, that the most revealing and unself-conscious piece of video that, to my knowledge, exists of Jimmy Savile – a mumbled confession of criminal acts committed in the sixties – should have been recorded by Will at a time when I was oblivious, in another room, trying to sleep.

We had resumed early in 2000, first – like a man dipping his toes in freezing water – with a day of charity work in Doncaster that was drizzly and uneventful and only gained us some shots of Jimmy lugging a huge cuddly bear on and off a train; and then – plunging in, knowing there was no turning back – a more ambitious week-long rail trip, that took us on a tour of three of Jimmy's homes – Leeds, Scarborough, and Glencoe.

As before, Will was mixing two formats: using a full crew for the bigger scenes, and filming intimate scenes and after-hours material on a small DV camera (nicknamed 'the toy camera') that he operated himself. The idea was, as much as possible, to stay close to the ground, blend in and make ourselves inconspicuous, like anthropologists trying to film a remote tribe.

We started, once again, in Leeds – though this time with just Will and myself present. The three of us ate at Adriano's Flying Pizza, a restaurant near Jimmy's penthouse that was his default hang-out.

Jimmy was on celebrity duty, presiding over birthdays, ferrying cakes to tables, conducting the singing like André Previn in a tracksuit.

'It must be bittersweet having fewer and fewer opportunities to spread this kind of happiness,' I said.

'Me and the Pope can never retire,' he replied. 'When he wakes up he's the Pope. I wake up and I'm me. That's the way it is.'

After dinner, we took a taxi back to Jimmy's. I turned in early for an uneasy sleep on a too-narrow bed in a spare room full of knick-knacks: a cuddly lion, a portable Sony TV, a trophy with a tarnished little plaque glued to it that said, 'Presented to Jimmy Savile OBE on the occasion of the opening of the Trinity Shopping Centre, Leeds, by Laing Development Company Ltd, on Tuesday 3 July 1973'.

The next day, I woke to the sound of Jimmy knocking on the bedroom door, then cackling as he walked away.

We took the train to Scarborough. Jimmy's flat there was in a grand old Victorian building, high above the seafront with a view across Scarborough bay, the waves rolling in, and hills off in the distance. Inside it was like passing through a portal into the seventies. There was white shag carpeting on the floor and suede wallpaper, a zebra-print sofa and pink cornicing.

I had been pinning a lot on the idea of the Scarborough flat. It was here that he'd lived with his mother, who he called the Duchess and where, to this day, he'd kept a wardrobe of her clothes, dry-cleaning them once a year. After the days of Jimmy's evasions, the idea of the Duchess's wardrobe felt solid – something properly odd that Jimmy would have trouble dancing around. His mother had been the only woman for whom Jimmy had ever expressed anything like love. After his father's death, he had taken to wearing his wedding ring on the third finger of his right hand. His mother had died a few years after, and Jimmy had once memorably described the five days he'd spent with her open casket, at a wake at a sibling's home, as the best time of his life. 'When she was dead she was all mine.'

All of these details I hoped to reflect somehow in our programme and they crowded in my mind, looking for a chance to join the conversation. But I was underslept after the night in the guest bed, and a little grumpy, and so intent on being forensic and focused that when it came time to pick up filming I tipped over into a mode that was closer to being badgering and rude.

On a narrow balcony, Jimmy puffed his cigar, wearing an aquamarine tracksuit and a chunky gold watch and wraparound Oakley glasses, and talked about life with the Duchess.

'Did you argue much when you were living together?' I asked.

'Never,' Jimmy said. 'No point in arguing.'

'And what if you had a girl with you?'

'She would have actually killed the girl.'

We walked back inside and Jimmy closed the balcony doors.

'Did that not cramp your style a little bit, since you couldn't bring girls home because your mum wouldn't let you sleep with women?'

'Didn't want to sleep with them. Good heavens!' Jimmy said with feigned shock. 'Anything more than two hours, brain damage.'

'Did that not cramp your style, Jimmy?' I repeated.

'I'll answer the question,' Jimmy said, pointing outside. 'If you see over there on the horizon, a caravan camp. I had a caravan there. So that was the love nest.'

In the Duchess's bedroom, appropriately grannyish with its dark pink bedspread on the double bed and genteel furnishings, he opened the doors to a small freestanding wardrobe against one wall, revealing a rack of clothing sheathed in dry cleaners' plastic.

'Now, all this gear was gear she wore,' he said. 'So instead of slinging it away, I thought I'd hang on to it because these make better souvenirs than photographs.'

This was my moment to elicit some vulnerability from Jimmy and I tried to slow the conversation down.

'Can we take some of them out?' I asked.

'What do you want to take 'em out for?' he snapped. 'Do you want to wear 'em?'

He moved towards the door, making as if to leave.

'I sense this is an emotional thing for you and you don't want to share it and I respect that,' I said.

'No, it's not emotional, it's a friendly thing,' Jimmy said, going on to explain the difference between *emotion*, which he seemed to regard as suspect – gloomy and incapacitating – and *friendliness*, which was positive and healthy. 'When I come in I always go, "All right, darling?"' he said. 'It's a friendly thing. It's not morbid. It's totally friendly. So there.'

I questioned him a little more, telling him he was being passive-aggressive, as he attempted to move the conversation away from the subject of the Duchess and her clothes. 'I'm just thinking of the time factor,' he said, and it was only later, viewing the rushes, that I noticed that the recollection of his mother appeared to bring him close to tears. Resigning himself to staying in the room, Jimmy sat back in a reclining armchair, affecting a pose of bored tolerance. I pulled photographs from an overstuffed drawer – pictures of Jimmy with prime ministers and stars and anonymous young women. I was aware this moment might be my best hope of addressing Jimmy's sexuality – the mystery of whether he was gay or straight or celibate or something else – and more generally how it was that for so many years he had kept a veil of secrecy over his romantic life.

'Your love life has never been discussed in the press, has it?' I said. 'Why do you think that is?'

'Probably because I've never been linked *to* anybody.'

'Do you mean you've never had a girlfriend?'

'Friends that are girls, eight million. Friends that are girls, yeah, but "girlfriend" in the sense of today, i.e. you are together, you don't bother with anybody else, et cetera – no, never.'

At the time, I took him to be saying either that he was celibate or that he had legions of lovers dotted around the country, but neither scenario seemed very plausible and I considered that the riddle of his sexual interests remained unsolved.

• • •

The rest of the day involved a saunter around Scarborough as dusk came on. We visited an amusement arcade on the seafront, run by a friend of Jimmy's, filled with machines that cascaded 2p coins, and then a fish-and-chip shop, where Jimmy was approached by a young woman.

'I've wrote to you loads of times,' she said.

'I know,' he replied. 'If you'd have put "if I ever meet you I shall fall madly in love with you", that would've been OK. I read the letter. I thought, "She won't even fall in love with me." So I slung it in the bin.'

Jimmy was approached in this way almost any time he went out in public.

That night I slept in the Duchess's bed.

The following morning the crew left and went home. For the next couple of days, it would just be me and Will and Jimmy, and I was imagining it would be quieter now. The only thing in the diary was a plan to film Jimmy recording a tribute for an episode of *This Is Your Life* featuring the DJ Dave Lee Travis.

And then, at the hotel, Will approached me with the air of someone with a secret.

He had something he needed to show me, he said, a piece of footage he'd shot two evenings earlier at Jimmy's penthouse after I'd gone to bed.

He scrolled around on his camera, and I peered into the viewfinder. In the clip, Jimmy, seemingly unaware that the camera was on, slouched back on his sofa, cigar in hand, watching a natural history documentary on TV – you could hear soft animal growls. There was video of me saying goodnight to Will and Jimmy and then, with me off stage and out of earshot, Jimmy appeared to relax. He reminisced to Will about his days in the sixties as a nightclub manager in Leeds. 'I invented zero tolerance, me,' he said. 'In the nightclubs, if there was any nonsense, I wouldn't tolerate it.' He explained that if any young men misbehaved at his clubs, he'd lock them in the boiler room until closing time. The police had spoken to him about it. 'Your daughter comes in here,' he'd told them. 'Tell me and I'll let them slags have their way with 'em. And they said, "All right, Jim, you didn't give 'em half enough." And they never nicked me for it. And I never altered.'

Of all the things I'd expected to uncover about Jimmy Savile, the idea that he might confess to more or less kidnapping customers of his dance halls was not high on the list. Also surprising was his manner of speech, which was mumbled and unselfconscious, still recognizably him but a more understated version. Even allowing for exaggeration, it hinted at a much darker, more brutal figure than the one the world knew. I didn't doubt he had been questioned by the police, and his steeliness and sangfroid were telling. He hadn't just imprisoned his customers, he'd sent the police packing when they questioned him.

Nothing else that happened on the shoot quite rose to the strange surprise of the discovery of Will's secret footage – though the days had their rewards, and in filming terms we basically got what we thought we needed: material of Jimmy at his Glencoe cottage, where he'd hosted Prince Charles the previous July; a visit to a pub where a local scallywag flashed Jimmy on camera (a rare instance of some-one being sexually inappropriate *to* Jimmy Savile); a sequence in which Jimmy, having fractured a leg, went to hospital but not before notifying a local photographer with a view to making it a national news story.

We had made a plan for Jimmy and I to spend the night together in a camper van, but in the event he refused my company, opting to stay on his own. But there was a small incident I cherished which we captured, when Jimmy emerged from the caravan and stumbled over his crutches, evoking – at last and for once – the air of pathos and vulnerability of the elderly and reduced man he was.

On our second or third day I asked Jimmy about the 'zero toler-ance' tape during a walk in the Highlands. We shot the conversation in an extreme wide – the two of us ascending a hillside next to his cottage – thinking some distance from the camera might encourage him to speak more freely.

He did not show any disquiet when I told him that we'd filmed him boasting about tying people up. He said he'd been speaking figuratively. 'It's like when you say "I could kill him." You don't mean you really want to kill him.' This was patent cobblers but evidently the best defence he could think of in the moment.

After the Scottish trip, we shot two more outings with Jimmy – visits to Broadmoor and Stoke Mandeville. He had lodgings at both hospitals with the same sort of memorabilia as was in his penthouse flat: awards, framed newspaper cuttings. But under questioning, for whatever reason, Jimmy was obtuse in his answers, his patience for my interrogation after so many days of filming having perhaps worn thin. I had the impression in both places that staff viewed Jimmy as an irritant, a presumptuous interloper turning up and expecting the run of the place. That, too, may not have helped his mood.

By the end of filming I'd arrived at an assessment of him as a rather remote figure, annoying, self-involved, but that those negatives existed alongside more surprising qualities of intelligence and acuity. For a man whose persona was so cartoonish, any subtlety of insight tended to come as a surprise. He had what seemed to be a watertight and self-contained outlook on life, involving logic and a certain understanding of psychology, and perhaps more than anything a quality of toughness, an ability to weather any kind of negative attention.

His self-image was as a steely kind of Yorkshire *Übermensch* who, through mental strength, had transcended the normal human need for relationships, for love, for the ties of convention – be they trivial, like tying one's shoelaces or packing clean underwear or having a cooker, or more profound, like the love of children or a wife.

He had made the decision to be unruffled by the crosswinds of fate and misfortune. As long as his most basic needs were met – unfussy food, shelter, cigars – he considered himself well taken care of. As for the demons of loneliness, anxiety, melancholy, he gave the impression of having banished them through an act of will. From somewhere he had learned habits of emotional self-reliance. He regarded himself as something of a guru on the subject of applying logic to human predicaments. More than once, during filming and after, he said to me: 'Call me when you have your nervous breakdown.'

When the time came to say goodbye, with no real expectation of seeing him again, I felt not so much a fondness for him as a kind of grudging respect.

Given all the pressure I'd felt to shake Jimmy up and rattle his cage, it's perhaps both surprising and unsurprising that, when the time came to edit the material, one of the challenges was not to make *me* look too bullying or inconsiderate.

Reaction from one or two friends and colleagues to a couple of early cuts was that I was being too mean to Jimmy. Sarah told me she felt I was insensitive in grilling him so cold-bloodedly about his relationship with his mother, right there where he kept her clothes, and we ended up toning the exchange down a shade. I showed a sixty-minute cut to a colleague while on location in India – we were doing a story about religious gurus. He was from Lancashire and I had the impression that, possibly because of some native northern loyalty, he found me overly rude to Jimmy.

But other than these niggling tonal issues, the film came together with surprising ease and, even in its earliest long cuts, was engaging throughout. One of the pleasures was the discovery that Will had left the camera running during various meals we'd had, capturing moments of candid reality, natural exchanges between the three of us. During one such dinner at a pub in Scotland Jimmy had picked up the camera while Will and I were off somewhere else and delivered a secret message, an odd sentimental little paean to our group, designed to be discovered by us at a later date, in which he expressed how much he was enjoying the filming. 'This is very, very pleasant,' he said. Then, addressing imagined accusations of being saccharine, he said, 'Might be a bit yucky for *them*' – meaning us. As an unsolicited Easter egg, it made a strange and telling counterpoint to the zero-tolerance footage: Jimmy 'on' and 'off'; the Jimmy who loved innocent good fellowship and the one who used to lock up 'slags' in his boiler room.

Of the hours we spent at Broadmoor and Stoke Mandeville, almost nothing was used, with the single exception of a section from a car journey in which Jimmy addressed the rumours of paedophilia. This exchange, which I probably would not remember had it not been in the show, later came to be much repeated. It was odd because it was only at his prompting that I raised the question of the rumours. We were sat in the back of a car and for the moment – possibly knowing it was our last day of filming – he was 'off' and being, for him, uncharacteristically obliging: listening, and answering questions.

'Why do you say in interviews that you hate children when I've seen you with kids and you clearly enjoy their company and you have a good rapport with them?'

'Because we live in a very funny world,' he said. 'And it's easier for me, as a single man, to say, "I don't like children" because that puts a lot of salacious tabloid people off the hunt.'

I'd asked if he was referring to rumours of paedophilia.

'Oh, aye. How do they know whether I am or not? How does anybody know whether I am? Nobody knows whether I am or not. I know I'm not, so I can tell you from experience that the easy way of doing it when they're saying "Oh, you have all them children on *Jim'll Fix It*", is to say "Yeah, I hate 'em." . . . That's my policy and it's worked a dream.'

When we'd arrived at a fifty-minute version, Will travelled up to Leeds to show Jimmy, as had been agreed, as a professional courtesy.

It's worth putting oneself in Will's place, arriving back at the penthouse, joking to disguise his unease as he thinks ahead to the reaction that will greet the film. He pops the DVD into the machine and for fifty minutes the two of them sit through a strange parade of images showing Jimmy as a lonely, occasionally sinister figure – 'Norma Desmond in tracksuit and trainers', as one journalist later put it – tramping the twilit Scarborough seafront and trotting out the same one-liners and catchphrases to an ever-thinning audience of passers-by. Not to mention that in the film – in addition to the host of exaggerations, impostures and outright lies he is caught retelling, and the ridiculousness of his general deportment, the clothes, the jewellery, the jokes – there is also his confession of criminal behaviour in his nightclubs in the sixties.

'That's good, that is,' he said when it had finished.

He then talked for some length about the 'zero tolerance' footage. His earlier explanation, that he'd been speaking figuratively, went by the board. Now he said, yes, he'd locked up some lairy characters in his boiler room, but they'd been asking for it, and the British public would understand.

When Will told me Jimmy's reaction, I was mainly relieved that he wasn't annoyed – not that it would have caused us to change anything in the finished film, but I don't like to make any more enemies than is strictly necessary. Unlike other contributors who have raged or sworn vengeance, Jimmy took the punch. He swallowed whatever hurt he may have felt, and declared the documentary another triumph.

David titled the documentary *When Louis Met Jimmy . . .* When it went out, I had the sense that we had made something compelling and strange. There was a richness to the encounters – the endless game-playing and cat and mouse – that put it in a different class to our other documentaries: his evasiveness and unwillingness to let the mask drop; my stolid and literal-minded perseverance. We had managed to capture on television for the first time something we as a society had all known but never quite nailed down: the flat-out weirdness and sinister quality of a celebrity who until recently had sat close to the power centres of British public life.

Most reviewers were complimentary, many responding to the sense of pathos Jimmy projected, a man addicted to fame, increasingly left behind – as we all eventually must be – by fashion and tastes and without the consolations of a spouse or a close loved one. One or two dissenting voices came from people who found the film overly critical of its subject and insufficiently appreciative of his charitable endeavours.

Oddly, given how much debate there was later about 'who had heard what', what no one seemed surprised by – on TV, in reviews, out and about, or anywhere that I'm aware of – was the reference in the programme to 'rumours of paedophilia'.

Chapter 16

# Celebrity Roundelay

'There's nothing real about you,' Sarah said to me late in 2000, a phrase that went around in my head for years afterwards, resonating in an awful way with a put-down Jimmy Savile delivered around the same time: 'Ah, insincerity. Your speciality.' Sarah and I separated not long afterwards. That sad passage of intimacy mixed with awkwardness and grief – the open secret of knowing we were splitting up while we continued to live together – was like hurtling over a cliff edge in extreme slow motion, not so much frightening as it was surreal and melancholic: falling through the air, knowing we would at some point weeks or months in the future smash against the ground, but in the meantime watching episodes of *Trigger Happy TV* and *The Sopranos* and making each other cups of tea.

We'd been together twelve years – our very own two-person Club 18-30, if they offered holidays where you stay at home and get high and play backgammon. I felt like the embodiment of the cliché of someone ditching his long-suffering supportive partner the minute he becomes successful – my guilt so heavy that I didn't even have it in me to call time on the relationship except in the most passive-aggressive way: by waging a devastating, attritional war of non-commitment. In the end, it fell to her to say the words, that we were splitting up. For face-saving purposes, we called it a trial separation. One afternoon in December 2000, I went out and watched a movie – *Chopper* at Whiteleys Odeon in Bayswater – to give her time to move out. I came back to find the flat half-empty and a note saying she hadn't been able to find her digital camera.

It was a sad winter. I never learned the knack for being single. I have that man thing of needing someone around – not so much to talk to, which might lead to intimacy or negotiation, but just to have a friendly looking body in the house. A bit like Jeffrey Dahmer keeping the corpses of his victims propped up on chairs around the flat.

Technically, we did everything correctly. There was no one else involved. It was a mutual decision. And at some level it was confusing to me that you can be honest with someone, try to be kind, try to do everything right, share your life for years, end things by agreement, only to have it all *still* end up being painful and wrong. At another level, of course, it made perfect sense: at *that* level I was neither kind, nor right, nor honest, depending on how you define those things. But I felt I had tried hard to do things correctly and later I wondered if the urge to conduct one's emotional affairs correctly was part of the issue.

I never had many more dealings with Sarah. I wished her nothing but the best. A few months after we'd split up David called me into his office at work, where the TV was on, and tuned in to a call-in programme hosted by Richard and Judy. 'It's Sarah!' he said, and it was – her voice talking about an unnamed celebrity ex-partner who was – I can't remember the details – possibly a narcissist or monster of ambition or a just an emotional cretin. I didn't mind – I assume she was helping out a friend, a producer on the show, and I owed her at least that – and in fact, without the ballast of a steady home life with a long-term partner, I was about to get exactly what I had wished for: a life blissfully empty of distractions, dedicated to work, and increasingly unhinged.

• • •

We'd moved offices by now. No longer in a groovy canal-side build-ing in Westbourne Park, we were installed in a block-like structure on an anonymous stretch of Wood Lane, next to the A40 and oppos-ite the warehouses of Unigate Dairy. The place looked like a child with limited imagination had constructed it out of huge grey Lego bricks. Its only human feature, an internal courtyard, was closed off because shadowy figures in health & safety had decided there was a risk of objects falling from the sky – meteorites, presumably, or frozen turds jettisoned from planes.

Kevin, my exec, was no longer with us: he hadn't died but taken a big job commissioning current-affairs documentaries at Channel 4. David had returned, combining his exec role with a lofty enter-tainment job that meant he was rarely around. In practice, the day-to-day running of the production fell to a new series producer, Gabe Solomon.

Without the tug of a home life, I floated around the rectilin-ear corridors, often chatting with the Irish TV journalist Donal MacIntyre. Donal had made a series of undercover reports, using hidden cameras, with the result that his highly secret face was now nationally famous. He too was trying to figure out a way forward, like an agent whose cover is blown and is now living out an aimless life in an apartment in Soviet Moscow.

After the success of the Jimmy Savile programme, and then another profiling the magician Paul Daniels and his wife Debbie McGee, word had come down from executives at the BBC that I should focus on more profiles. I should leave Weird America behind and make a series on modern celebrity. There was a celebra-tory dinner with the BBC2 controller at a west London restaurant. These occasions always feel haunted by the ghost of a notional future *Daily Mail* investigation into excessive BBC hospitality. One glass of wine only and check who else is having starters. I mentioned I'd been enjoying Rory Bremner's new series. 'You're bigger than Rory

Bremner,' the channel controller said. An unsolicited and faintly sur-real compliment. *Bigger than Bremner.*

I signed a new deal with the BBC for a vast number of pro-grammes, as usual without looking at the contract, with the attitude of a man at a cliff edge who doesn't want to see how long the drop is. Then production went into high gear, finding fresh celebrity can-didates for 'Louis Theroux' documentaries.

After the ease of getting to Jimmy Savile and Paul and Debbie, the feeling was it should be straightforward to get some more episodes underway. Our first forays were faintly worrying, however. The light-entertainment personalities and intriguing public figures were not leaping at us with open arms. Still, the early names in these situations are usually unrealistic – channel executives suggesting you spend a week bunking up with George Bush or the Duke of Edinburgh.

'That's a great idea. We'll make an approach.'

'Or Arnold Schwarzenegger, I just think you'd really be funny with him.'

'Yes, good one. Schwarzenegger. *I'll be beck.* Heh heh.'

Trying to keep my feet in the realm of the real world, I made a list of famous people who were interesting and who might actually agree to let me tag along after them for ten days. The list wasn't very long. One name on it was Uri Geller, the Israeli psychic. I phoned and we played tag for several weeks. Then one day, having called and gone through two different Israeli male voices, I reached the nation's favourite spoon-bender.

'I saw your Paul Daniels documentary and I really enjoyed it,' he said. 'You don't need to send me a tape because I love what you do.'

He went on to pitch a 'one-hour, or two-hour, or three-hour' pro-gramme that would be made from footage from his personal archive. It could be voiced by me, he said, 'or you could use *my* voiceover, which would be even better.'

'I have people on tape admitting that I worked for Mossad,' Uri went on, 'which I can't talk about myself, and talking of knocking out Egypt's radar system due to my intervention . . . How we are going to incorporate you, I really don't know. Maybe you can overlook the whole project, but in a serious way. I will have final approval or whatever.' As to the idea of me doing a regular, in-my-own-style documentary about him, voiced by me 'or whatever', Uri was not so keen.

We tried to keep the faith. Dauntlessly, a team of two or three APs and a couple of directors pounded the phones and brainstormed possibilities. The production offices rang with the music of a never-ending roundelay entitled 'What about?' The lyrics went something like this: *What about Tony Blair? What about Jerry Lewis? What about Carlos the Jackal? What about Cannon & Ball? What about Chenjerai 'Hitler' Hunzvi? What about The Krankies?* This refrain sometimes continued after hours with my mum, my brother, and close friends joining in. 'Hi, Louis, I was just thinking: what about Debbie Reynolds? What about Idi Amin? What about John McCririck?'

A blizzard of requests went out, trumpeting my 'non-tabloid approach' and 'six million viewers'. Reponses varied. Silence was a common one. Also, polite demurrals. And not so polite ones. Alan Whicker sent a four-word fax: 'Thanks but no thanks.' When a friendly rejection came back, it felt like a result. On those rare occasions when we received an actual 'yes', faced with the suddenly real prospect of two weeks of filming, often we'd realize we weren't as keen as we thought. An awkward phone call would follow in which we would explain that, in spite of having invited them, we didn't now want them to be in a non-tabloid, immersive documentary watched by six million people.

Sometimes contributors put themselves forward, which was always a bit weird. Bill Wyman's agent threw Bill's hat in the ring. The football club owner and porn magnate David Sullivan volunteered himself in a letter. *I thought you did a good job interviewing*

*Jimmy Savile and I would be willing to be in your programme.* Will went and recced him at his huge house in Theydon Bois, the Citizen Kane of Zone 7. He and his wife lived in separate buildings. He took Will on a tour of his quarters. 'Every day I check the papers for what films are on. If it gets at least three stars, then I tape it.'

The DJ Tony Blackburn expressed interest, as did Malcolm McLaren, Steven Berkoff, and Norman Tebbit. Tebbit's letter was memorable because he expressed some reservations that he might be too boring. The puppyish TV presenter Keith Chegwin was on board – he was launching a round-the-clock streaming channel from his home, entitled Cheggers' Bedroom – but his wife Maria didn't want to be on camera, which was a deal breaker for us.

Churning through rejections was like a groundhog day of phone calls and letters to light-entertainment has-beens and deposed foreign despots. Booking celebrities turned out to be a bit like dating. The people you want won't have you, and the people who'll have you you don't want.

At work, with Will Yapp.

It was tempting to conclude I was a victim of my own success. I'd done too good a job of stripping the secrets from the celebrities I'd already profiled. Or possibly I'd exposed them in a cruel way that no one in his right mind would willingly submit to. The truth is, it's a lot to ask of anyone to film for days on end, with or without the involvement of a puckish BBC inquisitor.

Eventually, after tireless efforts, a couple of names came on board. First, the excitable musical pioneer Ike Turner, who was mainly known for physically abusing his wife Tina. Then the multi-world-title holding boxer Chris Eubank. And a little after that, the diminutive Conservative politician Ann Widdecombe.

The Ike Turner film was a misadventure. His exquisite sensitivity meant he was singularly unsuited to a format that required him to engage in cheeky badinage with a BBC interrogator. There was a slow shrivelling of the access – at one point I was tailing him on a comeback tour but was forbidden from asking any questions because he was too stressed and anxious. In the end we knocked it on the head, if that isn't a tasteless way of putting it.

Chris Eubank had the hallmarks of being more TV-friendly. A love–hate figure of the sports world, reviled by many for his pose of arrogance, he was also one of the greatest British boxers of all time and riding a wave of recognition and public curiosity due to an eccentric appearance on *Celebrity Big Brother*. He'd monologued *at* Big Brother, speaking directly into the cameras to confess his vulnerabilities, seemingly finding the fictional concept of 'Big Brother' more relatable than any of his physical housemates.

In a way he was – with his nineteen successful world-title defences and his tabloid profile – a better booking than we had any reasonable right to expect. Having put his sporting achievements behind him, Chris was now plying his trade as a kind of children's role model, public intellectual, and style guru. Another way of putting it would be 'professional celebrity' but Chris had an elevated approach to his new public position. He saw himself as a teacher and truth-teller.

I once read a description of him as 'an intelligent man who thinks he's a genius', which has something to it.

He had several poems that he knew by heart and would declaim them when the opportunity arose, and carried little books with the sayings of Nietzsche and Oscar Wilde. More than once he recited an apophthegm of Wilde's: 'All women become like their mothers. That is their tragedy. No man does, and that is his.' Then, with a gleam of triumph, he would say, 'But I *did* become like my mother!' Another favourite phrase was: 'You've let yourthelf down.' He said this to me many times, in particular if he took against a line of probing – as in: 'You've let yourthelf down with that quethtion.' Also: 'Do with me azth you will. I am defenthleth.' He had a total confidence in his own ability to handle any kind of questioning and in fact he told me several times that he had a specific reason for agreeing to our project. 'I want you to find the chink in my armour.'

I filmed him over several weeks, having first met him in the grounds of his two neighbouring houses in Hove that he shared with his wife Karron and their four children. He was in full Edwardian dandy persona – jodhpurs, monocle, Windsor knot – and speaking with exaggerated precision though just occasionally little glimpses of the London street kid he'd once been peeped through. We spent the whole day together, touring his house, meeting the family, driving along the Brighton seafront in his huge Peterbilt truck. Much of the time Chris pontificated about the importance of bringing positive messages to children. His upbringing had been difficult: raised in Peckham, running wild, then sent to New York to straighten out, where he was saved by the boxing gym. He was keen to stress his considerable achievements but without being seen to do so. He seemed to feel underappreciated in his home country; I sensed that he was a little put out that there weren't statues of him on street corners.

On our second day, we took a train up to London where Chris was appearing on the light-hearted sports quiz *They Think It's All Over*. He did the show in full guru and role-model mode, coming off as deluded and self-important. In hindsight, I wonder whether twenty-four hours of our continuous attention had spun him into a hypomania of grandiosity. The other celebrity panellists on the quiz – David Gower, Rory McGrath – turned on him and mocked his speech impediment and a funny little hat he was wearing. Afterwards, Chris was mournful and a little bruised. But the positive upshot was he mellowed towards me. He relaxed and became slightly more normal.

The challenge, as filming progressed, was how to get past the pontifical persona to a more honest and grounded version of the man. We had a meeting in the office to discuss ways we might do this. It was agreed that he seemed most 'normal' around his family and that his wife, Karron, in particular, came across as approachable and no-nonsense. We decided we should banish the big camera and the sound recordist, and with just two of us present – the director Alicia and myself – we would film an evening chez Eubank as they did their evening routine with the kids, followed by food, which we would order out, so as not to impose.

What followed was a domestic scene both familiar and bizarre, with four young children all making claims on Karron's attention as she rushed up and downstairs signalling her exasperation, and Chris, in an almost surreal way, stood in the hallway in a handsome tailored suit and tie, seemingly doing not much of anything. I asked Karron if she wished Chris would help a bit more. 'Yes, he's lost the plot on that, I'm afraid. Totally and utterly. And I don't mind telling the world about that. Useless. As most male men are I'm afraid.'

As it became clear that Karron was going to broadcast her feelings of frustration to the world, Chris's face took on the hooded look of an Easter Island statue, and weirdly I couldn't help feeling a degree of sympathy for him – self-styled role model to an abstract concept of the nation's youth, dragged into an undignified domestic squabble on national TV about a more concrete kind of childcare.

Once the kids were in bed, Chris and Karron and I ate our take-away in the kitchen. Chris was in a dress shirt, tieless now, with the sleeves rolled up. Seeming stung, he admitted to a style of parenting that was out of keeping with the modern way prescribed, as he saw it, by *Richard & Judy* and political correctness. He pleaded guilty to having almost never kicked a ball with his children. Then he said, 'My father – can I remember my father playing with me? No. My father never played with me . . . I can remember my father telling me he loved me – behind a closed door, he was on the other side of the door – once.' He paused, appearing emotional. 'I give probably 80 per cent more to my children than my father gave me. And still it doesn't come up to scratch. Well, what is scratch? That's your perception. That's your reality . . . I don't feel guilty. I'm doing as much as I need to do.'

Afterwards, off camera, Chris said to me, 'So you got what you wanted.'

I said my on-camera goodbyes to him and Karron a few days later at their house. I went in for a hug – 'You're too thpindly to hug,' Chris said, and asked again whether I had found the chink in his armour. I told him, with a little flourish, that I *had*. The chink . . . was the armour. His obsessive need for self-protection was a weakness he needed to overcome. He didn't think much of this analysis. He told me I hadn't found the chink.

When the film eventually went out he was jubilant. 'I've had all thortth of people coming up to me to tell me it'th a total win for me,' he said. 'You let yourthelf down with the documentary.'

Chris separated from Karron a few years afterwards. I still have a soft spot for the film, though it's been a while since I watched it. I have a soft spot for Chris, too.

Ann Widdecombe was a difficult subject for me for very different reasons. The documentaries that had tended to work best so far were those that placed me as a straight man in a strange world – in subcultures that were alien or amongst people who were

With Chris Eubank.

flamboyant or egotistical. Ann's eccentricity was more low-key, genteel rather than outlandish. She was not a performer or a light-entertainment 'turn'; she was a politician; the world of Westminster and MPs she inhabited was much more guarded, and her instinct for risk more finely tuned.

She was famous at that time for having been prisons minister and defending the shackling of pregnant inmates in hospitals. Later, as shadow home secretary, with her devout Catholicism inform-ing her political positions, she had opposed gay marriage, opposed the equalization of the age of consent for men, opposed abortion, but *hadn't* opposed the death penalty – a hanger and a flogger, she wanted that brought back. All of this might have made her unlikeable, but some found her uncompromising and antediluvian moral outlook appealing, possibly because of the unlikeliness of her physical appearance: tiny, rotund, with massive breasts but oddly slender limbs, and a small and delicate head that was crowned with a pudding bowl of hair. She was, as they say, a 'conviction politician', utterly sincere and a little unworldly.

The most intriguing factoid about Ann may have been that she was, so it was said, *virgo intacta* – like Edward Woodward in *The Wicker Man*, a possible candidate for a placatory offering to the gods. I don't think Ann ever confirmed this but the rumour was widely circulated, based on her strict religious morals and her having never been married. I'd been told that she didn't like addressing questions to do with her sex life – or rather her lack of one. Out of pique at this restriction, when filming commenced one morning at her house in Elephant and Castle, I made 'the virginity issue' an early question, figuring it was better to derail the project on the first day rather than waste each other's time pussyfooting, ahem, around. We'd been looking at the furnishings and knick-knacks in her front room – plates with teddies on, pewter-wear, antique maps and ceremonial swords – when the subject was raised of what it was about her that had excited my interest.

'You're an intriguing public figure,' I said. Then I asked, 'What will we see in the documentary?'

'If you tell me what intrigues you, I'll tell you what's coming up.'

I mentioned her outspokenness, then slid into an observation about her having announced she would never marry, landing gently on, 'You've said you're a virgin.'

'No, I haven't,' Ann replied. 'People ask impertinent questions, then make deductions. But I always tell people to mind their own business.'

'Do you?' I ventured. 'I read last night a quote, and this surprised me, "If anyone says I'm not a virgin, I'll sue them."'

'As I said, I'm not going to go any further than I've just gone. I don't regard it as anybody else's business.'

'Well, I'll winkle away at that one.'

'I was actually told you would not,' Ann said, her head turning now to invoke my director Kate. 'I said I wouldn't agree to the documentary if it was along those lines. Frankly, I regard it as an impertinence.'

We weathered that wobble, for the moment at least, though Ann nearly pulled out a couple of days later due to a feeling that my questions were insufficiently serious – possibly it was an aftershock of the virgin question. Kate and I were summoned to an off-camera summit at Ann's offices to get the project back on track. Ann said she'd felt badgered and bullied by my questions. She said that during one conversation, as she drove, the distraction of attempting to answer had caused her to break a traffic regulation – possibly she veered into a bus lane. For her, a stickler for law and order, it had been embarrassing and she held me responsible for beguiling her into criminal activity.

I took all of this on board and felt rather bad, particularly at the idea that I might have 'bullied' her – though there is an irony somewhere in the idea of a strident disciplinarian feeling 'bullied' by cheeky questions. She went on to mention her consternation at – as I saw it – a harmless bit of small talk when I'd spent the day with her in her Kent constituency and visited her home in a tiny town with a name like Zazie-dans-le-Métro. While waiting for someone, parked up in a car, I'd asked about the difference between the Duke and Duchess of Kent and Prince and Princess Michael of Kent. How was it possible to have a duke and duchess and a prince and princess all of the same place? Wasn't it likely to lead to civil war? Or were they in fact the same people? She didn't seem any clearer than I was and, I suppose, as a royalist and Kent MP, she found that a little embarrassing.

Filming resumed, though there was always the lurking sense of her having mixed feelings about the project, enjoying the attention but hating and resenting any question that hinted at salaciousness or even carnality. It was difficult for me, since I'd always regarded a person's sexuality as a key to their personality and an exploration of intimate romantic relationships as the most reliable way of understanding who someone really is. With Ann that was all off limits, my hands were tied, and more than once I reflected on Anatole France's observation, 'Of all sexual aberrations, chastity is the strangest.'

The most intimate moments with Ann came during a cruise on a Norwegian liner. Kate and I had finagled tickets at the last minute – I suspect one of the aged passengers had passed away – and we flew to Tromsø to join the ship halfway through the cruise, spending a night in the nacreous summer light of the Arctic Circle before we boarded. Ann had brought her mother, Rita, who was as cheeky and playful as Ann was stolid and withholding, and also a female friend of Singaporean heritage whose name I don't recall – no sapphic interests are implied, I think they were just friends. Rita had written a poem about Kate and wanted to read it to us on camera. It began, 'Kate ate a cake, Kate ate a jelly', but how it went after that we will never know because Ann kept interrupting, telling her mother to be quiet, seeming to feel that to have a family member declaiming nonsense verse on TV would be a blot on the family honour.

At the end, when filming was completed, I felt we'd got away with it, just about, and had enough material to make an entertaining fifty minutes of television, but that we hadn't broken through the crust of her carapace of self-protection. I was aware Ann probably regretted taking part in the programme, which didn't feel great, but I didn't dwell on it. By now I had bigger things to worry about, and for once it wasn't the struggle to get programmes going, but something far weirder: the fact that a programme, having got going, had unexpectedly *gone too far*: blown up, and become a national news story, with me in the middle of it.

Chapter 17

## Professional Objects of Curiosity

Making a documentary is like surfing. I imagine. I don't surf. But there is a similar combination of applying skill and technique to elements that are outside your control. The 'waves' in this metaphor are the vagaries of life itself. You follow stories and people that have a likelihood of leading to actuality-driven scenes – a porn star failing to get wood on set, a confrontation provoked by a homophobic cult. On occasion you arrive at the beach with your board, having read reports of monster waves, only to find the sea as calm as a millpond. You keep coming back and usually, eventually, you get what you need. Or sometimes you don't. And then on occasion the unexpected happens, and your contributors are accused of a bizarre sexual assault at a swingers' party in Ilford.

The Hamiltons had been among the names we approached without thinking that hard about whether or not we really wanted to film with them. At that time they were fixtures of a low-wattage celebrity circuit. Neil Hamilton, a former minister of arch-Thatcherite views, had been forced out of politics for allegedly taking bribes in return for asking questions in parliament. He'd become a poster boy for what was termed Tory sleaze and had lost his seat in a high-profile election. His wife, Christine, had featured prominently in the coverage. Whereas Neil seemed mild and slightly robotic, she came across as fierce. She had helmet-like hair that looked as though it had been glued in place and when her dander was up, which was not infrequent, a scary basilisk gaze.

The accusation that Neil had taken bribes came from the owner of Harrods, Mohamed Al-Fayed. Fayed said he'd given Neil money in brown envelopes. Neil disputed this and brought a libel suit against the *Guardian*. He lost the suit, and a subsequent appeal, to the tune of several million pounds, finally declaring himself bankrupt a few months before we commenced filming.

At the time we approached, they were attempting to make lemonade from the lemons of their disgrace, plying their trade as 'professional objects of curiosity' – Neil's term. Any money Neil earned was siphoned off to pay his legal debts; Christine wasn't technically bankrupt so she could keep her fees for media appearances.

And there had been one or two suggestions of non-mainstream romantic practices, including an Oxford student who'd gone public to say that, during a speaking engagement at the university, Christine had snogged him.

They weren't busy. As documentary material, it wasn't a lot to go on. Still, they made an intriguing couple – there was something about them, his otherworldly quality and her intensity – and we weren't exactly spoiled for options.

I arrived one summer morning, getting lost on the stairs leading to the top-floor flat in a modern block in Battersea. This was their London pied-à-terre. They also had a large rambling house in Cheshire but they were in the process of selling that to pay their legal bills. As was our custom in those days, we started with a tour of the place, chatting as we went. The Hamiltons were friendly, forthcoming, conscious of the need to perform for the camera.

The flat, which overlooked Battersea Park, was cosy and piled with knick-knacks and books. A mug in the kitchen said, 'I am a naughty forty'. There were prints and portraits on the walls, and old political cartoons – several of them referring to a libel suit Neil had brought against the BBC. In 1984, a BBC *Panorama* documentary entitled 'Maggie's Militant Tendency' had alleged that Neil was part of a cabal of right-wing extremists that had infiltrated the Conservative Party – he'd sued and the BBC had settled, paying him £50,000 in damages.

Not having much to go on, other than the allegations of Neil's corruption and Christine's snog, I was nibbling away at the idea that they might be sexual boundary-pushers in some vague way. We went into the bathroom, which was also cluttered with books and tiles with Willie Rushton caricatures of fat naked ladies running around. Not quite knowing what I meant by it, I asked Neil if he and Christine were 'saucy'. His reply became the opening exchange of the finished documentary. In words reeking of prophetic irony, he said, 'No, not at all. It's been a permanent source of regret that the one thing I've never been involved in is a sex scandal.'

A few days went by. We filmed a sequence of Christine getting her hair done at a salon in Mayfair called Michael John, and another of me and Neil working out together on a 'trim trail' in Battersea Park. In their front room we watched a pilot of a TV show they had appeared in entitled *Posh Nosh*. A strange cookery-cum-travel format, it showed the Hamiltons descending upon a big unruly family in a council house. Christine whipped up a gourmet meal while Neil did duty as a butler.

We filmed a trip down to the South Coast somewhere to meet a friend and supporter of Neil's, an influential academic called Lord Ralph Harris or Ralph, Lord Harris – I'm honestly not sure how you write that. His name was Ralph and he was a Lord. An economist and disciple of Milton Friedman, Lord Harris had a comical tweedy air about him. He seemed a man born out of time – he should have been stepping out of a flying machine, smoking a pipe. My chief recollection from the visit was of Lord Harris leaning in and confiding his sense of confusion that his academic protégé and his wife had been reduced to going on a Channel 4 programme – *The Harry Hill Show*, as I knew it to be – 'dressed up as *badgers*'. It was one of a handful of times in my filming career when I've laughed involuntarily.

Then their diary went a bit quiet for a few weeks. It wasn't quite clear what else there was to do with the Hamiltons and there was a dawning possibility that they were so unbusy that we might need to let the project slip gently away.

At dinner one evening – it may even have been after the Lord Harris visit – Neil and Christine made an elliptical reference to a new commitment, something in the diary that was causing them a lot of stress and anxiety. They couldn't tell me what it was, they said. I was fairly sure it didn't involve dressing up as badgers. But off camera – possibly off-the-record – they told Will my director a little more. He in turn told our executive producer David, and there followed a weird few days when they knew what 'the thing' was and were in a position to tell me more while I was keen not to know. I was a bit more of a purist in those days and I liked the idea of being informed about 'the thing' – whatever it was – for real on camera by Neil and Christine themselves.

Still, I couldn't help wondering.

'Is it big?' I asked.

'It isn't Cheggers' Bedroom, put it that way,' David said.

'Will it have implications for the documentary?'

'Yes.'

'Is it something we can follow?'

'Yes.'

'Well, that's good, because fuck knows we need something.'

'Yeah, quite,' Will said.

'Is it animal, vegetable or mineral?' I asked.

'Look, what harm can it do for you to know?' David said.

'Well, I'll have to act.'

'All you have to do is say "shit!" or something like that.'

'It's just more fun like this,' I said. 'It's tantalizing.'

The result was, on 10 August 2001, I stood on a road near Harley Street and was blindsided by Neil telling me that he and Christine were about to drive, with their lawyer, to a police station in Barkingside, where they would be arrested, by arrangement, on an accusation of indecent sexual assault.

A woman, about whom they knew little, had alleged that Neil and Christine had raped her at a swingers' party in Ilford in Essex. As unlikely as it sounded, the police were taking the accusation seriously. They'd had three months to check the information. (The Met would later claim that they had twice invited the Hamiltons to provide alibis, which would have forestalled the arrest. The Hamiltons deny this.)

The drive to Barkingside involved a long circuitous car ride through the capillaries of east London's traffic system. We were in the company of the Hamiltons' lawyer Michael Coleman, in his car, license plate: '1LAW'. Despite the Hamiltons' evident stress and anxiety, Coleman was having trouble hiding his own relish for the impending battle with the police and media. 'This hasn't got anything to do with law,' he said. 'Principally what this is about is a psychology game.' He referred to the Hamiltons as a mere 'ball' in a grudge match between himself and the authorities. Christine, in one of her stock phrases of disapproval, said, 'Well, thank you very much.'

The strange sense of the stakes involved gave the car ride a surreal quality. I wondered how long they'd known about the allegation. Whether they had or hadn't done it, both options struck me as horrendous. The heightened reality of the occasion meant I thought I could feel them both improvising the drama in different keys: jolly and serious and sad. Neil kept making off-colour jokes. They had been at Lord Longford's funeral earlier in the day.

'Perhaps they'll be accusing us of necrophilia next,' Neil said.

'Neil, will you *stop*,' Christine said.

At the police station we split up. Will and I waited outside while the Hamiltons went into the station to be interviewed. For a while all was quiet. I wondered whether the story would be kept hush-hush. Then, slowly, a few reporters appeared, followed by a few more, until a full orchestra of camera crews and paparazzi were arrayed, as though tuning up for a big performance.

A few hours after they'd gone in, the Hamiltons emerged. Michael Coleman gave a statement.

'It's said that Mr and Mrs Hamilton were in a flat when a young woman was raped,' he said. 'It's also said that Mr Hamilton was masturbating onto her whilst another man, as yet unidentified by the police, was also masturbating onto her and Mrs Hamilton was squatting on her face.'

As he said this, Neil and Christine flanked him, both looking impassive.

'I take it, Mr Hamilton, you deny this?' asked one reporter.

'We deny this absolutely categorically,' Neil said.

Christine put her arm around Neil. 'I'm very happy to put my arm around my husband,' she said. 'The whole thing is an absolutely monstrous fabrication and a lie . . . You can all get your photos.'

After the press conference, surrounded by a scrum of press, we climbed back into Michael Coleman's car. Christine put the car window down, and I leaned back so the photographers could get a couple more shots of the unhappy couple. Then we drove off.

In his statement, Michael Coleman had said that during their interviews the police had brought up the name Max Clifford, the celebrity publicist famous for brokering kiss-and-tell stories with the tabloids.

'The whole thing's an absolute nightmare,' Christine said. 'As we thought, Max Clifford! Why would the police ask us about Max Clifford? Course he's behind it. He's got what he wanted. Whatever happens now, if we never hear another thing about it, we'll be all over the papers . . . Six policemen are combing our house! Opening every door, every cupboard. They're searching in all my clothes for a blue dress . . . It's absolutely monstrous.'

She became weepy. Then, noticing Neil was on the phone, she said, 'If that's the *Guardian*, just put it down, darling. Don't even talk to them!'

'Sorry, I can't talk any more now,' Neil said into the phone.

'The only identifying characteristic she could come up with was a blue dress?' I asked.

'She doesn't even know if I'm circumcised or not,' Neil said.

'Oh, for Christ's sake!' Christine said and put her hand over her face.

'We asked that question of the police,' Neil said. 'Needless to say they hadn't thought to ask it.'

'Do you know, at one stage they were going to lock us each in a cell?' Christine said. 'Can you believe it? Just because Max Clifford and some tart have invented this allegation!' She started crying again. 'We've had enough to put up with in our lives without all these lies.'

Trying to be helpful, Michael Coleman said, 'Take it in your stride.'

'Oh Michael, it's just a game for you. It's my life. It's my reputation. What a ridiculous thing to say. "Take it in your stride."'

Her voice was quavering and she covered her face again as Neil stroked her forearm with the tips of his fingers in a stiff up-and-down gesture.

Back at Michael Coleman's house there were drinks. Christine had several fortifying glasses of wine. Then the four of us – Neil and Christine, Will and me – continued on to the Battersea flat. Neil was driving. Christine was feeling the effects of the alcohol.

'I think we need to have something to eat,' Neil said. 'I hesitate to say you need to get something inside you.'

'Oh, for God's sake,' Christine said. 'Will, if you broadcast that I shall come round personally and stab you.'

At their flat a gauntlet of press – six or seven camera people with top lights on – swivelled in unison without saying a word. They were like alien creatures or robots. Upstairs we watched the news of the arrest on television. I had a glass of red wine to alleviate the stress and strangeness of the day's events. Then I had a few more. By now we'd been joined by a journalist from the *Mail on Sunday* called Paul Henderson, who declined to go on camera and lurked in the kitchen. I had the impression he was 'babysitting' the Hamiltons, with a view to landing their exclusive story.

'Paul's on side,' Christine said. 'Paul's helped us a lot.'

I had a whispered conversation with Paul outside the kitchen. I was – to use the technical word – slazzered at this point and feeling magnanimous.

'It just seems so unlikely,' I said. 'I mean, I really don't think they did it. It would take such brazenness on their part if they had done it to then go and invite our camera in. I mean, who is capable of that kind of sangfroid?'

'Well,' Paul said, rolling his eyes, 'anything's possible. I've been doing this job so many years, seen so much. I'll tell you, nothing surprises me any more. Nothing.'

A little later I went to the loo. Will came in to have a covert conference and then, possibly feeling a little emotional himself, he did an impression of Neil Hamilton masturbating onto someone at a swingers' party.

It being August, news was in short supply. The allegations against the Hamiltons were a sensation. The story was across all the news channels and in the tabloids, quickly mutating into a meta-story about the ludicrousness of the 'media circus' itself. This struck me as a little unfair: if anyone was responsible for turning the story into a media circus, it was surely the media.

My feelings at this point were complicated. I suppose I should have felt grateful that the Hamiltons had allowed us to continue filming, though I was also conscious that it was potentially helpful to their case to be seen cooperating with press. It could be taken as showing that they had nothing to hide. At the same time, many people regarded the Hamiltons' appetite for coverage as a further example of their supposed shamelessness and another count against them. But mainly I was confused by the turn of events and bothered by the strangeness of finding myself now a part of the story (as I increasingly was). In almost all the coverage there was a photo of me with the Hamiltons as we drove from the police station, with a reference to me as 'wacky TV personality' Louis Theroux, the fact of us making a documentary prefaced with the phrase 'in a bizarre twist'.

Among my friends and colleagues the prevailing attitude seemed to be that I should feel lucky to land such a scoop, a few going so far as to suggest I'd been part of making up the allegations to help our story along (as if). But I was also struggling with a sense of self exposure. One of my impulses in making documentaries had always been an urge for invisibility and escape. This time my escape route had led out into a spotlight on the main stage.

I was also surprised at how many people thought the Hamiltons actually had taken part in the rape. It was fairly clear to me early on that the case against them didn't add up. Whether or not they went to swingers' parties, they didn't go to them in small flats in Ilford. And in fact, within a few days of the arrest Neil had found several receipts placing him at Waitrose and witnesses to support his contention that they'd been hosting a dinner party on the night in question.

Still, there was no question of not continuing, and so, two days after the arrest, after a day off from filming, Neil, Christine, Will and I drove up to the Hamiltons' Cheshire pile. There we stayed for three days while the media camped outside. It was a little like *The Masque of the Red Death*. We drank and talked and Will filmed while a contagion of irrationality rampaged outside.

Forced together with them in the surreal circumstances of the media siege, and having lost my bearings as to what exactly my journalistic role was, I found myself enjoying the company of the Hamiltons in a more or less straightforward way. Neil's robot-like exterior belied a droll sense of humour. I would slip into my own robot-like mode, and we would compare notes about subjects we were both interested in: the American anarcho-capitalist philosopher Robert Nozick, the historian Thomas Carlyle, and Nietzsche (of whom Neil was a great fan and had done a line drawing which hung framed on the wall). Given the accusations made in the *Panorama* programme, I was on the lookout for evidence of far-right leanings, noting the many books by Enoch Powell. Neil would do impersonations of the famous 'Rivers of Blood' speech in Black Country tones. 'Like the Roman, I seem to see the River Tiber *foaming* with much blood.' He was knowledgeable about minstrelsy and enjoyed talking about various dubious blackface vaudevillians of the belle époque. In a sublimated attempt to derail Sacha Baron Cohen's then-flourishing career, I encouraged Neil to write a piece about him and whether he could be said to occupy a place in the minstrel tradition for the *Daily Mail*.

Christine was up and down – stern and fierce one minute, dissolving into tears the next, which to be fair, seems a reasonable reaction when accused of rape. 'I'm having a bit of a dip,' she'd say. In her up moments, she was reminiscent of dominatrices I've met, especially when she'd had a drink. If you interrupted her train of thought she'd snap 'Shut up!' or slap your leg.

In many respects, their match-up was of the classic Mars-and-Venus variety: him, stoical and underplayed; her, buffeted by emotional turbulence.

I began wondering why anyone might possibly fixate on the Hamiltons as the object of fantasies. I recalled that, before any of the rape allegations, a colleague at work had said, 'There's something about that couple', implying by her tone that she thought they might have unusual sexual interests. The first night in Cheshire, over a dinner – for which Christine made the same Bloody Mary jelly as she had for the alibi-providing party – I put it to them that people felt there was a mystery at the heart of their relationship.

'For some reason you have a hold over the public imagination,' I said. 'And there is a sexual dimension to it.'

'Why do you think that?' Neil asked.

'When I mention "the Hamiltons" people say, "Oh yes, there's something funny about that couple."'

'I simply don't believe it,' Christine said. 'Tell me *anybody* who's said that.'

'I think there's a belief that there's a secret at the heart of your relationship that no one knows,' I continued.

'I don't know what you're talking about,' Neil said.

'May I ask a sensitive question? Are you sexually quite normal?'

'Yes, completely, a hundred per cent normal,' Christine replied. 'We have no deviations. Absolutely nothing. Very happy with each other. We have no problems, we've never had any problems. A great life, thank you very much.'

Meanwhile the media frenzy continued, hitting ever higher levels of absurdity. On the first morning in Cheshire, a man turned up, a one-time TV reporter who was now a truck driver and the creator of the website neilhamiltonisinnocent.com. He had brought a banner with the website name on it and was intent on using it to give the website a plug on national TV – he persuaded Neil that he and Christine should carry it while marching out to the waiting reporters in a kind of procession. I counselled against this. I was aware that – as a journalist myself and supposed disinterested party – it wasn't really my place to advise but I couldn't help myself. For a while it turned farcical, with Christine freaking out that the banner was lying crumpled out on the drive in view of the cameras. In the end, they made their statement with no banner. In the live coverage Will and I were just visible lurking in the background, like a couple of shabby stagehands who have strayed into shot.

That night, after supper, I was reclining in a sofa when Christine came and sat next to me. Neil was out of the room. She began strok-ing my cheek.

'You haven't shaved,' she said.

She must have been aware Will was filming and I wondered if she was doing it for the camera.

'You do like to flirt, don't you?' I said.

'Who doesn't like to flirt? I mean, if you can't have a little fun, come on!'

I felt a familiar sort of doubling: immersed in a weird situation but aware that it was probably helpful for the documentary. I hope I am not being unkind to Christine when I saw it was a little reminiscent of being hazed by the wrestlers at the Powerplant.

Neil returned from the kitchen and, noticing us, did a comical double-take.

Later, after a couple more drinks, Neil decided he should go up the driveway and deliver a statement to the waiting cameras. Will and I followed him. No one was there.

'I've got a statement,' Neil shouted into the darkness. 'I love Will Yapp!'

After a few days the story ebbed away. The accuser, who went by Nadine Milroy-Sloan but whose real name was Emily Checksfield, turned out to be a troubled young woman from Grimsby. A fanta-sist, she had been visiting sex chat sites and became convinced that two of the people she conversed with – 'Lord and Lady Hamilton' – were Neil and Christine. Smelling a financial opportunity, she'd visited Max Clifford, who'd told her she could sell a sex story about the Hamiltons for six figures but would need proof. In short order, she arranged a visit with her online correspondent – a pensioner in Essex called Barry Lehaney. It was on an evidence-gathering trip to see Barry Lehaney that she said the sex party and the rape took place.

Lehaney's account of the visit differed markedly from Milroy-Sloan's. In his version he'd picked her up in his Ford Granada and taken her on a tour of London sites. They'd bought some food and wine at Tesco's then watched *Trigger Happy TV* at his flat. He'd offered her the sofa but she'd asked to sleep in bed with him. The following morning, unprompted, she'd masturbated him.

The detail that strikes me now is that Milroy-Sloan complained of feeling woozy after drinking a glass of red wine brought to her by Lehaney. Police found a strip of Rohypnol at Lehaney's flat, though Lehaney claimed it was planted. In any case, having made up the tale of the group rape, Milroy-Sloane's allegation of being drugged was thereafter unlikely to be believed.

On 13 July, Nadine Milroy-Sloan was convicted of perverting the course of justice and given three years. The judge commented: 'It's becoming all too easy for people to sell fake allegations about well-known people to the press, and the courts have to deal with it firmly.'

*When Louis Met The Hamiltons* marked a kind of weird high-water mark of my professional fortunes. Other people may have different barometers, but for me you are too famous when your image and likeness are thrust into the consciousness of people who don't like you. There is a lot to be said for being avoidable. But for a couple of months, for those who read papers and watch TV, I was

With Neil and Christine Hamilton.

hard to miss. One night at home, stoned, I was watching a dating show. The young woman said she didn't want to go on another date with the specky bloke. 'He looks too much like Louis Theroux,' she said. Had I become a byword for a certain kind of unattractive man with glasses?

What felt especially untoward was to have achieved success with a programme that hinged on nothing *I'd* done. A bizarre piece of happenstance – a lightning strike of misfortune that zapped Neil and Christine Hamilton – led to events that we were lucky enough to be around to document. All the excitement it created – at the BBC, among my exec and his higher-ups – felt to me like a prison sentence. David was in ecstasies over the success of the show. Nearly five million viewers. Stories in all the papers. But it worried me since there was almost nothing to be learned from making the documentary in terms of process – you can't choose your subjects based on whether they might be accused of rape by a deluded young woman. Meanwhile, I had an unfamiliar sensation of being *in demand*. Offers of 'at home with' photo features in magazines. *GQ* invited me to be their TV personality of the year, which I politely declined. In Edinburgh for the TV festival, the channel controller of BBC1, Lorraine Heggessey, fell into step beside me in the lobby of the Caledonian Hotel.

'So tell me about the Hamiltons,' she said. 'I think we might want that for One.'

All the attention and the sense of approval had a paradoxical effect, making me wonder about before. Did people not like the shows then? I began feeling morose, sensing that I was completely out of sync with what everyone else seemed to think I should want. My appetite for the sort of programmes I was doing, already in decline, dipped precipitously around this time. But I was a success, creating impact, and so there was no getting off the bus. And besides I had a ton more shows to make, and no sense of how I was supposed to make them.

Chapter 18

# Jimmy Links

'Well, yet again we are destined to speak by machine,' said the message in familiar northern tones. 'Greetings from the Glen. The mountains are high, the snow is good and everybody is huddling together, which is very social, to stay warm and not freezing, and it's woooooonderful, and you're down there in that *sub-tropic south* where nothing *means* anything – up here everything means something and it's ten to ten and it's Wednesday morning and of course we will speak together eye to eye, face to face, or whatever probably before the next millennium, but who knows?' *Beeep!*

I listened again, copying it into my notebook, wondering whether it might add something to the book-thing I was supposed to be working on and not thinking too much whether he was still a subject or something more like a friend.

The first contacts with Jimmy that were not strictly journalistic had begun around the time we were called upon to promote the original documentary. We'd done a couple of interviews at a hotel in King's Cross. After that there was a trip up to Leeds for some more publicity for another project or to record some DVD extras – the exact sequence is hard to piece together now. In a box of material from that time I have some cuttings, dated April 2001, that resulted from our joint publicity efforts for a DVD release of the *Best of*

*Weird Weekends* – two cover stories from colour supplements, the *Glasgow Sunday Herald* and the *Yorkshire Post*, featuring photos of me and Jimmy. One says: 'Ows about that, then! It's the Jimmy and Louis show'. The other: 'The Odd Couple: How Jimmy and Louis got Fixed up'. And so, without quite realizing it, I entered into a strange, mutually parasitic quasi-friendship, quasi-deep-cover investigation into his dark side.

The exact nature of the quasi-whatever-it-was is hard to parse in hindsight. The view is too clouded by the revelations. Certainly he was using us for a sense of relevance, and possibly with the hope of doing further projects. But it's also probably the case that he enjoyed my company – and Will's, since we always saw him together. And on our side there was also a mixture of impulses: using him for publicity; later, for material for a possible book that might attempt to fathom the riddle of who he really was; for the strangeness and diversion of the experience – of having a story to tell.

In a way it was all an after-effect of his being on board with the film. From that moment, all sorts of other decisions flowed, to do with a feeling of having him in our corner, a deployable ageing celebrity, a satisfied profilee, who came packaged with his own unintended irony built in. 'My friend, the weird and slightly creepy ageing DJ Jimmy Savile.' It made good copy, whether or not it was strictly true.

Jimmy naturally enjoyed the interest in him stemming from the documentary, and when it led to me doing further celebrity profiles, he began taking on a kind of protective interest in my work. After the profile of Paul Daniels and Debbie McGee, he called to complain: 'You are a Formula One car. You never got out of bleedin' first gear.' He was also troubled by a conversation I'd had with Debbie about her reproductive choices in which I'd mentioned that she'd never had children and that perhaps that was one of the reasons she had kept her svelte figure. 'A gentleman does not fucking ask a lady why she has not had children,' he told me with some heat, albeit erroneously, given that I hadn't in fact asked that question.

Drumming up publicity with Jimmy Savile.

The success of *When Louis Met Jimmy*, followed by series three of *Weird Weekends* and then the Paul and Debbie film, meant my stock was rising and I don't doubt that this also factored into Jimmy's thinking. He viewed himself as a co-author of my success. Thanks to him I'd been catapulted from the niche confines of chronicler of weirdness into mainstream visibility.

At the beginning of 2001, I signed a contract for a book. It was to be a kind of celebrity diary detailing my star-studded encounters, the glamorous social carousel of a young TV presenter making the scene.

I had been ambivalent about the idea of writing a book, for various reasons, not the least of them being that I wanted to focus my time and energy on TV. But I had a romantic attachment to the notion of being an author, and the idea of a diary forestalled some of my fears about not having much time to write. I figured it meant I didn't have to think of an actual idea, I just had to keep a journal.

The only trouble with this scenario was that I didn't lead a glamorous existence, nor did I make the scene on any regular basis – my life was pretty boring. I had a new girlfriend by this time and of a night she and I would stay in and watch repeats of *The Larry Sanders Show* or sometimes go out for meals in restaurants close to her flat in west London. Other than that, I worked. And so my celebrity diary was thin on material. I attempted to remedy this by writing descriptions of the off-camera dimension of the production – the celebrities we were approaching and for the most part being rejected by, the little bits of shooting we were doing – but this had its limitations. How much detail does anybody want or need about the process of booking talent for a TV show? 'People want to know what goes on behind the scenes,' the editors said. But the whole notion of my documentaries had been, insofar as possible, to broaden the frame enough so that all the interesting stuff took place on camera. The in-office stuff largely took the form of: 'We heard back from Noel Edmonds. It's a no, I'm afraid.'

I diligently kept the diary all the same, sometimes with the feeling of writing something interesting, just as often with a sense of attempting to subsist on my own effluent like a one-man human centipede, my lips sewn tight around my own sphincter. The idea of the diary went in and out of focus. At times it felt like a dumping ground for my worst insecurities. Since some of these were to do with the idea of doing the diary, a lot of the writing was a kind of feedback loop of anger and anxiety directed at my editor and at the book itself – which is pretty weird when you think about it: a book full of abuse directed *at the book*. But the book was protean in its conception, and in one of its more stable forms it was a meditation on Jimmy Savile and an attempt to go further into unravelling his enigma.

And so, alongside the opportunistic outings up to Leeds for interviews to promote programmes and DVDs, was another motivation to keep up with Jimmy, the idea of generating copy for my diary-book-thing. I wrote entries about the trips to his penthouse and made notes every time he called on the phone with advice or just wanting to pass the time of day. All of which also shouldn't cloud the inconvenient fact that Jimmy Savile's company – when he dialled down the Savilisms and was on his home turf of his penthouse – could be quite pleasant. He'd recline on his sofas and play host with the minimum of fuss in his overgrown bachelor pad, offering chocolates and coffees or glasses of red wine, always with some anecdote of recent vintage to do with an advertising campaign he'd just done or an interview in a high-profile national glossy. 'Ere, did you see *FHM* this month? Five pages, with a great big full-page photo. "Lock Up Your Daughters".'

There was almost always some pretext for the visits – a bit of taping, some publicity, plus whatever bit of copy I thought I might extract for my book – but there was also a social dimension, and for my purposes the line between seeing him professionally and personally was somewhat blurred. There were maybe four of these visits – possibly three of them involved an overnight stay. Will would sleep on the sofa; I'd sleep in the spare room. Invariably there would be a trip to the Flying Pizza – usually we would come up on a Thursday, which was a busy night there, and then stay for a few hours on Friday morning to sit in on the Friday Morning Club, a talking shop of elderly male friends of Jimmy's – unpretentious neighbours and local characters setting the world to rights.

Those trips to the Flying Pizza all blur together somewhat, but there tended to be a set routine. He'd always ask that Will bring a camera, so we could film him going into the restaurant celebrity-style. There was no film in the camera, since the point wasn't to record the occasion but to create a sense of TV glamour and excitement. Jimmy would stand around trying to attract attention, meet and greet anyone who was interested, sing happy birthdays, and then when he'd exhausted the celebrity duties he'd settle down and eat and we'd catch up.

Mainly he talked – about whichever cruise he'd just been on, which TV commercial or celebrity profile he'd just done. This suited me since I never felt that comfortable telling him much about my own personal life. I'd be listening out for anything I thought might be revealing – references to girlfriends, which did occasionally crop up, this or that woman who would be coming to visit, a female photographer to whom he'd 'given the Jethro – Jethro Tull – pull' earlier in the day, or anecdotes about local friends of his, all of whom had nicknames, like Jim the Pill or his hairdresser The Yosh or Marvellous Marvin.

One anecdote he told involved a young female reporter who joined Jimmy on a cruise in the hopes of ensnaring him into a relationship for a putative kiss-and-tell story. In Jimmy's recounting, the reporter confessed all and they ended up having an affair that remained their secret. I filed this story alongside many others of Jimmy Savile provenance under the heading Probably-Bollocks-Might-Not-Be. Jimmy's attitude to the opposite sex always had a strange side – and in fact he generally seemed to enjoy affecting a slightly chilling detachment, bordering on callousness, from the normal emotional reactions, but which he would have characterized as a clear-sighted and logical attitude.

Referring to a mentally ill young man who'd written him a fan letter, he breezily said, 'He's never getting better.'

'Seems a bit bleak,' I countered.

'Excuse me. I'll say it again, he's never getting better.'

There was an occasion – apropos of God knows what but possibly his volunteer work at Leeds General Infirmary and his interactions with sex workers when they'd come in to get patched up on the weekends – when he said, 'A psychologist will tell you that there is something in all women that wants to be a prostitute.' And another when I pointed out an attractive woman who may have been in her thirties or forties, and his response was: 'Grandma.'

'What?' I said.

'Grandma,' he said again.

Jimmy was also given to the usual sorts of racist speech typical of many of the older generation; possibly he delighted in offending my delicate sensibilities with his occasional references to 'schvartzers' and 'poofs' and 'cripples', though it's worth saying that he just as often was likely to make statements in favour of fellow feeling and tolerance. On one occasion during filming in Scarborough, before going out for dinner with a gay friend of Jimmy's, he said, 'Ere, Eric's a shirtlifter, right, so no jokes about poofters.' I'm not sure this qualifies as sensitivity but it seems to me marginally on the right side. He had – by his own profession, at least – a natural affinity with the Leeds Jewish community. He called Jewish people 'Wejs' – which is 'Jews' spelled backwards – though I'm not sure if this was his coinage. 'I'm looking forward to some good Wej verbals,' he'd say en route to a meeting with some Jewish friends.

Another time he called up to chat and share a couple of jokes: 'Ere, why does Michael Barrymore not need ashtrays? He puts his fags out in the pool! Heh heh.' Also: 'What do you call a shampoo for gypsies? Go and wash.'

I didn't laugh, but I also didn't judge too harshly, seeing the jokes as the private expressions of an old-school sensibility and part of Jimmy's natural inclination to shock. He enjoyed dark humour generally. When the police were looking for clues to the identity of the Yorkshire Ripper, for several days they had a large team searching Roundhay Park for clues, or possibly remains, complete with a catering van, close to Jimmy's flat. 'When I saw Peter in Broadmoor, I told him thanks for burying that brass in Roundhay Park,' Jimmy said. 'I ate free for a week!' Nietzsche wrote, 'A joke is an epitaph on the death of feeling,' and with Jimmy's dislike of emotionality, his jokes were a statement he was making about his detachment from normal human affect.

The trip up to record the 'Jimmy links' for the DVD collection *Best of Weird Weekends* was another time Jimmy gave hints of dark interests. We'd gone up the night before and made our ritual visit to the Flying Pizza. Then the next morning we sat watching the four episodes of the shows as Will filmed us in a locked-off shot. For nourishment, Jimmy had laid on a packet of Frazzles and some chocolate biscuits.

In typical style, Jimmy showed a yeoman-like commitment to the task at hand. It would have been easy to fast-forward and drop in some comments at salient points but he was set on watching all the shows all the way through – he also said he'd watched them all the day before as preparation. One of the *Weird Weekends* episodes, about gangsta rap in the Deep South, featured a Mississippi-based rapper called Mello-T, who styled himself a pimp. Mello was a troubling figure, charismatic but macabre and given to pronouncements like: 'Somehow when a woman has a gun pointed to her head, seems to make her think better.' Jimmy was quite taken with him. On camera, for the links, he expressed a weird concern that girls who saw the programme might be induced to take up careers in prostitution. Off camera, he commented about Mello: 'A man after my own heart.' Again, I noticed this then rationalized it as a bit of Jimmy Savile provocation disguising a deeper truth to do with his view of women as irrational.

After the four episodes of *Weird Weekends*, as a *pièce de résistance*, we watched *When Louis Met Jimmy*. It was almost eerie how easily we slipped back into our respective roles.

'Petulant!' Jimmy said, in a sing-song voice, of my attitude in an early encounter. I teased him for his weird inconsistencies and evasions, and the commentary devolved into the same childish repartee as the original programme. 'You're tricky,' he said, 'but I'm tricky too.'

When he learned that I was working on an entire series of celebrity profiles, Jimmy made semi-regular calls to offer suggestions or advice. Some part of him was probably keen that we should keep it to celebrities of similar calibre to him. He enjoyed Chris Eubank and tried to take credit for it. 'Ere that were a good idea of mine, the boxer kid.' When we briefly toyed with a profile of the presenter Esther Rantzen he was dismissive: 'With Esther it's just all about Childline. Total snooze.'

He regularly suggested profiling the strip-club manager Peter Stringfellow, who he said was a friend. Stringfellow never showed much interest in our overtures and, as proved the case more than once, Jimmy's vaunted connections led to no material advantage whatsoever for the production. Based on my experience, if the ability to deliver subjects for a series of puckish first-person TV profiles of intriguing public figures is any guide, Jimmy Savile had as much clout as you'd expect for a deranged-looking man in a tracksuit and a string vest. Among the other people he bruited as candidates for profiles were: then-manager of Leeds United football club, David O'Leary; the singer Lulu; the Romany impressionist Joe Longthorne; and the Kray brothers' enforcer Mad Frankie Fraser ('Don't call him mad'), who had once been resident at Broadmoor and whom Jimmy professed to be tight with.

Jimmy's suggestions were neither helpful nor unhelpful but revealing in what they said about his interests and the image he had of himself as a kind of behind-the-scenes fixer.

For a long time I imagined that some of the questions I had about Jimmy might be answered if I could just induce him to take an off-camera excursion with me to Broadmoor. I knew he had an interest in criminal mental health but it wasn't a subject he talked about much.

In the complement of his showbiz interests and charity work, his involvement with the killers and psychopaths at the hospital was the closest thing to something solid. 'Not criminals, patients,' he would say. He claimed to be 'the entertainments officer' but was hard-pressed to describe what entertainments he'd actually organized. It was said he used to have tea with Peter Sutcliffe but he was cagey on the subject.

I also had the impression he had made visits to Ashworth, the forensic mental hospital where Moors murderer Ian Brady was detained, and another time, when it was in the news, I asked what he made of 'the Myra Hindley story'. 'I am the Myra Hindley story', he replied gnomically and without elaborating.

I wondered if an outing to Broadmoor would at least be a chance to see Jimmy in a different context, in which some of his contradictions might make more sense. But, despite me asking him several times, no invitation was ever forthcoming and it began to be a bit embarrassing so I stopped bringing it up.

One of the few revealing pieces of information about Jimmy and the truth about his private life came in May 2001, in the middle of the period when I was in sporadic friendly contact with him.

A pair of middle-aged women who said they had been his girl-friends in the late sixties had got in touch by letter shortly after *When Louis Met Jimmy* originally aired. The letter was from both of them – let's call them Beth and Alice – and described how they had been part of a group of girls who sometimes helped out with jobs, all of whom were involved with Jimmy. Some left, moved on; others remained in his circle for years. 'There was never any jealousies', they wrote.

It seemed, mainly, a bid for recognition. In the film Jimmy had claimed he'd never had any girlfriends. I assumed this rankled them and that they wanted someone to know that Jimmy had had relationships – which they characterized as casual and 'fun'. The letter, which I showed to others on the production, appeared to put to bed at least two hypotheses regarding his sexuality: that he might be gay or simply asexual. Other than that, however, it didn't seem to promise much in the way of revelation and, with other work to do, almost a year passed before I called Beth on the phone and set up a rendezvous.

By this time I was working on my celebrity diary-book-thing, so my main impulse may have been to generate some material for that, though there was also a personal sense of curiosity about what light

Jimmy's girlfriends might shed on his character. Will, my director, came along too. We met at the Langham Hotel, on Regent Street, close to Broadcasting House. They walked in, a few minutes late, two smartly dressed women in their mid-forties, both slightly nervous. It soon emerged they were worried that Jimmy might find out we were meeting.

'Are we being filmed or taped?' was the first question from Beth. And then, 'Why did it take you so long to get in touch?'

Beth led the conversation and was the more voluble of the pair: she'd known Jimmy longer and had occupied a sort of leadership position in their little group, as organizer and diary-keeper. They painted a picture of a coterie of teenage fans who would meet in studio dressing rooms and caravans to socialize and catch up. Trying to get my dates straight, I asked one how old she had been. 'You sound like Jimmy,' she replied. 'That's the first question he would ask. "How old are you?"'

'Why?' I asked.

'Why do you think?'

We bought Cokes and sandwiches. 'It's more than we ever got when filming,' Alice said. 'You might get a cup of tea in a transport cafe and a voucher for your train home if you were lucky.'

I asked about the sex. 'Very quick,' one of them said. 'I wondered if that was why he wore those elastic waistbands,' said the other. 'You knew when he'd had enough of you and wanted you to go away . . . He'd just say "Good morning!"'

The impression I had was that the sex was something they tolerated as the price of being part of his inner circle, and the complaints they had were less about – as they characterized it then – his sexual ineptitude and lack of consideration and centred more on his weird absence of manners: the fact that he didn't see them out or buy them anything to eat or arrange transport back home. Alice said she had only once spent the night with him.

As our conversation went on, I began to sense that Beth and Alice had slightly different attitudes to their experience: Beth still seemed loyal to Jimmy, slightly in awe of him and keen to highlight the fun they'd had; Alice was more ambivalent. 'At the time it was great fun. A lot of laughs, but there were negatives as well,' she said. 'Looking back, I wonder if he gave a shit.'

They'd brought old ticket stubs and photographs, including some that had been taken just a few years previously at a reunion of the group which Jimmy had hosted at his flat close to Regent's Park. In the pictures they were laughing and clowning – there was one in which Jimmy was making an antic display of imposing himself on Alice, and another of Alice in the kitchen against the wall and Jimmy pressing up against her – you could only see his back and his white hair and her hand poking out from his shoulder. 'He's joking in that one,' she said, pointing at the first. 'But not in that one.'

In hindsight, it's tempting to pull out the most telling parts of what they said, those details that support what we later learned, though I worry it gives a misleading impression of an encounter that more took the form of a quizzical and bemused pooling of information – we were like a quartet of puzzlers standing over a ten-thousand piece jigsaw. Each of us gave our impression of the Savile mysteries in a freewheeling bull session. I shared the rumour about his being a necrophile, which they hadn't heard. They talked about his mafia connections, which they took seriously, and which added to their sense of paranoia.

I sometimes wonder what would have happened if I'd appeared more shocked by what they had to say about the callous and inconsiderate sex, but I still had in my head the tone of the letter and the references to reunions and fun and so I didn't hear what was undoubtedly also there, especially in Alice's recollections: a persistent sense of resentment and unease about how he had treated them. And there was also an explicit instruction that they would never tell friends about their relationship with Jimmy. They didn't want their children to know.

Towards the end of the lunch, Alice described approaching Jimmy about taking her child to *Jim'll Fix It* – this was years later, in the late eighties. Jimmy had arranged tickets on the condition she came up to see him beforehand and she'd met him in his hotel room. He'd propositioned her. 'But I was going out with someone at the time,' she said. 'I pushed him away. If I hadn't been, I might have given in. He said, "You must love him very much." Which was a sensitive thing to say. For him.'

'He's so clever,' Beth said. 'A genius really. But also mad.'

On the pavement outside, we said our goodbyes. The session seemed to have relieved some of their animus, and my sense was that we all felt better having compared notes. 'Sometimes I feel like confronting him,' Alice said just before the two of them walked off down Regent Street. 'But he's so clever, I know he'd make mincemeat out of me. It'll all come out after he dies.'

In August 2001, when Neil and Christine Hamilton were arrested for rape while I was filming with them, Jimmy was fizzing with excitement at having, as he saw it, an inside line to the story through me.

After the documentary went out, Jimmy called to congratulate me.

'I have spoken to a whole lot of people from all walks of life and they all give it ten out of ten,' he said.

'What was your take on it?'

'They're a pair of swingers.'

'How do you mean "swingers" exactly?'

'They're a pair of swingers. They're quite given to having a bit of sexual philandering given half a chance.'

Jimmy was firing on all cylinders. Maybe it was excitement at the programme – that it was being chattered about, and the way his association with me put him vicariously at the centre of things. Jonathan King, the musical impresario and TV presenter, was then in the news, too, being accused of sex crimes against underage boys, and Jimmy began talking about that.

'It's six of one and two threes of another,' he said. The accusers were all rent boys, he said, who were out for cash. 'Part of the compensation culture.'

'Ere, what about a thing on rent boys?' he went on. 'All you have to do is buy them a sandwich and they run off at the mouth. Half the time, it's them that gets the punters at it.'

That August I was invited to do a keynote presentation at the Edinburgh television festival, involving clips from old shows and work in progress. For some added value, someone – possibly David or Will – had the idea of making an all-access mini-documentary from the point of view of Jimmy interviewing me: *When Jimmy Met Louis.*

By this time I'd moved out of my Shepherd's Bush flat and had bought a house in Harlesden, a said-to-be up-and-coming area of west London. I think at some level, having recently been in a twelve-year relationship and on track to have children, I was carried by a kind of lifestyle momentum into a young-couple arrangement even though I was now single and living alone. My habits of thought hadn't changed and I still saw myself as a budding family man. But the upshot was that I found myself with a large house and no real sense of what to do with it, other than live in it like a squatter.

When the time came to film the documentary, I'd only been in the house a couple of months. It was big and empty – no sofas, no rugs, no pictures, no comfy chairs, no kitchen table. Just a futon and some clothes on a rack. This may also be one of the reasons I was comfortable having him over. I still didn't like him knowing too much about me, didn't quite trust him, and there wasn't much in the house to give me away.

Will directed. He contacted Jimmy, who agreed to the idea, asking only his usual '*pourboire*' – his term for a collection of high-priced cigars – from a shop called Dunhill in Mayfair.

Will met Jimmy at King's Cross, and filmed him in the taxi to the BBC offices in White City. It was midsummer, warm, and Jimmy was wearing a string vest and running shorts. He was by this time seventy-five years old, still bedecked in gold rings and necklaces, his long white hair pulled back in a ponytail. He had with him a knapsack.

He arrived at my offices at a moment when I'd stepped away, and he poked around my small closed-off section, playing the role of an intrusive investigator. 'What a dreadful tip this is!' He wrote 'Louis' Tip' on a piece of paper, then took a Polaroid of himself holding it, leaving the photo on my desk. Then, when I turned up, we sat down and he interviewed me, which was a strange experience. He had no natural curiosity, nor did he like to admit to not knowing something, so his questions followed the rhythm of a cross-examination rather than a natural conversation.

We had lunch at the BBC canteen – Jimmy discoursing on the nature of celebrity. 'Success is a three-legged stool,' he said. TV, radio, newspapers. 'If you have all three you can do what you want. But if you only have TV and radio captured, you'll be dependent on newspapers to print nice things about you. I wrote for the *Sunday People* for nearly twenty years and I found that when I was doing that none of the other papers were keen to have a go at me because it was like having a go at their own, right? So they went and had a go at somebody else.'

The subject of the Hamiltons came up. Jimmy viewed the story as an object lesson in how those in the public eye are vulnerable, and he impressed on me the need to be careful now that I was 'at the top of the tree' of broadcasting and prey to all sorts of prurient tabloid enquiries.

'Does it perturb you at all that you are actually in that category where somebody can have a go at you?' he asked. 'They don't care whether it's right, wrong, true, false – so long as they've got names, baby, they'll have a feast. Say, for instance, you were interviewing me on an allegation of something that was not nice, right? And you said to me, you're alleged to have de-dum-de-dum-de-dum. My answer would be, "It would be a lot worse if it were true."'

As ever, I found the idea of being held to ransom by the tabloids for alleged misdeeds a fanciful thing to worry about and I didn't much like the idea of being clubbed together in his imagined category of embattled ageing celebrities. To wind him up, I said, 'Well, they do say no smoke without a fire, don't they?'

After lunch we drove up to my house. With Will filming, Jimmy did a faux-investigative tour of the almost-empty premises. In the middle of one of the bedrooms, as a provocation, I'd left the little wooden box in which I used to keep my hash and rolling paper – I was still then in the habit of smoking a joint at night to help me sleep. I was curious to see Jimmy, whose trademark was his glibness and unflappability, faced with illegal narcotics up close. I had to point it out to him, though I'd left it in the middle of the floor. 'I'm an Indian tracker,' he said when he spotted the box. He opened it up, then finding what looked like a small fragrant clod of dried mud, exclaimed, 'Bleedin' 'ell fire!'

In the other rooms, Jimmy made a show of attempting to discern evidence of lady companionship.

In a top-floor bedroom, I'd hung some old photos showing Jimmy as a young man. 'This is your bedroom, if you ever want to come and stay,' I said, not quite meaning it, knowing he would never take me up on the offer, but also, if I'm honest, not completely *not* meaning it either.

My main recollection was the sense that he was mentally counting the minutes until he could head back up to Leeds. Downstairs, as I showed him out, I said: 'Thanks for coming by.'

'OK, good morning!' he replied.

'And if you ever do need a place to crash in London, you've seen you've got a room upstairs.'

'Thank you very much. I appreciated that. I'm just going to check that it's safe out there.'

Making a show of looking up and down the road, he ventured out, then hopped into the taxi that had been ordered for him. As he drove off, three children who had spotted him – though they would have been too small to remember *Jim'll Fix It*, so how they recognized him is an open question – chased his car down the road shouting, 'Jimmy! Jimmy!'

And in fact around this time, the tabloids and the gossips *did* start taking an interest in my private life. It came to the attention of the press that I had been married, and a reporter from one of the red-tops rang Sarah's doorbell at her new home. They got a photo of her looking bewildered in a long shot with her finger in a copy of a book I recognized as *About the Author* by John Colapinto.

Among my reasons for being precious about my own privacy was an awareness of what a private person Sarah was, and that grainy apparition of her in a newspaper, clutching a book, came to symbolize some sense of collateral damage wrought by my willingness to embrace fame too readily, to crave success, to be an emotional cretin – I wasn't quite sure exactly what, I just knew I felt guilty and implicated.

Of all the themes least likely to appeal to a general audience, I realize 'I'm too famous! Wah! Wah!' is high on the list. So be it. There are many worse things in a person's working life, like losing your arm in a threshing machine or getting black lung or sustaining a brain injury in a body slam in a wrestling bout with Rowdy Roddy Piper. Let's just say that, as I look back at the protracted climacteric of that time and the sequence of trivial incidents that were for me small landmarks of unhappiness, the one that was most surreal was the day Jimmy called and said I wasn't to worry but a paper had been asking him about 'Louis Theroux's secret wife'. 'They had no chance,' he said. 'Because against me the punter isn't born that has a chance.'

I felt relieved, and then in quick succession came a feeling of disbelief that my life had come to such a pass: having Jimmy Cigar-smoking Tracksuit-wearing Now-then-now-then Savile as a kind of ally and gatekeeper to my private life.

Chapter 19

# You Can All Fuck Off

It was towards the end of 2001. There had been a series of false starts and abortive projects – one involved embedding with a troupe of eighties pop bands for the 'Here and Now' tour, another on John Noakes, the ex-*Blue Peter* presenter. Uri Geller briefly came back into the frame, yet again, and the boy band 5ive.

For a while we were having serious conversations about dedicating an hour of network television to a profile of Linsey Dawn McKenzie, a glamour model whose fame was based on the enormous size of her breasts. She was going on a 'boob cruise' with a paying clientele of breast appreciators. An AP went out to Essex to recce her. I can't remember the specifics. But since we didn't make the programme, I conclude that her breasts just weren't big enough to generate a full hour-long programme.

By now all my anxieties and doubts about making celebrity profiles had coalesced into a kind of disgust. Having started out as a journalist, a humble trapper and skinner of stories with a certain knowledge of his hunting grounds and how to bag his quarry, I found myself in the position of wandering around the woods with a silver platter, waiting for a roast chicken to fall onto it. Day after day we were joylessly pushing the button on a slot machine, its wheels marked with celebrity names, hoping for a payday.

Not to mention that the whole diary-book-thing, which had seemed such a good idea, had now by its very formlessness taken over my life. In my work I'd always tried to expand the frame of enquiry, capturing more reality and greater authenticity by including those moments at the edges of an encounter that are in some ways the most real. But with the diary it felt as though I'd expanded the frame so wide that it was no longer clear where the edges were. My waking hours resembled a life-support system for a project that required me to have conversations with my celebrity ex-subjects and take notes. Of all the conversations, as ever, the weirdest and most interesting were with Jimmy Savile. But, even with him, I found myself in a place of diminishing returns, never getting closer to making his parts add up.

Then, in amongst these failures and missteps, there came an expression of interest from Max.

When he died in his cell at HMP Littlehey, Cambridgeshire, Max Clifford, the star publicist, was three years into an eight-year sentence for multiple counts of indecent assault. His death was an ignominious end for a man who had once been one of the most powerful people on Fleet Street. His stock in trade had been kiss-and-tell stories. Max would sell the tabloids scoops about nights of passion with celebrities. Rebecca Loos, a personal assistant to the footballer David Beckham, had used his services when she'd alleged that the two of them had been having an affair. The actress Antonia de Sancha had gone to him with her account of being the mistress of the conservative politician David Mellor. Max also worked for celebrity clients who wished to keep their names *out* of the papers. He would use his influence among editors to spike articles, usually by supplying alternative stories about stage-managed relationships.

Clifford's scoops sometimes involved colourful headlines of his creation. The most famous, 'Freddie Starr Ate My Hamster', was a mostly fictional *Sun* cover story about an unpredictable comedian eating a rodent sandwich while staying with a friend.

Though he would have disliked the comparison, Max Clifford resembled Jimmy Savile in some ways. Like Jimmy, he had a leathery toughness and lied without compunction – for advantage or to amuse himself. Also like Jimmy, he was a dedicated and high-profile charity fundraiser. And he was an undiscovered serial predator who – in 2001 – agreed to spend ten days with me for a documentary profile.

Max's interest in doing a programme came with a condition: he insisted we meet off camera before filming. Going back to *TV Nation* and *Weird Weekends* days, it was my policy not to do this, to preserve some authenticity to the encounter. But by now, with production in the doldrums, I was relaxing some of my old rules.

His offices were on the fifth floor of a building in New Bond Street: open-plan, overlooking the rooftops of the West End. A half-dozen or so mostly female workers sat at desks – 'Max's Angels'. On the walls were framed front pages of his greatest hits and photos of Max with some of his celebrity clients.

I arrived with my director – Alicia, from the Eubank film – and an AP, Helen Sage, to find Max in his glassed-off corner office, gabbing on the phone. 'Have you seen today's *Tatler*?' he was saying. 'It's going to be huge.'

He was silver-haired, in his sixties, in a blue short-sleeved shirt that showed his ex-boxer's arms and chest.

Once off the phone, he explained why the documentary wouldn't work.

'You want a big scandal, I know what you want. But these people who come to me with stories, they don't want their faces shown. They don't come to me because they want to be on TV. They come for two reasons: because they want to make big money, or they want revenge.'

This led into an inventory of his life and a cascade of unverifiable gossip, all of it off-the-record: an anecdote about a Westlife stag party and something else about Prince Edward. He kept mentioning names and then giving a little smile as if to say, 'Oh, I could tell you things,' and turning his lips as though secrets were wriggling to get out.

'In 1962, EMI sent me to look after an unknown band,' he said. 'They were called The Beatles.' And: 'Let me tell you, Paul Daniels and Jimmy Savile are egomaniacs. Max Clifford is not an egomaniac. He's got an ego but he's not an egomaniac.' And several times this exchange: Me: 'Do you think so?' Max: 'I don't think, I know!'

I was aware that in seeing him prior to filming I was already setting a dangerous precedent, signing up to his rules of on- and off-the-record. I knew that part of his technique for getting people on side was this kind of journalistic double bookkeeping – the truth versus the version we are agreeing to share – and that it created an unhelpful complicity. And so, as much as I was tempted to trade gossip, I held back and tried to say as little as possible. At the end of the meeting, Max said, 'Remember, you can make me look like a prat in the editing room but I can make you look like a prat after it goes out.'

In the lift on the way down, Helen said, 'He gave us the same exact spiel last time we saw him.'

We began filming a few days later – with the usual tour-and-chat, though of his office not his home. Max, in crisp blue shirt and rimless spectacles, gave off a measured sense of indifference bordering on uninterest as he touted himself as a rainmaker for his clients, a fixer and packager of rising talent. I asked if, in theory, Max might represent me.

'Well, if you could afford us,' he said with a suggestion of impatience. 'We start at ten thousand pounds a month. Secondly, as to whether we would represent you, initially it would depend on the chemistry between you and I. If you didn't like me, I didn't like you, it doesn't get started.'

The idea of me as a prospective client whose career Max could help – and also a potential enemy whom Max could hurt – seemed a fruitful theme for filming and we continued the conversation on a taxi ride down to Rochester, Kent, where a client of Max's, nine-year-old singer Declan Galbraith, was performing at a pub. (For some reason Max insisted on calling him 'Decland', as though he was a place.) In the back of the taxi, I teased Max about whether he might take his revenge on me if he didn't like the finished documentary.

'Oh, if you took liberties, then you've started a fight,' he said.

'Then what?'

'Then I'd fight back,' he said. 'If that day ever happens then you'll find out soon enough.'

Over the next few weeks, I prodded away at this idea as filming proceeded with a day here, a day there. Though known for kiss-and-tell, most of Max's work involved a random and less tantalizing assortment of people and products: an R&B outfit called Damage; the strip club Spearmint Rhino; a man who who'd been molested by Jonathan King; a new kind of smoke alarm that screwed into light sockets. Of Max's stable, most interesting by far was an A&R man and creator of novelty records who was just then breaking into television as a talent-show judge – Simon Cowell.

'Simon is obviously looking – as most people are that are suddenly getting a lot of media attention – to try to control it as much as possible,' Max said.

Still, there was something baffling about Simon's retaining Max's services. He was, presumably, already wealthy from his music career. His profile was high, and it was also the case that there were enough weird stories about Simon already in the papers to make you wonder what exactly Max was managing to hold back.

Hoping to flesh out the Max–Simon relationship, we arranged to film a charity event at Royal Marsden Hospital in Surrey at which we knew Simon would be appearing. And by coincidence the day before, a tabloid called *The Sport* ran a story about an alleged night of passion between Simon and a glamour model called Alicia Douvall. The article included the detail that Simon had folded his socks before the lovemaking. It was confusing – the question of whether it was a story planted by Max or one that slipped by him – and faintly ridiculous, when you thought about it, that there might not be much difference between the two scenarios.

The hospital was throbbing with the pheromones of excited children from local schools, with Max off to one side, somewhat incognito, though in control – less a ringmaster and more like a maître d' at a crowded restaurant. Declan, the child singer, was there with his mum. When Simon arrived – shortish, broad-shouldered, in a jumper somehow too revealing around the neck – he signed autographs, looking as though he wasn't quite sure why he was there.

I said hello. I'd never met him before though the production team had had some dealings with him when we'd been considering a project with the boy band, 5ive. I took an immediate liking to him: he was friendly and down-to-earth. I would meet him several more times and he'd always be pleasant, in a way I assumed was sincere, though who can ever be sure? (At one of our last encounters, I would ask Simon why he no longer wore his clothes so tight, and he'd say, 'I saw you on TV the other day and I thought you looked absolutely brilliant and I wanted to adopt more of your look.' Which was laying it on a bit thick – I suspected he might be doing some Jedi-level social-influence-through-flattery trick.)

On this occasion, though, at the hospital, there wasn't much-chit chat before I whipped out the copy of *The Sport* I'd brought with me and read out the cover line: 'Page Three Babe Sex With Pop Idol Judge in Full and Explicit Detail.'

'Bye!' Simon said, and laughed.

'Simon has been a busy boy for the last twenty years,' Max said. 'And now he's become a celebrity his past is catching up with him.'

'I haven't seen that actually,' Simon said, gesturing at the paper. He read it, then laughed. 'Unbelievable!'

'Did you have sexual relations with her?' I asked.

'Oh yeah, I did,' Simon said. 'Once.'

Max, the highly paid media handler, then went into turn-the-tables mode. By this time my Hamiltons programme had gone out, with its scene of Christine cuddling me, and he seized on this for ammunition.

'Ask him about Christine Hamilton,' he said. 'Christine was the special one.'

Simon asked Max if he'd consider me as a client. 'If he came to you and said "Keep me out of the papers," would you take him on?'

'I asked that,' I said. 'He said, "It depends on the chemistry."'

'Chemistry was your expression,' Max said incorrectly. 'I said "If I like him".'

A little later, the boy band Westlife arrived. Professional amid the mayhem, they stepped out of a minivan like investigators at a crime scene. The excitement of the children reached fever pitch and, along with Max, we made our escape.


The Royal Marsden visit was also notable for being the first occasion on which the Max Clifford prankster mode made an appearance. Alicia and I had been travelling back in Max's car when a call came in on the speakerphone from a friend of Max's at the hospital. They made small talk about the visit. Then Max said, 'What was interesting – you know Alicia was up there filming Louis?'

'Yes?'

'She was telling me he was shagging Christine Hamilton.'

The friend on the phone was confused.

'You're joking!' she said.

'Yeah! Unbelievable! You can see why there was that chemistry between them! She said that he likes older women.'

'Not that old surely?'

'Yeah, hopefully they never film the Queen Mother! The things you do for your art!'

I jumped in at this point, alerting the woman on the phone that she was being pranked and that I had never (as I hope I hardly have to say) had sexual relations with Christine Hamilton, and there followed an awkward moment of realization.

'Oh, Max, you're such a bastard,' she said. 'I feel really ill now.' But it seemed a revealing exchange – the way Max's humour relied on power and withheld information, a joyless kind of practical joking that seemed more about the pleasure he took in discomfort than anything comic.

'Why were you doing that joke about me sleeping me with Christine?' I asked when we were back in Max's office. 'That's just silly, isn't it?'

'Depends if you enjoyed it or not,' Max said.

'You want information on me, don't you?'

'To tell the truth, not at all. For what?'

'So I don't stitch you up?'

'No. If you do that, then so what?'

'That hurts even more,' I said, as a joke.

'The pluses still outweigh the minuses,' Max went on. 'It's a bit like being bitten by a gnat, isn't it. Not nice at the time but it's gone. Too many good things out there.'

I had been a little worried, before filming, about Max's dealings with me: what kind of relationship we would develop. For all their foibles, most of my other profilees – Paul Daniels, Chris Eubank – had a certain show-business charisma. Max was cut from different cloth. His manner was reminiscent of a nightclub bouncer who hasn't found your name on the list. It said, *Nothing personal. You're just not very important.* He told me several times he felt apart from the world of celebrities. 'I'm not interested in the tittle-tattle and the gossip.' Given that he name-dropped constantly and took an overweening pleasure in the exchange of secret information (which was, after all, his business), this was hard to credit. At the very least, he saw fame and status as a currency that he could use to get what he wanted. I suspected it was more than that though – that it represented a professional and emotional sustenance.

But as a documentary subject for me, Max had the saving grace of being thick-skinned, and his bullying and love of secrecy and control meant that, despite his mistrustfulness, we settled into a back-and-forth of sparring that was quite enjoyable. He liked to tease but even his jokes – like the Christine Hamilton prank – weren't simply attempts to be funny but also a chance to exercise power. He made occasional ironic remarks but these were delivered so mirthlessly that he came across like a police officer who's taken a course in sarcasm as a suspect-control strategy.

And so, conscious that it was a way to keep the programme moving, I continued to maintain a certain level of tension in our interactions, aware it might go too far – that Max might take against me or try to take revenge – but not worrying about it too much, until it happened.

One afternoon we visited Max at home, a large detached house in a gated community in the Surrey commuter belt. The neighbourhood was prosperous and lifeless, reminiscent of high-toned American suburbia. We were hosted by Liz, Max's wife of thirty-four years – a woman as genteel as the model-home furnishings that filled the enormous house: pastel colours, plates with puppies on them, porcelain figures, a statue of a spaniel, and a real spaniel called Oliver. Liz seemed to be filming on sufferance and there was a muted atmosphere as she announced her lack of interest in tabloids and show business. 'It's a load of old rubbish, isn't it?' she said, and sipped her tea.

Through our weeks of filming, Max had been continuing to share off-the-record information with my director Alicia – principally about the way in which he'd been orchestrating a fake relationship for Simon Cowell involving a dancer from the strip club Spearmint Rhino. It was a classic bit of Max cross-promotion: celebrity client dating a stripper from a business Max represented. But being told about it off camera placed me in exactly the sort of compromised position I'd been hoping to avoid. Instead of documenting his PR efforts, we were becoming adjuncts of it. In his kitchen, during filming, I raised the issue.

'You told Alicia that they hadn't had sex,' I said.

'Oh, well, I was protecting her innocence.'

'Why can you tell Alicia off camera but you can't tell me on camera?'

'Well, as I explained to you when we first started to do this, there's an awful lot of things that you can't be privy to.'

I pressed further on the question of Max's machinations and it was striking, looking at the scene afterwards, that his shoulder began twitching up and down as though his repressed irritation was causing a physical reaction.

'You're quite defensive,' I said.

'No, I just say it as I see it, that's all,' Max said. 'But let's put it this way. I don't intend to make it easy for you.'

'To do what?'

'To come out with the things I don't want you to come out with.'

Afterwards we went to a Chinese restaurant – Alicia, me, the Cliffords, and the impressionist Bobby Davro and his wife. Max teased Davro about a tic or a twitch he'd developed which he said had put paid to Davro's TV career. I wasn't sure whether it was banter between friends or an insensitive joke or maybe both. Then the subject of alleged showbiz miscreants came up.

'Michael Barrymore'll top himself in a few years, and good riddance,' Max said. 'He's a sick animal and that's what you do with sick animals.'

The waiter, who was Chinese, spoke heavily accented English. Several times Max asked him if they served 'hairy muff' for dessert, to the man's understandable incomprehension. We were filming and

I sensed he was attempting to share 'the lighter side of Max Clifford' with the viewing public.

After the meal, Max drove us back to his house, pointing out his neighbours. 'Mick Hucknall lives there, Geoff Hurst lives there. The Beatles used to live here . . . That's my tennis club. Cliff Richard's also a member.'

If there was a poisoning of my relationship with Max, it probably dates from the conversation in the kitchen. A day or so later, having been summoned to film a scene with Simon Cowell and his lap-dancing 'girlfriend' at Spearmint Rhino, in which they would be photographed together for the newspapers, I was surprised when dancers kept draping themselves around *me*. Photographers snapped away as I squirmed. Then a full-page story appeared in the *Mirror*: 'GOT THEROUX: 3AM Girls turn tables on TV inquisitor . . . and he's lost for words.'

It had been a set-up, Max's warning shot across the bows, but it was surprisingly irksome – in particular, the substance of the article, which was that I could dish it out but couldn't take it. Probably the most irritating part was that there was some truth to the story: he had dished it out, and I'd found it uncomfortable. But it was, at least, good material for the documentary. And in fact thereafter there was an almost daily drip of items about me in the gossip pages – placed by Max and designed to pique and irritate me. Thanks to the success of the Hamiltons programme, interest in my irrelevant doings was then at its apex. I was turning down most publicity requests, attempting to keep a low profile. Meanwhile, Max was inviting press along to our every outing.

Matters came to a head when, by prior arrangement, we filmed Max doing his grocery shop at a Sainsbury's, only to find that there was a small gauntlet of reporters and photographers waiting for us outside, including a *Guardian* journalist, Simon Hattenstone, who'd approached me the previous week about following me around for a print profile. I had turned him down, so it was utterly confusing to see him there. I retreated to a quiet spot to conference with Alicia, at which point she heard on the radio mike Max and Simon talking about *us*.

'You think we should level with him?' Simon was saying.

'No! I'll never hear the bloody last of it if you tell him!' Max replied.

'Because I wanted to do a follow-round with him, but he wouldn't want that—'

'I know. That's why I said come down. He's paranoid about everything.'

'Why did you let him do it?' Simon said, meaning the documentary.

'Why not?'

I went back in, camera rolling, finding them in the banal environs of the fruit-and-veg aisle. My heart was beating fast. I'd been lied to, and it felt strangely personal.

'I wish you'd level with me,' I said, and then to Simon, 'I know you're here because I'm here, and you shouldn't have to lie about that.'

'Nobody's lying to you, Louis,' Max said, giving me a gentle pat. 'You mustn't get paranoid about these things. Just relax.'

To Simon again I said, 'Is that the whole truth?' It seemed to irk Max that I was talking to Simon instead of him, and I suspect he'd twigged by now that he'd been caught out by his wireless mike.

'Talk to each other, then!' he said, agitated. 'If you're going to be silly about it then you can all fuck off!'

With that, he ambled off, wheeling his trolley. Then, realizing he was still wearing his radio mike, he turned and came back and stripped it off, fiddling in his pockets to find the transmitter.

'That's it. Thanks very much,' he said and stalked off a second time.

The scene of Max stomping off became our ending to the film, but it wasn't the end of my dealings with Max. As with all our celebrity subjects, we had an awkward pre-transmission screening in his offices, Max fidgeting in his chair, fiddling with his pencil and not laughing while the little coterie of his female staffers pressed at the interior window to try and see what was on screen.

At the end he said, 'You know and I know what you did. Fine. I can handle myself. I'm old enough and ugly enough to deal with it. But let's not pretend it's something else.'

'We have a hundred per cent track record with all our contributors,' I said, attempting to gaslight him into thinking it was basically a positive portrayal. 'We've not had one person who didn't like his film.'

'Well, good,' Max said. 'You must be very happy. You've done what you've done. You didn't have to do it but so be it. You've made an enemy and I will come back at you. Might not be today, or tomorrow, but one day when you're not expecting it, I'll repay you with interest for that programme and it won't be nice.'

*When Louis Met Max* turned out to be the last of the celebrity profiles I made, and for years I was grateful that I'd gone out with a documentary that had some toughness to it. Having been lost in the woods of some light-entertainment netherworld, it felt as though I had – for one last outing – got the eye of the tiger back: returned to the ring and gone toe to toe with a Fleet Street heavyweight, winning on points with a flukey twelfth-round knock-out.

In the years afterwards, I would sometimes muse on his threats against me. He made some barbed comments in a ghosted autobiography – claiming an ex-wife had been in touch with him, which I doubt. Occasionally I'd joke, in talks I gave, about his animus against me and living life with a sword of Damocles dangling over my head.

But what I didn't realize, until years later when it came out, was how many secrets he still had.

## Chapter 20

# When Louis Didn't Meet . . .

In February 2002, I stood on stage in front of the assembled great and good of British television, accepting a second BAFTA, for Best Presenter for the *When Louis Met . . .* series, with a peculiar mixture of gratitude, despondency and fraudulence. 'I'd like to thank the Metropolitan police for arresting the Hamiltons during our film-ing', I joked, then shuffled off stage and re-joined my mum – who I'd brought as my date – and spent the rest of the evening wondering how quickly I could get home.

It's a strange feeling getting an award for completed work knowing your work-in-progress – or more accurately work-in-stoppage – isn't going well. Like seeing the light of a star that you know to be extinct. And the star is . . . *you-oo-oo-oo.* (Echo continues as we crash-zoom into eyeball.)

Another relationship ended with a girlfriend I'd been seeing for about a year, which wasn't helping my frame of mind. I was famous in a way I'd never wanted to be, but more confused than ever about what I was supposed to be doing in my programmes.

One day in the spring of 2002, exhausted by the dissonance of treating him in a friendly way while taking notes any time we spoke, I found myself on the phone to Jimmy, telling him that I was writing a book in which he figured. He reacted in typical Jimmy style. His advice was that I should come up to Leeds and we could work on the manuscript together. Well, that didn't happen. I was confused but not *that* confused. I spoke to my editors and said I'd changed my mind about the celebrity diary.

For me, whatever happened next couldn't help but be an improvement: failure on my own terms being preferable to the feeling of helplessness that went along with trying to base a TV programme on the lottery of trying to book celebrities. At the same time, I felt out of step with my own collaborators – my producer and his higher-ups – for whom my increased visibility, more coverage, and higher ratings for the shows was an unalloyed good. More and more I felt like walking away from television.

In early 2002, the production went into a phase of attempting to figure out what to do next. We had a story meeting at David's house in Acton, west London.

'We need to have the Hamiltons programme as a benchmark of the kind of impact we are looking for,' David said.

This worried me. I'd never regarded 'impact' as something to aim for. Rather, it was something that sometimes happened when you followed your instincts.

'Well, I'm not sure how we're supposed to research stories based on how likely someone is to be accused of rape,' I said.

'I accept the Hamiltons may not teach us anything in terms of process,' David said. 'I am just talking about how many people watched and talked about the programme.'

I found myself growing irritated, feeling as though I'd been served a great steaming helping of pressure when I was already full up.

'I realize we are unlikely to necessarily get the really big names,' David went on. 'But we are at a stage now where that may no longer be important. We can take the leap of faith that the audience will come with us, if we show enough ambition in our choice of subjects.'

He asked what subjects I would do if, in a dream universe, I could cover whatever I wanted. Without needing to think very hard, I said, 'Michael Jackson and the Church of Scientology.'

And that was that. Without really knowing how it would work, in a spirit of build-it-and-they-will come, we went into production on a concept that was in essence *When Louis Didn't Meet . . .*

The Michael Jackson project – which aired under the title *Louis, Martin, and Michael*, for reasons that will become clear – ended up taking more than a year from conception to completion. It was either a qualified triumph or an interesting failure – or something between the two.

Like the rest of the world, and the tabloids in particular, I'd been interested in Michael Jackson on almost every conceivable level for almost as long as I could remember: a peerless talent – singer, dancer and performer for the ages – and also a human curiosity: a self-created sculpture of ambiguous sexuality and ethnicity. His face was a battleground, bearing witness to one man's refusal to be limited by the body he'd been born with. A crime-scene report in which the victim was also the perpetrator. An elegy on man's mastery over nature and its limitations.

It was a story full of grace notes – the messianic pop videos, the Neverland compound that, with its joy rides and the demented and uncared-for animals, befitted a Roman emperor. And at the heart the question of Michael's sexual interests: the unlikely relationships involving grown women – Lisa Marie Presley, Debbie Rowe – and the all-too-plausible romances with young boys who slept in his bed at his Neverland Ranch and travelled with him on tour.

I'd been living in New York in 1993 when Jackson had been accused of molesting thirteen-year-old Jordy Chandler. He'd ended up paying what was said to be $23 million to buy the boy's silence. Later I'd read *Michael Jackson Was My Lover* by Victor Gutierrez, which included documents from the investigation, with drawings Jordy allegedly made of Jackson's penis. The book made a persuasive case that Jackson was a paedophile. Weirdly, it made this argument from a pro-paedophilia perspective.

Firmly of the view that Jackson had predatory sexual interests, I hoped one of the boys – some of whom were now men – might agree to talk to us. Then came the reality check of who we would realistically film with. Without access to the man himself, we thought we might embed with some of his fans. Jackson had just released an album, *Invincible*, which was selling less well than expected. Jackson and his supporters blamed lack of promotion by the record label, Sony. Fans were being encouraged to demonstrate against Sony at its London headquarters.

We flew to Germany – Will, me, and an AP called Natalie – then rode back to London overnight in a convoy of coaches filled with rabid German Jackson fans who were taking part in the demonstrations. We got zero usable material. Deranged German Michael Jackson fan sounds funny as a phrase. But in the flesh it was simply depressing: a motorcade of *Untermenschen* in trilbies, one glove each, moonwalking in desultory petrol station forecourts.

Michael was staying at the Renaissance Hotel in Holborn, so Will and I booked a room there. For several days I talked to the fans and impersonators camped outside and to visitors who were coming and going from Jackson's suite, including Mark Lester, who as a child actor decades earlier had played the title role in the film *Oliver!* I wrote MJ a short letter and left it with a bodyguard seated outside his door – nothing came back – and then on day two or day three Michael hired an open-top double-decker bus and drove around the West End as the fans went into a delirium of excitement. The closest I got to the man himself was on his last day in London, chasing after a limo and sticking my hand in the crack of the window and for a moment holding his feminine ungloved hand. Then he flew back – I assume – to Las Vegas, where he was living with his children – Paris, Prince, and baby Blanket.

It wasn't a promising start. *Remember when I spent the night in*

*Jimmy Savile's mum's bed?* I thought. *Remember when I was inside the Hamilton's country pile during that media frenzy? I was the king of access. Now I'm chasing limos like a sad fan . . .* Still, we persevered. Will and I flew to Las Vegas with a vague idea we might hang about outside Jackson's apartment block, or whatever it was, Nick Broomfield style. With leads thin, I interviewed an impersonator called E'Casanova, who was promoting an inspirational song with the unintentionally comic title 'The Laughter in We' and it was then we had a small break in the case. We discovered E'Casanova's manager, Majestik Magnificent, had once been Jackson's personal magician and remained a friend and helper to Michael's father, Joe. For a fee of $5,000 Majestik would set up an interview with Joe.

If we couldn't get to Michael, it seemed a reasonable consolation prize.

A failed musician-turned-manager to The Jackson 5, Joe occupied a central and somewhat controversial position in Jackson family mythology. He was credited with recognizing the musical potential of his children, forming them into a group, shaping their career and driving them to succeed. But it was also said he'd been physically abusive. Michael in particular had viewed him as a terrifying figure. He had once commented in an interview he was so fearful of his father he would 'regurgitate' before seeing him. It was also claimed that Joe had teased Michael about the size of his nose – supposedly he would compare it to a pepper. Some speculated that the teasing might partly explain Michael's obsessive plastic surgery.

We met Joe late one evening outside a hotel-casino, the Golden Nugget, in downtown Las Vegas. In his seventies, slow-moving and soft-spoken, he had a louche reptilian air. He was wearing earrings, a necklace and bracelet, and had a pencil moustache. He looked somehow too groomed to inspire complete confidence.

He was with Majestik, who was acting as personal aide. We took them up to a suite we had booked, then just as we started the interview, the phone rang. A Filipino Michael Jackson tribute group called The Front Page that Joe was managing were in reception and wanted to come up. Then another protegé of Joe's arrived, a lissom teenage singer called Krystal.

And so it went on, with more false starts and disruptions. I kept losing the train of the conversation, and after two hours of filming almost nothing of substance had been gained from our $5,000, and it was hard to shake the feeling that instead of a step forward the entire 'didn't meet' format was a major downgrade. Especially once it became clear that at the same time as we were *not* filming with him, MJ was providing all-singing, all-dancing access to the ITV journalist Martin Bashir. When Bashir's film, called *Living With Michael*, duly appeared, it was an extraordinary piece of work, with scenes of Jackson climbing trees at Neverland, running up a huge bill in a toy store, and shouting 'Yoo-hoo!' in a high-pitched voice. It also featured a creepy interview with Michael and one of his young friends, a cancer-stricken child named Gavin Arvizo. The scene was so troubling it led to molestation charges being brought against the star. That was 'impact'. So much so that we abandoned our own project. The material of me riding in coaches with fans and interviewing his personal magician suddenly looked very lame.

Now, about ten programmes behind on delivery, I felt like a striker who's been signed for huge sums and can't find the back of the net.

For a few months we persevered with the Scientology idea. If I'd been looking for a way to waste more time, I couldn't have picked a better subject. The websites and online databases dedicated to Scientology are so labyrinthine and detailed that you can lose entire weeks reading up random accounts from disaffected ex-members with allegations of ill-use: polishing floors with toothbrushes, running around trees until they collapse, and descriptions of Scientology rituals, walking around touching walls for hours at a time and saying 'thank you'. (Is this a good place to say that the Church of Scientology disputes these characterizations? Lawyers – will that do?)

I watched some old documentaries. Most followed a similar formula involving interviews with ex-members who describe having naively joined out of a spirit of selflessness, then found themselves pressured either to keep paying for more services (therapy, classes) or to join the Scientology clergy, the 'Sea Org', sign a billion-year contract, live communally, work endless hours for very little money. Sometimes reporters went undercover and made secret recordings of Scientology 'registrars' trying to upsell them on more expensive courses and classes in communication. In a few there were testy interviews with senior Scientologists, which the members of the Church filmed with their own cameras. This had the effect of making the Scientologists look, if anything, even weirder. Almost always there was a visit to a fence at the edge of a base and quite often the crew would film itself being tailed by PIs in blacked-out cars.

Then, to my surprise, one of Scientology's LA-based PR people – Linda Simmons Hight – expressed some interest in speaking to us. We sent over a copy of *When Louis Met the Hamiltons* and made arrangements to meet up.

At the beginning of 2003, with a director and AP, I flew to Los Angeles. For a week or so we holed up in the Roosevelt, a beautiful old hotel in the heart of Hollywood, and tried to strategize our way into the world's most secretive religion. I had an inkling it was probably a fool's errand. I spent the mornings doing laps in the pool and push-ups in my room to keep my sanity. I bought time in an Internet cafe on Hollywood and La Brea and did research online about other examples of religious weirdness to see if I could find an alternative subject if the Scientology story fell down, as I suspected it soon would.

One morning Linda Simmons Hight invited us to visit the Church's Celebrity Centre. The centre had once been a long-term hotel for West Coast jetsetters, the Château Élysée – a beautiful 1927 building, on Franklin Avenue in Hollywood, with turrets and high windows and precipitously sloping roofs, redolent of a seventeenth-century

French castle. But it fell on hard times, and in 1973 it was bought by the Church of Scientology and was now its VIP facility for the religion's frequent fliers. I know there are other more serious misdeeds imputed to the Church of Scientology but, still, it's worth thinking for a moment about a spiritual organization that advertises that it affords better amenities to those of its believers who are famous.

Linda, small and chirpy, toured us around the gardens and a high-windowed orangery, and showed us upstairs to the rooms where the therapy, called 'auditing', took place. I have a recollection of saunas downstairs, where adepts would take mega-doses of niacin and sweat out impurities in their system as recommended by Hubbard in his 'Purification Rundown', but at this distance it is all a little vague in my mind.

'Write up a wish list of what you feel you would need for the documentary', Linda said at the end. 'We'll see what we can do.'

We went back to the hotel and wrote a wholly unrealistic pie-in-the-sky list: *interview Church leader David Miscavige; ride on motorbike with Tom Cruise; visit secret base near Hemet.* 'But these are just opening thoughts and we are completely open to any ideas you may have.' The conversation fizzled out soon afterwards, the whole episode disappearing like a half-remembered fever dream with almost nothing to show for its ever having been real. I never heard a peep out of Linda Simmons Hight ever again, nor have I ever seen her in any subsequent coverage, although she does still appear on a Church website. I sometimes worry that she may be pumping bilge at a Church punishment camp somewhere or polishing doorknobs on the Scientology cruise ship *Freewinds*. (The Church denies these allegations, etc.)

For some reason, what stayed with me after that was a conversation on the phone in which Linda spoke about watching the Hamiltons film. 'I saw the HA HA HA! show you made about the politician and his wife and I just HA HA HA! thought it was great, it was HA HA HA! very funny but I couldn't see how that kind of tongue-in-cheek irreverent sending-up approach would ever fit with our Church.'

'Well, it was basically an affectionate portrait,' I burbled. 'Obviously a very different sort of subject.' But what I was thinking about was her laugh: there was something about it that was off, it felt artificial and willed, almost as though it were part of some training she'd done on how to use chuckling to build rapport.

It was now a year since I'd a made a show. We were Napoleon's army retreating from Moscow, decimated, drinking horse piss for hydration, an emaciated remnant with nothing to show for all our pain and effort. Now, finally, we saw sense and either I or David called time on the 'Didn't Meet' concept. With no choice – I think the higher-ups were bearing down on David by this time, wondering what exactly we'd been doing with the licence-payers' money for the previous twelve months – we retreated to familiar terrain: American weirdness, more or less. I made a show about a legal brothel in Nevada and another on neo-Nazis in California. These films were less antic in tone than *Weird Weekends*. We took the more organic and less plotted approach of the *When Louis Met . . .* programmes and applied it to weightier but still strange American subjects. We didn't plan a narrative. No cards on the wall. We just called and got access and then jumped in.

Though they were conceived in a spirit of desperation and of 'making shows that we can make', *Louis and the Brothel* and *Louis and the Nazis* remain among my favourite programmes. I took it as a lesson: that sometimes good work arises from the absence of other options and that fate rewards those who hold their nerve when things aren't going well.

Having shot those, late in 2003 we still needed to deliver another programme. An idea about the proprietor of a topless magazine called *Perfect 10* starting a boxing league of glamour models had – amazingly – turned out not to have the weight and complexity to sustain sixty minutes of TV. So I dusted off the Michael Jackson material. The feeling was that we were far enough now from Martin Bashir's film for ours not to appear too embarrassing. I got back in touch with Majestik Magnificent, the magician, who put a call in to Joe Jackson. They agreed to a second interview – Majestik conceded the first one had been a fiasco, or at least suboptimal – and we flew to New Jersey, meeting them at a rundown mall where Joe was appearing as himself in an ultra-low-budget movie. After several hours of hanging around, Will and I repaired back to our hotel with Joe and Majestik.

It was now close to midnight. With time short, and exasperated from all the waiting around, I found myself taking a more confrontational approach than usual. I asked Joe about Michael's claim that he would regurgitate with fear whenever he knew he would be seeing him. He and Majestik seemed familiar with the topic. From off camera, Majestik said, 'All the way to what, Joe?'

'He regurgitate all the way to the bank,' Joe said as Majestik giggled.

I paused to take this in.

'I'm not quite sure I know what you mean when you say that,' I said. 'You mean you don't believe that he does or you don't care?'

Joe tapped his finger on the side of his easy chair. 'Do I really care? I really don't.'

'Michael's on record as saying you beat him with switches and belts,' I said.

'I never beat him,' Joe replied. 'I *whipped* him with a switch and a belt. I never beat him. You *beat* somebody with a stick.'

'It's also been written that you would tease Michael and call him big nose.'

'Did he say that? I don't recall calling him big nose. If I did it was out of a joking situation. So, you know. Whatever.'

With each question, the atmosphere was becoming more strained, but after my failure to pull off the interview in Las Vegas, I knew this was my only chance to get something usable for our film, and so I ploughed on through the bad vibes.

I talked about Michael's bizarre qualities. His apparent inability to relate to people his own age. His friendships with children. I said he seemed in need of help. Joe batted all of this away with languid disdain. 'I will get up and walk if I have to talk about Michael's nose on the BBC,' he said. ''Cause he wouldn't like that.'

Then he said: 'Michael is sorta like a kid himself. He never really grown up.'

We talked some more about Michael's nose until Majestik said, 'Don't ask that question again.' This led to a conversation about the perception of Michael's eccentricities. Finding a theme he could warm to, Joe momentarily came to life, decrying the tabloid moniker his son had been saddled with, which he slightly misremembered as 'Jacko Wacko'. 'You need to stop that,' he said.

And then, with the inevitability of a hit man whose time has come to finish the job, I raised the subject of Michael's romantic interests.

'Would you like to see Michael settled down with a partner?' I asked.

'What's a partner?' Joe said.

'A loved one.'

'A *wife*?' Majestik asked from off camera.

'A boyfriend or girlfriend,' I clarified.

'A *what*?' Majestik said. 'You tryin' to say Michael's gay now? Turn the camera off.'

A verbal squabble ensued, with Majestik saying several more times, 'Turn the camera off,' as Will, who was filming, protested and I persevered.

'You askin' me the wrong question,' Joe said. 'If I'd known this was going to be talked about I would never give you the chance to do this. *Never* . . . We don't believe in gays. I can't stand 'em.'

There were more expressions of outrage and dismay. Joe seemed to be struggling with the basic concept of homosexuality. 'Are you saying having a *boyfriend* as a *girlfriend*?'

I wasn't sure how to answer this. 'No,' I said. Or was I? *A boyfriend as a girlfriend.* I supposed I might be. 'I don't know what Michael's romantic interests are,' I said. 'I don't know which way he goes.'

'Well, certainly I'm tellin' you right now it's not with no boys,' Joe said. 'It's not that. OK?'

Then he said, 'Anyway, Majestik, I'm going to have to end this.'

'I tried to warn you,' Majestik said. 'It's over.'

And it was.

It had felt like a revealing interview. A small contribution to the picture of the cloistered and backward-looking world Michael had grown up in. An upbringing in which, whether due to the culture of the time or the strict Jehovah's Witness beliefs his family professed, the idea of men loving other men was beyond the pale.

When the time came to edit the film, we were still self-conscious about playing second fiddle to Martin Bashir's astonishing effort, so we decided to make a feature of Martin's presence. I made mention of my feelings of demoralization as I saw him coming and going from Michael's hotel suites. Hence, too, the title: *Louis, Martin, and Michael.* We delivered the programme in late 2003, along with the two others. I felt like Santiago, the fisherman in *The Old Man and the Sea*, arriving back with his raddled tuna carcass hitched to his boat. In a qualified and equivocal way I had broken my dry spell and earned back some measure of honour. It wasn't the Hamiltons or Paul and Debbie, or anything resembling the impact I was supposed to be aiming for, but it was *something*.

Then I pushed my battered skiff back out to sea and paddled far, far away from television.

## Chapter 21

# Nancy

I fell in love with her the first time I saw her dance – it was our third or fourth night out together and we were at a club in Soho. 'What's Luv' by Fat Joe came on and it was as though she passed into an alternate state of effortless motion, traversed a portal and arrived in the Groove Dimension, a place where gravity and time operated differently. It was a dimension I had trouble finding my way into, then and ever since.

Her name was Nancy and she was an AP in the BBC history department. She had the high cheekbones and sad eyes of a French chanteuse – she was film-star beautiful, but wore it lightly, as though her beauty was something she had never noticed about herself, and I admired her as she passed me in corridors on endless outings to smoke cigarettes in front of the White City building.

We first spoke at a BBC Christmas party. I was wearing a blue party wig and my opening line was, 'Oh yeah, I've seen you around.' Later she would impersonate it in a voice of gormless, obviously feigned disinterest. She told me she was working on a programme about Martin Luther King. I tested her on key dates in the Civil Rights Movement – the Montgomery Bus Boycott, the date of King's death – and when she answered I had to confess I wasn't sure if she was correct since I didn't know the dates myself.

We went on a date at a pub in Willesden, where Nancy mentioned her active role in campaigning against the war in Iraq and told me about her chant, to the tune of 'Who Let the Dogs Out?': 'Who let the bombs drop? Bush, Bush and Blair!' She expressed an admiration for the film-maker and journalist John Pilger, though she allowed that it was a shame about his hair. I took it as a reassuring sign that she was political but still had a healthy sense of perspective. On a second date we played word games over dinner and – this is a little weird in hindsight – did binary arithmetic on the restaurant's paper napkins. She teased me and I had the feeling of not being taken too seriously and having to stay on my toes. Later, when we fell in love and I marvelled at my good fortune, I sometimes wondered whether, as with John Pilger, she'd been able to see past the hair.

We saw each other through the following year. When I was staying in Hollywood, making my overtures to the Scientologists, she passed through on assignment with her own BBC project. Despite my visits to LA over the years, I was still learning the city, and with Nancy I felt I was imprinting it with our budding romance. Then, for a chunk of time, I was living at a legal brothel in Nevada for an immersive documentary. It could have been awkward for the relationship – in fact it *was* a little awkward, especially when I had to show her a rough cut of me getting a half-naked 'sensual massage' with one of the working girls – but she was much too cool to be seen to let it bother her. 'You know, you *are* flirting with her,' she said, as though it was a matter of only technical interest. It was one of many occasions between us when she outmatched whatever sangfroid I imagined myself capable of, and hinted at a capacity for detachment that was – if I'd thought about it – slightly terrifying.

She moved in a few months later, in late 2003, and then, when I gave up my TV job to travel around America for a book about meeting up with the subjects of some of my old shows, she left the BBC to come with me. For six months we traversed the country in a 1993 Dodge Dynasty – Nancy would do research and transcribe tapes in the evening while I wrote up my notes. In Mississippi we stayed in a converted shotgun shack that had once been home to a plantation worker who'd raised eight or ten children in it; now, along with a number of similar structures, it had been refitted for tourists as part of a plantation-themed novelty motel of questionable taste. Here Nancy sat at a piano and, more than a year into our relationship, revealed that she played to an almost professional standard.

At the end of the trip we settled in Los Angeles. She found work making television documentaries while I sat in our apartment, growing demented under the pressure of writing, constantly staring down the barrel of the fact that it didn't come as easily as I thought it should, freaking out that the book was showing signs of being no good, and thinking that I was thirty-four, the same age my father had been when he wrote his bestseller and travel-literature classic *The Great Railway Bazaar*. Often he would call and offer advice: 'Lou, let me take a look. I know a thing or two about books. If you want help. I don't want to impose.' I wondered if I was writing as an act of impersonation. I fended him off. At the same time I realized his input probably would have been helpful, but I couldn't bring myself to accept it.

In the evenings, as I worked, Nancy would play Chopin and Mendelssohn on a Yamaha electric piano I bought her for her thirtieth birthday. In the winter, torrential monsoon-like rains flooded the Los Angeles streets and beat down on our small rear balcony that overlooked a motorcycle repair shop and a Sizzler. One night we watched *Sunset Boulevard* and I delighted in the strange synchronicity of listening to the downpour as the disillusioned journalist and screenwriter in the film is forced by similar Hollywood rains to move from a guesthouse into the mansion of the ageing star – like Michael Jackson, she too had a chimpanzee as a pet – and the romance that ensued between them led to her descent into psychosis and his death. The film struck a chord with me – it seemed to deal with so many themes I had explored: stardom and delusion and love – and maybe too I identified with the central characters, the grandiose has-been and the jaded hanger-on. Like them, I felt a little like a leftover, a refugee from my TV career, though I was happy that night, watching a film that was so strange and funny and sad, with Nancy.

Eight months after we'd settled in LA we found out she was pregnant. We decided to move back to Harlesden, the cacophonous polyglot corner of west London where my house was, and where I'd hosted Jimmy Savile. Albert arrived on Valentine's Day, 2006. After a heroic forty-eight-hour labour at Northwick Park Hospital in Harrow, he was delivered by emergency Caesarean. The medical team hailed from points all around the world and the radio was playing and, with the music, I remember thinking it felt a little like a mechanic's garage: they were working under Nancy's bonnet, and then he emerged, huge and handsome, though understandably upset, his head faintly conical from all the hours of battering at Nancy's cervix. For a moment there was a weird feeling of self-recognition: this was what the start of life looked like, I thought, how I once was, how everyone once was, but the emotion I had I didn't recognize as

With Nancy and one-day-old Albert.

simply love so much as awe and mystery and responsibility and pride that we had produced something so perfect.

Having a child brought out a latent bourgeois side that I hadn't known was there. I started worrying about littering and anti-social behaviour. I would take photos of the piles of rubbish at Willesden Junction and email them to local councillors. The bins had been removed in the wake of the 7/7 bombings, presumably to forestall further attacks, but no one had given any thought to what would happen to the rubbish, which people now left in piles where the bins had once been. The bushes on the embankments were decorated like Christmas trees with crisp packets and energy-drink cans. The road bridge was illuminated with graffiti. I called the council to complain. 'Is the graffiti racist?' asked the man. 'Er, I don't think so,' I said. 'In that case there's not much we can do about it.' It crossed my mind to go down there one night with a can of paint and *make* it racist so they'd remove it. I would have to write anti-white slogans since the alternative didn't bear thinking about. Still, it wasn't ideal. It might look like I was trying to claim victim status or stir up racial tension.

All this went on in my head.

I had a great fondness for the area. Unloved, unfashionable, in need of a little care and attention, it felt like a metonym for the world's disadvantaged and overlooked. At the same time, it was hard not to feel abraded by the day-to-day jostle and noise of living there – foul-mouthed schoolchildren, Polish and Romanian build- ers sat on their front garden wall drinking between jobs, teenage drug-dealers. Its historic music venue, the Mean Fiddler, had closed and been turned into a hostel for the homeless. The junk shop at the corner of our street became a kebab joint – Master Kebab – with strip lighting and a kind of kiln built into the countertop where they baked fresh naan. Outside there was a little pipe that dripped efflu- ent onto the pavement. Even the McDonald's closed down – which seemed ominous: I'd never heard of a McDonald's closing down; I thought they only opened. I studied the houses in our street for signs of other families moving in. Builders went to work on a house diagonally opposite ours, and my brief sense of hope was dispelled when I saw that a bell with seven buttons had been put up – the dreaded 'multiple occupancy'.

But I also wondered who was this person – this stranger – who had taken up residence *in my own soul*, who cared about people's front gardens and whether there were empty tins of Red Bull on our front wall and mattresses in the street and the civic fabric, the crumbling streets and endless betting shops and mobile phone mini-marts and places advertising 'money transfers'. I began to resent him, and then in a circuitous way I came to blame the area for incubating the uptight litter-exasperated man inside me.

Weekends revolved around the local park and endless hours push-ing roundabouts and swings. Sisyphus himself would have goggled at the monotony of the amount of pushing I did. At least the boulder didn't cry and scream. He didn't have to talk to the boulder in a funny voice and say 'Red light! Stop!' The boulder didn't keep taking off its mittens and then cry because its hands were cold. Presumably it just kept rolling up and down the hill, mute and cooperative. Then we'd warm up watching videos of toys – penguins sliding down ramps and jack-in-the-boxes – that were supposed to turn your child into a genius. At bathtime, I'd squeeze his thighs to make him laugh, and the way his head tilted back showing his toothless gums melted my heart. His room was blacked out to help him sleep. We'd put white noise on a detuned radio to drown out other sounds, though some-times the radio would find stations on its own, filling Albert's room with surging, staticky foreign-language broadcasts, which miracu-lously tended not to wake him. Even after he was down I'd creep in and check on him, marvelling at his beauty and the unlikely trust the universe had vested in us by allowing us to have him.

For a year or two, a little gaggle of drug-dealers set up shop at the corner of the road. I felt an urge to dob them in to the author-ities, but I was also aware of a slight sense of hypocrisy, given how many hours of my teenage years were spent trying to score in similar areas of south London. Occasionally – once every six months or so – street fights would break out outside the house. Of an evening, trying to watch the latest box set with Nancy, I'd become aware of noise outside. If I'd had enough to drink I'd venture out in my dressing gown and pyjamas to remonstrate with the teenagers over the road. Sometimes they recognized me from the TV – Somali kids saying, 'You're that bloke! Lewis Froo! Ah! Ha ha!' – which somehow made it worse. I started a local chapter of the Neighbourhood Watch. I put up the stickers but couldn't be bothered to hold any meetings. I kept a written diary of all the activity outside our house, making notes about trivial incidents – 'fourteen-year-old offered me "ganj"', 'seven to ten teenagers, violence seemed to be in the offing', 'said my child was trying to sleep. Subject said he would "put me to sleep" if I didn't shut up.'

With so much going on at home, the unexpected dividend was that I was more focused at work. Coming out the front door and clambering onto my bicycle, I felt a surge of relief mixed in with a contradictory sense of missing my family already. Nights on location were like restorative trips to a high-end spa. Later, when I moved on to darker stories about crime and mental illness, cultists, and paedophiles confined in a maximum-security mental hospital, my guilty secret was that the trips were blissfully stress-free, remote from my daily concerns. My contributors' lives of chaos and despair dwarfed my more banal worries, and the accoutrements of filming were, after the chaos of home, luxurious: long flights in which I could read unmolested, meals in decent restaurants, consecutive nights of uninterrupted sleep.

The demands of domestic duties seemed to keep me balanced – I was forced to weigh my neurotic desire to get involved in story development against a home life involving a baby who didn't nap when he was supposed to. Albert would become increasingly manic and wild-eyed through the course of the day, while Nancy would make phone calls for emotional support that I did my best to give, inadequately and self-consciously, in a quiet BBC office surrounded by co-workers.

My life had a centre of gravity. There was a non-negotiable quality to the needs of the family that was stabilizing. As time-consuming as they were, it eliminated the possibility of choice. There was a war on: a benign war being waged against a relentless adversary, liable to attack at any time, in any place, with his capricious needs for snacks, amusements, nappies, changes of clothes – in which I, a small but doughty nation, was in an alliance with a mercurial superpower who sometimes doubted my commitment to the fight.

In saddling up again, none of us had quite known what kind of programmes we'd be making. In fact it's embarrassing to acknowledge how much presumption I showed waltzing back into my old job, having had a perfunctory meeting with the BBC2 channel controller Roly Keating at which I said little more than, 'I'd like to come back.'

'Any ideas?'

'Not really sure. Maybe slightly more serious than the old stuff. I was wondering about child soldiers in West Africa.'

Roly's only request was that, instead of the floating title of 'Louis and' or 'When Louis Met', we should now christen our specials 'Louis Theroux' colon – which didn't seem a lot to ask, given that's my name – and also that we would now, for reasons to do with scheduling, be working at the length of an hour rather than fifty minutes. A contract was drafted, for ten programmes over three years, and so, like Doctor Who, I regenerated back at the BBC, albeit in the same body – give or take some fat on the midriff and some hair on the shoulders – and instead of a young glamorous sidekick, with a new production team.

We were working now out of Bush House, the huge art deco megalith on Aldwych, which gazes with faded imperial grandeur up Kingsway. Inside was like a cut-rate United Nations, a labyrinth of low corridors and cramped offices dedicated to tiny language services. After a few months of the usual faffing and false starts, we finally got an idea going about gambling in Las Vegas, and then another about the Westboro Baptist Church, an extreme religious group in Kansas. The Church was then – under the influence of its bigoted and contrarian pastor, Fred Phelps – engaged in a campaign of pickets of the funerals of celebrities, and soldiers killed in Iraq and Afghanistan, at which they would hold signs of unbelievable crassness and insensitivity: 'God Hates Fags', 'Fags Eat Poop'.

That film, which came out under the name *The Most Hated Family in America*, was a hit – watched by millions, and briefly a water-cooler talking-point. With the support of my young family at home and a talented group of co-workers, I felt I was finally hitting my stride as a programme-maker.

## Chapter 22

## Behind Bars

The night before the first day of filming at San Quentin, I drove down from my hotel just north of San Francisco to a nearby Walmart on a mission to buy a pair of tan slacks. My director Stuart had advised me that visitors to the infamous California prison are forbidden from wearing blue jeans, since some of the inmates wore denim-blue outfits and the authorities didn't want to mistake any visiting civilians for runaways and shoot them by mistake. In a way it was a helpful wake-up call – it focuses the mind knowing that you might get sniped for wearing the wrong colour trousers.

It had been an idea of obscure provenance – possibly I'd been watching one of those American reality series that all feature the word 'Lock' and a preposition in the title: Lock Up, Lockdown, Lock-in, Lock-out. They tend to be overheated, full of grainy footage, gravelly voiced narration and ramped-up danger. Or I may have been thinking it would be funny to see pale bespectacled me out of my element in a world that promised menace and high-octane masculinity – like me and Nazis but more so.

Over the years I'd also seen a couple of documentaries about prisons, Paul Hamann's *Fourteen Days in May*, about a man on death row in Mississippi in the lead-up to his execution; and Liz Garbus' and Jonathan Stack's Oscar winner *The Farm*, about Angola

State Penitentiary (its stand-out scene shows a man in full clown costume visiting the inmates on death row to cheer them up on Christmas Day). Neither of these films is very funny and in fact *The Farm*, from my recollection, is a tiny bit boring. But around that time an American friend, a *TV Nation* alum, recommended a work of participatory journalism by the American writer Ted Conover called *Newjack*. It recounted his months working undercover as a correctional officer at New York's Sing Sing prison, and what came across was the bizarre sense of incarceration as a kind of cooperative endeavour in which the prisoners, in their way, had as much power as the guards. Instead of the usual view of prison as an us-and-them environment, in which the prisoners are beholden to the authorities' goodwill as they attempt to get back to normal life, I began thinking of it *as* 'normal life'. I saw the officers and inmates as settled in a routine, existing in a symbiosis that was respectful as well as predatory; brutal but in its own strange way mutually sustaining and even occasionally affectionate.

I mentioned the idea to my new executive producer, Nick Mirsky and series producer, Stuart Cabb. An AP was assigned. Over several months, calls went out to a long list of American prisons, and Stuart did a whistle-stop tour across the US of the five or so most promising possibilities, alighting on California's legendary San Quentin as the best option.

The entire complex of San Quentin is more like a town than a prison – there are a vast number of outbuildings: a post office, a museum, a fire station, employee residences, all ringed by an outer perimeter fence. In a concentric ring within, sitting atop an outcrop overlooking the San Francisco Bay, is the maximum security prison, with its yards and playing fields, its vast hangar-like multilevel blocks with rows of metal tiers running up the sides, its dining halls and laundry facilities and chapel.

The four of us – me, Stuart, a sound recordist, and Laura the

AP – arrived on a sunny morning in the summer of 2007. The day started, as would all subsequent days, with our passage through the 'sally port' – a little like the gate of a medieval fortress, though equipped with a metal detector. The gate opened out onto a large courtyard.

Our chaperone for the visit was the prison's public relations officer, Lt Eric Messick. Knowledgeable and good-humoured, Lt Messick had done his time as a prison guard, and his confidence in his position there and his knowledge of prison life meant he took a relaxed attitude to what we could see. In general, I was pleasantly surprised by the amount of leeway we had to film inside the prison. The only places that were off-limits to us were those related to execution – the roughly 700-strong Death Row, the execution chamber itself – and the area for those inmates deemed the biggest threats to officers (spookily named the 'adjustment centre'). Nor could we request to speak to specific inmates by name. This last rule, apparently, stemmed from a legal prohibition known as the 'Charles Manson law'. Manson had become so popular among ratings-hungry journalists that they had had to outlaw the practice.

On that first day we made our way to the Carson Section, San Quentin's 'hole', for inmates who had assaulted other inmates or officers. The CO in charge, Officer Jaime Alejos, equipped us all with stab vests. 'These guys have a tendency to either spear you or dart you,' he said. 'May as well protect your major organs.'

With its lofty ceiling and its three or four tiers stretching up one wall, Carson Section had an exalted feel, like the nave of a cathedral. But the crudeness of its infrastructure – pipes visible, everything bolted together and roughly painted – brought the place back down to earth and made it resemble something agricultural: a facility for livestock – which, I suppose, is what it is. The cell openings had bars, which in turn were covered with mesh grills. Behind them were shirtless men, their bald heads and moustaches just visible. As we processed down past the ground-floor cells, whoops and heckles were audible. I was conscious of being seen by a thousand eyes, and that the possessor of any single pair might take against me and dart me.

'It's all show,' Officer Alejos said. 'They're gonna make all kinds of noise.'

'Do you actually quite like dealing with them?' I asked.

'Yes, I do.'

'Why?'

'Because most of the stuff that they say is amusing. It makes you laugh.'

Officer Alejos steered me towards a 'frequent flyer', a young man whose name he gave as Playboy Nolan – not, I suspect, the name he was christened with. Playboy looked to be twenty-five or so. Short, with narrow eyes and unnaturally pale skin, he was elf-like in his appearance – if elves went bad and shaved their heads and got tattoos written in grandiloquent script on their necks. He said he was in for three years for carjacking. It seemed a long time.

'You used a weapon?' I asked.

'They said I had a weapon,' he replied.

Alejos explained that Playboy had been sent to Carson for 'gassing' correctional officers – I knew this meant spraying them with effluent, but I needed more information.

'You assaulted COs with what?'

'Any kind of liquid substance you could put together.'

'Faeces?'

Playboy looked confused. 'He say faeces?'

'Poopoo,' Alejos clarified.

'Nah. I ain't goin' that far.'

'Urine?'

'Yeah.'

'Your own?'

'It's not nobody else's! Heh heh! But sometimes I been in predicaments when I had nothin' in my cell, and the only way to get my point across was to come up with some kind of combination . . . Five or six officers I gassed.'

'Would you ever gas me?' Alejos asked.

'Nah!'

'Why wouldn't you gas Alejos?' I asked.

'I known him for a long time, so.'

From his body language, I could see Alejos took this as a compliment – the idea that he might be exempted from Playboy's effusions of bodily waste. Greater love hath no man than this: that he should not spray his friend with some kind of combination of piss and poopoo.

'You seem almost a little proud that he wouldn't do that to you,' I said.

'No. I've known Playboy about seven years now. Since he was seventeen years old. I've seen him at his freakin' worst. Unbelievable. You just want to go over there and hit him, tell him to shut up.'

'And now I sense you have a pretty good rapport.'

'Oh, we always had.'

'This is calm for me right here,' Playboy said.

This emotional flavour, an unlikely sense of camaraderie and paternalism in a place where one might expect to find only antagonism, set the tone for much of my visit to San Quentin: guards who found the shenanigans of their inmates diverting, who took a protective, almost teacherly, attitude towards their charges; and inmates who had evolved a grudging tolerance for the guards, allowing that for the most part they were just guys doing a job.

This was, on the one hand, tactical: it's not in the interests of either party for inmates and guards to antagonize one another for no reason. The prisoners can retaliate; so can guards. But it also spoke to a deeper quality, something I tend to think was simply symptomatic of who we all are as people: our need to get along; the way in which physical proximity tends naturally to breed a certain comity, so that relationships that might seem at first to be utterly opposed are in fact more mixed up and complicated.

This turned out also to be true of that other archetype of brutality: the prison gangs.

A little like the porn world, its remoteness from the mainstream had brought out an unvarnished racial polarization at San Quentin. No shame attached to racism: it was just a fact of life. The inmates ganged together by colour – whites, blacks, and several groups of Hispanic prisoners: Norteños, from Northern California; Sureños from the South; and a third group called the Paisas who tended to be native Mexican, and for some reason struck me as the most approachable and least threatening.

The gangs appeared to exist largely for reasons of self-protection: you needed back-up in prison; otherwise you were vulnerable to extortion or sexual bondage. At one point I was told there was a possible exception for guys who are very bookish – that there was a certain leeway for those who are super-literate or super-religious to go their own way. Needless to say, if I *do* ever have to do time in San Quentin, I'd definitely be aiming for that loophole.

For those signed up to gangs, membership had its privileges but came at a price. Specifically, you had to observe the esoteric racial code: not sharing food or lodgings or anything of value with anyone of another race and being ready to knife any other gang member who does so.

At yard time, there were unofficial areas for different groups, demarcated with invisible boundaries. During our first week of filming, we found ourselves amongst a group of twelve or so skinheads, guys mostly in their twenties and thirties, several of them shirtless and heavily decorated with ink. 'We're the white guys,' one said when I walked up. He was muscular, shaven-headed, with the ghost of a horseshoe moustache. He seemed to be the spokesman of the group.

I asked whether they were in a gang, and they began muttering and pointing to their tattoos. 'BBH,' said horseshoe-moustache man. 'Barbarian Brotherhood.'

'Do all the different races have different areas?'

'Yeah. That's like the black area over there, the Norteño area over there, white area over here. Indian area over there. We keep it segregated.'

'How come?'

'Keep a clear line, pretty much.'

'We don't want to programme with them,' said another. 'White power.' Then he made a noise that sounded a little like a goose honking. *Skronk!* And then: '707!' – referring, I think, to a Northern California area code. There were some more *skronks!* and some laughter before I carried on.

'In the outside world people tend to rub along. Different races get along, more or less. How come inside it doesn't work like that?'

'For no confusion. So we don't get confused. Between races and stuff. We just stay away from them.'

'We just don't want to live with them,' goose-honk man said.

'Is there someone in charge?'

'No one's going to say that.'

'Why wouldn't anyone say that?'

'Cos then they'll high-profile us and put us in the hole.'

'Are most of you here on parole violations?'

'At least fifty per cent of us are here because of meth. At least the white guys.'

Hovering on the edge of the group was a much younger-looking inmate, slight of build, with his top on. He looked lost. A nineteen-year-old, he explained he hadn't gone to trial yet. He was here for a ninety-day observation, having picked up thirty-one charges related to a robbery. He was looking at a possible thirty-eight years.

'How did you hook up with these guys?' I asked.

'He's white,' one said. 'We take care of our own.'

Talking to the guys, I had the impression of something marginally more benign than you might expect from the term 'prison gang' – a mutual aid society, a family, a club, a support system of a brutal sort in a place in which to be alone was an invitation to be preyed upon. I'd also been pleasantly surprised by their willingness to entertain my questions. It should probably be mentioned that the Barbarian Brotherhood appears to be a very small gang – specific to an area of Northern California – and should not be confused with the far larger and more homicidal Aryan Brotherhood.

I had more questions about how it worked, but before I could ask them yard time was over. Like schoolchildren at the end of playtime, the Barbarian Brotherhood traipsed back to their cells.

A few days later, having come in at the crack of dawn to film inmates getting breakfast, I spied two of the Barbarian Brothers again. I joined them at their table for a bite of prison food.

We were seated in a vast and sonorous hall. It was early enough that it was still cold outside and the inmates all had their shirts on now, pyjama-like, billowy orange tops.

'If you were black and you offered me a bite of that food I couldn't take it,' horseshoe-moustache man said.

'Why?'

'Just part of the rules, man. If you did, you'd get beat up.'

'Who'd beat me up?'

He paused and then said: 'Me.' He laughed. He looked at his fellow gang member, who had tattoos of flayed skin up his neck. 'This guy,' he said.

'You would really do that?'

'Yep. We'd be out to gitcha. We'd tell you not to do it first. Then we'd have to gitcha.'

'How?'

'Probably just mob ya. Like two or three dudes would just attack you.'

'How bad?'

'Till the cops stop 'em.'

'You really mean that?'

'Yep.'

'Why would you do that?'

This seemed to stump horseshoe-moustache man, or possibly he was tired of answering questions.

'Tell him, Nick,' he said to his friend.

'It's just how it is,' Nick said.

We finished our food and I followed the two of them back to their cellblock, each of them carrying their brown-bag lunches. Inmates in general population, as they were, only got yard time twice a week – they would be cell-bound for the whole rest of the day. When I look at the sequence now, what strikes me is the strange contrast – after all the talk of violence and enforcement – of the warm embrace they give each other as they say goodbye and go off to their respective cells.

I met several other gang members during my San Quentin sojourn. All could recite the rules but, when asked for the reasoning behind them, none had much in the way of an explanation. 'Politics,' they would say when pushed. In time I came to my own conclusions: the importance of protection; a clinging to skin privilege in a place where people had so little to hang on to for status; the need to promote order in a world that was on the verge of being a Darwinian free-for-all. It was the brutal prison version of keeping peace.

One of the weirdest examples of the code of gangs came on the last day of filming. We'd been allowed into a yard for inmates in need of protection – mostly gang dropouts, trans inmates, and sex offenders. I spied a skinhead – bald, shirtless, tattooed – whom I'd spoken to once before. I asked why he dropped out.

'It was a situation,' he said. 'They wanted me to stab my cellie, and I only had fifty-nine days left, just because he borrowed a black guy's dominos.'

'Why didn't you do it?' I asked.

'Because my mother was gettin' ready to pass away. And I wanted to get out and I only had fifty-nine days left.'

I had the impression it wasn't so much the principle of stabbing the cellmate that bothered him; he mainly just didn't want to add to his time.

In the end, the clearest statement I got on the place prison gangs occupied came from Playboy Nolan, he of the 'gassing'.

I met up with him again, on a day when he got his yard time. Playboy, it turned out, was also a gang dropout, from an offshoot of Nuestra Familia called Northern Structure. For his protection he was kept away from other inmates, and his outdoor area consisted of a cage resembling a zoo enclosure – a 'walk-alone' – which he was allowed into for a couple of hours once a week. We shot him, awkwardly, through the bars. I asked why he'd dropped out and he gave the stock answer: 'Basically because of the politics. I just don't like being told what to do.'

'There's gang members on the bigger yard right now. If we put you in there right now, what would happen?'

'Oh, there would be conflict. There would be a big, big fight out there. Big melee out there.'

'They'd get you?'

'I'd probably get them first.'

'What do they *do* here?'

'The whole point of being in a gang is to orchestrate unity as one, together. If I need food from someone? My white brother will give it to me. If I need security, back-up? My white brother will give it me. Drugs, they take care of for you. All that kind of stuff.'

Now, having left the gang, Playboy had a target on his back.

'Do you worry when you get out that the gang might still be after you?' I asked.

'The threat is very high. When you drop out your name goes onto a list, called the Bad News List. And those people right there are supposed to be killed . . . It's a list that's written down from every single prison, from every person higher up . . . And the objective of the individuals on the streets is to control the drugs and the money and to kill these certain people.'

'What was it that got you involved in the gang in the first place?'

'My brother for one – he's still affiliated to this day, right? But not only that. Me growing up on the streets, that acceptance feels good, you know? When someone says they love you – "oh right, I love you, I got your back" – it just made you feel good.'

'They haven't got your back any more.'

'Nah, nah, nah, I got my own back. But it's all right though. I be all right, I know that. I been alive this long. Who says I'm not going to live fifty more years?'

The experience of making the San Quentin film landed on me with the force of a revelation, reminding me, in its combination of the strange and the familiar, of a sculpture of the human body with the skin off and the organs on display. The violence, the tribalism, the lust – all of it was in full view, ugly and shocking, and at the same time, if I was honest, redolent of the darker recesses of my own soul. It was a world without hypocrisy, in which the depravity humans are capable of was laid bare, and which, for the same reason, could also surprise you with acts of tenderness, unlikely friendships, and small moments of connection.

Long afterwards, I tried to keep something of San Quentin with me – that sense of having seen through the veil and the knowledge that the restraints of civility are thin and fragile. Most of us will do what we have to when we need to survive.

The film got six million viewers when it went out. It was the most watched documentary of the year anywhere on the BBC. To be fair, I think there was something hopeless on BBC1, so in a sense the figures were altitude-assisted, our version of Bob Beamon's epic long jump in Mexico City in 1968. Like Beamon, we never again came close to that number, setting ourselves up for a sense of failure whenever our ratings came in. Years later, I finally kissed goodbye to the heady heights of six million and accepted the lower slopes of 2 to 2.5 million as our natural home.

The bigger lesson, though, was that we were probably right not to worry overmuch about being funny. Other stories were suddenly possible – stories that looked at the psychology of criminals, the ecology of law-breakers and law-enforcers, their unacknowledged Janus quality as mirrors of each other, the chaos and violence of the agents of the state, and the paradoxical peace-keeping effect of the code of the streets.

Now, with the endorsement of six million and the confidence it brought, we had the licence to explore a darker kind of terrain. Having more or less escaped the shackles of 'weirdness', the production went on the hunt for stories that promised jeopardy and menace.

Chapter 23

# We Want to Burn Him

If this were a documentary I would montage through the next few years. Working with my team, we produced a series of hard-headed programmes in high-crime and high-conflict areas – Philadelphia, Johannesburg, Lagos, the West Bank of Israel/Palestine – that looked at the outlaw code of the streets and the practices of the police, and the way in which they reflect each other. It was Max Weber who defined the state as that institution that has a monopoly of 'legitimate violence'. In a real sense, according to Weber, the government and its enforcers are simply the biggest gang, running a protection racket, which we happen to call taxation. For another perspective, there is the lyric in NWA's 'Sa Prize (Fuck Tha Police – Part 2)' that says, 'Motherfuckers from high-crime areas view the police as a threat and that's some shit you better not forget.'

In amidst all of this, halfway through filming the Philadelphia doc, our family expanded again. In February 2008, at Queen Charlotte's hospital in East Acton, our second son, Fred, arrived via C-section. We took him home a couple of days later. Albert, still not yet two, greeted him with a pile of toys he thought the newborn might enjoy playing with. It was faintly heart-breaking: the knowledge that he had no inkling of how his life was now altered – condemned to getting half of our attention, at most, forever more. The toys seemed an attempt to propitiate an angry, squalling deity. As with so many similar acts, it was in equal measures honourable and utterly futile.

First time round I'd learned certain baby skills, based on a single book, with a theory about replicating the conditions of the womb. It involved tight swaddling, semi-violent rocking and loud shushing. As weird as it sounds, it worked surprisingly well with Albert. But Fred was somehow immune to the technique and found it distressing. I tried swaddling him even tighter, pulling the ends of the blanket practically with my knee on his chest, and rocking more violently.

'I think if I can just tuck this in here—'

'He's a different baby,' Nancy said. 'He likes it if you're just gentle.'

'I'm not getting the swaddle tight enough. The old blanket was better. This one doesn't hold the knot.'

In March, when I re-engaged with work, it was probably a relief for everyone.

By now a directive had come from the empyrean echelons of the BBC. The new, more dangerous stories we were doing required me to go on something called a Hostile Environments Course. I'd heard tell of these courses. They were whispered about in BBC corridors. 'Have you done the Hostile Environments?' The way they said it, it was a little like people who've taken magic mushrooms or bungee-jumped, a feeling that you were in on something, a certain rite of passage requiring reserves of bravery. Another analogy that springs to mind is the Agatha Christie play, *The Mousetrap*. Like *The Mousetrap*, part of the mystery of the Hostile Environments Course was that it entailed a twisty ending that those who'd taken the course were pledged not to reveal.

I had by now done enough years at the BBC to treat diktats about safety and procedure with a certain level of scepticism. One of the discoveries when I first began working in television was the 'risk assessment' form. I remember reading one that said: 'Hazard:

presenter may be doing some driving; Proposed solution: will stick to speed limit and drive carefully.' Undoubtedly they served a purpose some of the time. But a lot of it seemed disconnected from the reality on the ground. Of course we would drive safely. Did we really need to worry about a visit to a lawfully accredited gun range, of which there are thousands operating safely across America? And as to the real possibility of risk: who honestly knew what would happen at the White Supremacist compound or riding around Jackson, Mississippi with a pimp? *Hazard: pimp may attempt to turn me out. Proposed solution: shake my money-maker and stay on that grind until Daddy is happy.*

The Hostile Environments Course took place in April 2008. The closest thing I can compare it to is a school trip or possibly a not-that-fun stag do. There were fifteen or twenty of us – BBC staff from all over the organization, news reporters, fixers on foreign bureaux, World Service producers – bunking up for two or three nights in an annex on the grounds of a shabby old stately home somewhere outside London. In charge of the course were two ex-army instructors, one specializing in security and danger; the other covering medical know-how. The days were divided between classwork – reminiscent of school, with whiteboards and group discussions – and field exercises. One outing involved using a twig to pick your way out of a minefield, another navigating around the grounds with a compass and an Ordnance Survey map. There was also quite a lot of running into darkened rooms, finding badly injured plastic dummies and shouting: 'He doesn't look good. I'm checking airways! I'm putting him in a recovery position. Panda eyes! Elevate his leg!' The instructors had little pumps that squirted blood from the dummies' arms and legs. 'Oh! Nasty! Tourniquet that!'

The medical stuff was useful. The war zone stuff was less *immediately* relevant for me – not many mines or Ordnance Survey maps in Philadelphia. Very occasionally I had the sense the instructors might prefer it if we didn't make any programmes on location but stayed in our hotel rooms, memorizing our acronyms. But I am being a little unfair, and in fact in subsequent years – after doing stories in Lagos and the West Bank – I had cause to think back to what I'd learned and find it helpful.

Probably the most memorable bit of instruction had to do with dealing with roadblocks: that you should resist the urge to be overly accommodating; don't roll down your window unless asked, and even then only a crack. If possible don't let them into your car. Present polite resistance at every stage. It sounded in some ways counterintuitive: I had always made it a habit to placate and appease police. Yes, officer. No officer. I'm so sorry, officer. But in fact every act of power involves a kind of negotiation. By giving a little, you are inviting more trespasses, putting yourself in more danger.

It occurred to me that the roadblock and the car was a metaphor for power in general: how bullies and predators depend on us to cede authority to them, and that those without power should never forget how much it is still up to us to fight back, to not give in. In the words of the French philosopher Jean Baudrillard, 'Power is a seduction.' Even violent force depends on a kind of giving-in. (I can't find that quote on Google, which means I may have made it up. However, it is true.)

The last day of the course – a kind of grand finale – took place a couple of weeks later. It was an ambitious, fully realized role-play event in a fictitious country with its own currency and a made-up recent history. There were rebels and government forces and we were issued little cameras. The idea was to get in and do some reporting, record a piece to camera and get out. In childhood, I'd played a little Dungeons & Dragons and had an unfulfilled yen to do LARPing – Live Action Role Play – as a knight with a foam sword going round a castle, with people dressed as orcs lying in wait. The last day of the Hostile Environments Course was the closest I ever came to this dream.

The event required quite a bit of staging and support personnel.

Some of the extras were local soldiers for whom, I can only imagine, the whole exercise was a welcome change of routine. At least one or two had gone method in their approach to the performance: smelling of booze and shouting in an authentically deranged way: 'Wind your fucking window down and show me your papers! You're in the Republic of Raristan and we don't take any shit, all right?'

The final exercise involved being pulled over at a roadblock, bundled out, and having sacks put over our heads. This – being taken as a hostage – was the *Mousetrap* twist. The act of being blinded and frogmarched and shouted at, though you knew it to be fake, was surprisingly disconcerting. You had to stumble a little way from the vehicle then, with the sack removed, try to plead for your life. The lesson, I recall, was to not stop talking, don't look away or submit, maintain eye contact, keep being a human to your captors and not someone ready for death. 'I have children waiting for me. Their mother is dead. They depend on me. I have a picture in my wallet – please! Do you have any children?' and so on. When my time came, and the trainer raised his gun, it miraculously jammed and I made a run for it.

My most abiding recollection of the experience was the input from some of the BBC fixers and producers from far-flung places who'd already faced extreme hazard while reporting on wars in the field. Towards the end of a field exercise, one producer from the Middle East or North Africa asked with touching sincerity for advice on how to triage the casualties in a car after a serious crash. 'Because one time, after our vehicle was blown up in Libya, we didn't know which one to help first,' he said, 'and one of my colleagues died from bleeding.'

A couple of weeks after finishing the course, with our newborn, Fred, now if not exactly pitching in around the house then at least being somewhat more manageable – not in reality, but certainly in my own febrile self-justifications – I flew back to Philadelphia for two weeks to finish that programme, and then to Johannesburg for a couple of weeks for a new project about vigilantes and private security.

I look back at emails from that time and marvel at what Nancy had on her hands. Her messages are mainly short expressions of regret that she shouted at me on the phone or that she is tired and that Fred still isn't sleeping through. Mine are long diaristic accounts of how the day has gone, apologies for not being around more, and lamentations that we aren't getting much in the can.

The idea with the Johannesburg film had been to do a companion piece to the Philadelphia doc and to put them out as a two-parter. All we needed was to get access to the police. Alas, the BBC had burned its bridges with the Joburg police department, after running a scorching piece several years earlier that depicted its cops as violent and out of control. For lack of other options, we began thinking about a doc that looked at the burgeoning world of private security and the way it intersected with crime. I'd read accounts of home invasions of almost unimaginable brutality taking place in the suburbs. The private security firms were – apparently – taking up the slack from a police force that was outmanned and outgunned by the criminals.

And there were other leads: I'd seen a short Channel 4 piece about a grassroots vigilante group called Mapogo. In one of the scenes, a Mapogo official whipped a 'suspect', apparently unperturbed by the presence of a camera, bizarrely describing the punishment as 'medicine'.

Then, a few days before we were due to fly, a spate of xenophobic violence convulsed South Africa. The disparity of income in the country was higher than it had been under the apartheid regime. Up to thirty per cent of people of working age were unemployed and many locals viewed immigrants from neighbouring nations like Zimbabwe and Malawi as interlopers who were taking their jobs and driving down wages. It was reported that angry mobs would corner those suspected of being foreign. Sometimes they'd ask them to pronounce certain words – the Zulu words for 'elbow' and 'buttonhole' – knowing it would betray a non-native speaker. Or they based their assessments on hairstyle or vaccination marks. Those identified as outsiders might be beaten up or burned to death.

I was at the airport waiting to fly when my brother called: 'The riots are all over the news!' he said. 'You're in the catbird seat! You're in pole position! It's the Hamiltons Part 2.'

His enthusiasm was so over-the-top, I was pretty sure it was insincere and that he was attempting to put some kind of hex on me. If so, it worked. Danger levels in South Africa were so elevated that it was virtually impossible to get into the townships to do any filming. Locals resented all the disapproving coverage. They viewed media as the enemy and were liable to turn on them.

We whiled away the days filming with security firms in largely white areas doing the rounds of houses and shops. This was singularly unproductive. No calls came in. 'I don't understand it,' the guards kept saying. 'It's usually non-stop. You should have been here last month.'

After a week or so, the threat level in the townships dipped somewhat. We got the go-ahead to film and the BBC risk team assigned us a security detail of a couple of burly Afrikaners who looked like the physical incarnation of the old Apartheid regime and who, in addition, spoke no black African languages. Rather than protection, it seemed likely our Boer bodyguards would make us more of a target. There was an abortive attempt to film a walkabout and interview in a vast and volatile township-cum-shanty town north of Johannesburg called Diepsloot. We passed a shebeen. The drinkers became excited seeing a crew, and surrounded us. They seemed mainly happy, though amid the shouting and jostling it was hard to be certain. 'We've got to get out of here,' said the guards. 'Evacuate! Evacuate!' Afterwards none of us was sure whether we'd just had a narrow escape or had massively overreacted to a bit of high-spirited bonhomie.

By the end of the shoot, the only scene of any power we'd managed to capture was with the Mapogo vigilante, William. He'd arrived for a pre-arranged interview at his offices with a badly beaten 'suspect' in the back of his vehicle. It was shocking and upsetting. The man was bloodstained, his expression impossible to read. I asked our local fixer, Sidney, to try to speak to him but he refused to talk.

'This is the medicine,' William said, waggling a long leathery stick called a sjambok.

The whole situation – the casual, on-camera acknowledgement of corporal punishment; the bloodied man – was bizarre and seemed to bespeak a world in which death, violence, and injury were all part of the daily currency of life.

Still, for ten days' work it was thin pickings. Back in the office in England, we went through the rushes with a funereal sense of gloom. The main takeaway was that we were unlikely to find our story in the suburbs and needed to take a different approach. No more Afrikaner security guards. Instead, we would ask Sidney to help organize protection using men who spoke at least two or three of South Africa's black languages. Sidney was a consummate connector: he could speak to anyone, gathering intelligence and building trust. We hoped that with his help we would be able to get into the life of the townships in a deeper way, defusing situations simply by talking and letting residents know we were there to tell their story.

We returned. It was still slow going but little by little the scenes accumulated and a picture emerged of a world, in the townships and squatter camps, where mob justice was endemic. Despairing of being helped by the police, townspeople would round up suspected rapists and robbers, corner them, truss them and burn or stone them to death. 'People are killed like chickens,' a community volunteer called Walter told me. Another man recounted being shot and the police doing nothing about it. With a rueful air, he added: 'Even myself, if they say, "This one is a robber," I can assist to kill.' To my knowledge, the story of mob justice in the townships hadn't been told before and I felt proud that we were bringing it to light, in all its strangeness and cruelty.

The most surprising moment of filming – and eventual climax of our documentary – came late in the shoot when, one morning, a call came in from William, the Mapogo vigilante who dispensed 'medicine.' He was, he said, at that moment, in Diepsloot, cornered by an angry mob of local people grown sick of his practice of physically assaulting men in his custody. He thought they might be about to kill him and was hoping we might help.

We drove to Diepsloot, arriving to find an unruly gathering of local residents on a dirt road with rough corrugated shacks on either side. Sidney advised us to hang back while he went to speak to the crowd. Within a few minutes he returned, looking concerned.

'William is in trouble,' he said. He described how William and a co-worker had apprehended a supposed suspect in the area, detaining him inside a van. 'While they were trying to drive out, the community turned against William.'

Sidney said he'd talked to the people in the crowd, reassuring them we were there to document but not to critique. He felt confident we were OK to film. But he added: 'When we go in, you mustn't mention William's name as if we know him. They will turn against us.'

We walked up the road to where the crowd was gathered – a hundred or so. There was shouting, and William came into view, standing next to a police van, looking terrified. A couple of officers, in blue caps and jackets, carrying rifles, were attempting to marshal the crowd to no discernible effect. People dressed in t-shirts and dusty trousers and woolly hats were blowing whistles, and in among them was a man holding a rope that seemed intended for trussing William.

At the forefront of the mob was a young woman.

I asked her: 'You're saying this guy, William, beat someone up that you know?'

'Yes, he beat Donald Lekgwati. Because this guy, this William, says he's going to burn him. Truly speaking. William told us that he's going to burn Donald Lekgwati. So we can't allow him to burn Donald Lekgwati.'

William was bustled into the police vehicle, protesting his innocence in the affair at hand. 'I can't use my hands on him,' he said.

Turning back to the young woman and Sidney, I asked: 'What do they want to do to William?'

With a wry smile, Sidney said, 'They want to kill William.'

'Yes,' the young woman agreed.

'They want to burn him,' Sidney said.

'Yes, we want to burn him. Because he told us he is going to burn that Donald Lekgwati.'

It was an extraordinary scene: the surreal juxtaposition of people who came across as personable and thoughtful, expressing in a matter-of-fact way a desire to burn a fellow human being to death. It was also a testament to Sidney's soft diplomacy, his ability to reassure and placate and negotiate. In the high-risk theatre of the mob it was a thousand times more useful than a phalanx of bodyguards.

The phase of work in which our main output of stories was of a slightly more dangerous stripe – 'pushing the jeopardy button,' I used to call it – lasted a couple of years. A documentary about meth users in Fresno followed. It sticks in my mind as one of the only times I was forced to make four separate filming trips over the course of many months to get what we needed. Unlike the prison, where everyone is bored and already convicted, the streets were much harder to get into, and less safe. It was inordinately hard to film someone actually smoking or injecting meth, and over the whole endeavour hung the unwelcome spectre of the *Brass Eye* drugs special – when oh when were we going to find someone out of their gourd on Yellow Bentines or Clarky Cat?

We shot a film about gangstas and hoodlums in Lagos – two trips of two weeks each, two weeks being the deal I'd made with

Nancy for the longest allowable filming trip. The Lagos film was memorable because our climactic scene – the result of an election that we were fairly sure would lead to unrest – coincided with a family holiday in France: a villa had been rented somewhere near a town called Verdun-sur-Garonne, where, apparently, the 'Theroux' clan originally came from, before they migrated to Quebec. Nancy, the kids, my brother and his family were all coming; my dad had flown over, which was unprecedented. He rarely came to Europe, and never for holidays, but he was enticed by the idea of a road trip to the ancestral spawning grounds. But I bailed on the holiday to film in Nigeria, which went down in the family ledger – a metaphorical accounts book in Nancy's brain largely dedicated to my domestic failures and unkept promises, times I left outings early, missed parties – as The Time Louis Didn't Come On A Family Holiday.

Then, during the unrest, which took the form of a ragtag procession of 'area boys' – local youth – jogging along in a loose-knit and motley street procession, at least one or two of them armed with broken bottles and dripping blood, at the point it was decided we had what we needed and should clear the area, the director Jason and I managed to forget our AP, Guy King, leaving him amid the melee as we bundled into a waiting vehicle.

All these programmes had their merits. I began to think of myself as making good on the awards and visibility I'd won too easily in former years – I was earning out the advance of my early promise. More importantly, our working practices at last felt sustainable: we were back to making shows in a way that was enjoyable and offered something different in the TV landscape. Having let go of comedy as a dominant flavour, the stories flowed steadily. I began to see that there was nothing so dark that we couldn't handle it, and with each outing we edged a little further into more difficult material. 'Go dark but cast it light,' I would say. You know you've attained some higher grade of knob-hood when you have your own little professional mantras that you repeat to your co-workers. It meant, choose stories whose themes are filled with the possibility of misery and angst, but make sure your contributors are sympathetic and open.

Another thought experiment I sometimes found helpful was whether I could imagine a given subject being featured in a reality format. If yes, then it was a sign it didn't have enough of a knotty or dubious dimension: drugs, crime, serious mental illness. You weren't likely to see them in a programme devised by Endemol involving sexy guys with six packs and ladies in bikinis. I tried to dodge the ever-present threat of obsolescence by taking on topics that were just too weird and questionable to be treated in 'normal' TV.

I kept venturing gingerly forward. Well, we did that. Can we do *this*?

## Chapter 24

# This Is What I Do

A friend once told me she thought the problem with working in television is that it's too much fun, with the result that it makes relationships unstable. The TV widows and widowers – the ones left behind to do childcare and cope with tantrums and keep on top of laundry – can't help resenting their other halves off filming in far-flung locations, with buffet breakfasts and heated swimming pools. Early on, Nancy and I developed a few rules we tried to stick to in an attempt to ease the pain a little: I wouldn't go away for more than two weeks at a time; I tried to call every day; almost without fail I would write a longish email home. But it wasn't easy.

Since Nancy and I had met at the BBC, it wasn't as though my being a programme-maker came as a surprise. Still, as time went on, and our commitments – also known as 'children' – multiplied, she made it clear she had an issue with me going away as much as I did. More than once she said, a little ruefully, 'I always promised myself I wouldn't get involved with someone in TV. I've seen it fail too many times. Husbands and wives spending too long apart. Directors having affairs with their APs . . . It never works.'

Like many couples, we fell into familiar patterns in our arguing. They were like songs – duets – without the music. Many centred on the idea that, unlike her, I had made no real concessions to family life. I was still going away, still doing the same job, as if nothing had changed.

'I've sacrificed my career and changed my life but you've given up *nothing*,' she would say. 'You've had everything your way. Name one thing you've given up!'

'Not true. I leave work early. I'm never back after six. I'm usually the first one to leave the office.'

'Your workmates don't have kids, Louis. *You do.*'

'I've made lots of compromises.'

'Name one!'

In the background to these arguments were certain phrases that I discovered, to my cost, I wasn't supposed to say. But inevitably I would say them, because – to my mind – they were self-evidently true and important. One was: 'But this is what I *do*, Nancy.' There were other variations of this that were equally inflammatory. 'I was doing this when we met.' 'You knew what you were getting into.' And so on. They never failed to increase the tensions.

'What was I doing when we met? *I was making programmes, too.* I wasn't sweeping up bits of rice from under the table. "This is what I do." *Change* what you do! Do something else. It's not part of who you are. It's bullshit.'

Another phrase was: 'Why don't we get more help?'

'Get help – so you can *not be a dad*? It's not about "help", Louis. It's about you being a father to your children.'

I suppose we all bring into our relationships certain assumptions based on how our parents were. I'd grown up with au pairs who'd lived with us in our house. Both my parents had worked. My dad had travelled for weeks at a time. The way I rationalized it, I wasn't expecting Nancy to stay at home. I didn't have an issue with her travelling for work – though as it happened, she didn't travel for work as she had taken a break from full-time paid employment to be around for the kids. Still, I wasn't expecting anything from her that I wasn't also prepared to give. And so, to my mind, it was all equitable and fair.

Given the limitations I was working within – the fact of having commissions and needing to make programmes and suffering from the human frailty of only being in one place at one time – I did my best to keep my end up on the home front. I didn't 'help' at home, since that was another trigger word. 'I *help!*' Help implied you were supplemental. 'You do it and I'll help.' 'Wow, that's amazing, you're *helping* with *your* kids. Has it ever occurred to you that might be *your job?*'

One part of me – a nasty little voice in my head – would say, *So work is a luxury now. I'm selfish because I work. What happened to, 'He's a good provider'? I'm supposed to count myself lucky that I'm allowed to keep doing a job.*

Sometimes I would look enviously around at other couples and how much licence they gave each other, how much they could get away with – long hours, frequent trips, self-indulgent hobbies. *Golf? Rock climbing? Whaaaat?* For a while, my brother and I got into an unhealthy habit, whenever we were together with our families, of needling and picking at each other's supposed masculine entitlement. 'Ooh, doesn't do the school run! Did you hear that, Nancy? And how long were you away on your boys' walking weekend?' It was a little like some kind of grotesque metro-sexual update of the Four Yorkshireman sketch. 'You got up for four feeds in one night? *Looxury!*'

In arguments with Nancy, I tried not to cite examples of the latitude other male partners seemed to enjoy, since that never ended well.

'Jim and Joan have au pairs. Jim just got back from a two-month shoot in Tibet.'

'Maybe if you talked to *Joan* you'd know their marriage is in *serious* trouble.'

Before I went away I used to make batches of kedgeree and

bolognese and spoon them into little Tupperware tubs for freezing. Sometimes, on location, I would do an online Sainsbury's shop. When I flew back – more often than not on an overnight economy flight, landing exhausted and jetlagged – I'd be aware of the need to hit the ground running. I'd walk in with my bags, feeling like a zombie. Nancy would be tired and resentful. She'd have got into her own routines while I was away. I was an interloper and an encumbrance.

'You seem grumpy,' she'd say. 'Aren't you happy to be home?'

'No, I am happy, I'm just tired.' My little voice would be saying, can't I have a lie-down? 'I might have a little lie-down. I'm just so tired.'

'I've been looking after a baby and a toddler on my own for two weeks! But you're the one that's tired, OK, sure!'

'It's jetlag. It's different.'

'You just have no idea, do you? I make everything so easy for you. You have it all your way. You get to carry on doing what you do. I haven't had a night away from my kids in three years. You've never even done a weekend on your own with the kids!'

'Book a break! Take a week off! I would *love* you to. You've got an open offer! Just do it!'

In certain respects, we communicated better when I was away. Without the distractions of children, and with the imposed calm of distance and the interface of the written word, she would express her frustrations at the life she found herself backed into.

'I'm really lonely, Louis.' 'I feel I'm basically being a single parent.' 'I'm in half a relationship.'

For my part, I toggled between viewing myself as being unfairly victimized and put upon for making a living and – on the other hand – seeing Nancy's side and wanting to do my best to support her and not wanting to be the stereotype of the guy whose wife is angry with him all the time. As was so often the case, my brain was a parliament of fractious voices. There was the one saying, *Why can't*

*I retire to a man-cave and organize my collection of jam jars with screws and nails in them, and then emerge later to have wordless sex with my wife? Is that so unreasonable?* And, across the aisle, there was the honourable representative for Progressive South who found Jam-Jar Man revolting and retrograde. *What is your problem that you couldn't imagine being a house-husband and even find the phrase 'house-husband' a bit weird?* I found certain clichés of masculinity creeping into my thinking. It was like Bernard Manning turning up at the house wearing my dressing gown and slippers. What are *you* doing here? *Go away!* That couldn't be me. I was cool feminist guy. I was the guy who was *fine* with his girlfriend not shaving her armpits at university. I wasn't the guy who complained about his wife to his mates in the pub and wondered whether there might be ancient wisdom in sexist jokes.

Making it all the more complicated was a weird kind of ambivalence about myself. In the spirit of Groucho Marx, I had never been completely OK with the idea of someone being in love with me. It seemed a character flaw in them. In turn this led me, ever so slightly, to undervalue Nancy for being with me.

This was – in an unacknowledged way – lurking in the background of everything: the sense that if I was more committed, if I'd actually proposed all those years ago, somehow that would ameliorate everything. It was the double whammy of *travels a lot* and *never even asked me to marry him.*

I liked to think my resistance to being married was part of a bohemian attitude to do with the fatuity of weddings, their role as platforms for materialism and showing off, as bourgeois status showdowns. Possibly too some buried anger at my own parents and their marriage vows, which were – as they say – more honoured in the breach than the observance. But if I'm honest with myself, I also see a deliberate withholding, a misjudged sense that it might keep Nancy on her toes and possibly also, in a spirit related to my attitude to contracts, that it gave you some leverage if you didn't sign anything, that it wasn't all quite official, and you could walk off the job if it wasn't working out.

None of this was clear or consistent in my own mind. I loved Nancy. I loved my family. I wanted everything to work out. But other darker ideas and impulses hidden from me were moshing around alongside the healthier ones. And all the time the stress of children and work and daily life and feeling the impossible pull in different directions, of having to be around, of having to go away, bubbled up as the passive-aggressive anger of not quite being present.

Alongside these arguments – which were going on intermittently in the background of our lives for several years – was a sense at work that we were in danger of running out of road. One night, after the kids were in bed, I sat down with Nancy in our front room to watch a DVD of a rough cut of our programme about meth use in Fresno. Twenty minutes in, she said, 'That's the first time you've smiled.'

I didn't think too much of it. At the end she gave a few notes – she is a perceptive critic and a hard marker – and then said, 'I just think you should do what you are good at. There are plenty of reporters who can go to dangerous places. Your skill is building relationships.'

It may be that it took a while for the weight of what she'd said to sink in. Or that I was lacking other options. But the comment stayed with me – a sense that, in pursuing harder-edged stories, I was also in danger of losing something, that something needed to change, without quite knowing what or how.

In the spring of 2010, I turned forty. Our children were now two and four. We were getting a little more *help* on the home front. We'd recruited a childminder who came two or three days a week. Nancy had bounced back. She'd lost her 'baby weight'. She had a new job. An ineffable sparkle and lightness had returned to her.

For my birthday, we'd invited the wider family – uncles, aunts, in-laws – around to our house for a big lunch. It was hot. Nancy had bought six or eight wooden lawn chairs, flat-packed in cardboard boxes, which I started to assemble in the back garden. There were the other usual chores to do with hosting a large number of guests – moving tables around, tidying, running up and downstairs. Nancy had gone into her getting-tense-because-guests-are-coming mode. *Have you peeled the carrots? I thought I told you to get the houmous that has caramelized onions in it?* 'I'm just doing the chairs.'

I began feeling put upon. I was three or four chairs in, the sun was beating down, and I began wondering whose idea this party had been. Had I actually wanted a family party for my fortieth birthday? Had Nancy asked me or had she just decided that was what we were doing?

Time and my own sense of shame have obscured the details of the argument that followed. I shouted and she left. The party-goers arrived, Nancy returned, and if the photos are anything to go by, everyone had fun, reposing upon the chairs I had only recently put together, finding them adequately supportive and solidly con-structed. In the subsequent days and weeks I didn't think much more of the argument, but much later Nancy told me that was the moment she detached.

I should have known something was up when Nancy was com-plaining less than usual about my going away. For some reason, she was surprisingly relaxed about the two two-week trips to Israel to film in the Occupied Territories. Then the real warning sign, which completely went over my head, was her saying, 'You know, if you ever want to pursue an outside physical relationship, I would be OK with that.'

I thought, 'Well, that's nice.' Needless to say, I didn't do anything about it.

During a minibreak at a London hotel for her birthday – a posh restaurant, cocktails, a hotel dressing gown personalized with her name on it (yep, it was pretty classy) – she mentioned that she had had thoughts about other men. The way I saw it, the only odd thing about this was that she was telling me. If I were accountable for every passing thought I had, I'd be in deep trouble. The point was that you didn't endorse those thoughts. You let them drift away like balloons. What you *didn't* do was gather them together and present them to your boyfriend like a bouquet.

I'm not sure what I said in reply, but it may have been, 'Have you seen the dressing gown? It has your name sewn into the back.'

Chapter 25

## Look on the Dark Side

I took the step that felt as though it changed everything – bringing the possibility of a way of working that was, for me, unprecedented, and opening up new frontiers of programme-making – in 2011.

We'd made a series of programmes – about kids on psychoactive medication, Miami Jail, and Americans who keep tigers and chimpanzees as pets – and we were once again casting around for ideas.

A book called *Leisureville* had come out, an immersive piece of reportage about life at a vast retirement community in Florida. With extensions in people's age, many American elderly were now leading a kind of second adolescence, filled with sex, video games, and drugs. I wondered if it might be an idea for us. I persuaded myself it would be a welcome return to a lighter, funnier style of story, though I also worried it was too soft, that there wasn't enough to get my teeth into. We discussed including people suffering with Alzheimer's and dementia, to give it more weight. But that seemed a bit of a mismatch of material, and from there we drifted towards thinking about a show exclusively about Alzheimer's and dementia.

We ordered up a few programmes from the BBC archives. They were rather off-putting. One of them, an experimental documentary made in the eighties, featured a mixture of real dementia patients and carers who were played by actors and who *sang songs* about their work. 'It's been three weeks since he recognized his wife / what a life!' (That's not an actual quote since the usually dependable Google Video search has failed me on this occasion, but take my word for it, it was pretty odd.) Others were dull-but-worthy exposés about UK facilities where the residents didn't get enough activities and the staff had to pay for their own toast. My series producer, Emma Cooper, having watched a couple of these, began having misgivings about the whole idea and sent me an email saying, 'It better be more than Louis taking Doris to the loo.'

And then there was a deeper question, one that brought the project into doubt on a more fundamental level. My exec, Nick, raised it early on. Who exactly was doing anything questionable? Who was I going up against? It was the first time in my entire career of making programmes that I had taken a subject in which potentially no one would be doing anything the least bit ill-advised or wrong-headed or silly. I thought about this and realized it could be a serious stumbling block. For as long as I'd worked in television – going back to *TV Nation* days – I had looked for stories in which I was in some small way arrayed *against* someone. Who was that here? For a while I tried to persuade myself that there was a background question to do with the medical establishment making people live too long, warehoused in care homes. But even I wasn't quite sure whether I believed it.

Still, we needed to make something and I hoped that, despite the absence of a broader question of injustice or strangeness, there might be a story in the set of dilemmas faced by the loved ones of the family members with dementia: what were one's responsibilities to someone whose personality was dissolving? A wife who no longer recognized you and was pursuing relationships with other people? A parent who was becoming a liability – getting drunk, taking the car, becoming physically violent – but who didn't wish to be locked up?

What were one's duties to a parent who was seemingly incapable of any thought, expression, or recognition?

That was the idea. But I think we were all aware that we were venturing into new terrain.

It was agreed that we needed a residential facility where we could do the bulk of our filming while making sorties out to pick up other dementia-affected characters if needed. Given the bleakness of the condition itself, the brief became finding a positive supportive environment that would relieve some of the grimness of the subject and possibly teach us something about the newest best practice when dealing with those with dementia.

An AP, Gavin Whitehead, who'd recently come off the show *Top Gear*, did the research. Bit of a change of pace but it's still basically elderly people and wheels, I suppose. We settled on a place in Phoenix, Arizona, called Beatitudes. Gavin and a director called Dan Child went out and shot some recce tape, which we watched in the office. There were still some questions about how interesting it all was. When projects are slow, I am sometimes paralysed by the thought that we are, as a production, nominally free to pursue *any idea in the world*, and yet we ended up *here, looking at tape of old people with Alzheimer's drifting around in grey corridors*. But there was also a subtle poetic dimension, to do with the sadness of life's final stage. Recalling the myths of the ancient world, I was struck by the similarities between dementia and the waters of the river Lethe, in Hades, which, it was said, when drunk would cause the souls of the dead to forget their lives on earth.

One contributor jumped out, a dentist in his sixties, known to everyone as Dr Gary. Dr Gary was affable and funny and, depending on the fluctuations of his condition, believed himself to be living at an army base thirty or forty years in the past. He had a wife called Carla, some ten or fifteen years his junior, who still lived in the family home. But Gary no longer remembered being married.

He recognized Carla only as a friend and junior colleague – and he was in relationships with a couple of other women at the facility.

The film ended up centring on the strange world of Dr Gary.

'This is my workplace,' he told me the first time we met.

'Doing?'

'Dentistry or working on something dental. Whatever they put me to. I don't care. It's not really a medical building . . . But here we are. I don't ever leave it. It's kind of strange that way.'

His situation was at once fascinating, bleak, and also in its way heart-warming. He clearly enjoyed having a camera crew around. He liked making jokes and passing on esoteric bits of information. He was, most of the time, content to be berthed at the vague military base he imagined he was at, wandering the corridors, doing quizzes, the object of the many ladies' attentions. For a while he'd been stressed out about not having a wallet – he thought he must have lost it – so staff had equipped him with a dummy wallet, a prop with meaningless cards inside. He was living a curated reality in a benign matrix.

Sometimes, of an evening, he would experience the confusion and distress known in the world of Alzheimer's as 'sundowning'. He'd pack his bags and announce it was time he was moving on to his next posting, or he'd hover around the emergency exits, expressing a desire to leave. At these times, he would need 'redirecting'. The commonest way was to tell him your teeth were bothering you and ask for a quick check-up. This would distract him and soon the urge to leave would be forgotten.

I tried this one time when I noticed him loitering by an emergency door.

'"Push until alarm sounds",' he said, reading from a notice on the door. '"Door can be open fifteen seconds".' Then, with a tone of perplexity – his hands out palm up, expressing incomprehension, he added, 'That's a siren going for fifteen seconds. *You can't use that!*

That's ridiculous! What can I do?' He looked at the camera now for help. 'I'm screwed.'

'Someone told me you used to be a dentist,' I said. 'Would you take a quick look at my teeth? They're not very clean, though.'

'Well, you're a Brit, aren'tcha? You guys don't clean your teeth like we do. Bite down. You've got good occlusion. Cross-bite back there. I wouldn't do anything about it cos it's not going to hurt you now.'

And he was away.

The first week of filming seemed to go well enough. We flew back to look at what we had shot, and it was in watching the rushes with the rest of the team that I got a queasy feeling.

Some of the material with the dementia patients was somehow not quite right. It was a finely judged thing. When I asked questions like 'How are you?' 'How do you like it here?' 'I understand you've been having some memory issues?' it felt OK. But any question that appeared designed to elicit frailty felt very wrong. Anytime a resident's loved one or close carer was not present, the conversations could also feel problematic. But conversely, when a loved one *was* around, and when the dementia sufferer was part of a three-way conversation, with the vulnerable affected person included, the conversations were enjoyable and natural, and the foibles and funny phrases became part of a genial and warm expression of fellow-feeling. One was licensed to laugh and find them funny, which in turn created a sense of release, all the tension that went with the sadness of the affliction and the sense of embarrassment of not knowing how to talk about it was dissipated and replaced with a wonderful feeling of connection.

This became a rule of thumb in later years when doing stories involving people with disabilities: to always include the affected party in the conversation – even if it's a person in a coma or in a non-responsive state to attempt to make contact with them – and in general always to be aware of who is in the room and has a stake in whatever is being discussed, especially when it's someone who might be overlooked: children, the vulnerable, even animals.

The most touching encounter I had at that time was with a couple named John and Nancy Vaughan. They were ninety and eighty-nine years old respectively. They'd been married sixty-odd years, and in old photos they came across as a glamorous pair, a little like movie stars. Both were still healthy in body but, while John was mentally present and correct, Nancy had profound symptoms of dementia. Without children, it had fallen to John to be Nancy's main carer, a task as physically demanding as it was emotionally wearing.

Their house backed on to a golf course and the road was lined with cactuses and succulents instead of the usual lawns and trees. John came to the door wearing a nametag, a reminder for Nancy. He ushered me into the front room to meet Nancy. She looked me up and down and gave me a little tap.

'You're beautiful,' she said.

'Thank you,' I replied. 'So are you.'

'Ah! We're beautiful and beautiful.'

In the kitchen, we talked some more. Nancy was charming and friendly, playing host, using intonations and inflection that were appropriate. But her words were a different matter. They came and went or were half-made-up. When John asked her her first name, she struggled to recall it. Asked her second name, instead of the correct one, 'Johnson,' she said a little uncertainly, 'Bread.'

The overall effect was of someone being present, enacting forms and rituals in a way I recognized and that felt honest and warm, but that was also, in a way, illusory, and it was hard to tell how much I was projecting onto her of what I imagined she might mean.

Having, as I saw it, hit it off with John and Nancy, on our second trip we arranged that I should spend an afternoon with Nancy on her own. She was a feisty character who didn't hesitate to show her impatience with me, and my own feeling was that it was here – in being one-to-one with an unpredictable albeit charming and likeable dementia sufferer – that I would be tested. This was me, in a sense, 'going up against' someone, being challenged and experiencing the central dilemma of our story – the complexity of personal relationships with a dementia sufferer – at first-hand.

It was also, I should add, part of a solution to a problem of storytelling. Our documentary needed progression. In other stories, I had followed the ups and downs of my contributors, their dynamic trajectories, while also deepening my own journey, getting closer, understanding more, challenging more assertively. With dementia, the illness only goes in one direction, downward, at various inclines. So the afternoon with Nancy was also a helpful destination for the film, a moment of climactic participation, in a third act that otherwise threatened to be uneventful and dispiriting.

John had invited me to take over. For him, he said, it would be a welcome break, and also a valuable illustration of what he was up against. His break was semi-fictional in that we had arranged that he would be on stand-by in a back room in case Nancy needed the bathroom. In the event the day passed relatively peacefully. Nancy and I went for walk and got about twenty yards outside the house when she told me she'd had enough and wanted to go back. I made lunch but Nancy seemed to forget how to eat. Then she forgot who I was and what I was doing there, though without it causing her any distress. I tried to put some music on, grappling with a stereo on all fours on the floor. 'What are you doing down *there*?' she enquired with a little impatience. Then we looked at old albums of photographs in the front room and she fell asleep leaning on my shoulder.

I took an elegiac pleasure in her company and her contentedness. She was still beautiful, still kind and self-possessed, still present, while also being reduced, hollowed out, like a grand old hotel that had seen better days. The satisfaction she still took in life was evident.

When John returned I thanked him and told him and Nancy how much I had enjoyed the afternoon.

'How much of Nancy is still here?' I asked.

'Thirty per cent,' he said. 'But all of it is still in here.' He pointed at his own head. 'My memories of a great sixty-one years and an oath that said we were going to be with each other until death do us part. And it hasn't parted us yet.'

It seemed an almost philosophical question about quality of life. I'd heard people assert their preference for death over the addled existence created by advanced dementia. Later I would make a film about assisted suicide in which a contributor expressed his firm conviction he would prefer to be dead than alive with dementia. But I also wondered: by what right does a person claim to make decisions for a future self, a self who may have their own ideas about dignity and quality of life?

On an upper floor of Beatitudes was a residential area for those with the most advanced dementia. One woman, sixty or so years old, would wander the hallways uttering a continuous stream of noise that sounded like 'gulla-gulla-gulla-gulla-gulla'. Once a week, her son would visit. He'd follow her and circle around her, eliciting no recognition. We filmed as he waved photographs of her younger days, trying to register some small moment of reaction. There was nothing, or next to nothing.

'My sisters don't come any more,' he said. 'Because this is hard.'

He described a mother who had been a nurse, a caring person but also a worrier, self-conscious, assailed with self-doubt. In this telling, his mother's dementia – her slow departure – had also, in certain respects, been a release, mitigating her cares and anxieties. And then, as he was saying this, his mother paused, took his face in her hands and rested her eyes on him for a moment.

'And that's why I come,' he said. 'Because sometimes that happens.'

• • •

It would be hard to overstate how much of a sense of release it was, making a film that was engaging and funny and entertaining and which at the same time featured only good-hearted people doing their best in difficult situations. It felt like I'd arrived after a long circuitous odyssey at a place I never quite dared to dream existed. Imagine: a film you could show contributors and not worry over-much about their reaction. Films that were filled with strangeness, awkwardness, awfulness, distress, nightmarishness, but which were basically supportive of their contributors, sympathetic to their situations, on side with them in seeing the unfairness of what they were having to endure. Not that I imagined it was the only way I would work from now on, but it seemed to open up new seams, new possibilities, story ideas I'd nursed for years but never imagined I might be able to actually do.

Not long after we finished the dementia film, we started one on autistic children and their families. I'd heard a documentary on Radio 4 called 'Letting Go of James' about a family with several children, one of whom – the eponymous James – was autistic, non-verbal and prone to physical assaults on those closest to him. The documentary followed the ups and downs of the family as they came to the decision to put James into a full-time residential facility – the heartbreak of saying goodbye to one's own child, the love mixed with more complicated emotions. I was aware that much of what people commonly understood about autism stemmed from films like *Rain Man* and books like *The Curious Incident of the Dog in the Night-Time*, which tended to focus on protagonists less prone to physical outbursts, and whose challenges were compensated for by almost supernatural savant abilities. This struck me as not just a little distorted – taking the broad sweep of autism and its manifestations – but also unfair on those families involved with the more difficult types of behaviour, as if it was assumed they all had mini-Rain Men running around, memorizing phone books and helping them to win millions in gambling.

We ended up making the autism programme and putting it out alongside the dementia one as a two-parter. In an attempt to acknowledge the shows as being about families and relationships dealing with extraordinary sets of emotions caused by neurological conditions, we called it *Extreme Love.*

In the years afterwards, I toggled between stories that were more obviously about weirdness – a porn follow-up; another about sex offenders living surveilled lives in south Los Angeles – and human-interest subjects about ordinary people making difficult decisions in impossible situations: families tempted to keep piling on expensive, often painful, medical treatments for loved ones with life-threatening conditions; clinics for people with brain injuries or dealing with profound addictions or assailed by baffling mental health problems.

It is a privilege to be able to document some of the most intimate and harrowing moments of people's lives. I'm aware that may sound a little glib, or just ghoulish. I tend to see it as the opposite: an opportunity to make connections in the most unlikely places, a chance to find the comfort of friendliness and laughter in the dark.

When we were filming with dementia patients, several times their families and loved ones told me that the change of routine and the excitement of having a crew around had given them a new zest for life, lifting them out of the doldrums of an unchanging routine and a slow decline. Clearly that's not why I make programmes. I am a journalist, not a social worker. I am there to get the story. I am curious about life. I am fascinated by the awfulness that life throws at us and in awe of the resourcefulness ordinary people show in toughing it out. By bringing out the story, I hope to spread truth and understanding. But I also like to feel that where possible we do not make situations worse – and that, where vulnerable contributors are concerned, we are mindful of their need to be protected from further harm. And over the years I've been struck that people who are going through extraordinary, often awful experiences are grateful for the chance to share their travails with an outsider.

Sometimes I have the sense that I am trying the patience of the audience. No one has said to me, 'Why can't you go back to making funny programmes?' but I sense it, on occasion, in the reactions of friends or on Twitter. 'Why don't you make some more *Weird Weekends*?' people say. 'I enjoyed your programme – if enjoyed is the right word.' Very occasionally I get: 'Oh, too dark for me. Too depressing. Gloomsville.' It preys on my own mind, too, the idea that I may stray into terrain that is self-indulgent: 'I don't care if it's boring, it's *important*.'

My own feeling is that a subject should only earn its stripes by being engaging, watchable – and, yes, enjoyable. I never want or expect viewers to come to a subject out of a sense of duty. Is it a good watch or not? Is it shocking? Is it powerful? Is it wrenching? I *enjoyed* watching Joshua Oppenheimer's *The Act of Killing*. I *enjoyed* reading *If This Is A Man* by Primo Levi. I *enjoyed* Gitta Sereny's biography of the death camp commandant Franz Stangl, *Into That Darkness*, and also her account of the child murderer Mary Bell in *Cries Unheard*. I *enjoyed* Nick Broomfield's fly-on-the-wall film about a youth-offender institute *Tattooed Tears* and also Kurt Kuenne's documentary about a child murder, *Dear Zachary*, and other films and books – too many to mention – that look with intelligence and sensitivity on subjects of profound sadness and darkness.

I read a phrase the other day: the heartlessness of optimism. To look on the bright side is counted as a virtue, but to do it in an unthinking way can be also unkind and uncaring, especially to someone who is experiencing pain, who is feeling lonely and unheard.

Accept that life is unbearable and awful for many people at least some of the time. Laugh about it if you can. Look on the dark side and make the best of it all.

## Chapter 26

## Savile-Geddon

Nancy and I married at Marylebone Registry Office on Friday 13 July 2013 – the inauspicious date was the only one available at short notice. With nine years and two children already on the clock, the idea of a wedding was a little after the fact. The delay – which resulted from a combination of my inborn misanthropic qualities and a lamentable failure on my part to recognize how much I owed Nancy, how much I loved her and also how important a public declaration of love might be to *her* – in a way demands less explanation than my miraculously managing, against the odds, to see clearly what a plonker I was being.

I was – and continue to be – a confused person in many import-ant respects. I told myself I believed the best way to honour our relationship was for us to love one another and make it last, and that I viewed the idea of a public statement of intent, like a wedding, as attention-seeking and phoney. But undoubtedly amidst those inclin-ations was an inability to commit – certainly that was what Nancy felt – and it was only when I came face to face with the real risk of losing her that I realized what a calamity that would be.

The rapprochement that followed took months and involved relationship counselling in West Hampstead with a woman whose clear impression was that Nancy was right about almost everything – afterwards we would eat lunch at a Middle Eastern café on West End Lane in almost post-coital fashion. A few months after the counselling ended we were in a posh restaurant at the top of a skyscraper in Los Angeles when I finally did something I'd never quite been able to imagine myself doing.

I didn't have a ring. I've never been good at picking jewellery and with the knowledge that, worst case scenario, the ring would be on her finger for at least a few months – or, all being well, for life – the pressure was on. So, instead, I had the brainwave of presenting her with the business card of a Hatton Garden jewellers.

The idea was the card would speak for itself – I slipped it into a menu, and after we'd finished our main courses, I waved the menu at her in nonchalant fashion.

'Have you got room for something else?' I asked.

When she saw the jewellers' card, she looked confused. It didn't quite say 'big romantic gesture' in the way I'd hoped, so to remove any ambiguity I got down on one knee and said, 'Nancy, will you marry me?'

She smiled in a way that seemed to say it was both too late and welcome all the same.

The official part of the ceremony took place at Marylebone Registry Office. My dad had flown over from Hawaii with his wife, Sheila; my mum and her partner Michael were also there – there was something unifying about having all the parents and step-parents together in one place. Naturally we had included our two boys, then four and six, dressed in little linen outfits. The older one, Albert, was supposed to do a reading, a quotation about friendship from Winnie-the-Pooh, but he panicked and went dry. My brother Marcel, who was acting as best man, stepped in, hoisted him up and filled in, reading the text while holding Albert in his other arm.

After the signing of the paperwork we retired for a lunch at a grand Victorian pub in Kensal Green. Marcel gave a speech that took its cue from a Twitter handle I once used, 'Loubot2000'. Its conceit

With Nancy at our wedding, dancing to 'In Dreams'.

was that I was a temperamental bit of high-tech kit that needed a troubleshooting guide:

Congratulations on purchasing your new Loubot 2000! The Loubot 2000 is precision engineered to work straight out of the box and give you a lifetime's trouble-free use. If you feel that your Loubot 2000 is malfunctioning or faulty, please take time to read the following list of FAQs before contacting the helpdesk. 'My Loubot 2000 is unresponsive.' The Loubot 2000 is highly introspective and may sometimes go into power-save mode. To restore normal functionality, try asking one of the following questions: Was Jimmy Savile really a paedophile? What do Scientologists actually believe?

Are chimpanzees dangerous? This should reboot the system. 'My Loubot 2000 seems tense and anxious.' Try oiling your Loubot 2000 with red wine.

I then gave my own speech, expressing my love for my new wife, my awe at her intelligence, her kindness and humour. 'Nancy continues to sprinkle stardust on my life,' I said. 'One of life's mysteries is how I've hung on to her.' My cousin Justin was then in a relationship with the actress Jennifer Aniston and I recalled a conversation we'd all had one night at a restaurant in LA when Jen had compared Nancy to Cate Blanchett. 'Personally I think Cate Blanchett should feel flattered by the comparison,' I said. 'Jen didn't mention which film star I looked like,' I added. 'Probably because it might have been awkward mentioning Brad Pitt.'

Mid-afternoon we adjourned to a second pub, where we hosted a wider ring of friends and guests. My dad gave an idiosyncratic oration, involving one of his favourite themes: his mystification – pride mixed with pain – that there were places where I was better known than him, and his confusion that people sometimes approached me when we were together to express enthusiasm for my programmes and yet, being told he was my father, did not shower him with attention as progenitor of whatever talent I possessed.

He then recited a poem from memory by Robert Frost, called 'Provide, Provide', which describes an ugly old witch called Abishag, who works as a washerwoman, but who was at one time a beautiful Hollywood star. This is the normal course of human affairs, the poem suggests, and goes on to recommend dying early. It was, all in all, a weird message for a wedding and afterwards I asked my mum what she thought he meant by it.

'Oh, don't read anything into that,' she said. 'He only said it because it's the one poem he knows by heart.'

And it was here, at the second pub, with the music blaring as guests danced and ordered drinks from the bar and queued for a hog roast, that Will Yapp, the director of *When Louis Met Jimmy*, approached me, leaned in and confided, 'So, Beth's been in touch. ITV are doing a job on Jimmy. Big exposé for a new strand.' I was happy but not drunk and I had to strain to catch his words as he described what he knew about the exposé. It was to be a scalding tell-all: women were coming forward with stories. Even his charity work would be revealed as a cloak for self-enrichment.

I nodded and took it in, not thinking too much about it – it all seemed so vague and speculative – and then we were swept up in the music and occasion: my new wife and I dancing to our opening song of Roy Orbison's 'In Dreams'.

The last time I'd seen Jimmy had been in the autumn of 2005, after I'd come back from writing my book in America. Even before that there had been a distancing. After I threw over the diary-book-thing, the relationship with Jimmy had tapered down quite naturally. By the time I'd gone back to doing stories in America – the brothel, the neo-Nazis – there was no contact between us, neither friendliness nor ill will, just a sense that a strange passage of life had come and gone and – not to put it too cold-bloodedly – we had no further reason to see each other.

For that last 2005 visit, the invitation to travel up had come from Will. It was late in the year and, though I was back in the UK, I was not yet back making television – the only professional pretext for the trip to see Jimmy was to promote my book. A TV reporter filmed parts of the evening for a segment on the local news – our conversation at the house and an outing to the Flying Pizza. But I didn't take any notes. I have no recollection of what we discussed.

Friends of his, after he died, told me he'd continued to view me in a friendly way after we lost touch. But I also tend to think he felt a little bit abandoned. Our last conversation, when I'd called after a gap of several years, had been in 2009. I was booked on Chris Evans' Radio 2 breakfast show to promote a new documentary about prisons or mental health – I'm not sure – and I'd thought it might add a moment of surprise and intrigue if I could say I'd just spoken to Jimmy.

Jimmy had answered the phone himself, as he always did, with a noise that sounded like: 'Nyes?' But as we spoke, he'd sounded distant, a little cold.

'I'm going on Chris Evans,' I said.

'Ah, the height of fame,' he replied with a sarcasm that was a touch unfriendly.

As the years passed, from time to time, I'd hear little bits of information. I continued, whenever I gave interviews, to be asked about him and also to pump my interlocutors for anything they might know that shed more light on his hidden side. Once, when I was interviewed by the Radio 2 DJ Johnnie Walker, he made a veiled and vague reference to a young woman, or girl, who, he'd heard, or said he'd heard, had had a relationship with Jimmy, or a something, which for unclear reasons, had ended badly, with her feeling ill-used. It was that vague and, though it sounded a little ominous on the face of it, it was impossible to chase up or know how much to make of it.

In another interview, the DJ Phill Jupitus commended me on air for my work exposing people whom 'we know to be despicable'. I bridled at this a little, saying it wasn't quite how I saw what I did. 'Do we know Jimmy Savile to be despicable?' I asked. Off air he told me he didn't have the goods on Jimmy himself but that if I wanted to know more I should get in touch with the frontman of the rock group Slade, Noddy Holder. Noddy had told Phill personally that he kept a file on Jimmy 'this thick' – he made the appropriate gesture with finger and thumb – conjuring the unlikely image of the glam-metal icon sleuthing Jimmy's crimes between Slade gigs and adverts for Nobby's Nuts.

I did some half-hearted follow-up on the Noddy lead, but it went nowhere.

In early 2006, Jimmy made a cameo appearance on *Celebrity*

*Big Brother* series four. The house that year included the politician George Galloway, the glamour model Jodie Marsh, and a rapper from Wales called Maggot. Jimmy, looking stooped and ancient, held court in a red tracksuit, discoursing about show business ('Whatever The Beatles did, they wanted to have me not too far away. They reckoned I brought luck to them') and making insinuating jokes. 'Don't forget, ladies, I am available most weekends for home visits.' It was striking how much the housemates deferred to him. The retired basketball player Dennis Rodman took an unlikely interest in Jimmy – or maybe, given his incongruous friendship with Kim Jong Un, Rodman had a penchant for mercurial men with strange hair.

Later, a couple of victims were to say that it was this appearance that prompted them to go to the Surrey police. This in turn led to the one recorded police interview with Jimmy in 2009. The interview, published after his death, took place at Jimmy's office at Stoke Mandeville and was, on Jimmy's side, a masterclass in evasion, consisting of flannel, legal threats, bluster, and lies. The police investigation was dropped soon afterwards.

In my own mind, I had by the end settled on a view of Jimmy as simultaneously creepy and mysterious but also someone to whom I felt a degree of affection; a manipulator, with a troublingly detached and transactional attitude to human relations, but also, weirdly, as someone somehow dependable.

How strange it is to write that now.

When he died in 2011 Jimmy was still riding high as the nation's most famous charity fundraiser and icon of eccentricity. Celebrities and dignitaries queued up to salute him. His funeral was a jamboree in Leeds involving the usual Savile flare and showmanship: thousands of attendees, a gold coffin, a massive marble headstone. I had passed up an invitation to go to the commemoration. I'd like to think it was because I was too wary of being part of a tribute to a man whom I knew to be, at the very least, flawed and possibly far worse. But it may be that I simply didn't have the appetite to be a bit player in an over-the-top media spectacle.

I wrote a blog post of thoughts on his passing, mentioning my sadness and a mild sense of guilt that I hadn't seen more of him before he died. I talked about the dark rumours and how they had been my motivation for making the original film. I recounted the irritations of dealing with him, his evasions and pranks, his dark references to physical intimidation in the nightclubs but also the toughness I'd come to respect – the way he was 'unfazed by negative attention.'

I ended: 'He was a complete one-off. Wrestler, charity fundraiser, DJ, fixer, prankster, and professional enigma. He was also a plain-spoken Yorkshire philosopher and psychologist. There won't be another one like him.'

But I was also careful about what I didn't say. I turned down various offers to write a piece for a national paper or comment on the radio or take part in a Christmas TV tribute. My feelings were too complicated for me to know how to do them justice, and even then I was aware that, as much as we'd played the role of friends in newspaper profiles and even on occasion with each other, our relationship was chillier and warier than that, and at its base, on both sides, somewhat transactional.

Six months later a journalist for the *Yorkshire Evening Post* emailed a colleague, trying to reach me. She was preparing an official biography of Jimmy. 'I was a dear friend of his,' she said. 'He often spoke of Louis but did say he hadn't kept in touch recently . . . I read bidding prayers at his funeral and am really sad he has passed away as we had lots of fun together.' The working subtitle of the book was *The Life and Times of a National Treasure*.

I spoke to her by phone about my experience of filming and our friendship, such as it was. During the interview, I went off the record and asked if she'd heard the rumours that he had an unpleasant secret sexual side. The book, *How's About That Then?*, came out early in 2012, a benign appreciation of the man and his good works. She included a couple of pages on the rumours. It was, she later told me, 'the worst-timed book in history'.

In the months after he died I noticed one or two small news stories about Jimmy, referring to a *Newsnight* segment and allegations to do with an 'approved school' – a government-funded boarding school for wayward girls of high intelligence, Duncroft in Surrey. The *Newsnight* segment had been shelved, for reasons unknown.

In October, ITV aired *Exposure: The Other Side of Jimmy Savile*. Presented by Mark Williams-Thomas, it featured a series of women who spoke about his assaults on them as teenagers – tongue pushed into the mouth, unwanted groping, much of it taking place on BBC premises, a lot in NHS hospitals, and all of it dependent on a sense of celebrity and glamour conferred on him by his BBC TV shows. The women's defences were down; they trusted Jimmy Savile, and he assaulted them. Several of the contributors had attended Duncroft, where it was said teachers and staff turned a blind eye to reports of Jimmy's sexual misconduct.

Reaction to the programme was immediate and overwhelming. A dam had burst and a torrent of further allegations from other women – and some men – crashed over anyone who'd ever had any dealings with Jimmy. The BBC was immediately in the firing line – not just for its failure to stop Jimmy in all the years he was assaulting women on its premises but also for the decision to pull the *Newsnight* investigation. Inquiries were set up, and within a few weeks I was on the phone to one of them, telling what I knew: principally about Beth and Alice, and the fact of their having had relations with him in the late sixties when one of them was fifteen, but also about comments made by Johnnie Walker and Phill Jupitus.

In those early days I imagined it might all be over quite quickly. In a kind of stubborn adherence to the facts as I understood them – and maybe in a spirit that was unconsciously having trouble facing the reality of having been friendly with a sexual predator – I tried to tell myself it couldn't be quite as bad as it seemed and I found myself parsing the data to find ways in which it might be questionable or speculative. But what I couldn't explain away or extenuate was the testimony of the girls from Duncroft – how plausible it seemed that he might take advantage of vulnerable girls – girls already so ill-used by life as to make them easy pickings for one so-minded, plied with cigarettes and sweets and the promise of tickets to the TV show *Clunk-Click* – girls who I could all too easily imagine him viewing as 'damaged goods' and grateful, in his transactional understanding of the world, for the attention of an ageing DJ and therefore, in his mind, fair game for his predatory attentions.

A BBC colleague told me that all the rushes from *When Louis Met Jimmy* were being viewed by an in-house investigator or maybe by the police. Requests to speak to various inquiries trickled in – a police investigation in Scarborough, another in Leeds. I spoke to these, confirming that I'd seen nothing during filming in the way of depraved or criminal behaviour. For several weeks after the *Exposure* piece, more of Jimmy's victims and survivors came forward, on an almost daily basis, in tabloid articles and in TV appearances: on morning chat shows, on a follow-up ITV documentary and a BBC *Panorama* entitled 'Jimmy Savile: What The BBC Knew'. This last one featured Kat Ward, whose interview for *Newsnight* had been spiked. The calm and measured detail of her testimony, its description of a quid pro quo of TV tickets for oral sex in the back of a Rolls-Royce, was utterly persuasive.

With each new revelation, the image of a free-ranging predator whose charity work gave him access to restricted areas with vulnerable people came into sharper focus. In many of the accounts I struggled to recognize the man I'd imagined I knew, but occasionally there were details that reminded me of him. One – an anonymous letter from 1998, sent to the Scotland Yard vice squad – alleged, 'His fundraising activities are not out of altruistic motives; but purely for selfish advancement and an easy living. He has slimed his way in wherever possible. He has tried to hide his homosexuality, which in any event is an open secret with those who know; but did you know that he is also a deeply committed paedophile.'

It went on to describe Jimmy getting involved with a rent boy who had blackmailed him and threatened to expose him for paedophilia, even alleging that it was Jimmy's practice to seek out rent boys after doing charity runs. 'Now I've had a run, I feel like some bum,' he would allegedly say.

I thought back to his conversation with me about rent boys. *All you have to do is buy them a bun. They run off at the mouth like they've got verbal diarrhoea.* Even – ridiculously – the rhyming motto had the ring of truth. *If it ain't a game it's a shame*, I'd heard him say many times. Was it possible in his strange, almost medieval, Catholic view of things – like a Medici buying indulgences before committing a crime – he viewed his vice as having been paid for by the good work of the charity run?

As it became clear how the BBC had missed the chance to expose Jimmy – alleged at the time to be because of a reluctance to disrupt the Christmas TV schedule, which included a *Jim'll Fix It* tribute, though this was subsequently disproved – the organization went into meltdown. The Director General was forced to resign and the Chairman of the BBC Trust came in for heavy criticism. News managers involved in the decision to pull the *Newsnight* piece were suspended. Suddenly, anyone who had ever heard a rumour about Jimmy Savile was under suspicion – which was weird given that, as far as I knew, *everyone* had heard rumours about Jimmy Savile, from the DG of the BBC to my mates in the school playground in 1983.

For having made an exposing documentary about him while he was alive that at the same time failed to out him as a paedophile and a predator, I now occupied an ambiguous place in the whole affair. From some, I got credit for having shown him as the weird creature of narcissism and detachment that he was. It was also pointed out that I'd been one of the very few people who'd raised the issue of rumours of paedophilia to his face. But in some quarters – principally those reposing in the area of my brain known as the 'self-doubt cortex' – I was also the person who hadn't managed to take him down despite two weeks of access and the resources of a TV production behind me. In general, I couldn't shake the feeling of disappointment that I'd failed to see him clearly for what he was when he was alive or that I'd missed an opportunity to unmask him.

The *Panorama* documentary played the clip from *When Louis Met Jimmy* in which I talked to him about the rumours of paedophilia. I was, of course, pleased to be able to appear prescient. But I was also aware how far from a *j'accuse* that moment actually was.

In amongst the victims that were coming forward were the two women I'd spoken to and had tea with in 2001, and what played most on my mind was the thought that, if I'd handled the conversation differently, they might have been able to say more. Looking over notes I'd taken at the time, I was struck by how many clues there were. How quick and unexpected the sex was. 'It would be up against the wall. In the dressing room or in his caravan at King's Cross.' 'Very persuasive.' 'One thing would lead to another so you didn't really know what was happening.' And the sense of secrecy and social pressure. 'Draws you in and draws you in.' 'Like a cult.'

At the time it had been wrapped in the tone of the original letter and the warmth of their conversation, which was about friendship and fun. It seemed so different in hindsight. Had they needed more of a nudge? But it was also true that I'd never had the sense I was supposed *to do* anything with what they were saying. They had just wanted to be heard. And I kept telling myself, if they'd wanted to out him as a predator, why didn't they just say so, and what was to stop them going to the police?

I was also conscious how much there was about Jimmy that wasn't being said – or that people weren't getting quite right. The number of victims kept going up and up, along with the luridness of the details. There were allegations of satanic masses and dismemberings of small children. The sense of outrage at his having got away with his crimes and his supposed closeness to the establishment had created a slingshot effect: the truth had been suppressed for so long, with victims' voices kept silent and complicit elements in the saddle, and now it was twanging violently back into a world of outlandish allegations in which everything was believed.

The person being depicted bore no relation not only to the man I'd known, but to anyone who ever lived. Someone with 'no emotions' whose entire life had been constructed with the exclusive purpose of committing crimes. The ancillary of this was that anyone who had dealings with Jimmy was under suspicion. How could they have not known when he was committing sexual assault on a daily basis? The leading investigator on a Metropolitan Police report said, 'He spent every minute of every waking day thinking about it.' One part of me took this as understandable hyperbole, given the sense of betrayal and anger that was flooding over the country. It was possible the nation needed to live through a moment of convulsive outrage. But at the same time, wasn't it also important to tell the truth – in a forensic way like, you know, a police detective?

In a weird way, it did Jimmy too much credit to imagine he was capable of doing that much evil – that he was, as some seemed to feel, on a par with Adolf Hitler and Ian Brady. Further, in reducing him to a monomaniac and a caricature, it did a disservice to those who worked and helped him in his programmes and his charitable works in good faith but failed to see his dark side. I worried that it short-changed his victims, some of whom had a more complicated attitude; and perhaps most serious of all that it made further abuse in the future by other predators more likely by removing them from the real world and putting them in the realm of Grand Guignol.

At the same time as I was feeling all these things, at a deeper level, I was also doubting them. What if my emphasis on the need for 'nuance', and 'truthfulness', and a 'forensic attitude' came down to an attempt to minimize his crimes in some way? Was I trying to protect myself because I had been one of those groomed – the journalist who spent two weeks with him and then stayed in touch with him and yet still somehow failed to see him for what he was? I began second-guessing my impulses – the most basic principles that had guided twenty years of work: the importance of seeing complexity and ambiguity, and understanding most of what we term evil as a by-product of a kind of self-deception and confused good faith or simple selfishness. What if my journalistic radar had failed me in my hour of greatest need and all my clever notions of showing empathy for people who least seemed deserving of it was dangerous sophistry – 'clever twat shit', to use a phrase of Jimmy's – and tortured apologetics for abuse and oppression? What if I had 'contextualized' and 'nuanced' myself into the profound failure of not recognizing sexual predation when it was blowing cigar smoke in my face? In my darkest moments of self-doubt I imagined myself as one of those ageing Nazis in Germany who spent decades post-Second World War quacking about 'the real Führer' and how much he did about crime and the economy.

In this spirit of over-sensitivity, soon after the first batch of revelations, I attended a charity function at the Globe Theatre on the South Bank with a smattering of random celebrities. In huddles in the bar, like an unofficial show-business conclave, we compared notes on the Savile latest. Part of my MO at that time was to air my own understanding of the situation, trying to make sense of it. In an attempt to explain their vulnerability, I made mention that some of Jimmy's victims had been 'star-struck', and that this had led to their defences being down. The look of incredulity on the face of a female actor I was talking to was chilling. What she seemed to have heard me say was, 'Those girls were throwing themselves at him.'

One part of me wondered if she'd lost the plot. But the greater part wondered if *I'd* lost the plot – the ability to navigate cocktail-party showbiz chat in a way that didn't sound like I was OK with paedophilia.

One April morning, in 2013, I was summoned to give evidence to the Janet Smith Inquiry, the BBC's all-encompassing review of its role in the Savile affair – assaults committed on BBC premises, against BBC staff, people under its care.

I was living in LA by this time, and the interview had to be done via some high-tech video-conferencing system on the umpteenth floor of the gleaming downtown offices of the international legal firm Reed Smith.

Dame Janet – snowy-haired and distinguished-looking, like the commander of a space ship on a progressive *Star Trek* spin-off – beamed in from her conference room in England somewhere flanked by young-pup legal aides, to ask about the circumstances of the documentary, how it had come to be made, how I'd found Jimmy, the rumours I'd heard before doing the show. The conversation proceeded in a friendly fashion for an hour or two and – bizarrely, given it was the question that preoccupied me – appeared to be over without me having been asked about Beth and Alice, the two girlfriends turned whistle-blowers, despite my having spoken about their letter and meeting them to at least two people months earlier who were working on the inquiry. Naturally my instinct was not to bring it up, since it was, I felt, my weak spot in the whole affair, but good sense prevailed and I tippled them to the meeting – 'tippling' being the sort of word Jimmy Savile liked to use.

Later I emailed Will Yapp to vent and express mixed-up feelings of confusion, shame and fear. We agreed to open a file to share documents – reports and newspaper cuttings relating to *l'affaire Savile*. It was like a scab I couldn't stop picking. Nearly a year after speaking to Dame Janet, I heard via Will that Beth was upset with me for mentioning her letter and possibly compromising her identity. Had I told the Inquiry her and Alice's real names? There was an awkward transatlantic phone call in which I told her I didn't think I had mentioned real names but I'd shared the text of the letter. Afterwards I thought about the strangeness of worrying about not having done more earlier with what I knew and now being told I'd said *too much*. I wondered why I had a low-level feeling of guilt when I hadn't, as far as I was aware, done anything wrong, and why was I racking my brains for something I might have done wrong. I thought about a remark of Nietzsche's, that witches killed in witch hunts were often, by the end, *persuaded of their own guilt.* 'So it is with all guilt,' he writes.

And at the same time, in spite of all of it, with an almost vertiginous sense of anxiety, I couldn't help thinking about a follow-up.

# Chapter 27

## Coffee with Larry

Vast and unsustainable, and teetering always on the edge of environmental disaster – mudslides, wildfires, earthquakes – Los Angeles is a strange city, though I sometimes wonder if other people take against the place for the same reasons I like it. It is in some ways idiotic and certainly self-obsessed– but also vigorous and unpretentious: the equivalent in conurbation form of the kind of deluded monomaniac that for a long time I made the subject of my interviews.

We had moved there because we wanted an adventure. It was late 2012. Nancy and I were not long married and had decided to consecrate our renewed commitment to each other with a major life change. Nancy, raised abroad in less rain-lashed countries, craved a break from another British winter. The children were open to the idea of a big move – or too young to understand what they were signing on for; while I, a professional observer of American culture, reasoned it could only be a good thing for my work if I lived in the midst of the people I was studying, in classical anthropological style.

The invisibility of being in LA, the fact that I wasn't often recognized, was also part of its appeal.

Any ambivalence I had about being famous – the fact that you sometimes got asked for selfies when your child was having a

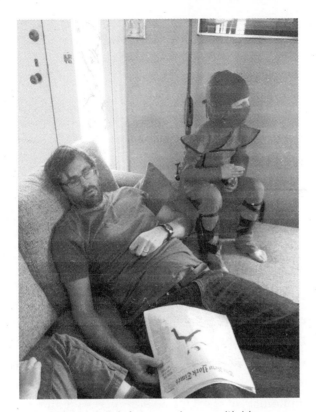

At home in LA, busy coming up with ideas.

five-alarm meltdown on the Tube, or found yourself outside a pub where a large party went into a FOMO panic and every person had to have a photo – was reversed. In LA I could wander around lost and not worry that someone had spotted me and thought, 'There's Louis Theroux. Why is he walking up and down and looking at his phone?' And those moments of recognition, someone asking for a picture or offering a compliment, being rare, were more welcome. In LA, I was in my twenties again, noticing that actors at parties didn't seem that interested in what I had to say. 'What do you do? Documentaries? Uh-huh. Cool.' *Scans room for escape.* It was like being back on Krypton – a planet where I no longer had my superpowers.

The 2008 crash was then still recent enough that property prices were depressed and we could just about afford to buy a house on the east side of the city, in a pleasant tree-lined area on the southern edge of Griffith Park called Los Feliz. Our children enrolled in a local school. The BBC arranged for a series producer to be based with me. A couple of APs were brought on and we rented a small office on a Hollywood lot, called The Lot, built aeons ago (in LA years) for Charlie Chaplin and Mary Pickford.

The first subject we looked into was California's network of mental hospitals. Based on a previous film we'd made about a maximum-security facility for paedophiles and sex offenders, the California Department of Mental Health had been receptive, and access had already been signed off at the top level.

My new series producer and an AP went on a recce, and the reports that came back made it sound fascinating: a unit full of stalkers of stars; another that housed patients with psychogenic polydipsia, a pathological compulsion to drink water. It was like hearing travellers' tales from explorers on a far frontier, describing lands where diamonds were strewn on the ground and men whose heads grew below their shoulders. Then the reports became less frequent and more laconic – the access was in doubt, for mysterious reasons – possibly one of our team had asked 'Where do you keep the psychopaths?' and the question had ruffled some feathers or more probably it was just a general sense of apprehension on the part of rank-and-file clinicians at the hospitals at the idea of featuring a vulnerable population of the mentally ill on a television programme. The project ebbed away.

Scrambling to make something, we front-burnered another idea we had been developing about end-of-life care and patients embracing long-shot medical treatments for life-threatening conditions. I'd seen the same subject done on the PBS documentary strand *NOVA*, but I felt we could do it with more focus on the human stories. I went into it knowing it was a further step along the road of grimness and I had moments of panic, wondering if this time we really were overworking the depresso machine.

We filmed at Cedars-Sinai Medical Center. For those accustomed to London's patched-up and retrofitted Victorian monsters, Cedars-Sinai looked a little like a futuristic rendering of a hospital complex, all clean lines and curves and shiny windows. There was a Spielberg building and thousands of museum-worthy artworks on the walls, Rauschenbergs and Warhols and de Koonings. It had a reputation as the hospital to the stars. While we were there, the rapper Lil Wayne was brought in. There were reports – denied by Lil Wayne himself – that he'd overdosed on recreationally consumed cough medicine, also known as sizzurp or purple drank. But Cedars-Sinai also served a local community of regular people, many there on state aid for the poor and elderly, and it was mainly among these that we spent our time.

Progress was slow. We were not allowed to wander the corridors, as we had done in other hospitals and prisons we had filmed in. At Cedars-Sinai, our AP had to set up filming with each contributor individually days in advance; only three of us could go in at any one time and there was no hanging about, which ruled out the possibility of finding new interviewees as we went, a type of serendipity we had always relied on. Not to mention that we were also – naturally enough, in a story about life-threatening conditions – at the mercy of the progress of the illnesses, the comas and the cancers, and they didn't always cooperate with our schedule.

Not for the first time, I wondered if I might have finally alighted on an idea that was too gloomy for even the most dedicated fan, but we soldiered on, and eventually accumulated a series of scenes I still look back on as some of the most awful and dramatic I've ever been present for: an aspiring x-ray technician called Javier who married his fiancée, knowing he was about to die, with the assembled family and officiator all in surgical masks and rubber gloves; a young comedian and actor called Donta being informed by his team of white-coated specialists, who entered the room like a firing squad, that they no longer held out any hope of recovery. Much of our filming centred on a college student and football player called Langston who was in an unresponsive state following a heroin overdose. Doctors felt it was only a matter of time before they would have to switch off the machines that were keeping him alive, though the family disagreed, praying over him, and several months after his accident, he came round and spoke to his family – later we filmed him walking into the hospital to thank all the staff who had cared for him. It was the only time I've been lucky enough to capture a miracle on tape.

As filming in the hospital dragged on, we thought about making more shows in LA and putting together a series that would be an oblique portrait of the city, its episodes infused with the quintessential themes of scattered souls, self-invention, disparities of income, and a culture of utopian aspiration jostling against a reality that was far more grim.

We were conscious we should probably – in a series about Los Angeles – also try to feature an idea touching on the world of celebrity and show business. We circled around the world of stand-up comedians, and filmed a couple of interviews: one with the alternative-comedy guru and podcast host Marc Maron, and another with a faded comic of yesteryear, Gallagher, whose act used to involve him smashing watermelons with huge mallets. These encounters had their moments, but I worried that there wasn't enough at stake in the story – just the possibility of professional failure and embarrassment. The world of the comedians didn't seem terribly different to my own world and I lost confidence in the idea.

As the months went by, filming on these and other programmes – about the Sheriffs' Department, the Department of Children and Family Services, the secret underground world of monitored sex offenders – proceeded with the rhythm of LA traffic: brief stretches of open road soon gave way to unending miles of stationary vehicles. Too late, I realized something I should have predicted: that LA, being an entertainment capital, could not be more ill-suited to an outfit like ours. Every state and local institution in the city has endured multiple approaches from reality-TV teams. Like a remote tribe that has had too much contact with the outside world, they are all savvy about show business, and now want payment before anyone will put on a grass skirt or do a rain dance. The one card we could play – the idea of a reputable documentary production providing some exposure, memorializing what you do – was at best quaint and more often hopelessly naive. *We don't have any shiny beads but will you put on the grass skirt anyway?* I remember coming to this realization not long after the LAPD turned down our access request. They had a standard filming contract that required productions to licence their logo. The licence expired every three years, meaning whatever you filmed would, in effect, be worthless not long after you made it.

Our lowest ebb came mid-summer. We had retreated to the world of stray dogs in animal shelters. *Here at least we won't be dealing with aspiring celebrities*, I thought. Within a few weeks we discovered that our favourite character, a dog trainer who lived in an industrial space in South Central LA, the leader of a small pack of dogs, had an agent and a lawyer and a deal for a high-profile reality TV show that was going into production any second. Even the dog trainers were too starry for us.

But for all its frustrations, working in LA also meant being able to film and go home at the end of the day – not to a hotel in a foreign country but to my family. I loved returning from work to find the kids in the swimming pool and jumping in with them less than an hour after I'd been at my desk and then barbecuing dinner with my towel round me like a sarong as the light went. The boys picked up situational American accents that they used at school and on play-dates but not with us. Nancy got a part-time job at a campaigning production company and found a new circle of friends who had no idea that I was someone on television, and who as a result seemed to see her more clearly. In the winter we took trips out to Joshua Tree and 29 Palms on the edge of the Mojave and dreamed about moving to the desert, with sand and cactuses instead of a lawn, with clear night skies crowded with stars and the possibility of a different life.

And in between TV commitments I was also nudging along another project, a long-nurtured dream shot of my own.

It had started at a documentary festival in Sheffield more than a year earlier. Late one evening, at the bar of the Mercure Hotel, where the film-makers and dignitaries gather for drinks after the films and sessions are all finished, I'd run into a friend called Simon Chinn. We'd been at Westminster together. Back then he'd been a sporty and self-deprecating ladies' man and an indifferent student – he had once copied a history essay of mine on Jean II and Philippe VI of France. But in the subsequent twenty-five years he'd emerged as a documentary-producer of international renown, the winner of two Oscars for his films *Searching for Sugar Man* and *Man on Wire*.

Simon asked if I'd ever thought of making a feature-length documentary for cinemas. 'Of course,' I said. 'But I don't have an idea.' A few weeks later Simon called to say he had an idea: 'Scientology.'

If you've been paying attention, you will have noticed in previous chapters I have expressed an interest in the mysterious and secret religion founded by the troubled sci-fi writer L. Ron Hubbard. From my visit to the L. Ron Hubbard Life Exhibit as a young whelp in the last century, through my tour around the Celebrity Center for an abortive TV documentary in 2002, and onward, I had seen Scientology as the *ne plus ultra* of cultdom, combining, as it did, show business, Americana, hucksterism, over-the-top religious commitment, and space aliens. (Have I mentioned that Scientology disputes these characterizations? If not, may I do so here?) And so, given my history with the subject, there was an irony or maybe just a coincidental quality to the idea of Simon suggesting Scientology *to me*. Simon's interest stemmed from a story he'd read in the *New Yorker* by Lawrence Wright, profiling a disaffected ex-Scientologist, Paul Haggis, and the Church's efforts to harass and silence him.

I met up with Simon at his offices in Fitzrovia and we discussed the idea.

'It's the holy grail,' I said. 'The ultimate story. It would be amazing. But how do you do it? They would never let us in.'

'Do you know that?' Simon asked.

'Ah . . . yes,' I said. 'The best they would give you is tiny amounts of meaningless access. A tour of the Celebrity Center. A heavily chaperoned visit to some warehouse where they make e-meters. Almost everything I've ever done has been based on access,' I went on. 'It's part of how it works. That sense of permission.'

But Simon's interest and his track record was enough to prevent me pooh-poohing the idea entirely. And so over the following months we kept in touch, reading up on the subject, meeting for coffees and comparing notes.

Since I'd last gone spelunking in the potholes of Scientology research – those vast databases of allegations about ill treatment in the Sea Org and crazed self-actualization techniques – the contours of the story had changed a little. Starting around 2004 there had been a stream of departures from the upper echelons of Church management. In a series of memoirs and newspaper articles, these disaffected ex-members – most of whom had worked at a secretive base in the desert a couple of hours outside Los Angeles – depicted a culture of violence and degradation deep inside Scientology. They portrayed Scientology's leader, the diminutive David Miscavige, as a brutal and unaccountable martinet who verbally abused his underlings and ran a regime that hinged on isolation of staff from loved ones, humiliation, control, and weird mind games. For several months at least, and possibly longer, they alleged Miscavige had forced senior staff to eat, sleep and work inside a double-wide trailer nicknamed the Hole.

This feels like another good place to mention that Scientology disputes all these allegations.

Miscavige had seized power soon after Hubbard's death in 1986 and, in the accounts of the apostates, he came across as a Stalin-like figure, someone who had none of the religious vision or charismatic charlatanism of the founder but who more than made up for it with a kind of genius for control and domination.

At the same time, what I was also struck by was the sense of world-changing zeal of the Scientologists and their sincere belief that they had all the answers to all the problems that had plagued humanity for decades – war, insanity, crime – and their complete conviction that it was down to them and them alone to save humanity. This explained their dead-eyed intimidation of journalists, their hounding of ex-members, and why so many of them were prepared to tolerate ill treatment: what was a few months of polishing door knobs in a punishment programme when weighed against the salvation of the universe? This notion of idealism being a close cousin of zealotry was central to what interested me about the Church – especially wrapped in the bizarre trappings of the sci-fi space opera – and it took me back, in a pleasurable way, to my *Weird Weekends* days of people passionate about nonsense in a way that was comical and troubling and sad, but with some of the seriousness and maturity of the later shows mixed in.

I wrote up a film treatment that developed these ideas. 'I love stories in which the best human qualities are put at the service of questionable projects,' I wrote. 'I find that the most shocking behaviour is motivated by very relatable human impulses.' As to how the film might work, I was a little more vague, and these parts of the treatment – for all the references I included about it being a 'landmark documentary feature' and 'my dream subject' – couldn't help disguising a certain skimpiness and desperation. *We'll meet a defector . . . and I'll do some Scientology with an Independent Scientologist . . . and I'll try to get into the opening of a new Org . . . and stand by the fence of the secret base . . . and we may even get some access to the Celebrity Center . . . Did I mention it is a landmark documentary feature?*

Maybe for this reason, there were troubling questions of who would direct the film. Simon had been keen to bring on a high-profile name – someone with 'feature documentary experience'. But the rarefied world of A-list theatrical documentary directors was not yielding up many names. In a way, it wasn't surprising that there should be few takers, in the premier league of doc makers, for a non-access-based Scientology film fronted by a presenter who specialized in access.

By the time I was living in LA, more than a year down the line from the first conversations with Simon, the project was still notionally moving forward – the BBC had committed money, the film was funded – but with still no director or coherent vision, we were arguably no further along.

One day at work a colleague, an AP who lived in LA and was connected in show-business circles, mentioned that the Hollywood comedy writer and director Larry Charles had seen and enjoyed some of my programmes. I was delighted, of course. My years of aspiring to write sitcoms were still near enough that the idea of praise from one of the original writers of *Seinfeld* and *Curb Your Enthusiasm* – a man who had also directed Sacha Baron Cohen's prank film *Borat* and *Religulous*, a satirical documentary about religion presented by the American comedian Bill Maher – felt like a kind of anointment.

A few weeks went by and then I had a thought. I suggested to Simon that *Larry* might be the director for our movie.

We met up at an organic coffee shop in Beverly Hills. Larry, then in his mid-sixties, arrived, long-haired, long-bearded, in a Homburg hat and baggy cotton trousers that could possibly have been pyjama bottoms. In Hollywood, scruffiness is an indicator either of homelessness or inestimable wealth. In Larry's case, I was fairly sure it was the latter. He was effortlessly funny, complimentary about my old shows – he mentioned the dementia one for some reason ('I loved that scene, the woman going "gullah-gullah-gullah", it's become a thing I do with my girlfriend') – and his conversations were a torrent of ideas so free-flowing that they bordered on the hypomanic.

On the subject of a Scientology film, he was immediately enthusiastic. He'd tried to do a bit on Scientology in *Religulous* – it hadn't made it into the film – but he felt the subject was ripe for a different approach. 'Little bit of prosthetic disguise on your face, you would be unrecognizable,' he said. 'You could go undercover as a dishwasher at the Scientology headquarters for two weeks.' Another idea involved producing a live musical celebrating Scientology and staging it in Hollywood. 'There is a way to expand on what you have done. Bring new elements into it, broaden the canvas, deal with larger themes and use humour, outrageousness, danger, spontaneity, emotion and film techniques to produce a scary and iconoclastic and fun ride.' Many of his ideas revolved around exploding the usual documentary storytelling tropes and using Hollywood techniques, especially re-enactments. 'I see re-enactments as being very important to this . . . I just want you to do what you usually do. My job is to turbo-charge everything to take it to the next level of it being a movie that can play in malls not just in art houses and festivals.'

After Larry left, Simon and I loitered behind, both dazed and excited by Larry's manic creativity and raffish bohemian glamour. 'I think we might have found our director,' Simon said.

More meetings followed between Larry and me, and in hindsight, the six months or so of brainstorming were like a lost weekend of Hollywood romance, a whirlwind affair with a mistress who I suspected was too attractive and intelligent for me, making me wonder when it was going to end or what dark secret about her past I would uncover. We would email ideas back and forth and occasionally meet in a cafe in West Hollywood. For my part, the idea of 'taking meetings' with a comic master felt exciting but also trepidatious. He talked about working with a tiny crew. I worried that his idea of a tiny crew was my idea of a huge crew.

During one coffee session, I explained my sense that the important material would stem from the Scientologists' reaction to whatever we came up with. They would undoubtedly view me as an 'SP'. A 'Suppressive Person' – the term is used often by Scientologists and is synonymous, more or less, with 'psychopath'. Scientologists teach that journalists are 1.1 on the 'tone scale', putting them on a par with 'sexual perverts' – which I think means gay people – and so they feel they are licensed to harass and confront them, especially those they view as disseminating negative information about them. The Internet is full of amusing videos of Scientologists 'handling' reporters in this way, and also tailing them in blacked-out vehicles. In fact one of the most revealing short documentaries on Scientology, John Sweeney's 2007 *Panorama*, was mainly composed of sequences of him being tailed and harassed and until he famously snapped under the pressure and went shouty-crackers during a tour of one of their facilities.

'We need to think about how we document them coming after us,' I said to Larry. 'It's a shame we can't make a film and then release it and then film them harassing and suppressing our film.' I mentioned Errol Morris's film *Tabloid*, about a woman in the 1970s who became erotically obsessed with a Mormon missionary, kidnapping him and allegedly making him her sex slave, and I went on, 'The most interesting part of *that* was that the woman later attended screenings at festivals to stand up and denounce Errol Morris – none of which you would know from watching the finished film. But can you imagine how much more interesting that would have been? The main character stepping up and taking control of the movie.'

'I love that,' Larry said. 'A film within a film. We could have a casting call for actors to play David Miscavige.'

This wasn't exactly what I'd meant and, intrigued as I was, I also worried that it seemed prankish, unmoored from any documentary reality. But Larry was off and running. What about instead of being one film within a film, there were several, each in a different mode? A religious epic. A sci-fi film. A Miscavige biopic. At this point, my head was starting to spin as I tried to keep up with Larry's runaway vision. But I'd spent enough time in Hollywood by now that I knew I should mask my confusion. 'Yes, I love it,' I said. 'Wow, interesting. Ha ha ha!'

One August day, I took a break from some filming I was doing in the South Central dog pound and Ubered up to some shiny offices in Century City, where Larry, Simon and I spent a morning interviewing editors. We talked about the re-enactments and the idea of doing things differently. It was becoming real and I was in equal measures excited and scared. A few weeks after that, I took off with the family to my dad's house on Cape Cod for a short break, and it was there that I received a message from Simon. It said simply, 'Larry's out.'

I called back straight away. 'Why?' I asked.

'He doesn't think you're on board with doing things in another way. I think he felt you were maybe a little unenthusiastic.'

'Did it seem that way to you when we were interviewing editors?'

'I've got to say it didn't. So I don't know what's going on. Maybe there's another reason. I don't know.'

I sent a message to Larry, hoping to change his mind. 'I am absolutely on board with another way of working . . . For me this is all about stretching myself and using different muscles.' But it didn't work. We were now nearly a year into our development phase and still without a director.

Chapter 28

# My Scientology Movie

It was March 2014 – more than six months after Larry left – before we shot our first scene on the film. Several times I thought about abandoning the project altogether. If I could have pushed a button that would have made the entire idea and any memory of it disappear, I probably would have done. The knowledge that there was another team also pursuing the subject didn't help. Alex Gibney, the director behind numerous Oscar-winning documentaries, had optioned Lawrence Wright's book, *Going Clear*. HBO was paying for his film. It was likely to make a big impact. It was liked spying Amundsen and his huskies speeding towards the South Pole while you're still walking around Millets looking for thermal socks.

In October, the family took an RV trip, driving from Los Angeles across Southern California to Nevada, Arizona, and Utah. I felt like the quintessential American dad piloting the vehicle, which was the size of an aircraft carrier and about as manoeuvrable. It was the kind of holiday I'd dreamed of taking as a child, in the years when my brother and I would spend our summers going mental sequestered in our dad's house while he worked and we stared at the static on the portable black and white television. Now I was making it real for my children, even though bits kept falling off the RV. There was an aerial on the roof for the flat-screen TV that went up and down with a hand crank but it got stuck in its 'up' position. Then I had a fight with the metal rods that supported the fold-out awning. I figured I'd be driving a metal carcass by the time we got back – the mechanical equivalent of a whale skeleton.

In Southwestern Utah we found an RV hook-up on the edge of Bryce Canyon National Park. During the day we hiked the trails, admiring the hoodoos – mysterious red rock formations carved by the wind that looked sometimes like totem poles or manikins or erect ginger roots. At night, when the temperature plummeted to near freezing, we roasted marshmallows, and after the boys were in bed Nancy and I watched a documentary that had been causing a sensation at festivals, Joshua Oppenheimer's *The Act of Killing*.

We digested it in half-hour chunks over three successive nights. It told the story of a wave of mass killings in Indonesia in the late sixties, doing so from the perspective of the killers themselves who were shown on sound stages directing scenes that re-enacted and celebrated the tortures and murders they had performed. Bizarre and shocking, it struck me as a new way of thinking about non-fiction storytelling. One had the sense, by the end, that the re-enactments had become an almost redemptive technique, allowing the principal culprit Anwar Congo to confront his crimes and, seemingly, think about them in a different way.

Later, I discovered there are precursors to this approach – Mohsen Makhmalbaf's *A Moment of Innocence*; Rithy Panh's *S21: The Khmer Rouge Killing Machine*; *Punishment Park* by Peter Watkins. Joshua Oppenheimer himself has pointed to the films of the French director Jean Rouch – which involve semi-scripted self-re-enactments – as an influence.

Watching the film in the RV, I thought about a different way of seeing the re-enactments that Larry Charles had talked about for the Scientology film. Instead of spoofs of genres, or exercises in poking fun at Church practices, or simply ways of visualizing Church practices and events, the process of making the re-enactments would be the point. They would work as a kind of therapeutic role-play for our contributors, bringing their memories to life, forcing them to examine their own consciences, which in turn would allow me to interrogate their choices.

A month or so later, back in LA, I received a call from Simon saying he had another director in mind, John Dower, a respected veteran of several theatrical documentaries, including the definitive film about Britpop, *Live Forever*. John was intrigued by Scientology, which he described as being like a religion invented by Thomas Pynchon, and he liked the film-within-a-film idea. Still, he had some misgivings. He wasn't explicit on the subject but I supposed they were the understandable ones of someone used to running his own ship jibbing at the idea of crewing with a co-captain whose name and likeness were carved into the vessel.

He wrote a treatment setting out his vision for the film. It would be a documentary about me, Louis Theroux, as I attempted to make a fictional feature film about Scientology. The 'Louis Theroux' in the treatment seemed a different person to the one I'd known – well, *been* – for forty-plus years. He was like a made-up character. I couldn't get my head round the concept. I didn't want to make a fictional film about Scientology. I bridled at the idea that I wasn't a co-author of the actual 'outer' documentary.

We had a slightly awkward conference call. He was jibbing. I was bridling.

John left the project. Then he returned. Then he left. This hokey-cokey dance went on for several weeks, in-out, in-out, until I sent an email not exactly shaking it all about, but making it plain that I wasn't trying to replicate my TV documentaries and that I was as keen as he was to try a different approach. I threw in the words 'improvised re-enactments' and 'therapeutic role play' for good measure. I don't know if those exact phrases did the trick but John came on board again – this time for good – and we settled into a concept in which we were making a film about Scientology, more or less as equals,

Selfie with my Scientology director, John Dower.

that would use re-enactments and the Hollywood process of casting, location scouting, directing, improvisation to shine a light on Hollywood's sci-fi religion.

The collaboration with John, while it had its bumps, in the end turned out to be more fun and more rewarding than I could have imagined.

Filming took place over the best part of a year. A few days here and there, possibly twenty or so shoot days in all.

At the beginning – and to an extent all the way through – there remained unknowns about how the re-enactments would work. One of the few consistent features was the feeling that they would hinge on the participation of an ex-Scientologist named Marty Rathbun. He featured in almost all the coverage of Scientology that had appeared in the wake of the wave of defections starting in 2004. At one time he'd been the Inspector General for the entire church, responsible for enforcing orthodox practice at all the Scientology churches and missions – though Scientology disputed this, claiming he'd been a lowlier figure. He'd audited – Scientology-speak for counselled – celebrity Scientologist Tom Cruise (maybe you've heard of him?). Marty had worked closely with David Miscavige for years: they'd been brothers-in-arms of a spiritual sort, but they'd fallen out. Marty had fled the Church and now he was a spearhead of anti-Scientology. In my mind, Marty would be our Anwar Congo: the troubled and charismatic warrior still processing complicated feelings.

John had made contact with Marty. When asked about the idea of taking part in another Scientology documentary, he said he was burned out on the subject. Then John mentioned the re-enactments idea, and Marty was sold.

On our first day of filming, a bright spring day in Los Angeles, I drove to the airport in a car rigged with a piece of scaffolding that carried a fabric sunshade and a couple of cameras, including a huge one that was shooting back at me. It felt like proper show business. 'Don't go over forty miles an hour,' John said. 'Got it,' I replied, and it was only a half hour later, distracted by the rig and the excitement, that I drove onto the freeway by mistake. At high speed the sunshade acted like a wing, I could feel the lift – it was either going to detach and kill a random passer-by or, best case scenario, we would take off and travel to our destination by air. But we made it, and I picked up Marty – the camera apparatus meant we couldn't open the front doors and had to crawl inside – and on the drive to Marty's motel we chatted in a friendly way as we filmed. In the motel room, I read him a letter from the Church in which they declined to take part in my documentary.

Marty was polite enough, intelligent and self-possessed – in his fifties, going grey, a little paunchy, he had the air of a high school basketball coach whose life hasn't gone to plan. He wore rumpled shirts with lots of pockets, like a fly fisherman, though I can't recall if he was wearing one that day, and behind an apparently laid-back

314 GOTTA GET THEROUX THIS

exterior was a contradictory figure: part spiritual seeker, part back-yard brawler.

John and I had agreed that, while we had no clear idea how the re-enactments concept would develop, a first step would be to film – as Larry had once proposed – a series of auditions for the role of David Miscavige, with Marty sitting in and offering input and direction. The day after the chat at the motel, at a studio in an anonymous stretch in the west of the city, we sat in a windowless room for several hours as one by one thirty or so young actors performed lines from the Scientology leader's only network-TV interview, on the American current-affairs programme *Nightline* in 1992.

In footage from the show, Miscavige – then around thirty-four years old, with Vanilla Ice hair and shoulder pads – gives off a steely intensity as he attempts to explain the basic concept of the Church – no easy task given the vagueness and calculated mystery of its doctrine – and tries to quash allegations of dirty tricks that had recently appeared in a *Time* cover story, subtitled 'The Cult of Greed'. 'Scientology. The word means study of life,' he says, with surprisingly broad unpolished Philadelphia vowels. 'Study of knowledge. And that's what it is. It takes up all areas of life itself. Things that are integral. Maxims that are related to life and very existence.'

Fresh-faced and vulnerable, several of them visibly nervous, the young actors came across as touchingly eager to please, offering different reads, placing their trust in us. They seemed to embody the age-old Hollywood dream of making it and it wasn't hard to imagine them as exactly the kind of starry-eyed hopefuls that Scientology has traditionally sought to recruit, with promises of show business connections and the prospect of becoming the next Tom Cruise. From the off, Marty lit up and took control, feeding lines, offering suggestions on how to embody the right level of contained rage and righteousness.

He encouraged the actors to improvise foul-mouthed abuse, with either him or me standing in to take it. 'Get personal. Dress the guy down. Call him a four-eyed son-of-a-bitch cocksucker. *Louder.*' He told an actor to shove me against a wall – it was oddly bracing – and could barely conceal his pleasure at the spectacle of play-acted physical violence. 'This is really good,' he muttered.

During all this, I also plied him with questions about his involvement in the Church, how it was that he'd stayed in for so long and become an adjunct to a regime that was so oppressive. What was it about the beliefs and about Miscavige's personality that had appealed to him? He described the intoxicating danger of an all-encompassing religious vision, and there was a piece of him that still tapped into that thrill of being part of a Spartan band of holy warriors. All of this flowed naturally from the process of the auditions.

After that day, I was confident the re-enactments idea – though

Holding e-meter cans during filming.

we didn't know where it was leading or how it would pay off – was a goer.

For the rest of that year, every few months, Marty would fly out to film short sessions with our actors. As we became comfortable around each other, we settled into a kind of *48 Hours*-style double act. I was Eddie Murphy: puckish and immature. He was Nick Nolte, the grizzled vet who was too old for this shit. Still, he seemed to enjoy aspects of our time together. It was clear he was obsessed with Scientology – and, in particular, David Miscavige – and he enjoyed giving vent to his obsession.

'Ultimately, it's as if he literally, in his warped mind, is begging me to end all this for him,' he said. 'He knows I'm the truth, man. And that is the scariest thing in the world to him.'

Marty believed that it was his leaving, in 2004, that snapped Miscavige out of an alleged spiral of abuse. He said it was possible that the secret base he and Miscavige worked at could have 'gone full Jonestown' if Marty hadn't blown the whistle and spoken to the papers. He maintained that Miscavige was obsessed with *him*. This may well have been true. It was documented that a committed band of Scientologists had filmed and harassed Marty and his wife for months on end after he left the Church. They called themselves 'the squirrel busters' and wore goofy hats with cameras on top of them. It was commonly assumed they were operating on orders from Miscavige.

A part of Marty still viewed Scientology as valuable. He saw aspects of the tech as therapeutic and insightful, and he seemed to pine for the world-saving mission and the paramilitary dedication of the Sea Org; knocking heads, pushing people around, shouting and motivating. In filming with our actors, it was a little as though Marty had been gifted a small cult to imprint his spiritual thinking upon.

A month or two after the Miscavige auditions we held another casting call for the role of Tom Cruise. This time we enlisted the help of an ex-Scientologist named Marc Headley – he'd been audited *by* Cruise when he was still inside, living at the Church's secret base in the California desert. Then, with our Miscavige and Cruise now cast, we took them, and twelve or so other young actors, and put them through a day of Scientology 'drills' on a hot soundstage in an area of LA called Silverlake. This – we hoped – would be a way of exploring what Scientologists actually do: how they instil the ultra-disciplined, glazed-eyed attitude that is the hallmark of the true LRH believer. But it was also something Marty had suggested – he presided over the instruction – and the day turned out to be revealing not only for the content of the teaching itself, which mainly involved taking turns staring at each other in pairs and shouting abuse, but also for the way it led to an unintended blow-up between Marty and me. He objected to my suggestion that we follow Scientology protocol and applaud an imaginary portrait of Hubbard at the end of the day. 'I advise you guys not to do it,' he said. 'I'm not participating in that shit.' And walked off in a huff.

That Marty found me irritating created a helpful dynamic for the film and prevented it becoming too cuddly. I tried not to take it personally, and truthfully it wasn't just about me. He would often say he was fed up with the whole subject of Scientology and especially the world of anti-Scientology: the usual suspects of the prominent critics making claims about abuse and cult tactics. 'I've graduated from Scientology. I'm done.' His position reminded me of William Shatner, in the famous comedy sketch that showed him telling attendees at a Star Trek convention to 'get a life'. Marty didn't want his existence defined by his time in the Church and resented the role he'd been assigned as champion of the cause and official scourge of Scientology. He'd recently remarried, and he and his wife had adopted a young infant. The child seemed to represent a rebirth for Marty: a part of his life that was untouched by anything to do with Scientology.

• • •

The Church pushback began not long after the first round of auditions with Marty.

Mainly it came in the form of sheaves of legal correspondence from Scientology lawyers. The gist of the letters was that I was a religious bigot; that I was basing my reporting on unfounded allegations by a handful of apostates; and would I do the same sort of reporting about the Archbishop of Canterbury, Justin Welby? They heaped scorn on the idea of using Marty Rathbun, a 'disgruntled apostate', to help cast our actor for the role of Pope Dave. I had the impression they might be OK with our doing re-enactments if we had a more suitable casting director, which was an unexpected development – the idea that they might seriously think about coming on as collaborators. But my main reaction was to wonder how they knew about the auditions and the presence of Marty, and to speculate whether it was possible we had a Scientology mole on our team.

I wrote back making the point that: 1) I wasn't a religious bigot; 2) there was an open invitation to any Scientologists who wished to speak to us and help with casting; and 3) yes, I probably would do the same story about Archbishop Justin Welby if he was dogged by multiple allegations of physical assault and human trafficking.

This was all true as far as it went, although – with respect to the Welby question – I had to acknowledge that Anglicanism probably *was* less intriguing than a UFO religion with Tom Cruise and a secret base. Whether it's bigoted to find a sci-fi writer founding a religion in the mid-twentieth century weirder than a Galilean preacher in the outer reaches of the Roman Empire is, I guess, a matter of opinion.

I was ready to post the letter, when John, with his director's hat on, possibly thinking it might provoke a reaction and certainly mindful that it was more visual than me popping it in a letterbox, had the idea of hand-delivering a copy to someone at Scientology's secret base. We were now a couple of months into filming and while I had been reluctant to be seen to be goading the church or trolling them – I kept thinking about where the line was between reasonable journalism and gratuitous provocation – John and Simon had a more pragmatic and ultimately more sensible view of the need to proactively put ourselves in the Church's crosshairs. We made the two-hour drive through the desert and arrived at a collection of buildings just visible behind trees that straddled a rural highway, with low walls at the edge of the road and, around the perimeter, higher fences with razor wire and floodlights. It all seemed normal enough, as alleged mind-bending secret cult headquarters go; no groans or clanking chains were audible. There were lawns and a golf course and all in all it could have been a very large high-end rehab clinic and country club. Except maybe for the razor wire. And the floodlights.

At the front there was a small gatehouse with a sentry and I went up to it, peering in and mouthing, 'I've got a letter!' I couldn't hear much back so I tugged on the door and then the sentry tugged back – he seemed discombobulated, or 'enturbulated' to use the Scientology word – so I backed off, a little confused, and we drove down the highway to a small side road to ponder our next move. It was here, a short while later, that a fierce-looking middle-aged woman in dark glasses and a uniform of white shirt and slacks drove up with a tall cameraman in tow. 'This is not a public road,' she said, with some heat. 'This is not a county road. This is our road . . . You now need to leave.'

I protested that I was only trying to deliver a letter, to which the lady said that I'd trespassed 'several times'. I resented this – I don't regard going up to a gatehouse to deliver something as trespassing – and despite various resolutions I'd made to remain respectful whatever transpired, a little part of me now started to go a tiny bit John Sweeney. Not that I shouted, but I was aware of no longer being calm and at one point, knowing it might irritate her, I slipped into Scientologese. 'I have not trespassed several times,' I said. 'Clear the word "several"!' ('Clear' being a Scientology word for 'Look up in the dictionary.')

There was some more back-and-forth, and the police arrived soon after, having been called by the Scientologists. They were friendly enough – we debated whether or not the road was public or which parts of it were – and a little after that we left and drove back up to LA.

As the months passed, the need to plan a climactic scene of re-enactment became more pressing and eventually late in the year we settled on a concept: the most troubling allegations made by Marty and others were that Miscavige had been physically abusive to his staff and, specifically, that he'd shut them up, for months and possibly years, in a virtual prison known colloquially as the Hole. It seemed natural that we should, with Marty's help, depict the Marty version of what the Hole might have been like.

It was towards the end of the year by this time. I'd moved back to London. Meanwhile letters had been continuing to arrive from Scientology's lawyers – cc'ed to various senior people at the BBC – to the effect that I was an unserious journalist, a tabloid provocateur and that the contributors I'd lined up were disgruntled apostates, fantasists, who were kicked out of Scientology for incompetence.

There had been a couple of further engagements with agents deployed by Scientology. A glamorous European woman and a cameraman had appeared outside the studio where we were filming one day. They were filming us setting up from across the road but refused to identify themselves. 'We're just making a documentary about *beeble*,' she said, meaning 'people'. I'd started filming *her* with a Flip video camera and she'd run away. We had spent one whole day being tailed by a car with smoked-out windows – almost certainly a PI hired by Scientology lawyers. It was memorable, not just for the weirdness of being followed in a creepy fashion by people in the employ of a self-described *religion* supposedly dedicated to spreading peace, understanding, and happiness (would Justin Welby do *that*?) but also because we took elaborate measures to try to corner the driver where he or she had momentarily parked so I could get out and interrogate whoever it was, and when the moment came I messed up, stopped our car just a little too far back, giving our tail enough space to slip away.

John and I, and our DP Will Pugh, went back and forth about where we should shoot our Hole re-enactment, though we tended to agree that there was a purity and logic about doing it in the desert close to the real Scientology base. John suggested a recce of possible locations, and bringing Marty with us, and maybe our 'David Miscavige', a talented young actor named Andrew Perez. Since being cast, Andrew had gone method in his approach, devouring books on the subject and he'd expressed an interest in making a visit to the base, to get a feel for the place. We could kill two birds with one stone: scout the desert and take Andrew on a Scientology field trip.

'Well,' I said. 'If we're going to do all this we should shoot it.'

And so Marty flew out from Texas again and we drove out to the desert one last time – him and me and Andrew – with the crew filming as we went.

Marty was in a state of more or less on-going semi-grumpiness towards me by this stage – possibly I'd asked him the same question four or five times too many which is an occupational hazard of interviewing the same person over the course of a year. He kept mentioning that everyone else's questions – the production assistants, the runners, the extras – were better than mine: more spiritually informed and more acute. This was fine by me – drama is conflict – though I did sometimes feel a little like his ill-treated and long-suffering spouse, undermined and belittled, and told constantly how much better he could do than me.

When we arrived at a spot not too far from the Base, an expanse of sand and creosote bushes with bare brown mountains in the distance, Marty pointed out, reasonably , that it looked nothing like the grounds of the Scientology secret HQ, which had neat landscaped lawns and spreading trees. Besides, he said, regarding the Hole, 'It was all inside. So you could literally recreate it anywhere . . . It's going to be a logistics nightmare out here.'

We chatted a little more about the feel that we were looking for. 'You've got to create that claustrophobia,' Marty said. 'It's a nondescript cheap-ass sort of office set-up.' Andrew and Marty ran some lines that Miscavige had allegedly said, and then, with the light starting to go, Andrew and I drove a few miles down the road to the Base, the same spot where we'd had the police called on us before. It was dark when we got there. In the months since I'd last been there a gate had been erected, but we'd done some research and double-checked with the local authorities that the road was open to the public, which it was. We even had a filming permit. We climbed over, and we were by the fence when security lights started going on and off. The action of the lights was slightly spooky: they didn't seem to be motion-activated and I wondered if we were being filmed by hidden cameras. Still, they had the side benefit of allowing us to see more clearly.

Then a loud commanding male voice rang out from the main road, 'You guys are trespassing. You need to leave or I'm calling the cops.'

We headed back up to our vehicle and that's when I saw the same woman, once again accompanied by a tall man holding a small camera.

'The road's closed. You're trespassing. You need to leave,' she said.

'Apparently it's a public road,' I replied and waved a copy of the filming permit.

'No it isn't.'

'And we have a—'

'No, you don't. See that thing that says "Road Closed"? What's your name? Lewis? Loo-ee? Are you so stupid that you can't see the sign that says "Road Closed"? Do you know what a road means? It's *closed*.'

By now I knew the woman's name – Catherine Fraser – and I began using it liberally, hoping it might irritate her.

'Catherine, Catherine. What is the issue here? We don't want to cause you any upset, Catherine.'

'I don't want him filming me,' she said. 'Tell him to stop.'

'But you're filming me,' I pointed out.

'Tell him to stop,' she repeated.

'You tell him to stop and I'll tell him to stop,' I said. This was a bluff. If she'd agreed, I would have been in trouble, given filming was the express purpose of my being there.

'Catherine, my deep desire is to speak to someone from the Sea Org,' I said. 'This is good. Let's just keep the conversation going.'

She retreated to her car but her cameraman stayed outside, filming me. I got out my trusty Flip digital recorder. It was too dark to see anything in the viewfinder but I figured it might intimidate him. Then I intoned: 'Are you making a documentary too? And if so, who is your one for?' But no answer came back and so we just filmed wordlessly, in the dark and lit only by the crew car's headlights and the sweeping beams of the cars passing us on the road.

When the time came to film the scene of the Hole re-enactment, there was a part of me that was amazed we'd got to the end without Marty bailing. A few weeks earlier, I'd been trying to think up other ideas for our little team of actors to re-enact and my mind had turned to allegations of physical abuse that involved the Sea Org members running around trees for hours in the hot desert. It was part of a drill created by Hubbard – the 'Cause Resurgence Rundown' – that had allegedly been turned into a punishment by Miscavige.

I had suggested this in an email to Marty.

'You running around a tree with actors, I guess, tells me where you are going,' he replied. 'It is where I have expressed repeated concerns about – let us do our all to be as entertaining as possible by clowning. As I have explained to you on numerous occasions (I am sure providing you with miles of great footage of entertaining impatience and frustration), to John from the outset, and even to Simon two and nearly one-half years ago, I don't really want to participate in such a project – let alone devote, what, five or six out-of-town weekends to it while raising an infant. I am rethinking whether the December trip is worth anyone's while.'

John had had to step in and send some long pacifying email to smooth Marty's feathers.

Marty had also experienced a nasty Scientology encounter at the airport one afternoon – after doing some filming with us – when three Scientology executives had showered him with weird abuse. The Church later tried to claim that the executives had been there by chance and that Marty had first abused *them*, though I found that a little hard to believe. Marty filmed some of the encounter on his primitive mobile phone. Smudgy digital images showed two men and a woman in executive dress: 'You're a loser!' the woman said. 'You're nothing! Why don't you stop committing suppressive acts and live a real life?' It was a surreal display: the naked antagonism in the name of spirituality and ethics.

Marty uploaded the video to his blog. It went viral. For a while the satisfaction of having a hit video seemed to quell some of Marty's disgruntlement towards me and the project. But that soon passed and instead he came to see it as a side effect of his doing our film – which it probably was – and then by extension to resent me for, in a roundabout way, fomenting the trolling and making his life miserable in order to generate material for the film.

We had brought back our little band of actors one final time – including Andrew our Miscavige and our Tom Cruise – and rendezvoused at a West Hollywood studio where a set had been created: a cheap-looking conference room interior, little more than chairs and a table and a window with bars, and an easel with a flipchart. Marty had written a rough script, and the day started with him presiding over a bull session in which he explained the background to the scene: the Hole, how it had worked, how he had been sent there and how he had reached his breaking point. He also described the particular day that the script depicted – when Marty had (allegedly) seen Miscavige beat up his friend Tom DeVocht, causing Marty to make the decision to flee.

When the time came to do a take, Andrew Perez, our Miscavige actor, went full curtain-chewing loco, delivering a freewheeling rant based on Marty's words, pushing subordinates around, hurling abuse. 'Get down! Lick the fucking floor! You fucking mental midgets! You fucking degraded beings don't get shit done!' At one point he grabbed the leg of the flipchart easel and smashed it on the table, causing it to shatter into a thousand pieces – for a moment I worried he might have put out somebody's eye. 'How do you handle an SP. *You handle him roughly, OK?*'

'That was a command performance,' Marty said afterwards. 'It was as if he was channelling that guy.' John came down to congratulate the actors. I asked if he thought we needed another take 'Uh, no,' he said, looking as though I must be mad. 'There's a guy in the control room who actually seemed quite disturbed.' Maybe he was worried about Andrew smashing another leg. Either way, there was for a few minutes a feeling of relief that we'd done the main job of work we were supposed to do – that it had revealed something about the creed that Marty had espoused and advanced for so many years – and more than that, if true, the existence of the Hole was arguably an expression of something inside Scientology itself: a logical consequence of the most extreme form of its totalizing worldview and fanatical intensity.

I was wrapped up in these thoughts when I happened to wander outside to find Marty in conversation with two older guys with white hair and beards who looked like Kenny Rogers and his session bassist.

'What's an SP like you doing in a place like this?' 'Kenny' said to Marty.

'How much is the BBC paying you?' said Kenny's friend.

'Between the foster care and what the BBC is paying you, is that enough for you to cover your nut?' Kenny asked. 'Do you get paid enough for the foster care?'

Scientologists have a gift for pushing people's buttons. In fact, you could argue the most compelling evidence that Hubbard may have been onto something is how effective they are at causing people anguish: John Sweeney losing his shit during filming; me by the side of the road. And now, Marty, with the mention of his son.

They turned and left. Marty looked shaken.

'This is really sick, man,' he said. 'None of these things just happen. David Miscavige had to direct this. He scripted it and he directed it.'

'We probably shouldn't tell the actors what happened,' I said. 'It might upset them.'

'Welcome to my life, Louis. I have to live this life where I can't really share what happens to me on a day-to-day basis. We can't make friends. It's very difficult to say, "Hey, come on over for a barbecue, but realize you might be being surveilled and it might be going into the archive of the most pernicious, dangerous cult the Western world has known for the last fifty years."'

I've thought a lot about what I did next. I'm still not sure whether it was right or wrong. I chose this moment of Marty's vulnerability to bring up his misdeeds in the Church. 'You ran private investigators,' I said. 'Some of these techniques were things you did to other people.'

Marty paused and looked away.

'You're so wrong,' he said. 'It never even crossed my mind to think about bringing a person's child into something.'

'You had PIs pretending to be people's friends while secretly—'

Marty was now wandering off, seemingly in disgust.

'Isn't that a fact?' I said.

He stopped and turned. 'You're a fuckin' asshole. That's a fact,' he said. 'Fuck you.'

Almost immediately I felt bad at how startled and betrayed he looked at my questions. He paused now, clearly angry and upset.

'You know, I'm sitting here having my child brought into this thing and you want to make me defend myself?' he said. 'Fuck yourself.'

'OK, I consider myself fucked,' I said. 'I don't know what to say now.'

'This is really offensive. I'm really fuckin' offended by it. I'm telling you I have no life. I can't even make friendships. I am unemployable. And you start giving me this shit?'

Then we stood in silence for a bit, there on the pavement outside the studio.

We filmed one or two more scenes: our David Miscavige playing backgammon with our Tom Cruise (we figured, having cast a Tom Cruise, we needed to use him in something); a final triumphalist oration by our David Miscavige, taken from a speech he gave at a Scientology gala in 2004.

But in that moment with Marty, after he'd been emotionally ambushed by the two Scientologists, I was confident we had an ending and, therefore, a film.

Chapter 29

## The Fart

When they raised the baby's head, tiny, cross-faced and smeared like a bagel in what looked like cream cheese and jam, I glanced at Nancy and could only think, *We're not doing this again.*

He'd arrived after a harrowing C-section one October afternoon at St Mary's Hospital in Paddington. Nancy looked half-dead afterwards, as pale as a vampire; the procedure had been delayed and delayed for mysterious reasons – we'd felt like passengers whose flight keeps getting pushed back, the same sense of boredom and impotence, though with an admixture of fear. Then when it was going on, there was a worrying atmosphere of hushed urgency, and muttered conferences, vital signs were dipping, and my mind naturally went to the worst-case scenario and I cursed myself for the foolhardiness we'd shown in taking Nancy through the blood-letting of another round of life creation.

Getting to term had been a trial. Two had ended in miscarriage. There were tears on a weekend away in Yosemite. We'd been through nothing like that before. The language of grief and the social forms I was versed in didn't seem adequate to the occasion. The sadness was completely private, between us, and even I – if I'm honest – didn't really understand what she was going through. It still seemed abstract to me, whereas to Nancy the babies had already become real.

Seven months into a new pregnancy we moved back to London, thinking it made sense to be close to family, arriving back in our old house in Harlesden to find the area had perked up a bit. The high street had been pedestrianized. A Specsavers and a Subway had opened up. Then came a Holland & Barrett. When Costa Coffee arrived in 2015 it felt a little like something magical was happening. A *Costa*? We hadn't dared to dream we'd see the day. We were *literally* in a land flowing with milk and not honey but reasonably enjoyable coffee with a publicly accessible toilet. It might not seem like much, but to have some kind of recognized national chains felt like the green shoots of a comeback. There were still itinerant bands of street drinkers and shuffling medicated men emanating from half-way houses, but now they were sharing the pavements with young families sipping lattes. It was a mixed blessing, since many of the new arrivals seemed to avoid the local shops, treating the area like a bedroom community, but it was also a welcome addition to the mix – 'Music and Movement with Little Beep Beeps', Bouncy Castles on Friday at the Willesden Sport Centre . . . Even the 'Pound Man', a hyper-aggressive local cadger, was no longer in evidence (months later, I ran into him during a carol service in Wormwood Scrubs prison).

Being plunged back into baby mode was both wonderful and bizarre – a kind of regression to a previous life stage. In my mind, I compared it to going back to primary school as a grown man, the closest I've ever come to time travel. This time, though, we had Albert and Fred – the two big boys – so we were in a sense straddling time zones. They more than anyone had been excited to visit him – baby Walter – and just about managed to conceal their disappointment to find him, in those early days, a squeaking and floppy creature, an overgrown grub, blinking and squinting with unfocused eyes, who woke them in the night.

Alas, I'd sold a lot of our old baby paraphernalia on eBay – which Nancy liked to bring up, as though I'd passed up a chance to snag a priceless Mondrian at a junkshop or buy shares in Apple in 1976. So I had to re-buy everything: baby-change table, crib, sterilizer. Miraculously the baby monitor still worked. The first few months were a cascade of moments of recognition, each with its own emotional cue: will he feed? Why is he crying? When did he last poo? Why won't he nap? What's wrong with the fasteners on this baby-grow? Is he teething? Does this look like a rash? HOLD HIS HEAD! Burping and winding. Swaddling. Creeping around the house, putting him down so gently it was like doing bomb disposal, and the heart-stopping feeling of being stalked by random noises – is he awake? Third time out, we were lazy, overmanned by the other children, and all about the path of least resistance: dummies if he cried, let him eat what he likes, put him down when he feels like it and let him climb in with us if need be – let's just relax and enjoy our farewell tour of babyland.

Somewhere around this time Nancy reminded me that I had agreed I'd only make programmes in the UK. I had no recollection of saying this, but it was definitely true that I'd campaigned for a third baby so I had a certain obligation to make myself available.

I had my doubts about doing UK shows. From the earliest days, I'd suspected that a certain amount of culture clash was an intrinsic element of the formula. Other than the celebrity programmes, I had never made a documentary in the UK – or never successfully, since there had been a couple of abortive starts. Was I still seen as a TV piss-taker? Was my brand toxic to contributors? Occasionally I'd recall a story in the Arabian Nights called 'The Historic Fart' about a man who breaks wind noisily at his wedding. He's so embarrassed he flees the city. Ten years later, he feels he may have served out his exile and returns with a little trepidation and finds himself in the market place, where to his dismay, the *very first conversation* he overhears is a recollection of his now-legendary flatulence.

And what about me? Were my farts still at the forefront of people's minds?

Forced to engage more seriously with UK ideas, my mind turned to subject areas that exist in a more extreme form in the UK than in the US. From there it was a short hop to Islamic fundamentalism. I spent several months reading, and watching videos of so-called hate preachers. The *soi-disant* caliphate of Isis was in its considerable heyday around that time. The reports of life regimented according to strict eighth-century Islamic practice, with brutal punishments, and taxes on Christians, and slaves, was reminiscent of *The Pursuit of the Millennium* by Norman Cohn, which I still hadn't read, or millenarian sects described in histories of the English Civil War. I downloaded issues of *Dabiq* – Isis's English language propaganda magazine – marvelling at its marriage of up-to-date desktop-publishing software and medieval theology. It featured full-colour photos of a Syrian air-pilot being burned to death in a cage – alongside numerous paragraphs of references to religious authorities that looked, to the outside eye, rigorously footnoted and sourced. Another issue ran an almost *Smash Hits*-style Q&A with the captured pilot before death.

I wasn't seriously thinking of visiting the area – too dangerous – but I wondered about meeting the nexus of UK Isis supporters. Among the most visible British Isis advocates was Anjem Choudary. As a student of medicine at the University of Southampton, he'd gone by the name Andy and had a reputation as a party boy – a famous easily googleable photo shows him laughing in front of a table laden with beers next to a copy of the men's magazine *Mayfair*. But later, after graduating, he'd fallen under the influence of the preacher Omar Bakri Muhammad and embraced a violent interpretation of the Koran. He'd pop up on Fox News and Channel 4, evangelizing – in a way that was oddly bland and legalistic – for a wholly Islamic sharia-based government in the UK.

When it came to trying to pin him down for filming, Anjem proved elusive. He'd talk to our A P, seem flattered by our attentions, then go quiet for weeks. Once or twice he notified us at the last minute of the locations of his weekly street ministries – where he did 'dawah'. One Sunday, in the shadow of the City of London skyscrapers, we turned up to find his ragtag band of street preachers handing out leaflets to a bemused multicultural public, alternately preaching at them and berating the many hecklers. We got almost nothing usable out of the encounter. During our only significant conversation, Anjem fired questions at me while a minion or colleague filmed us. They put the conversation up on YouTube, editing out most of my answers.

A few days after that, an associate of Anjem's, Abu Baraa, which means 'father of innocence', invited us to speak to him at his community centre. Abu Baraa was a little younger than me, of Pakistani heritage – he'd been born Mizanur Rahman and grew up in London. He appeared thoughtful and intelligent, explaining in mild tones that we'd fallen prey to Western propaganda in our view of the Caliphate: yes, there were 'beatings' of wrongdoers but we had to understand they weren't being hit very hard; 'slaves' was a misnomer, he said, and you couldn't rape your slaves anyway, they had to consent to sex; and besides, he continued, didn't we have slaves in the UK? Weren't the people locked up in prison 'in bondage' as slaves?

He went on the attack, asking what was the foundation of my supposed moral outlook? How did I distinguish right from wrong? If I did not look to the Koran or the Bible, what was the framework by which I judged actions? Suddenly I was on the back foot. I thought about saying, 'I'm asking the questions', and dodging the debate but at the time I felt the ballsier move was to belly up and engage – make a case for a rational system of values founded in 2,000 years of philosophy, ethics, the Enlightenment – but I was struggling to do it cogently. I heard myself appealing to a Western liberal tradition, human rights, opposition to torture and capital punishment, but it was all pretty vague and the moment I invoked the idea of 'the

West' I was aware I was already on thin ice. 'Who gets to decide?' he kept saying. 'So it's Western civilization is it? The West decides?' Afterwards my director Jamie Pickup told me: 'You got owned.'

When filming prospects are looking unpromising, I can usually salve my concerns if there is at least one contributor I feel positive about – someone compelling and different. And here there was: an Irishman named Khalid Kelly. He had been a nurse, named Terry Kelly, in Saudi Arabia. Imprisoned on a drinking-related offence, he'd converted behind bars, becoming increasingly radical after he was released. He was now back living in Ireland and his soft lilt of an accent and his amiable manner made a striking contrast with his radical views. All the signifiers were at loggerheads with the usual image of the jihadi – he sounded like he should be sharing a Guinness and talking up the craic to be had in Dingle. Alas, after showing some interest in our project at first, as time went on Khalid Kelly got cold feet, possibly for fear that he could get locked up for 'glorifying terrorism'.

And there was a second stumbling block with UK ideas: there seemed to be three other documentary crews chasing all the stories we were interested in. The tiny handful of Islamists we might have been able to film with were already involved with other producers, who would whisper in their ears in self-interested fashion that they shouldn't do any other publicity. For a while we pursued leads among Muslims advocating a conservative non-jihadi brand of Islam. I became interested in a YouTuber and Islamic provocateur who called himself Dawah Man, real name Imran Ibn Mansur. One of his videos was entitled 'Would atheists drink their dad's sperm?' I liked the cheekiness of his delivery – he came across like a Muslim Ali G and professed to have been, at one time, a rapper on the verge of huge success. But even he didn't want to tango with me.

Gradually, without the realistic prospect of contributors, the story withered and died. Abu Baraa and Anjem were locked up on convictions for advocating terrorism. They each got five years. Another man in their circle who I'd seen at the dawah in east London – Abu Izzadeen, born in Hackney as Trevor Green – was arrested on a train in Hungary, presumably attempting to migrate to Isis. A year after we were in touch, in November 2016, Khalid Kelly blew himself up in a suicide attack on Iraqi troops during the Battle of Mosul.

I regret that we weren't able to make that film on radical Islam. It feels like a gap – a lacuna in my oeuvre (and no one likes one of those). I've done programmes on extreme Christians, ultra-nationalist Jewish Israelis, white supremacists and black supremacists, but nothing on the most polarizing religious topic *de nos jours* – the threat, or alleged threat, posed by violent Islamism. In the end, it was a failure of trust. The atmosphere was so heightened – the fear of being locked up in the UK for 'glorifying terrorism', the sense of suspicion of outsiders – as to make it impossible. A few months later the other crews' efforts aired: Jamie Roberts' *The Jihadis Next Door*; Peter Beard's *My Son the Jihadi* and one or two others. As powerful and well-made as they were, even in them there was a vague sense of distance – a lack of intimacy – with the central element of the phenomenon, the home lives of the violent jihadis themselves, slightly missing.

In a practical spirit of thinking about shows we could actually make, I began work on a film about alcohol. Years earlier I'd seen *Rain in My Heart*, Paul Watson's harrowing documentary that follows the end stages of several severely addicted drinkers: two or three of them died during the course of filming and there is an unforgettable scene of a young man in his bedroom who necks an entire glass of red wine and then promptly vomits it back up again. 'Wouldn't *sipping*, if you have to have a drink—?' comes Paul Watson's voice from behind the camera. 'I don't *sip*,' says the young man, with a perverse pride.

My director, Tom Barrow, and AP, Grace Hughes-Hallett, secured access to the liver unit of King's College Hospital in south-east

London. For weeks they hung about, meeting the hospital's regulars. The recce process dragged on and on. The people who would agree to be filmed tended to be street drinkers – homeless older men – who, it was felt, would give a false sense of the nature of the problem: keeping it at a safe remove. Our contributors should be proxies of the audience: this could be you. One day in August, having just arrived back from a family holiday in America, my series producer called to say the team had found a young man they liked and we should film.

Thirty-one-years old, an academic administrator, Joe Walker had been found collapsed in a street by a stranger and brought to A&E. He was four days into his detox when I met him: lying in bed, battered by his recent dissipation, with weird bruising on his legs and a cut above his eye.

'That's never happened before,' he said in a shaky voice, looking at his legs. 'It's quite frightening.'

The nurse in charge of detox asked if he could walk and he hobbled around for a minute or so with the help of a stick.

'Definitely ataxia,' the nurse said.

'It started with a bottle of vodka a day,' Joe told me. 'Then it went up to two bottles of vodka a day.'

He'd been four and a half years sober. Then he'd been turned down for a job and gone through a break-up. 'I just thought "Sod it" and went for it.'

Joe became our central character. We filmed him intermittently over several months and alongside him a handful of other characters who appeared in the finished film – a big, soft-spoken South African called Pieter; a French and West African sometime waitress named Aurelie; an old-school Londoner and antiques dealer called Stuart.

Several weeks into filming, after he'd been released from hospital, I called on Joe at his flat above a parade of shops in Denmark Hill. He was doing well, on the wagon and looking for work. We talked about his life and his upbringing. He showed me some photos of trips he'd taken, including one to Australia – in the picture he was sunburned at the wheel of a boat; and in another, dressed in a red jumpsuit getting ready to go skydiving. 'I was out pissing it up, quite frankly,' he said, and mentioned a girlfriend he'd been horrible to through his drinking. There were books and CDs on his shelves that reminded me of my own tastes or the tastes of someone like me, a copy of *Goliath* by Max Blumenthal and the music of Nick Drake, and the feeling of similarity was only reinforced when I discovered he'd played Sky Masterson in a school production of *Guys and Dolls* – the only musical I think I can say I know almost all the words to, other than *Jesus Christ Superstar*. We sang 'Luck Be A Lady' together.

A few weeks after that, word came that he was drinking again. We entered a weird phase of production, aware that he was homeless and vulnerable, but unsure of exactly how we should attempt to tell his story. It would have felt strange and wrong to film him on the streets but he didn't seem to want to reach out to his friends and family. Off camera, my director Tom encouraged Joe to seek services, both for his own good, and also because we knew it was our best chance of getting a useable scene. And in fact, by a stroke of luck, a week or so into this phase, we happened to be at the hospital shooting a different sequence when we heard that Joe was in A&E, inebriated and behaving erratically, demanding and then refusing treatment. I found him outside on a front wall of the hospital on Denmark Hill, bruised and bloody, shirtless, wearing an overcoat. His hands were shaking so much he couldn't hold his cigarette. With one of the A&E doctors, a young woman, I helped him inside, into a small room, where he lay down on a hospital bed. His body was racked with the pain of withdrawal. He was buffeted by the craving for more alcohol, pricked by thoughts of lost loves, and almost crazed with self-pity.

'You've actually been to see us three times in the last twenty-four hours,' the doctor said. 'What are you hoping we might be able to do?'

'Detox,' Joe said, and hiccupped.

Then, after she'd gone, he asked, 'Can I have some Lucozade?' He looked frightened and awestruck, as though it was taking every reserve of strength to make the request. I went and got some from a vending machine. When I got back he was lying down, groaning, in his dirty pink jumper. His head wobbled as he drank.

'How are you feeling?' I asked.

'Withdrawing very heavily,' he said. 'It's like I'm dying as a person.'

'What was it that triggered you?''

'My ex. Wouldn't talk to me.' He paused, then said, with utter hopelessness, 'The most beautiful girl I've ever seen.' He lay back, closed his eyes and gave a series of heaving bronchial sobs.

I wasn't sure what to say or do, but knew he needed to hear something to boost his morale. Absurdly, I heard myself ask: 'Do you want some Lucozade?' Then I said: 'You can get back on track.'

'No, I can't, I think this is endgame.'

There was a pause. He looked at me. 'You must hate me,' he said.

I hadn't seen this coming. 'No,' I replied. 'No! What a strange thing to say.'

He brightened. 'Do you like me?'

'Of course I like you.'

The doctor and the detox nurse came back in to say that they'd agreed to admit Joe for another extended treatment, though they had some misgivings based on his pattern of coming and going. 'It's actually quite neurologically dangerous, Joe, to keep on detoxing someone. But obviously we're very happy to help this time.'

'Thank you,' Joe said with an air of performed sincerity. I assumed it was performed because he was having trouble holding himself together and was trying to converse appropriately but then, almost as soon as the nurses had left, Joe announced he was off. 'I just want to get a bottle of vodka and go to Ruskin Park.' I was a little shocked at the idea that, having just been admitted, he was now leaving again. I tried to dissuade him but he slipped past me, heading outside – for a moment he was forestalled by another nurse who spotted him and escorted him back – but then he was off again, making his way out into the crowds of the High Street, like a balloon wafting into the sky, watched by me and the doctor who'd been helping him.

We stood looking on with a sense of sad impotence – he had blown it, the doctor turned to go inside – and that was when he reappeared, with a bottle in his hands.

'It's only Perrier,' he said when he reached us. 'I didn't drink anything.'

We followed him inside again. This time he stayed.

Afterwards I reflected on how uncomfortable it had been, filming Joe in the depth of his crisis. The awfulness of his addiction and not knowing how to help. I thought about how much easier it would have been if he'd had a girlfriend or parent with him who would have been the lightning rod for his emotional outreach. I wasn't sure how to be a friend to Joe in his moment of need, nor whether it was

With Joe Walker, a few months after filming *Drinking to Oblivion*.

appropriate to try to be one. I was also aware how inadequate my expressions of support sounded. *Do you want some more Lucozade?*

And yet, later when I watched it, I realized my discomfort and impotence were what gave the scene its power. My awkwardness, the Lucozade, were both embarrassing and ludicrous but also eloquent expressions of what many feel when confronted with addiction.

When the film came out, titled *Drinking to Oblivion*, it seemed to touch people in a different way than other documentaries I'd done. I wondered if it was because it took place in Britain. It was – literally and figuratively – closer to home. But my deeper secret was that it had also meant something more to me. As a British person, a south Londoner, I'd come home and been able to make a programme close to where I'd gone to school; where my Mum had grown up; where my grandparents had met and married.

It felt like a very personal sort of vindication. I'd served out a sentence. My farts were forgotten after all.

# Chapter 30

## Programme Six

The idea of a programme revisiting the subject of Jimmy Savile – so long deferred, so feared at the channel, and so fraught with difficulty for me – became real in late 2015.

It was now year four in the Savile Disclosures Calendar, and the cultural landscape bore the imprint of everything that had followed from Jimmy's unmasking. An investigation had been set up by the police – Operation Yewtree – and a host of beloved, and not-so-beloved, T V and radio personalities had been rounded up. There would, in the end, be nineteen arrests – of DJs, actors, musicians – with around half resulting in prosecution, and seven eventual convictions. Most saw it as a necessary rectification of a historic injustice – the failure to listen to and hear victims and reassure them that their accounts of abuse and assault would be taken seriously – though there were also increasingly elements in the media and in the country that viewed the entire process as a witch hunt, an attempt to apply a present-minded moral framework to a more louche and free-spirited era, fuelled by compensation claims and a frenzied tabloid culture, whose resources would be better spent chasing up-to-date cases.

Either way, the post-Yewtree reality was the new normal. Rolf Harris, Stuart Hall, Gary Glitter were all in prison; the DJ Dave

Lee Travis had received a three-month sentence suspended for two years. The world had moved so fast that it was hard to recall that as recently as 2005 Rolf had painted a portrait of the Queen, from life, as part of her eightieth birthday celebrations. The BBC had filmed it for an hour-long documentary, called *The Queen, by Rolf*, and the portrait had been lampooned for its rendering of the royal smile, which showed her teeth on display in a rictus that recalled a silverback readying for battle.

Such painterly misdeeds were once the worst Rolf could expect in the way of publicity. Now he sat in HMP Bullingdon for historic sex crimes.

It had been a strange cultural moment to live through: exciting, salutary, a little voyeuristic, in certain respects confusing, and occasionally – for those, like me, cursed with a tendency to worry over moral wrinkles and hypocrisies – troubling. Certainly I took the view that it could only be a good thing for men and women who'd been assaulted to finally get some measure of justice; that a more enlightened and clear-sighted attitude to the reality of sexual exploitation was now prevailing.

But I also had concerns about the erosion of due process. Ageing politicians and civil servants had been hounded on flimsy or non-existent legal pretexts. Some stars had been kept in legal limbo for months while the police chased paper-thin allegations. At the apex of the panic about sex pests in high places, the police had announced that the allegations of a man known pseudonymously as 'Nick' were 'credible and true'. 'Nick' turned out to be Carl Stephen Beech, a shameless compensation hunter and paedophile, who – as I write this – has just been sentenced to eighteen years in prison for perverting the course of justice. But in 2015 his tales of stabbings and stranglings of children involving Leon Brittan and the MP Harvey Proctor were – unbelievably – being taken seriously and used as the basis for a credulous and expensive police follow-up.

· · ·

Max Clifford, my old sparring partner, had been arrested only a few months into the new era, in December 2012 – Savile Disclosures Year 1.

In the years since we'd made our programme there had already been some surprising revelations. His wife Liz had died of cancer, and afterwards he had outed himself in a profile in the *Observer* as a long-time frequenter of swinging parties. He'd amplified the account in a ghosted autobiography, *Read All About It*. He'd been a 'ringmaster' at the parties, he wrote, or ghost-wrote, 'a role I like to have in many aspects of my life.' If anything it helped to explain why he'd been so quick to believe that the Hamiltons might have attended a sex party in Ilford.

'I was too greedy to be faithful,' he continued. 'Almost anything went, including having two girls at a time. Having sex with girlfriends' mothers and watching others have sex.' He described tricking a girl into sex with a friend who was a plumber by telling her he was someone important in show business – seeming to view this as a blow for social justice and a fitting punishment for being over-interested in celebrity. The prank – if you can call it that – reminded me of the same qualities of insensitivity and the need for control I'd noticed during our filming,

Then, after the Savile revelations, he'd gone on TV to make a plea for an indulgent view of stars' sexual indiscretions. Celebrities were 'frightened to death,' he'd said.

'All kinds of things went on,' he'd gone on. 'And I do mean young girls throwing themselves at them in their dressing rooms, at concert halls, at gigs, whatever . . . They never really asked for anybody's birth certificate, and they were young lads.'

Among the 'young lads', presumably, Max had included himself, though he'd been in his forties when several of the allegations took place. His fall was precipitous and complete, and because of our association I took a more than usual interest.

At trial, one woman described how as a seventeen-year-old she'd visited him for career advice. Max had told her to remove her dress in his office. The assault took place while Max was on the phone to his wife. Even stranger, he had wanted the victim to accompany him to a dinner so that she could masturbate him under the table as he sat next to his wife.

Several times, according to accounts given in court, he'd impersonated James Bond producer Cubby Broccoli and Stephen Spielberg in order to create an illusion of power and influence.

Max denied everything, writing off his seven accusers as 'fantasists and opportunists'. Friends from the world of celebrity – Pauline Quirke, Des O'Connor – testified to his tireless charity work, as though good works were incompatible with being a sexual predator. He would still be attempting to have his convictions overturned when he died.

As the Yewtree juggernaut trundled on, with the idea of a Savile revisit apparently off the table due to continuing nervousness at the channel, I'd encouraged the team to explore the general subject area of old-school entertainers and allegations of historic sexual abuse. It seemed a natural subject for us – the queasy cocktail of cold-blooded exploitation, transactional sex, and the lines between the two.

But having put out some approaches, we got not much back. Surprise surprise. Being – as they saw it – railroaded for dimly remembered gropes decades earlier was not a subject the investigated and arrested stars were in a rush to spill their guts about on national TV.

The only celebrity who showed signs of cooperating was the impresario and sometime TV presenter Jonathan King. King had been convicted of multiple accounts of historic sex offences in 2001. In a way, he'd been the Ur-Savile, a show-business star-maker and eccentric who'd used his celebrity cachet and an instinct for vulnerability to prey on vulnerable boys. He'd been released on parole in 2015. But King had already featured in two documentaries – both of them forensic and compelling, one by Jon Ronson, another by Nick Hornby. In both he'd expressed his view that he'd done nothing wrong, an opinion he was entitled to, but expressed himself with such callowness and lack of introspection that he did his case no favours. The idea of another documentary put me in mind of the fate of the corpse of Oliver Cromwell, exhumed in 1660, two years after his death, so it could be hanged.

Around this time, a new BBC2 controller was appointed – Kim Shillinglaw. It was strange to reflect that she was the sixth I'd served under. When a new one came in, I had the feeling of being seen like a smelly cat that came with the house. One or two people said, 'She really liked that autism film you did.' I wondered if that meant it was the only programme of mine she'd seen.

One afternoon I was invited up to the seventh floor of New Broadcasting House, the BBC HQ on London's Portland Place, to meet her. *There was a time when my bosses were from an older generation*, I thought when I saw her. But we were around the same age – she was, by the standards of British television, rather glamorous. We talked about some of the ideas my team were working on. Alcohol. Another about brain injury. The perennial subject of celebrities came up, whether there could ever be another *When Louis Met . . .* I made as if to take the idea seriously. *Julian Assange. Blah blah. Nigel Farage. Ha ha!* Then, with the same lack of expectation of someone checking the coin return of a random pay phone for loose change, I mentioned the idea of doing something on Jimmy Savile.

'It's very strange having known him personally, and realizing this side was hidden from you,' I said. 'It feels a little like being friendly with Jack the Ripper. It's hard to square the two parts of him and I wonder if that's partly how he got away with it.'

To my surprise she said to go for it.

A slightly weird interim followed. Production on a particular film doesn't go into high gear until the series producer hires a director. My seniors at the BBC mooted various candidates, including one friend and contemporary whose reaction to the idea when I spoke to him on the phone was resolutely negative.

'We know how Savile got away with it,' he said. 'He intimidated vulnerable people and he charmed those in power. What else is there to say?'

I made my case that he'd become a figure of such grotesquery that we were in danger of making him not quite real, which carried its own risks: firstly, in not telling the whole truth, and secondly, by extension, making it harder to spot Saviles of the future (which, incidentally, would be a good name for an avant-garde band, especially if they weren't looking to get many bookings). I tried to hint at the need for an understanding of the case that went beyond a simplistic view of perfect victims and perfect perpetrator. I mentioned the existence of victims of Jimmy's who had, in some cases, been friends or quasi-friends. There were many facets to the case that were less clear-cut and might allow a fuller understanding of how abuse takes place.

And what about the consequences of his crimes on those around him who feel they should have seen more and now are in the position of realizing they spent years of their life with a man unmasked as a sexual predator: his long-term girlfriends – of which there were said to be a couple – how were they to deal with all of this? His family? All of those who knew him, or thought they knew him, people for whom their association with Jimmy Savile and his celebrity and his charity work was one of the defining facts of their long lives – what about them? It seemed to me there were all sort of awkward dilemmas that we might be able to interrogate.

To all of this, my director friend, making a topical reference to the leader of Isis who was then much in the news, said: 'Yeah, well, you might have been friendly with al-Baghdadi, but that doesn't mean you should make a film about what he's like behind the scenes.'

'Personally, I think that sounds really interesting. I'd watch it in a heartbeat.'

'Well, the Isis victims might have other ideas.'

We ended the call in a way that was personable and polite but the clear message was that the documentary was wrong-headed and probably immoral. 'I really question why Kim has commissioned it,' he said.

The conversation wobbled me – not regarding the appropriateness of doing the documentary but it made me wonder quite why it was that, when I spoke about 'the need for nuance and a forensic attitude', people sometimes heard special pleading or an urge to extenuate and excuse. I thought back to books and films that made an impression on me. Their power and resonance hinged on their uncomfortable details and the awkward quality of the moral ecology they described: victims who couldn't help but become adjuncts of their predatory conditions; suffering that was in no way ennobling; a strange symbiosis of oppressors and the victimized that ended up immiserating everyone.

Without quite finding the right form of words, I was fumbling towards an understanding of Jimmy's crimes that did not shame his friends, his colleagues, his family, and most of all his prey for failing to push him off with enough strength, for failing to see more, for failing to cry out, for failing to speak up – for failing to fit into a neat moral category that, for good or ill, is not how many, or even most, people behave.

Embarking in earnest on the second Savile film also meant I could chase down the little clues and leads I'd had about Jimmy over the years and finally answer some of my what-ifs: what if I'd aggressively pursued the little hints that had been shared with me?

One of my first calls was to Noddy Holder, lead singer of Slade, about whom the comedian Phill Jupitus had said 'He has a folder *this thick*.' I made approaches from various angles, via friends of friends and colleagues of colleagues. Word came back that he had nothing to say. I received an email that said, 'I really never had any time for

Jimmy Savile nor knew him.' Putting myself in Noddy's shoes, I could see that a call from a strange journalist asking about your relationship with a reviled sexual predator would not bring you pirouetting to the phone. Still, what about the file?

I ended up writing a letter, which was passed on to him. To my surprise he called – Slade frontman, glam-rock icon, 'Mama Weer All Crazee Now' scribe Noddy Holder. He said he'd met Jimmy a handful of times, doing *Top of the Pops*, and that Jimmy had struck him – as he did many people at that time – as being 'cock of the walk', self-important and an egoist, but he couldn't recall a conversation. More to the point, Noddy had had no inside knowledge of sexual wrongdoing: when the *Exposure* programme had aired he'd been as surprised as anyone else. The thick files turned out to be a misunderstanding, based on a conversation backstage at Phill Jupitus's show *Never Mind the Buzzcocks*. Someone had said they'd heard the journalists on Fleet Street have a file on Savile 'this thick' and Noddy had agreed, saying he'd heard the same thing.

Several other calls ended up in a similar place. In a diary from 2001 I'd found a reference to Keith Chegwin describing Jimmy Savile as 'evil'. I called Keith – he was on his mobile, puppyish as ever, scampering up Oxford Street. He didn't remember describing Jimmy as evil, though he allowed he might have heard something from another Radio 1 DJ, Tony Blackburn, in the eighties about Jimmy being arrested. 'One day he'll have his comeuppance,' was the attitude at that time, he said. Keith said Tony Blackburn might be someone to contact, which I did. It was an off-the-record chat in his agent's offices and so lacking in content that I didn't bother writing up the notes. There were a handful of other calls that went a similar way and the upshot was oddly unsatisfying. I'd been telling myself that Jimmy Savile's story was there waiting to be told – like a thread, it just needed one tug to unravel. But the reality was different: the missed opportunities weren't so missed after all. Either that or there were people who were keen not to be seen as having known more, for fear of being tied into a perceived web of complicity.

Then there was a further more awkward development. I'd been hoping we'd be able to include contributions from friends and family of Jimmy's. I'd been in touch with a self-appointed spokesperson for an underground network of Jimmy supporters – I'll call her Sally. 'They call us deniers,' she said. She didn't like the term. Sally had stayed out the spotlight, for obvious reasons, but had run a campaign of letter-writing and behind-the-scenes organizing attempting to rehabilitate Jimmy. She was also a gatekeeper to various friends and girlfriends of Jimmy's.

By this time a director and AP had been assigned to the project and we'd shot our first interview, appropriately enough, with Kat Ward, the woman who'd set the whole train in motion by writing an online memoir in which she described his visits to Duncroft and then later by being the first to speak up in a spiked segment for *Newsnight*.

I'd got in touch with Kat via Facebook and the interview had gone smoothly but Kat, as was her right, had told a friend who happened to be a journalist, and he'd rushed out an article about me doing a follow-up documentary. In its haste to stay ahead of the story, the BBC put out a press release, which I didn't see until it was too late, that couldn't have been designed to be more alienating to contributors who already had fears of being tarred as accessories to his crimes after the fact. The press release suggested friends of Jimmy's were holding on to secrets. There was also a gratuitous reference to Jimmy as 'the man who hoodwinked' me – somehow taking a programme that still had a plausible claim to being the most revealing portrait of Jimmy while he was alive and turning it into a testament to failure.

The friends and family – Sally, lines that were out to one of Jimmy's long-term girlfriends, other long-time friends who could have shed light on his nature – quickly evaporated. A lightly amended press release went out a few hours later but by then the damage was done. The four or five of us working closely on the project were called into a meeting with the executive producer and a BBC2 executive at Broadcasting House to sift through the wreckage. The channel executive made the case that we should see the press release as a positive, since it had forestalled the need for an awkward conversation with contributors about what was in the programme. He missed out the fact that such a conversation would only have been awkward because the contributors would have featured in the programme, which they now wouldn't.

It is hard to overestimate the amount of paranoia and anxiety that surrounded our Jimmy Savile film. By this time another documentary was already in the works – this one for BBC1, designed exclusively to honour the victims. The other film was to be so victim-focused that Jimmy's face would be deliberately obscured throughout out of a sense of respect for their feelings. My hope was that the existence of this other film might take the pressure off us and free us up to make something more – I suppose – perpetrator-focused. But it was also clear that the wounds were still raw – BBC brass were both keen to be seen to be treating the crimes with their proper gravity but also, behind that, there was a fear that the subject was so radioactive that it should be locked away in a lead-lined box and buried in the deep bosom of the ocean.

As a way of preserving some privacy, the BBC had procured us some quiet offices in Maida Vale away from the hubs of TV-making. We were also taking the precaution of referring to it as 'Programme Six'.

By this time – late 2015, early 2016 – there were numerous reports in the public domain: novella-length accounts of the findings of in-house investigators. They were published online and had the look and layout of actual books. The police ones came first – the Met, Surrey, West Yorkshire, North Yorkshire, another by the Crown Prosecution Service to determine why the 2009 Surrey Police investigation had gone nowhere. Several NHS reports followed – Leeds General Infirmary, Broadmoor, Stoke Mandeville. Others came later – any school or children's home Jimmy had been known to have visited was required to conduct an investigation, and the Department of Education supplied an online template for how their published write-ups should be organized. In the final tally, there were a total of thirty-two hospitals, ten local authorities, plus several charities including Barnardo's and Action for Children. There was also the magnum opus that was the Janet Smith Inquiry.

It has occasionally struck me as odd that these reports aren't better known, especially given how much money and effort must have gone into writing them. It is true that the local government ones are thin gruel. There are quite a few in which, having been alerted by an ex-pupil that Jimmy may have made a visit to a school sports day or fete, the investigators appear to have spent weeks making enquiries without managing to find a victim while being under an obligation to record every remembered detail from forty years previously. Jimmy lifting up a teenage girl's skirt 'by a few inches' with a hockey stick in 1971 or 72 in a spirit that the person had regarded at the time as 'insignificant' was the subject of an entire twenty-five-page report from Saxondale Hospital in Nottingham.

Yet the reports from the hospitals – and Leeds General Infirmary in particular – are another matter. If there was a moment when I felt I took on board the full import and enormity of Jimmy's crimes, it was when I set a few hours aside to read them, finding myself oppressed with sadness and guilt and foolishness. At the same time there was a weird tension as I struggled to resolve the image of the person I knew with the person being described in the incident reports. It may be that television and newspaper accounts can't do justice to the crimes of Jimmy Savile. All the sensationalism disappears amidst the accumulation of forensic detail from victims who, with the candour afforded to them by anonymity, can share their accounts of incidents that – in many cases – affected them for life. There is something in the colourless prose of the reports that gives an added power to the stories.

For the LGI report, sixty-four people shared accounts of abuse – incidents spanning nearly four decades, from 1962 to 1999 – and involving men, women, boys, girls. Most were in their late teens and early twenties, but plenty were outside those ages. What is striking reading them – other than the sheer numbers of victims – is the effrontery of his offending, its shameless and almost incontinent quality. Many accounts involve him touching the victims' genitals, under clothes, under bedclothes, when a mother has left the room or sometimes with a nurse or doctor close at hand. 'The doctor told me to do this.' 'Has the pain gone away now?' 'Uncle Jimmy will sort it.' 'Uncle Jimmy will look after you.' Or just as often it is a wordless act, an intrusion so bizarre and unexpected that the victim doesn't know how to react. In my own work, having interviewed paedophiles who preyed on children, their own and other people's, I am well aware of the grooming techniques that allow abusers to confuse their victims and lower their defences. But the odd thing about Jimmy was that he didn't groom much of the time – or he did some version of speed-grooming, based on his celebrity, projecting a sense of authority and, above all, permission – so that, even on those occasions when he was sworn at, pushed away, shouted at, there is no sense of his having been chastened, just a comment: 'He scurried away' or 'He left quickly.'

Many of the victims describe being in pain, being on their way in to surgery or coming out of it, coming round from unconsciousness, confused, dazed, completely off-guard. In this vulnerable state, they were assaulted by a white-haired man in a porter's outfit or scrubs, someone many didn't recognize as Jimmy Savile but assumed was a hospital employee. But it's also the case that his offending was so indiscriminate that it's hard to generalize about its qualities. Many incidents were opportunistic, relatively fleeting, taking place in corridors and on wards; but some involved a level of forethought and planning, meetings with parents, rendezvous, invitations to the porters' offices, or in at least one case his mother's flat, followed by what sounds like a massive physical overwhelm, Jimmy using his considerable physical strength to overpower and rape his victim. Some – especially the later ones, the ones that took place after his peak offending period of the sixties and seventies – were seen as relatively trivial, simply annoying or creepy, at the time and then reconsidered in hindsight. Given the overall impression of compulsivity and predation, one tends to be struck by those handful of occasions when Jimmy is fended off – a young woman who spent the night at his flat, having been invited back to a fictitious party, while wearing her ball gown, and successfully kept him at bay while sleeping in bed with him. One reads the less serious accounts and imagines the Savile deniers holding on to them as their scintilla of evidence for his forbearance and kindly behaviour.

Reading the reports was anguish-inducing but also felt salutary for me personally – a long-overdue inoculation against whatever residual sense of fondness I'd felt towards Jimmy. I discovered I had perhaps felt more attachment than I'd realized, some sense of investment in his not being an indefatigable sex offender. Otherwise why was there so much distress and guilt? Or was it perhaps a normal reaction to the accumulated sense of violation, the pain and distress all those people – adults and children – carried with them? And was it normal, too, to resist believing the worst about someone until faced with the incontrovertible truth? In the reports' accumulation of clinical detail, they provided a breathtaking portrait of the relentless predatory behaviour of a man who appeared compulsively dedicated to grabbing, groping, fiddling, and intruding.

It was also a shock to see cruelty arising from actions that had almost nothing in them that was reminiscent of good faith – not even the cousin of good faith that is honest selfishness or greediness. Over the years, I'd come to see how much wickedness was a by-product of a kind of self-deception: sincere fascists working towards a bright Aryan utopia or zealots dictating intolerance on the basis of God's holy word. Even the paedophiles at the mental hospitals I'd visited had, for the most part, persuaded themselves that the children they abused were capable of consent, that they 'enjoyed it', and they cited passages from Ancient Greek texts or practices in Papua New Guinea to suggest that it was a modern peculiarity to fetishize the innocence of children. 'All great deceivers . . . in the actual act of deception . . . are overcome with belief in themselves,' thus spake Nietzsche. To persuade others, you first have to drink your own Kool-Aid. But how had Jimmy – with his rampant grabbings and rapes – ever imagined that he was being anything other than vicious?

Chapter 31

## Horrible Stuff

When the time came to speak to the victims myself, I made it my habit on the way to the location to re-read passages from the reports, to make sure the gravity of the offences was in my mind during the conversations.

In selecting contributors, we were – as ever – at the mercy of who was willing to go on camera. We'd been in contact with Liz Dux, the lawyer at Slater and Gordon who was handling compensation claims. It was around this time that the figure of over a thousand victims was being bandied around in news reports. Liz Dux said, with regard to claims she was dealing with, it was closer to a couple of hundred. She wasn't sure where the larger figure had come from.

She sent out a form letter from the production to alert people to our project should they wish to speak. We'd been keen not to obscure victims' faces, which limited our pool even further – the idea being that it can look shady and unsatisfying to hear testimony from people whose faces you can't see.

For me, the second Savile film represented a new way of working. One of the axioms of my programmes, going back to my *TV Nation* days, had been that I looked at contributors who were making questionable decisions: the Klansmen, the Westboro Baptist Church members. Even in those later shows about addiction and mental illness, the subject of enquiry was people facing impossibly difficult choices, of how best to support troubled loved ones. To speak to victims of sexual assault was new ground for me and, especially given my history with the man, I was trepidatious.

Alongside the new interviews with victims, we would be drawing on the abundance of archive from the original show, the forty-odd hours of rushes, the material shot in the years afterwards, the DVD 'Jimmy Links' rushes, the rushes from the tongue-in-cheek mini-doc *When Jimmy Met Louis*. Ancient battered boxes were brought down from an old storage facility and combed through. All of this was different to our normal way of working. It was also felt that, given my different role in the story, I should be interviewed on-screen by the director, instead of simply voicing the programme.

Early on in the process, I watched some of the rushes from the original documentary. I had always wondered whether there might have been clues that I missed. Possibly in a bid to salvage my image of my own acuity, I recalled that I had pushed him harder at various points, in particular, in the scene at his mother's flat in Scarborough about his sexual interests and his relationship with the Duchess.

The rushes had been transferred onto DVDs and I watched them at my desk in the open-plan BBC offices in White City.

*[From Roll 022, filmed in the Duchess's bedroom]*

LT: Did the Duchess not give you 'brain damage'?

JS: No. I was fifty-five when she died. We were more like pals. Duchess and me were best pals.

LT: Did the closeness to the Duchess mean you didn't get married?

JS: No. Nothing. Every day Christmas day, every night New Year's Eve. Rock and roll, baby.

There followed the conversation, which we'd used in the film, about his 'girlfriends'. Some had been friends for forty years. 'I was a pirate,' he said, who had never wanted exclusive relationships.

> LT: Do you think your relationship with the Duchess was
>    anything like a marriage?
> JS: That is a non-question. Only a funny fella would ask
>    a question like that.
> *[LT: keeps at it, asks JS to explain it.]*
> JS: We were the most normal family in the world . . .
>    When you find someone that loves you they'll do it
>    for you.

More or less at random, I dug out Roll 74 and Roll 75. Though they were higher numbers, the tapes dated from an earlier occasion – they'd been shot by Will on the toy camera. With just the two of us present, me and Will and no crew, there was a chance this material would be more intimate and more revealing.

The images showed me and Jimmy wandering around a leisure centre in Doncaster, the one where he'd donated a large cuddly toy bear. 'JS does a slightly weird lower lip thing on a woman's hand,' I wrote. 'Two blokes. JS says, "You're better looking than me so bollocks."' I watched on: there was some more wandering; we climbed into Jimmy's limo; we made chit-chat about charity work. 'JS says, "Don't play with the switches, 'cuz it knacks all the business up." JS begins doing a Souza marching-band song.'

I don't know quite what I'd been expecting from watching the rushes. Maybe that his deviant qualities would be more evident. Or maybe I'd just wanted to see him again with the knowledge of his crimes so that I could merge the two people into one, or just so that I could look at him again knowing what he did. But it didn't happen: the two people refused to become one, and instead of resolving them

I was thrown back into a time before the revelations, into a state of mild boredom, enduring the harmless windbaggery of a faintly ridiculous ageing DJ.

The interviews for what came to be called simply 'Savile' took place over several months. It was a far cry from the immersive mode of working I was used to. Instead of the sense of being in a world, we interviewed contributors piecemeal as they became available.

We featured four victims, all female, and representing a spectrum of his offending. We had hoped to film a male victim, but only one was comfortable coming forward, and he had changed his story in significant ways, which I worried would be an unhelpful distraction in the film.

Our first interview was with Kat, the ex-Duncroftian. Now in her sixties, and living on borrowed time in the aftermath of bowel cancer, she lived in Gobowen, a village in Shropshire close to the Welsh border. I took a train up. In her front room, with her long-term partner sitting by for support, she recounted the matter-of-fact details of a young teenager, so abused by her mother and her mother's boyfriends, that being asked to give a blowjob to a forty-something DJ in the back of his Rolls in return for some tickets to a TV show was, as she put it, 'not that big a deal, really'.

In subsequent weeks I interviewed others. Cherie lived in Bournemouth, close to the seafront. A talented artist, her home was filled with her oil paintings, seascapes, animal portraits, and numerous pictures of the singer James Blunt. She described how, in 1973, she had been recovering from a breakdown and serious surgery at Stoke Mandeville when he came in through a ground-floor window. He'd stuck his tongue in her mouth – one of the hallmarks of his offending – and, disorientated and with her arms bandaged, she had been unable to fend him off.

Susan, an optician in Leeds, had been delivering some spectacles to Jimmy's house. He'd invited her inside, kissed her on the mouth, dropped his trousers, and uttered his catchphrase, 'How's about that then?' She'd told co-workers back in the office, who'd laughed. For years afterwards she'd made no secret of the encounter – processing it as a funny story rather than as an assault, and only after the revelations did she come to see it with clear eyes as abusive and frightening.

In Aylesbury, not far from Stoke Mandeville, I spoke to Sam. A woman roughly my own age, she had, as a young girl in the late seventies and early eighties, attended Sunday service at the hospital chapel. From time to time, Jimmy – an intermittently observant Catholic – would show up. Sam described being in the vestry, aged twelve or so, having helped with the collection, where Jimmy would grope and molest her, penetrating her with his fingers, brazenly and almost in view of other church-goers. Sam, too, had been abused by her grandfather, who had raised her. Softened up, her defences scrambled and worn down, she had put up little resistance against Jimmy.

'I never said to him "don't",' she told me, 'because I knew he could.'

With all the victims, there was the slightly uncomfortable moment of soliciting their opinions on my original documentary. In my self-involved state, I still imagined there might be a chance they'd recognize the programme's revealing dimension and give me credit for going as far as I did. Yeah, that didn't happen. At the same time, it was oddly bracing to feel the force of their unvarnished feedback. 'I remember thinking "*poor Louis*",' was Kat's reaction. She said she felt I'd been 'hoodwinked' by him. Cherie remarked on how 'silly' I seemed, being pushed around by a puffed-up celebrity. But the overwhelming impression they gave was a sense of guilt. They felt bad for not saying or doing more to speak out. Each had thought she was the only one. If only they had known, they said, they would have raised the alarm. They would have tried to bring him to justice.

Alongside the victims we interviewed others – associates, colleagues – who'd worked with him in a friendly way for many years. One was a BBC producer called Gill Stribling-Wright who'd started out in a junior capacity on *Clunk-Click*, then moved on to *Jim'll Fix It* and stayed in touch as she moved up the TV ladder, doing *Parkinson* and ITV telethons. My director on the original documentary, Will Yapp, had interviewed her for background back in 1999. At that point she'd described Jimmy as a 'tarnished saint', someone with a fascination with what makes people tick, which explained his visits to Broadmoor, and who had an interest in philosophy. 'I don't think there's anyone who really knows him completely, someone who he confides all in,' she'd said. 'I think there are various people who know a little bit and all of them participate in the compartments that he's placed them in.' Now, sixteen years on, she told me that in the years she worked with him she never saw anything that caused her concern. Had she read the reports? No, she said. 'Because I don't know what I'd *do* with it.' His private life had been obscure, though looking back little clues stood out. 'Part of his persona was the fact that he would tread very close to the line, in hindsight.' She mentioned, when asked if he'd ever shown anything other than a professional interest in her, that she would have been too 'walnuttish' for him – a word she'd heard him use, which meant dry and wrinkly. She would have been in her mid-twenties at the time.

Another colleague, a senior nurse at Stoke Mandeville called Sylvia Nichol, still had a trove of memorabilia, including an oversized last birthday card that was never given to him and a larger-than-life Jimmy Savile bust made out of Lego, which she kept in the shed. She'd spent the greater part of her working life raising money for Stoke Mandeville's Spinal Injury Unit and described the moment she called Jimmy because the roofs on the cheap hospital buildings were leaking, and how that had let to him spearheading a charity effort that raised £10 million. All that work was now rendered suspect – seen as a smokescreen for his offending. 'Sometimes I do say, please can you fix this?' she said, standing in the shed with his Lego bust. 'Because I reckoned he could fix anything.'

And then there was Jimmy Savile's personal assistant, Janet Cope.

Janet had been fired unceremoniously by Jimmy after twenty years' service – told simply, without explanation, 'You're out' – around the time I'd done the first documentary. She had worked as Jimmy's diary-keeper and factotum. By her own account, she organized events, cooked for him, and covered for him when necessary. When he'd felt lonely on an around-the-world cruise because it was full of Americans, none of whom recognized him, she'd spoken to him on the ship's phone every day to keep his spirits up. Unlike Sylvia and Gill, Janet had read the reports. She viewed the incidents described as either trivial ('a pat on the bum') or simply made-up.

Like the colleague at Stoke Mandeville, her life's work had been tainted from its association with Jimmy Savile. Her way of dealing with it was simply to refuse to acknowledge the truth.

Re-entering the world of Jimmy Savile was like travelling across a landscape ravaged by a hurricane. The survivors were making sense of what happened in different ways, but no one was untouched by what they had lived through.

As filming progressed I was in touch via email with Beth, the woman who had written me a letter describing herself and her friend as 'girlfriends' of Jimmy's. I'd been hoping to feature them in my follow-up programme. But both were publicity shy. They had family members who still didn't know about their association with Jimmy and they were worried about their real identities becoming known. Still, negotiations proceeded. Methods of preserving their anonymity were discussed. Beth was also insistent that she should know the names of everyone involved with the production. Emails she sent were stamped with legalese about their confidentiality and her sense of anxiety ebbed and flowed depending on what was going on in the news. She described the toll the unmasking of Jimmy Savile had taken on her. She'd had a nervous collapse after giving testimony to the Janet Smith Inquiry and another after seeing the Jonathan Maitland play *An Audience with Jimmy Savile*.

We met – first just Beth, myself and Will. Then later Alice came along as well – nearly fifteen years on from our lunch at the Langham, both of them a little nervous. Both had endured serious illnesses, Beth in particular looked grey and drawn and gave off an anxiety so intense that it was hard to differentiate from low-level passive aggression.

What was odd was that they seemed to have reversed positions in the intervening years. Beth, who'd seemed more protective of him in 2001 and inclined to recollect the happy parts of their association, could now barely bring herself to think about him, so great was her hatred. Remembering some of their encounters brought her to tears. It made me wonder whether, in the scheme of things, the uncovering of Jimmy's crimes had been worth it for her personally. Alice, on the other hand, seemed lightened by the revelations, still angry, but the anger didn't seem to eat at her the way it did Beth.

She talked about some feelings of guilt at having done interviews and been part of the posthumous process of unmasking Jimmy. She said she still had some residual fondness for him and talked about the first time he'd taken advantage of her – he'd been forceful but not violent.

'It wasn't the worst kind of "rape",' she said, doing air quotes.

'Why did you do air quotes?' I asked

'Because the first time was so unexpected and quick. It was only later that I viewed it as rape. But the other times, I don't view them as rape, because I went back. I knew what I was getting into.'

She described a man who was awkward, who lacked finesse, and she said this in an almost indulgent, pitying way. She said she had dreams about him, since the revelations, in which he came to her crying and she'd feel sorry for him.

'When we sent you that letter, I think I wanted you to do something, but we didn't want to be involved . . . Who did you show it to?'

'My executive producer. I can't remember who else exactly. But it was an open-plan office. There was no sense of secrecy around it.'

I had the sense Alice might be thinking there was someone who 'suppressed' the letter – who stopped me from doing more. I tried to explain that the letter said so much about 'friendship' and 'fun', there was nothing in it to make me concerned.

'I took it as, OK, he had girlfriends. He's not gay. He's not asexual . . . But beyond that, it didn't feel especially like news . . . There was nothing in it about sexual assault. And in fact, it talks about a thirty-year friendship.'

'We put that stuff about being friends in so you knew we weren't crackpots,' Beth said. 'To show we did know him.'

Alice said that when Jonathan King had been convicted in 2005, she'd sent Jimmy a caravan-shaped postcard, saying, 'Worried you might be next?' But they had harboured fears about Jimmy's underworld connections. His boasts of friends in the mafia, his joking references to himself as '*il capo di tutti capi*', she'd taken at face value. 'We all agreed nothing could be done while he was alive,' Beth said. 'He was too powerful.'

I thought: *I didn't agree nothing could be done while he was alive.* But I didn't say anything.

'Why didn't you go to the police?' I asked.

'We wanted something much bigger and more public than that.'

It occurred to me that a police investigation would have led to something big and public, but I didn't point this out, and we all left a little later, having talked for two and a half hours.

I saw Beth a few times afterwards. She'd asked us to keep her involved, and I sent her emails letting her know how the TV project was progressing. It was by now four years since the revelations, but the BBC1 documentary about victims and the appearance of the Janet Smith Inquiry meant there had been a spike in Savile coverage, which took a toll on her health. She'd been going through therapy and on one occasion she suggested I join her for a session – I think to help me understand what she'd been going through – but I declined.

I never saw Alice again. Before our meet-up, I'd sent her a list of questions via Beth. In return, I got a two-page document with thoughtful answers to each of the questions. She described meeting him, when she was aged fifteen, through a friend, at his radio chat show *Speakeasy*. His first question to her had been, 'How old are you?' He'd sexually assaulted her up against the wall of a BBC corridor, and then, a few months after she turned sixteen, he'd raped her in a hotel room.

'I hadn't got a clue I was being taken advantage of at that time but I knew it was wrong somehow,' she wrote. 'It was only later that I saw it for what it was and became very angry and emotionally confused about it. Although it sounds sick, at the time I even felt flattered at the attention of someone so famous. I felt I was special to him and was fond of him.

'I am glad it is out in the open as it has helped so many people come forward to report abuse . . . However, as for it being "therapeutic" I would say no. It has been immensely stressful . . . I now realize with vivid clarity I meant nothing to him but that I was taken advantage of, used and abused; I was one of hundreds. I know he was an absolute bastard but another part of me (weirdly) feels I have betrayed him. I am still looking for some understanding of my own experience and emotions. I know I am not to blame but I carry shame and guilt about what I feel I "allowed" to happen.'

Chapter 32

## Gotta Get Theroux This

It started, like the hiss and whisper of train tracks announcing a coming train, with bits of noise on social media. On Twitter, there was a murmur of interest in my old programmes, some of which had turned up on Netflix. Young people tagged me in tweets expressing their appreciation for episodes of *Weird Weekends* – shows that were nearly twenty years old – and even, on occasion, avowed an unlikely amorous interest in that older version of me (if that two-sizes-too-big leather-jacketed gurning man-child *was* me, which at this distance I wasn't sure it was).

Then a more unexpected development: unlicensed merchandise. T-shirts, Christmas jumpers, pillows, birthday cards, mugs – some of it frankly baffling on conception: one of the mugs showed me, for some reason, with large breasts – and often with the legend 'Gotta Get Theroux This' or 'Sleep Tight Theroux The Night'. I had spent years, nay decades, hearing people say 'Theroux the keyhole', 'Theroux the looking glass', even in the primary school playground – literally when I was about five years old – 'Louis *Theroux* the ball! Ha ha!' So I was by now anaesthetized to the comic effect of that particular *jeu de mots* but I was, nevertheless, grateful for what I took to be an appreciative sentiment.

Every now and then I'd hear of someone who'd got a tattoo of me

Louis Theroux with Tits

A mug of me with tits? Sure! Why not?

on a leg or arm, which I found flattering but also stressful. Being emblazoned permanently on someone's body seemed to carry with it certain responsibilities, and it was far from clear what those might be. Another darker part of me, the part that liked it, seemed to think that perhaps *more* people should be getting tattoos of me, and the notion even flitted through my head of incentivizing them with free signed DVDs.

A waitress on the West Coast of Ireland birthed a Twitter account, @NoContextLouis, with screen grabs from shows and the relevant piece of dialogue: one showed me apparently saying: 'She said there was no dick too big', another 'Can I work the swan tonight?' One of my pleasures in my years of making TV had always been getting into situations where I was forced by circumstances to say something ludicrous or asinine with a straight face. 'He called you a bald-faced fucker.' 'Do you want some Lucozade?' I enjoyed @NoContextLouis as a celebration of those moments.

There was also a Twitter account – @louistherouxbot – that used a computer algorithm to generate random bits of 'Louis Theroux commentary' of a wholly nonsensical sort. Sensing a PR opportunity, I announced on Twitter that I would record one of the lines if I got enough retweets, and ended up using my best 'serious VO' voice to announce, 'I'm in Amsterdam to meet Hannah, a former IT expert turned cybergoth who believes that Hull is a portal to Hell.'

Peak ironic-Louis-appreciation – I still haven't found a catchy way to describe the phenomenon – may have been a series of Louis Theroux-themed club nights around Britain. I didn't delve too deep into the details – it has always felt unseemly to be over-interested in whatever cult status I may or may not enjoy – but I did stumble across a short video clip of ten or fifteen people on a dance floor, grooving around while wearing masks with my face on. I can only compare my feeling to the scene in *Being John Malkovich* when the eponymous main character enters a portal in his own head and arrives in a world in which everyone looks like him.

It was hard to judge the exact tone of some of the appreciation. It definitely wasn't nasty. At the same time, it was clearly partly tongue-in-cheek and playful – naturally so, since it revolved around a kind of fiction, a constructed TV identity and not the real me, whoever that may be. Nancy researched the company that was making some of the merchandise. I'd wondered who else they featured on their iPhone cases and pyjamas, hoping it might be philosophers and revolutionaries like Jean Genet and Hakim Bey. I was a little disappointed to find their other honourees were David Hasselhoff and a Sky Sports commentator I'd never heard of. Nonetheless, it was basically flattering, and it was only strange to achieve some kind of ambiguous elder-statesman status when I felt my grip on success was still so tentative, my sense of security so fragile.

And the serendipitous part was that the slow percolation of interest among younger viewers coincided with us finishing up *My Scientology Movie*.

• • •

The film had been edited through the end of 2015 and beginning of 2016 – spending more than six months in the cutting room, four months longer than any of my TV projects. It had been a beast to get under control – for a while John and Simon had kept me out of the edit altogether. 'I like to give my directors a little space to play with the material,' Simon said when I called to ask what was going on. I felt like Colonel Sanders after he'd signed his name and image rights away to KFC and wasn't allowed to open another restaurant, pressing my face against an imaginary screen door and saying, *Hey, guys, remember me? Can I help fry the chicken tonight?*

Then, having 'played' their way to a standstill, they invited me in to collaborate, and I threw myself into helping, which seemed only to make matters worse, at least for a while, until gradually the four of us – me, John, Simon, and Paul the editor – found a way through the material: an opening that set up the idea of Scientology as something beguiling and mysterious, the introduction of the device of the re-enactments, the story of my relationship with Marty balanced against a mounting sense of intimidation from the Church, and the final-act moment of confrontation with Marty on the street outside the studio where we'd filmed the recreation of the Hole.

In the last few weeks of the edit, we sent the Scientologists a list of all the allegations the film made. There was then a process of reflecting the Church's denials and 'clarifications' using on-screen text. I had slightly dreaded this, worrying it would emasculate the story – clutter it up and weaken it with qualification. In fact, in the end, the inclusion of the Church's counter-statements strengthened the drama by giving the viewer more access to the Scientologists' mindset, shedding light on how they explain their actions to themselves.

Among the claims in the letters from the Church was the delightful explanation that they had filmed us at various locations only because they were working on their own documentary *about me.* I couldn't help finding this idea flattering and intriguing, though at the time of press there is still no sign of *My Louis Theroux Movie* by the Church of Scientology.

The BBC legal and compliance teams for the most part let us say what we wanted. The only significant point of contention for them was that the scene of Tom Cruise playing backgammon was too close to the re-enactment of the Hole and that it might be construed as suggesting the star of *Risky Business* and the *Mission Impossible* franchise knew about David Miscavige's alleged abuse and that he was around when it was allegedly happening. (Scientology denies any abuse in the Hole, or the existence of a Hole. Or the existence of a film called *Holes* starring Shia LaBeouf. Have I mentioned *that*?) To placate our lawyers, we tweaked some commentary and moved the backgammon scene a little further down the film. This still wasn't enough. In the end the decision was referred all the way up to Danny Cohen, the BBC's then Director of Television. From his Olympian roost, he ruled that yes, it was OK to show Tom Cruise and David Miscavige playing backgammon.

Along with its letters and rebuttals, the Church also sent a thick ring-binder full of printed papers in individual plastic sheaves. It was entitled 'Letters from Executives and Staff who have been at the Gold Base since the 1990s'. It contained a hundred or so written testimonials from Sea Org personnel, in a variety of fonts, many with jazzy photos of the correspondents grinning and looking as though they were trying a little too hard to telegraph *freedom* and *self-expression* and *definitely-not-in-a-cult-ness*. What was eerie was the way the letters all hit the same talking points. Every one described the luxurious conditions staff live in and featured a vignette depicting Miscavige's wonderful personality. 'He is the most selfless person I have ever met.' 'He is the most compassionate man I have ever seen.' 'I will never forget the first time I met him . . . He came and personally spoke to me and asked me my name.' 'He is the most caring person I have ever seen.'

I imagined the orders coming in. *Here is what your letter should look like. Here is a template but make it your own!* The accumulation of over-the-top praise was so formulaic it had the effect of sounding utterly false.

In late 2015 the film was accepted into the London Film Festival, and it was around the same time that we sent a link for Marty to watch. We'd maintained a cordial long-distance relationship in the months of editing. There had been some talk of possibly flying him out for the premiere, and though that idea was dropped, we were still hopeful he would support the film and view it as a fair-minded albeit warts-and-all portrait. He wrote back to say, in somewhat muted terms, he had found it 'clever' and to congratulate us for being true to our word about showing the conditions in the Hole. A few days later he wrote again. This time he wasn't so complimentary. He said he hated the film and he blamed Simon for – as he saw it – conning him into participating in a project that was wholly different than the one that was promised. On the plus side, he seemed to regard me as too trivial and unserious to deserve the same level of vitriol – though he did call me an 'assclown'. He labelled John a 'rimless zero'. In subsequent months, he made other false allegations – claiming that I had egged him on to be more lurid in his scripting of the alleged abuse in the Hole.

Three years on, the biggest mystery remains the 'rimless zero' remark.

I couldn't find it in me to be annoyed at Marty. He had put a lot into the project and I could well understand why he felt hurt when it didn't turn out to be as uncritical of him as he might have liked. I also tended to see his turning against the film as part of his general disillusionment with the world of anti-Scientology. And in fact in subsequent months and years Marty would blog and post videos attempting to debunk any TV shows and movies that were critical of Scientology.

It was widely assumed that he had been paid off by the Church and was now, in effect, back working for David Miscavige.

The night of the premiere, I rode down to Leicester Square with Nancy in a fancy car laid on by the festival. John and I introduced the film, welcoming everyone and in particular any Scientologists that were there, as they undoubtedly were, and then I skipped out, feeling no need to see it for the hundredth time, and also a little anxious about being exposed so directly to the reaction of the audience. Afterwards we did a Q&A, and I found it difficult to judge the mood of the room. It was only later – when I joined my mum and her husband, Michael, for dinner at Pizza Express, and I saw their reaction and how much they'd enjoyed it and how proud they were – that I felt more confident about the film and its prospects.

Over the next few days reviews appeared, all positive, and I looked forward to a distributor imminently buying the film and giving it a wide release. What I didn't expect, though perhaps I should have done, was another pushback from the Church of Scientology.

It began in an almost comical fashion with a visit, one Sunday morning, by a pair of police officers. I'd been making pancakes for the kids, and I invited the two men into the kitchen. In the incongruous setting of our disorderly toy-strewn house – me wearing my pyjamas and dressing gown, with the two big boys watching *The Dumping Ground* in the other room, and Walter in his playpen – I heard one of the PCs say, 'We're here because a serious threat has been made against you, which has been passed on to us.'

'Right,' I said, waiting for the words to make sense.

'The threat was made in an anonymous phone call by a Mr X. It was made – as we understand it – in a phone call to the Church of Scientology, in East Grinstead. The gentleman in question had seen a film you have made and had taken a negative view of the film, saying it had caused him to wish to hurt you. The Church of Scientology was concerned about your well-being, so we're here to make sure you are OK. May I ask, have you seen anything out of the ordinary or suspicious?'

As he said this, I realized it had all the hallmarks of a Scientology scare tactic – in the guise of helping, but actually with the intent to cause fear and disquiet, they had invented a fictitious threat. In a weird way, it was almost gratifying to see the Scientologists still apparently working off their old 1970s playbook – like finding a collectable bit of kitsch from the seventies in a junk shop, a Rolf Harris Stylophone or a Speak & Spell. *Wow! Remember these?* I explained this to the police, though either I didn't persuade them, or professionalism required them to continue to act as though the threat was real.

'Any men lurking in the shadows, sir? Signs of breaking and entering?'

'No, I've just told you . . .'

They ended by saying they were putting me on a 'priority list' with a special phone number – presumably my calls would ring on a giant red phone on the Police Commissioner's desk. At the very least, I figured, it might help when there were unruly elements kicking off outside the house and we were trying to settle the children.

But the police visit was, in a sense, a mere tinhorn fanfare for the arrival of a more worrying development.

A message came in from Simon. Something in it made me think it was ominous and I called back, after the kids' supper one evening, from the quiet retreat of our top-floor bedroom, to hear him say, in a voice that was unusually grave, 'Yeah so, we've had a letter from David Miscavige's personal lawyers. Apparently you sent a tweet that they consider libellous and they are threatening legal action.'

'Oh dear,' I said.

'Yeah.'

'That's not good is it.'

'No. Sorry.' This was said in a manner so heartfelt and final that it suggested, not just that *this* threat to do harm really was serious but also that there wasn't much he would be able to offer in the way of help. It was my Twitter account and if I was going to use it to libel vengeful high-profile figures, that was on me.

He ended by suggesting I call Nigel, the media lawyer who'd worked on the movie, which I did. He also forwarded me the letter. It quoted from a tweet – or rather a retweet, since the words had auto-generated when I'd clicked on a button to share an article – that said, and I quote, 'David Miscavige is a terrorist.' Yeah. That wasn't good. I recalled tweeting the article – I'd had some misgivings on account of its overheated content and had wondered about erasing it, but a publicist we'd retained had suggested I didn't, since apparently that was seen in PR circles as a sign of weakness and would probably only bring more attention. What I didn't recall – and didn't think I'd ever actually read – was the wording of the tweet itself. *David Miscavige is a terrorist.* I pondered all this a little ruefully, then called my agent. In a tone not dissimilar to Simon's, she said, 'David Miscavige may be a lot of things but he ain't a terrorist.'

'But what do I do?'

'You need to get a good lawyer and get ready to spend a lot of money. Because I'm telling you now, this could be very expensive.'

A day or two later, another letter arrived from the lawyers acting for Miscavige, filled with more legal sabre-rattling and shield-clanking – 'false', 'outrageous', 'defamatory' – and a demand for an apology. This I might have thought about providing – given that I don't actually think David Miscavige is a terrorist – except my lawyer warned that the apology would not forestall a claim of financial damages, but in fact, only make one more likely, possibly to the tune of £100,000 or more.

My lawyer advised me to instruct a high-powered QC. A name was suggested, Heather Rogers. She had once been part of the legal team defending the writer Deborah Lipstadt in her libel defence against the historian David Irving, whom she had labelled a Holocaust denier. There were meetings – the QC was as impressive as I'd expected – and as she did her preparation, read the letters, read my tweets, the articles, and viewed the film, and as the bills came in and money haemorrhaged out, I found myself mainly reassured by her level of competence and only slightly distraught at the strangeness of having to pay someone hundreds of pounds to watch a film you've made, as research.

Around the same time – towards the end of 2015 – I was making trips up to MediaCity in Salford, where I was appearing on a Christmas edition of the quiz show *University Challenge*. On the train, I would brood about my own stupidity at sending the tweet and the likelihood of its having catastrophic consequences. I looked up the meaning of 'terrorist'. You could 'terrorize' someone without doing them physical harm, I reasoned. Though, as the Scientology letters pointed out, my tweet had gone out not long after the Charlie Hebdo murders, so I was sort of suggesting that David Miscavige went round stabbing journalists, which he hasn't done as far as I know.

I did a Twitter inventory to see how many of my followers were real people. It suggested I'd only published the tweet to a million people, not 1.8 million. And in fact only a few thousand had probably seen it. I told this to Nigel, the lawyer.

'Yes, I'm not sure how helpful that is for us,' he said.

The case motivated me to do well in *University Challenge*. I was getting a small fee for each appearance. If my team went all the way, I'd only need another £98,000 for the war chest, though come to think of it that wasn't counting legal fees.

In the final I got on a hot streak, answering questions on *Mad Men*, Tennyson, and Pope Linus I. We won. It improved my frame of mind for about fifteen minutes. Another legal letter came in from Miscavige's lawyers. We sent one back. Despite all the polysyllables and legal verbiage, it was, I realized, just a more sophisticated and more expensive version of two kids in a playground saying 'Come on then! If you want some!' 'You and whose army! Hold me back! Hold me back!' but neither of them really wanting to fight.

Still, it was stressful and not helping my equanimity around this time was the sudden onset of a debilitating pain in the groin and the realization, after I checked myself in the mirror, that one of my testicles had grown to roughly four times its normal size. It was a couple of days after Christmas by now. Nancy had made plans for us all to stay with friends in Norfolk, but I showed her the questionable testicle, and she agreed I should get it checked out while they began the holiday. They drove off, and I made my way down to an urgent health clinic and there followed an embarrassing procession around a sequence of A&E departments where a series of doctors stared at and felt my balls – then asked if it was OK to let the trainee doctors sit in and have a look – and tried to figure out why one of my testes was the size of a goose egg.

Finally, late in the day, with the light gone outside, the last doctor said with a smile, 'Yes, just an infection. Orchitis is the medical name. Antibiotics should sort that out, but you can't be too careful. I hope you don't mind me saying, I do like your documentaries. Anything new in the pipeline?'

I took the train to Norwich, where I joined Nancy and the boys, and the following morning I pushed Walter's pram around a hillside that overlooks the city, conscious of my testicle jostling in my trousers like a spiteful troll. The next night was New Year's Eve. We visited my old friend Adam Buxton and his family at their converted farmhouse, staying up and toasting the year ahead while I wondered inwardly whether I'd be remortgaging the house, and should I just apologize, or did that, as the lawyers claimed, lay me open to massive damages.

The next day we drove across to the easternmost edge of Norfolk, a little village called Sea Palling, whose buildings were mostly washed away in disastrous floods in 1953 that had killed seven people. Nancy and I and the boys whiled away the hours in an arcade filled with machines that cascaded two-penny pieces and spat out long snakes of tickets that you could trade for prizes, and I tried to forget about the legal case.

After a few days of antibiotics, the testicle returned to its accustomed size, presumably a little wistful about its brief visit to the big leagues. And by a strange quirk of fate, the Miscavige infection went down a few weeks later – finally succumbing to the weeks of high-dosage legal correspondence. Afterwards, along with the relief at the situation having gone away, I had the feeling of having been initiated, and that maybe this was the price of having been credited with more bravery than I deserved. Perhaps on occasion you had to weather misfortune that was undeserved – or at least, unglamorous, unexciting, and ten times more worrying than an angry glistening wrestler with nipples like rivets or an exasperated Klansman caught out with Nazi figurines.

Other than occasional attempts to hack my emails, which may or may not have emanated from Scientology, or the *News of the World*, or a Russian troll farm, things went largely quiet. Which was welcome, but there was still the question of whether anyone would ever get to see the film.

Chapter 33

# Half Old, Still Confused

I try not to be too worried about the success or failure of programmes when they go out on TV. You figure you made the show
you wanted to make, and it does what it does. Feature films turned
out to be a different story. Mainly the problem is that, if the distributors don't like the film, they won't buy it and the film won't go into
cinemas.

After the success of the premiere and the great reviews and word
of mouth, I was expecting a smooth passage for *My Scientology
Movie* into cinemas across the UK and then the world. But something strange happened . . . nothing. Well, maybe not quite nothing;
there was occasionally some little whisper or micro-step forwards.
A sales agent came on. An invitation to another festival. But the nothing soon returned. I found it hard to decipher the nothing – whether
it was a genuine nothing, or the nothing of bad news that I was being
spared having to hear, or whether the nothing was itself the bad news.
There were screenings for potential distributors, then what sounded
like the mumble of something but turned out to be more nothing.

In early 2016, our film showed at Tribeca Film Festival. John
Dower and I flew to New York and did a day of press in an air-
less office with a procession of reporters from online outlets whose
enthusiasm for our film persuaded me it might find an audience

in America. There were more good reviews – including a glowing write-up in *Entertainment Weekly* – followed by a couple more months of basically mumbles and nothing. So far I had been trying not to be too interested in what was happening as I thought it was probably annoying to Simon and definitely uncool to have too much staked in the film's success, but at this point I couldn't help myself. I pressed John to account for the lack of interest.

'It's weird,' he said, 'but I think there is a portion of the more high-minded docs world that can't help seeing you as a TV commodity. They're thinking, "It's not cinema." And it's bollocks but it's the way a lot of these people think.' He described meeting a high-end docs distributor at a Tribeca dinner. 'She was all sniffy and I asked if she'd seen how it plays to an audience. *She hadn't even seen the film.*'

I felt demoralized. I thought about all the small films and modest TV docs that get short runs in cinemas. Couldn't we just get a little art-house release for a week in a handful of cities? I lobbied Simon to do anything to get the film out there.

'We could just stick it up on YouTube,' I said. 'Let people pay to download it.'

Even as I was saying it, I reminded myself of a character in the film *Sideways*, a know-nothing who advises his writer friend, 'Publish it yourself! Get it in libraries! Let the public decide!' Judging from Simon's reaction, it was a risible suggestion and may partly explain why I am a TV presenter who specializes in getting out of my depth and not an Oscar-winning producer.

As months went by and there was still no sign of a distributor buying our film, I felt baffled and impotent. In July, with everything still quiet, Simon suggested we shake the bushes by taking the film up to Sheffield for the documentary festival. This would be our third major festival – I worried a little about whether it seemed a bit desperate. It reminded me of an elderly man I once saw in a bath house in west London. I was with my brother in the sauna and the man kept sauntering past and 'accidentally' letting his bathrobe fall open and then standing there with his willy out. (In this analogy, in case you are wondering, I am the elderly man and the Scientology movie is the man's genitals.) But I deferred to Simon's greater experience and agreed to go, let slip my bathrobe and dangle my willy-movie one more time.

By a happy coincidence, I heard Michael Moore would also be at the festival, promoting *Where To Invade Next?*, his latest film. Simon had thought it would be helpful for our film if we could get Michael to watch it and support it, and I also had my own reasons for wanting to meet up, and so through a mutual acquaintance I engineered a meeting.

He was crossing the foyer of Sheffield's Showroom Cinema when I spied him. He had a small entourage around him, opening doors, carrying bags. It was the first time I had seen him in the flesh in twenty years. He looked older, a little heavier, his face was retracted into his neck, and I noticed how he shambled, his legs folded in at the knees – he moved them almost without raising them – and I worried about his health.

We found some seats in a corner of an empty bar. He apologized, he hadn't managed to see our film, he said, and then without me having thought about it, I heard myself, as an opening gambit, burbling incoherent appreciation for what he'd done for me by taking me on as a correspondent all those years before. 'I never really had a chance to say thank you for taking the chance and putting me on the show,' I said. 'You changed my life and nothing that happened later would have happened without you.' To my surprise, I realized I might be emotional.

'Oh wow, that's nice of you to say,' Michael said. 'I'll never forget when you first came on board. I saw you around the office doing the photocopying and I said, "That British intern has something about him. We should give him a chance on camera."'

This recollection was at odds with my own memory, which told me I'd never been an intern at *TV Nation*, or done photocopying, but I didn't like to correct him and spoil a moment of bonding.

We moved to a crowded Italian restaurant across the road – Michael had shaken off his retinue and a seagull swarm of British TV executives. It was just him, me, and John, my director. Michael ordered a Kahlua and cream and a spaghetti carbonara and we talked, reflecting on the time that had passed. We were both old now. Both divorced. Well, I was kind of half old and half divorced. He remembered Sarah, recalling one of the few times we'd all socialized together – he'd invited us to a fundraising dinner for the magazine *The Nation* and Sarah had accosted him about my habit of going off on assignment on short notice, as though it were his fault.

We moved on to the subject of Trump, who was defying polls and emerging as the Republican frontrunner. Roseanne Barr, an old friend of Michael's and at one time a leftie – was among those climbing aboard the Trump train and endorsing right-wing conspiracy theories. Michael saw the whole phenomenon as symptomatic of the political class, right and left, turning its back on working people – he decried the lack of connection between the Democrats and the blue-collar folk in the Midwest who were showing signs of lining up for Trump. I was listening and trying to keep up, and say something relevant, but nothing much was coming to mind about Wisconsin and Michigan swing voters, and I had the feeling of trying to fall in and jam with a band on a tune I didn't know that well. With that same sense of wanting to impress him and make him laugh but feeling a little out of my depth, I reflected that nearly twenty-five years on, it wasn't so very different to that first ever meeting for a job interview at the Brill Building.

A couple of months after the Sheffield screening, Simon called with good news: a company called Altitude had signed on to distribute the film. We had a meeting at their offices in Soho; they were happy, I was happy, everyone was happy.

With a nod to the gonzo quality of the film, they had the idea of bringing in the gonzo illustrator par excellence Ralph Steadman to do the art for the poster. They also mapped out a reassuringly relaxed publicity strategy – a day and a half of interviews over a month or so. And there was mention of kicking off the opening weekend with a live event, with a Q&A at Royal Festival Hall that would be streamed to God knows how many cinemas – I had tuned out by this point – around Britain.

I was by then preoccupied with other matters – back on the treadmill of TV-making, reporting a series of programmes about crime and addiction in the US, murder in Milwaukee, heroin abuse in West Virginia – so I didn't give much thought to the film's release. I heard some more mumbling – emails from Altitude that I was cc'ed into and that I only half-read – but this time the mumbling was more positive: burble burble ticket uptake burble thrilled more cinemas burble very excited blah blah burble.

On opening night I was a little under the weather. I made my way down to the South Bank. I sat in the green room and signed some posters. Adam Buxton was there – he was doing the Q&A – and Ralph Steadman, hawk-faced, a little batty-seeming, with wild eyebrows and a jewellery confection of silver and lapis lazuli round his neck. I'd had a briefing call with him on the phone a few months earlier. He'd just watched the film and said, I think in a positive way, 'Oh God, it's so fucking depressing. Jesus, what a fucking nightmare. So awful.'

The evening was a blur. I felt typically anhedonic, ill, nervous, sapped of energy. I was still mindful that it was at heart a film about not getting access and that some viewers might be disappointed. But the crowd enjoyed it from what I could tell and the Q&A passed off without incident, and so it was with a feeling of pleasant surprise that I read, in a triumphalist email from Altitude early the following week, that the live event had been beamed into so many cinemas that in that one night the film had grossed more than most theatrical docs make in a year.

And so it went on. After its long period of languishing unloved, the film defied every prediction, selling well week after week, until it was the second-highest grossing doc of the year in the UK and one of the most successful of recent times.

Eventually, in early 2017, the movie came out in America. It showed in cinemas in New York and Los Angeles, and for about fifteen seconds it was the number-one film on the iTunes documentary charts. I did a short publicity tour, which mainly consisted of low-rated Internet broadcasts: print journalists who did web interviews filmed by the office tech guy. One woman literally interviewed me on her personal Facebook page, with questions coming from members of her family.

At a time when I had grown complacent about media interest, turning down interviews like Duran Duran in their heyday, it was a salutary reminder of what lack of interest feels like.

I did a couple of nights in New York. The ghost of my younger self seemed to be walking the streets, angry and resentful and wholly committed to making something of himself with no real clue as to what it would be. Being back with a middlingly successful documentary felt like a triumph of sorts, my fifteen minutes of the big time. I had the feeling of being both close to that hungry young man and far away, his dark energy muffled by a modicum of success but still throbbing underneath, still directionless and confused.

# Chapter 34

## The Last Mention of Jimmy Savile

All the time I'd been trying to keep faith that we'd find a distributor for the Scientology film, I was also plugging away on Savile, and it was by a strange stroke of dark synergy, that *that* project finally came to air only a few weeks before the South Bank screening.

Understandably enough, the BBC ran a low-key publicity campaign in the lead-up. No photos were released, nor did they put me up for any interviews. I was ten thousand miles away in Australia when the programme, titled *Louis Theroux: Savile*, went out. Not by design – I had a long-standing commitment to a speaking tour – though there were strong arguments for me being out of the country when I had a show on: it relieved some of my anxiety, and I worried less about whether people are calling and texting, or whether they weren't and why they weren't. With the higher stakes of the Savile revisit, this was all the more the case.

The main theme of the reaction to the show was that it had been 'brave'. The fourth or fifth time I heard the same word I began to wonder if it was code for 'rash' or 'foolhardy' or 'self-incriminating'. One dissenting view came from the *Mail*. 'One star' was their verdict – and I'm not sure 'zero stars' existed as a setting on their critical meter. The reviewer was annoyed that I'd suggested his former colleague Angela Levin might have done more to out Jimmy Savile, given that she'd told me in an interview in the programme that she'd had credible information that he was an abuser. Angela herself had pointed out that she didn't have the kind of evidence a newspaper would need before they'd risk printing such serious allegations.

Another brickbat came by email from Jonathan King, the convicted sex offender I'd been dallying with the previous year. 'I was truly horrified by your Savile fiasco,' he wrote. 'Surely your position should have been similar to Sylvia's – you had and have no idea whether the allegations and claims were true but all you saw made you consider him a friend. I only met him socially once (but must say I would never, ever have offered him a room in my home) – he struck me as a decent, hard-working saint. Here was the chance for you to be the boy who said the emperor was wearing no clothes. But your understandable mistake will have killed off your promising career, I fear. A terrible shame.'

There were also several letters in response to the programme, including one from an events organizer in Spalding who had booked Jimmy on several corporates in the nineties. The letter was full of bizarre punctuation and solecisms. 'I cannot fail to see how you didn't see from the word go . . . "Something isn't right here!" . . . Or were you also "bowled over" by the man?' he wrote. He'd known Jimmy was a wrong 'un when he came to the hotel room door in tiny black briefs. 'He didn't know us from "Adam"! It's not normal behaviour!' On another occasion he had taken vast numbers of boxes of the hotel's branded chocolate and charged them to his room. He wanted them for a children's hospital in Bristol. 'He thought he could do "anything he wanted" and "get away with it".' Yes, the *real* story, which I'd missed, was the vicious and premeditated theft of hotel chocolates.

There were also the usual fruit-loop letters, one about a self-published book promoting world peace, and a couple that boasted of random trivial connections with Jimmy. 'I worked as a cameraman on *Jim'll Fix It* for three years and found him incredibly vain. It annoyed me that he'd only arrive for the final run-through and show, yet take the credit for arranging fixes (it was the researchers).'

But in amongst them was a more troubling one.

The woman only gave her first name. Across several close-written pages, she recounted a passage in her life when, aged thirteen, over the course of a year she and her family been groomed by Jimmy – in the letter she'd referred to him only as 'The Man' – under the guise of him helping her dancing career. He'd visit every six weeks, giving the girl's mother fifteen pounds each time.

One night, after she turned fourteen, he'd taken her to a house, given her gin, and had sex with her, saying, 'Never forget your first time.' She'd become pregnant. The child, a girl, had been put up for adoption. The letter ended by saying, 'She has always been in my heart and I have always said "Happy Birthday, I love you" on her birthday. She knows nothing of me and it must stay that way. I would so, so much love to see her and to find out if she is happy. God, I hope she is OK. She must never know about him. There can't be anyone who wants to know he's their father. I will worry till the day I die. Don't worry about him. I think we know now that he was nothing but a narcissist and whoever was to meet him would be fooled.'

Maybe because I was working on the programmes at the same time, I found myself thinking about parallels between Jimmy Savile and L. Ron Hubbard. Both were mythomanes, inventing and exaggerating to embellish their own careers and pedigrees. Both had a magnetic quality that enabled them to persuade and beguile the vulnerable. Both amateur hypnotists, operating like stage performers prevailing and imposing upon the unwary either in the name of selling religious snake oil or to sexually abuse. In both I saw people whose qualities of charisma and intelligence were put at the service of exploitation and betrayal in ways they themselves were almost certainly not wholly aware of.

I also saw a great deal of common ground in the accounts of the victims, the survivors, the defenders, the friends: all sorting and interpreting overlapping experiences and sets of data. The spiritual bondage of being in the Sea Org – the long years of persuading yourself you were engaged in a mission of cosmic importance, enduring ill treatment, poor conditions, alleged episodes of physical violence – had similarities with those in the entourage of Jimmy Savile who imagined they were part of something glamorous and exciting, and hoped they were valued by him or even loved. And there was also the awkward grey area: a contradictory and confused middle ground, albeit possibly a small one, where the same facts were open to inconsistent interpretations, presenting certain survivors – the ones who hadn't experienced the worst – with a choice. They could view their experience as abusive and a violation or simply an experience that was unpleasant, something to be shrugged off, something that was outweighed by other factors, like the good they felt they were doing: spreading the gospel of Ron, or Jim.

And then I would remind myself of the significant differences. The scores of people Jimmy Savile preyed upon who *weren't* groomed: who weren't part of something glamorous or exciting, but were taken by surprise, groped, wrestled, overwhelmed.

In the aftermath of the two documentaries, many asked if I was still being trailed by PIs and Scientologists. I was always a little sorry to have to disappoint them. Scientology basically left me alone. There was a rather thin hit piece on one of their websites, which mainly consisted of them alleging that I was a useless journalist since I had failed to unmask Jimmy Savile. But, compared with their smear jobs on other journalists, it was very anodyne. By now there were other exposés in the works, including Leah Remini's American TV series *Scientology and the Aftermath*. I imagined Scientology's attentions like the eye of Sauron, swivelling away from me and towards the latest assault on their reputation.

The ghost of Jimmy Savile proved a more tenacious adversary.

I had hoped that making the second programme would help to exorcize him. It didn't quite. Mainly the ghost took the form of my own questions and self-recriminations. I was conscious of not having said everything I wanted to say. At the same time it wasn't quite clear what it was I did want to say. I felt alternately defensive, annoyed, apologetic, and self-critical. I was irked by the piety and self-righteousness of those critics who suggested I should have seen more. And I wished I had seen more. I felt proud of having unmasked him as much as I did in my original programme, and ashamed that I had begun to like him, and most of all that I hadn't done more to encourage the two women who came to me to go to the police and raise the alarm – that in some way I hadn't heard them.

There was also a feeling of irritation that he had become such a convenient and lazy shorthand for evil, for anyone accused of something or accusing someone of something. He had become the person someone is 'not as bad as': 'All I did was grope them in the office and they're making me out to be like Jimmy Savile.' He was also the shorthand for the person someone *is* as bad as: 'He is the Jimmy Savile of football/music/film.' Jimmy Savile had become a figure of complete evil: his purpose was now to make everyone else in society feel OK that they aren't him. He had become a thought-stopping device, and a way for creepy men to make themselves look better, to draw attention away from the myriad inequalities, small slights, acts of embarrassment and control.

At the same time, though I could say I had a rough idea of who he wasn't – black hole of pure evil, devil incarnate – I still couldn't say I had a clear sense of who he *was*. My ongoing project of attempting to make Jimmy into a single person still hadn't quite happened.

Occasionally I'd be asked whether, with all my exposure to deviant people and predatory worlds, anything still shocked me. Nothing would spring to mind and I would recall the line from Jean-Luc Godard's *À Bout de Souffle*, spoken by the small-time crook played by Jean-Paul Belmondo: 'Informers inform, burglars burgle, murderers murder, lovers love.' People do what they do. A world *without* crime, insanity, war – the dream promised by L. Ron Hubbard – now, that would be shocking. But was it shocking that people, given the chance, abused their power, gave vent to their darkest impulses, made themselves OK with selfishness and cruelty? It seemed the least shocking thing in the world. But then I'd catch myself and I'd recall the feeling of reading the reports into Jimmy Savile's offending. The strange queasiness – which somehow never diminished – of realizing someone you thought you knew and sort of liked would manipulate and deceive in a way that was so out of keeping with who you took him to be, and that part of you, to begin with, had resisted believing.

Epilogue

# Crooked Timber

In late 2016 I was cycling to work down Harley Street when I received a call from someone at the UK's documentary body, the Grierson Trust.

'Have you got a minute?' the woman said. 'We're very pleased to tell you the trustees have decided to give you this year's special award.'

'Oh wow,' I said.

'It's our most prestigious award. It was very unusual. The judges were unanimous, which doesn't often happen. I hope you're pleased?'

'That's wonderful,' I replied. 'Amazing.' I said, 'Wow!' again, and then I worried that saying it twice in quick succession might come across as awkward and insincere.

The truth was, when I ran a quick audit of what I was feeling, what was mainly coming back was blankness, mixed with an almost Tourettic urge to turn down the award, either because I felt I didn't deserve it or possibly I felt I deserved it too much, excessive humility being a close cousin to narcissism. These were all just thoughts drifting in my head, mental flotsam, and I accepted the award, of course, with abject gratitude, and possibly another 'Wow'. For years I'd hoped I might win a Grierson. I'd been nominated a couple of times and once or twice I'd thought I'd deserved one but been disappointed, and cursed the decision-makers for denying me. But it was strange, I was also overcome with imposter syndrome and on the night, a dark evening in late Autumn in a basement auditorium in East London, I gave an acceptance speech so self-effacing that it risked making a mockery of the decision to give me the award in the first place and came close to undermining the prefatory remarks given by the BBC executive, Charlotte Moore. The gist of Charlotte's speech was that I was much more than a TV presenter, while the gist of my remarks was that I was just a TV presenter.

Backstage afterwards, I bumped into Charlotte. 'We probably should have coordinated our speeches,' she said.

At the after party I got drunk and in a dazed state I did my best to hold coherent conversations with a parade of young producers and filmmakers who approached me in the spirit of pilgrims reverencing a statue of the Virgin Mary – if anything I felt less lifelike or intelligible than a religious effigy. Around midnight Nancy bundled me into a taxi and we made our way home where I wobbled into the kitchen and fixed myself another ill-advised glass of red wine. Then, upstairs, in the bathroom, I brushed my teeth and peered into the mirror and looked at the wrinkles around my eyes and my jowls and my hairy shoulders and a liver spot on the back of my hand, which reminded me of one my grandpa used to have when I was growing up, and in my drink-addled state I examined my own eyes, not quite recognizing them as mine and not understanding how my own mind could be dancing behind them, and I thought: *You live, you live, you live, and then you die. You're alive now and then you die.*

In August 2017 I moved with my family to Los Angeles – Nancy and I had been saying for some time that we had cut our LA stay short when she'd become pregnant with Walter, and that we had unfinished business with Los Angeles. 'One last hurrah,' she said, though I didn't like the phrase. What happened after a 'hurrah'? A 'foomf'? A 'pffffft'? Why couldn't your whole life be a 'hurrah'? The move was a huge upheaval and I wondered if it was worth it, but we did it, and I made a series of programmes based on the West Coast of America called *Altered States* that looked at new ways in which intimate connections and life-stages were taking place: a multi-million-dollar industry connecting parents hoping to adopt children with pregnant often indigent mums unable to raise their own babies; new laws allowing the terminally ill to end their lives at home when they wanted. There was also an episode about polyamory – consensual non-monogamy – in Portland, for which I visited a sensual eating party where I consumed strawberries and cheese while topless and blindfolded, and it was around then that I began writing this book.

From the outset, in making programmes, I tried to give people the benefit of the doubt. I tried to put a generous construction on wrongdoing where I found it: a lack of information; a misguided sense of priorities; an understandable urge to imbue one's life with a sense of importance. My working practice was to see evil as a side effect of misguidedness or selfishness or woundedness, but only very rarely as an active attempt *to do wrong*.

I also preferred to believe that people are capable of redemption and change, and that, even when they aren't, there are positive traits and small compensations in almost everyone. Good and bad are intermixed in people. They are – if I may borrow from the language of gender – non-binary. I don't even think the terms 'spectrum' or 'grey area' do justice to the Dulux colour chart of how people behave and make sense of the universe.

If I can make a single observation based on almost everyone I've interviewed, it's that we are complicated. We hate those we love. We feel exalted in being debased. Victims can be bullies. Suffering can feel comfortable. Insanity can make perfect sense.

'Everything I am I hate,' a pimp in Mississippi once said to me, quoting St Paul. I looked up the verse. It is from his letter to the

Romans. It runs, in the King James version: 'For that which I do I allow not. For what I would, that do I not; but what I hate, that do I.'

We feed ourselves lies – about the unconquerable strength of a mother's love or the ennobling quality of suffering. 'What doesn't kill you makes you stronger.' Uh-huh. OK. Unless it leaves you in a wheelchair, with PTSD and feeling suicidal.

And so where does that leave us? Just struggling forward, doing the best we can, with no grand answers, making tiny decisions to try to be slightly better.

Early in my career, journalists sometimes asked if I ever worried whether I might run out of weird subjects.

Surely there was an upper limit on the number of UFO cults and sexual fetishes in the world? I can't recall what I said, probably something to the effect that the carnival of human folly shows no sign of ending, nor does the crooked timber of humanity promise to straighten up any time soon.

Weirdness is built into the human condition. It is an inescapable fact of life. We are born. From somewhere invisible to us our consciousness emerges. It flickers for a few years, lighting up our crania like the flame inside a magic lantern, then sputters out. A once-thinking, once-feeling mass of humanity becomes inanimate. In the passage between those two points, we are slaves to a set of impulses hidden from us, both within us and without. Sex is weird, religion is weird, family is weird. Having sex with multiple partners is weird. Having sex with the same person for seventy years is also weird. Our emotions are weird, and not having emotions is weird.

Death is really weird.

I find it hard to imagine what a rational human would even look like. I am getting a vision of Spock, but he was half-Vulcan.

As someone who struggles with worry and self-doubt, it may seem odd that I fell into a line of work that brings me into contact with humanity at its strangest and most extreme. I tend to think the two things are connected: I enjoy the company of people whose lifestyles are outlandish or who are faced with situations freighted with psychological anguish, because it relieves the tension inside me. It's a bit like tinnitus: presumably the symptoms are relieved when there is actual ringing going on. I once remarked in an interview, in an uncharacteristic moment of insight, that the qualities that made me good at my job were the same ones that made me bad at life. I'm not too sure but I *think* I meant that I have a habit of seeing life as though from behind a glass. I allow other people to have emotions.

In my own life, I have tended to avoid living too much. 'As for life we have our servants to do that for us.' So says a character in *Axël*, a French drama famous mainly for that line. A part of me feels the same way about my documentary subjects. Or, if that is overstated, then at the very least that I think whatever angst and self-conflict they are living through convinces me that my own issues are small by comparison. I find relief in the reassurance that others are afflicted by the same turmoil and confusion as I am or by worse. But improvisation is a survival skill, in life as in documentary-making. Everyone is sad and confused and making it up as they go along, walking in their own way on the weird side.

And when I'm not working, when my gaze turns inward, I sometimes probe and doubt and investigate *myself* to the point of paralysis. To quote Nietzsche a final time, 'In time of peace the warlike man attacks himself.' I'd like to think I am getting better. My wife and children have helped me to see that there is life outside work. I am grateful to them for that and so much more.

I have managed to make a career in TV through a singular insight, made through instinct and rationalized after the fact: that the proper subject of documentaries is people doing things they're not supposed to do. The 'supposed tos' may themselves be wrong-headed; the people may be right in what they do. But the feeling of being at loggerheads with certain norms and conventions is always present. That is what I interrogate. That is what I am interested in.

Oddly – or not oddly – I made this the centrepiece of my work because of my own frailties: because I am overly hemmed in by 'supposed tos' and 'alloweds'. My fretted and oppressed wishes emerged in the work, in a kind of fixation with people forced through inclination or circumstance to behave in ways I have not or cannot.

One day in early 2018, while working on a story about rape on American campuses, I did an interview in New York with an artist, Emma Sulkowicz, who had been assaulted while at Columbia by a fellow student. We spoke in Emma's studio in the area of Brooklyn known as Dumbo. The studio was close to a bridge carrying subway lines and we kept being interrupted by the rumble of passing trains.

After the interview was over, with the afternoon free, I left my crew and, following the map on my iPhone like a dowsing-rod, I walked up to my old neighbourhood in Fort Greene. I had the feeling, being back in New York, of time travel into my past. But it was confusing: nothing was where I remembered it. I lost my bearings, turning around and around, not quite able to figure out from the phone which way I should be going. Then a video call came in from my youngest son, Walter, who was missing me. I turned the camera around to show him video of my surroundings and told him about the tall buildings and details on the street: the yellow taxis, a mail box, a tree that had grown around a metal railing.

A little later, I arrived at the apartment where I'd once lived during one of my break-ups with Sarah, and where I'd hosted the porn performer, the survivalist, the Christian evangelist and the space channel for my 'Weird Christmas', and I recalled how one night I'd cycled home over the Brooklyn Bridge and braked too hard, sending myself over the handle bars, and had woken up the next morning, barely able to move. I remembered watching On The Waterfront on my own and the Marlon Brando character had been the same age I was, twenty-eight. And then a memory came to me of visiting Sarah in the apartment in Williamsburg and filming her on a second-hand video camera as she made origami boxes.

I walked to the corner of the park. The old bodegas were now speciality coffee shops and trendy cocktail bars. I continued up to Clinton Hill, and at Clinton and Washington I went down into the subway station, waiting for a G train up to Williamsburg. All this time I'd been looking for a moment of recognition, and it was only here that it came: the smell of the air-conditioned subway was still the same, an indefinable mixture of metal and sweat and cleaning products.

Williamsburg was now forested with high-rises, shiny condo complexes, jarring amid the terraces of brownstones, the low-level thicket of old Brooklyn neighbourhoods. There were European tourists milling around, wearing backpacks. Everything was different and I resented the sight of people who didn't remember what I remembered. I thought about how awful it would be to live forever and be subjected to an onslaught of perpetual change, nothing ever remaining the way it was – a constant process of adjustment like a wall being overlaid with coat after coat of paint, or an old cassette tape being recorded over until it was crackly and inaudible.

And then I walked back down into the subway.

## Picture Credits